Reflections of an Economic Policy Maker

DATE DUE FOR RETURN

Reflections of an Economic Policy Maker

Speeches and Congressional Statements: 1969–1978

Arthur F. Burns

American Enterprise Institute for Public Policy Research
Washington, D.C.

Library of Congress Cataloging in Publication Data

Burns, Arthur Frank, 1904-
  Reflections of an economic policy maker.

  (AEI studies ; 217)
  Includes index.
  I. Inflation (Finance)—United States—Addresses, essays,
lectures. 2. Inflation (Finance) and unemployment—United States—
Addresses, essays, lectures. 3. Laissez-faire—Addresses, essays,
lectures. 4. Fiscal policy—United States—Addresses, essays, lectures.
5. United States—Economic conditions—1977—Addresses, essays,
lectures. I. Title. II. Series: American Enterprise Institute for Public
Policy Research. AEI studies; 217.
HG538.B938   332.4'973   78-21864
ISBN 0-8447-3319-9
ISBN 0-8447-3333-4 pbk.

AEI studies; 217

Printed in the United States of America

CONTENTS

Preface
Arthur F. Burns

PART ONE
FREE ENTERPRISE AND ECONOMIC GROWTH

PART TWO
INFLATION AND UNEMPLOYMENT

PART THREE
FISCAL RESPONSIBILITY

PART FOUR
SOUND MONEY AND BANKING

PART FIVE
INTERNATIONAL FINANCE

PREFACE

This volume owes its existence to Dr. Thomas F. Johnson, Director of Economic Policy Studies of the American Enterprise Institute. Soon after I took up residence at the Institute, he suggested that various of my pronouncements during the years I presided over the Federal Reserve System had relevance and usefulness beyond the occasion when they were made. I welcomed the suggestion and took advantage of his willingness to make a preliminary selection from the multitude of my public addresses and congressional statements.

The final selection includes all the items on Dr. Johnson's list. It also includes some others, among them two that extend slightly the time period he had proposed: an address of December 1969, delivered while I was preparing for my responsibilities at the Federal Reserve, and one recently given, which grew out of my experience in the System.

In making the final selection, I resisted the temptation to include only those items that may flatter or bring honor to their author. Much of what is contained in this volume is repetitious; passages here and there may appear to be, or actually are, inconsistent with others; some of the views presented I might now question or reject. Yet, even as they stand, these papers convey my strong conviction that inflation has become the most dangerous economic ailment of our times and that our country may be headed for disaster if we ignore the lessons won through hard experience. I trust that this collection also conveys something of my struggle to protect the integrity of the Federal Reserve and to wring truth from our troubled and rapidly changing economic and political environment. Such a personal accounting requires the suppression of editorial impulse, and I have therefore left the papers just as they were originally presented. They are here arranged—rather arbitrarily in some instances—in chronological sequence under each of five general headings.

I need hardly add that the papers were prepared in the course of an exacting official life that left little time for niceties of analysis or elegance in composition. Even so, they could not have been carried out without abundant help from highly skilled and devoted colleagues. The Federal Reserve is a collegial body of great moral and intellectual distinction. Whatever merit this collection of papers may have is attributable in very large part to the passion for objectivity and decency of these erstwhile associates of mine.

ARTHUR F. BURNS
September 30, 1978

PART ONE

Free Enterprise and Economic Growth

The Triumph
of Free Enterprise

It is a great pleasure for me to visit Japan again. Four years have passed since I was here last, and while I have heard much of the progress and prosperity you have experienced, it is good to see the evidence with one's own eyes. My personal knowledge of Japan goes back some ten years. During my last visit, in early 1966, the mood was not one of universal optimism because you were then experiencing a readjustment in the rate of production and profits. There are always those who find any economic pause a justification for pessimism about the future. I have not been one of those. I have long been impressed by the great resiliency of the Japanese economy. I believe that you have discovered a formula for economic progress that will continue to bring excellent results in the future as it has in the past. That is not to say that you will not encounter problems. You will. But your resiliency lies in the skill you have developed in devising solutions to problems and your ability to work together as a nation to achieve your goals.

This is a particularly interesting time for an economist to visit Japan. As I am sure all of you recall, fiscal year 1970 was designated as a target year in the economic plan unveiled by Prime Minister Ikeda in 1961. In what many people then thought was a fantastically ambitious design for the future, he calmly announced that Japan planned to double her gross national product between the years 1960 and 1970.

It is therefore fitting, as we are gathered here today, to take note of how the actual achievement of Japan compares with Mr.

Address in Tokyo, Japan, July 2, 1970.

3

Ikeda's bold projection of a decade ago. While his plan called for a national output that in this fiscal year would be twice that of 1960, it now appears that your national product will in fact be at least 180 percent above 1960.

The Ikeda plan projected exports reaching $9.3 billion this year, while imports would rise to $9.9 billion. It is now believed that exports will come to nearly $20 billion and imports to nearly $19 billion.

The Ikeda plan foresaw Japanese steel consumption rising to 45 million tons this year. It will actually be around 80 million tons.

According to the Ikeda plan, a big expansion was to occur in automobile production. But while it was then thought that the output of passenger cars, trucks, and buses would amount to about 2.2 million units, it now appears that well over 4 million vehicles will be produced this year.

I might go on with such comparisons, but it is not necessary to do so. Virtually all indicators tell the same story. Far from being overly optimistic, as many people then thought, Mr. Okita and his colleagues—who drew up the ten-year plan at Prime Minister Ikeda's request—were very conservative in their projections. However, I am sure that no one will find fault with them for that. They would not have been believed had they forecast the achievements that have actually come to pass.

It is interesting to recall that a few years before Japan unveiled its income-doubling plan, the Soviet Union had already singled out the year 1970 as the date by which its economy would surpass the United States in production per capita and in the standard of living. It may be worth recalling Mr. Khrushchev's precise words:

> The superiority of the U.S.S.R. in the speed of growth of production will create a real basis for insuring that within a period of, say, five years following 1965, the level of U.S. production per capita should be equalled and overtaken. Thus by that time, perhaps even sooner, the U.S.S.R. will have captured first place in the world both in absolute volume of production and per capita production, which will insure the world's highest standard of living.

To achieve this goal, the U.S.S.R. would have been obliged to more than double its per capita GNP even if the United States made no further progress and simply maintained its per capita output at the 1960 level. However, unlike Japan, the U.S.S.R. fell far short of the goal that Khrushchev had set for 1970.

The economic contest between the U.S.S.R. and the United States enters the year 1970 with the United States holding a commanding lead. In 1969, total output per person in the United States was nearly $4,600. This was two-and-a-half times the corresponding Soviet figure. Measured in real terms, the gap between the per capita GNP of the United States and the Soviet Union was more than 25 percent higher in 1969 than in 1960. While the Soviet growth rate was slightly higher than the American rate, the difference was so slight that if the same growth rates were maintained over the next 50 years, the per capita GNP of the United States would still be about double that of the Soviet Union in the year 2020.

The wide difference between the living standards of the Soviet Union and the United States is vividly portrayed by comparisons of the number of working hours required to earn enough to buy various goods and services. It turns out, for example, that the average worker in Moscow in April 1969 had to work nearly seven times as long as his counterpart in New York to earn enough to buy an identical supply of food sufficient to feed a family of four for one week. The difference for many nonfood items was even larger. The following are the multiples by which the cost of certain goods in Moscow exceeded the cost in New York, when cost is measured in terms of working time: for bath soap, 12.5 times; for nylon stockings, 14 times; for a man's shirt, 12 times; for a refrigerator, 12 times.

These comparisons are based on official prices in Moscow, not black market prices, which are, in many cases, far higher. For example, a Volga sedan costing the equivalent of $7,700 reportedly sells for 2.5 times that amount on the Moscow black market.

Although the U.S.S.R. has failed even to come close to the economic performance of the United States, the per capita output of Japan has probably already overtaken that of the U.S.S.R. The official figure for per capita GNP of Japan in 1969 is very similar to our estimate for per capita GNP of the Soviet Union. If the figures are adjusted to allow for differences in the purchasing power of the currency that are not adequately reflected in the exchange rates, Japan appears to have surpassed the Soviet Union in 1969.

There are important lessons to be learned from Japan's extraordinary economic success and the concomitant shortcoming of the Soviet Union. The rather high rates of growth recorded for the Soviet Union in the early postwar years have not been sustained because of deficiencies inherent in the Soviet system. In a free economy, the relative strength of the demand for goods and services determines the allocation of productive resources. In the Soviet system, on the other hand, the path that production takes is basically shaped by the decisions of economic planners in Moscow.

Important economic decisions in the Soviet Union have therefore not been guided by sensitive signals such as are constantly being transmitted by costs and prices in a free market economy. To make matters worse, until recently they were not even subject to correction by public criticism. Thus, economic success in the Soviet system came to be measured, traditionally, in terms of meeting targets set by the government, rather than in meeting the wants of consumers. This sometimes led to production of equipment that failed to work or to the output of some consumer goods far in excess of demand, while other goods continued to be in critically short supply. Such production might be expressed in a high rate of growth of GNP, but it did not spell progress in the elevation of living standards. In time, the waste involved in this process became a matter of grave concern to Soviet officials, particularly to economists and engineers.

As early as 1959, a Soviet econometrician, L. V. Kantorovich, pointed out that it might be advantageous if prices were allowed to play a bigger role in guiding the allocation of resources in the Soviet economy. Another Soviet economist, Professor Y. Liberman, proposed that profitability rather than achievement of planned targets be used as the measure of success or failure of productive enterprise.

Although the Soviet Union has tried some experiments with reforms along these lines, there has been no correction of the fundamental flaws of the Communist economic system either in the Soviet Union or in the satellite countries. In Czechoslovakia the frustration with the results of centralized decision making, which reached a climax during the industrial recession of the sixties, was an important factor in the reform movement in 1967–1968, but the courageous effort to rationalize the economy by giving greater play to individual decision making was brought to an abrupt end by Soviet troops and tanks in the summer of 1968.

This result was no great surprise to those who recognized that the reforms required to rationalize the Soviet-style economic system would weaken, if not totally destroy, the political control wielded by the Communist party. Faced with a choice between introducing economic rationality and the maintenance of their political power, the Russian rulers chose power. Unless and until they are willing to change their approach, it seems likely that their own economy and that of their satellites will continue to lag far behind the United States and other advanced countries of the free world.

Japan, on the other hand, has relied on the free market system, and that system has served Japan well. The Ikeda ten-year income-doubling plan, whose goals have been so conspicuously exceeded, called for basic reliance on the private sector and on free market forces. The document which outlined the plan stated:

> In trying to achieve the economic policies contained in this plan, it is desirable for the Government to count on the originality and devices of private enterprises and individuals. It should refrain, as far as possible, from taking direct control measures for the purpose.

The authors of the plan recognized, of course, that the government had the responsibility of helping to create a climate conducive to economic growth. They pointed out, in particular, that it was the duty of the government to stabilize the value of the currency and to minimize business fluctuations through proper application of overall fiscal and monetary policies. But they left no doubt about their determination that the conduct of production and marketing was to be determined by private enterprises acting on their own initiative, not through state enterprises or state controls.

Japan's faith in the free market system has paid handsome dividends. Yet there were many economists and statesmen at the time when Khrushchev made his extravagant predictions who took him seriously. They argued that freedom was a luxury

7

that poor nations could ill afford, and that these countries would therefore need to resort to authoritarian control of economic activity, if not also to outright governmental ownership of industrial enterprises, in order to augment their income and wealth. And, in fact, a number of countries in Asia did adopt in varying degrees the policy of turning over to the government the decision-making functions that are performed by private citizens in countries that practice free enterprise.

Those who adopted this approach overlooked the fact that Adam Smith, the father of the idea that freedom was more conducive to economic growth than governmental control, had addressed himself to the problems of a nation that was then very poor and very underdeveloped—that is, to the England of 1776. Two hundred years ago, English peasants, living at a subsistence level without any of the benefits of modern industry or science to ameliorate their condition, were probably worse off than their counterparts in most of free Asia today. And the French peasants lived in even greater poverty than the English.

Adam Smith examined the results of governmental intervention into economic activity in eighteenth century England and France with a perceptive eye. He came to the conclusion that the inefficient use of resources that he observed could be remedied and that wealth could be augmented if individuals had greater freedom to manage their economic affairs as they saw fit, instead of being tied down by minute and exacting regulations prescribed by bureaucrats. He saw that detailed economic regulations, often laid down by authorities far removed from the actual operations or needs of industry and commerce, produced undesirable results even though they may have been, or actually were, well intentioned. In time, as the force of Smith's logic and evidence won adherents among men of authority, his revolutionary ideas proved instrumental in sweeping away much of the irrationality that had retarded economic progress. This paved the way for the extraordinary increase in living standards that has occurred in the West in the past two centuries.

It has been said that those who will not learn from the errors of the past are frequently doomed to repeat them. This has been the fate of much of Asia in the period following World War II. The Communists took control of all of mainland China, and for a time the world was told in glowing terms of the great economic transformation they were effecting there. Indeed, it was widely believed for a time that the great political contest in the world between the advocates of democracy and the advocates of dictatorship hinged on the ability of the democratic countries in Asia to perform as well as authoritarian China. The attention of all Asia was reported to be riveted on this contest to demonstrate which system was economically superior.

The year 1958 was hailed as Communist China's "great leap forward." It was claimed that food output had been doubled in a single year, and that final victory had been achieved over hunger. However, these claims were soon exposed as wild exaggerations, as it became evident in 1959 and 1960 that serious food shortages had begun to reappear. Far from developing self-sufficiency in food and eliminating hunger, Communist China experienced critical food shortages in the early 1960s and was compelled to import huge quantities of grain from abroad to meet her requirements. The agricultural communes which had been so widely acclaimed as the realization of true communism were quietly abandoned or radically modified. Agriculture in China appears to have remained virtually stagnant throughout the 1960s. Although production figures have been withheld, the available evidence suggests that output may not even have kept pace with the increase in population. In the early 1960s, the food shortages were attributed by government officials to bad weather, but this excuse was soon dropped as food imports continued to be required year after year.

The failures of agriculture had serious effects throughout the Communist Chinese economy. It soon became necessary to retrench drastically the plans for industry and transportation. Resources were simply not available to push forward the grandiose schemes that were supposed to show the rest of Asia how a country could rise from agricultural poverty to industrial affluence by pursuing the Communist path. Official statistics on economic performance of Communist China became very scarce as the boasted "great leap forward" failed to materialize. Talk of competition between Communist China and free Asia dropped to a whisper once it became evident that the free countries were well ahead in the contest.

The countries of Asia that have retained the free market system and have avoided the centralization of economic decisions in the hands of the government have clearly been winning the economic contest. The countries that have done the least well have tended to be the ones that either rejected the free market or severely limited it by governmental controls.

The great economic success stories of Asia in the 1960s are found in countries like Japan, the Republic of Korea, Nationalist China, Thailand, Hong Kong, and Malaysia. These countries, in the ten years ending in 1968, have all recorded average increases in real output of 6 percent a year or more. Japan, of course, has been one of the outstanding performers, with an average annual growth rate of 11 percent in this period.

Rates of growth of GNP can be misleading, especially in countries where the underlying statistical data are inadequate and of doubtful validity. It is therefore desirable to check the growth figures of GNP against other records. One useful indicator of underlying growth is the trend of exports, since this is a measure of a nation's ability to compete in world markets. Export performance is a test of a country's efficiency in keeping up with the standards being set elsewhere in the world.

Professor Ota Sik, the architect of the short-lived economic reform in Czechoslovakia, called attention to the fact that the Communist economies have had great difficulty in meeting the test of economic efficiency posed by exports. As he put it: "On the foreign markets, Czechoslovak production is absolutely unable to adjust to changes in demand." This has been largely due to the tendency to neglect quality in production. Over-priced, shoddy goods can be sold in a market that is shielded from foreign competition, but they have little chance in export markets.

It is significant, therefore, that the countries in Asia that have achieved high rates of overall economic growth have also done very well in expanding their exports. The whole world knows what an outstanding record Japan has piled up in export markets. In the period 1958–1968, Japanese exports expanded at an average annual rate of 16 percent a year. It is perhaps less well known that the Republic of Korea, Nationalist China, and Hong Kong have also expanded their exports at phenomenal rates.

There are fascinating stories behind the export statistics of free Asia. I have just come from Korea, and I am very impressed by the remarkable change that has taken place there in just the last decade. Korea's expansion of exports from almost nothing to over $600 million last year is a modern miracle. I am also impressed by the fact that tiny Hong Kong, with a population of only 4 million, exported about as much as all of India in 1969.

The experience of these Asian countries in achieving such outstanding success in the face of what many people once thought were overwhelming odds illustrates how difficult it is for any economist, no matter how farsighted he may be, to chart the future course of a nation's development. I know that many of you could cite interesting examples from your own experience of the achievement of what once seemed practically impossible.

Some of you may recall the pessimism that prevailed in the years immediately after World War II about Japan's economic future. The development of nylon obviously posed a great threat to the future of silk, which had been one of Japan's leading exports before the war. No one foresaw at that time that Japan would become one of the world's great producers of synthetic fibers and fabrics and that Japan's exports of these goods would eventually far exceed the value of her prewar exports of silk.

Japan has demonstrated the shallowness of the belief that latecomers in economic development are unable to compete successfully with countries that have gotten a head start. I remember the late Prime Minister Ikeda telling me of the first tape recorder he had ever seen. It was on one of his visits to New York in the early 1950s. Neither he nor many of his compatriots then foresaw that tape recorders and other electronic products would play a major role in the tremendous expansion of Japanese exports that has occurred over the last decade.

One of the great strengths of a free economy is that it permits the development of the unexpected. Given proper incentives, the Japanese, the Chinese, and the Korean entrepreneurs have found new uses for their land, labor, and capital. In many cases, the raw materials, such as wood for the plywood factories of Japan and Korea, had to be imported from distant lands. There were failures as well as successes, but the end result has been the rapid development of production and exports that had not been dreamed of, much less planned.

The lesson to be learned from these experiences is an old one. Where men are given the opportunity and the incentive to make and sell the products of their labor in free markets, they will tend to act in ways that increase productive efficiency and thereby raise the living standards of the country as a whole. To be sure, freedom of entrepreneurs, workers, and consumers to make their own decisions is by no means the sole determinant of how well a country will perform economically. A nation must also pursue sound monetary, fiscal, and trade policies in order to achieve its economic potential. But there cannot be the slightest doubt, in view of the experience accumulated over centuries, that free and competitive markets are a major determinant of economic growth and widespread prosperity.

It is no accident that the Asian countries that experienced the slowest rates of growth in 1958–1968 were also the countries that leaned most heavily on centralized economic controls. The countries at the bottom of the scale in terms of growth of real GNP include Ceylon, Burma, India, and Indonesia. Each of these countries has experimented extensively with government ownership or control over economic activities.

Burma in particular has gone far toward economic authoritarianism. By exercising far-reaching controls over production, trade, and finance, both its production and distribution have been injured. Burma's main crop, rice, has been adversely affected by pricing policies that have denied producers adequate incentives. Over the past decade, neighboring Thailand has increased rice exports by 28 percent, while Burma's exports of rice have fallen nearly two-thirds. The result is that Burma's total exports are now running at less than half the 1963 level. The ability to import has fallen correspondingly.

Indonesia under President Sukarno followed economic policies that were in some respects more disastrous than those of Burma. In addition to establishing stifling controls over production and trade, Sukarno's government borrowed heavily abroad, largely to build up a military machine, but partly also to finance ambitious projects that in the end yielded little or no economic return. The productive capital of the country was therefore badly eroded, exports fell sharply, living standards declined, and the country found itself saddled with huge foreign debts and with diminished ability to produce the exports needed to service the debt. Fortunately, Indonesia is now in the process of liberalizing her economy, but the country will require many years to recuperate from the damage wrought by the Sukarno policies.

The adverse impact of authoritarian economic policies has also been felt in India, though to a much lesser degree than in either Burma or Indonesia. India over the past decade and a half has emphasized strong centralized control over investment, backed by extensive restrictions on imports and foreign exchange expenditures. Fortunately, the earlier decisions to emphasize heavy industry at the expense of light industry and agriculture are now being questioned. The failure to provide incentives to exports has left India lagging far behind many other countries, and has contributed to balance-of-payments difficulties which necessitated even tighter import restrictions. As a result, India has passed through a difficult period during which many of her industrial enterprises were deprived of the supplies and equipment needed to keep operating at reasonable rates.

Division of labor, territorial specialization, freedom of trade, and decentralization of economic decision making—these were key elements in the thinking of the founder of classical economics, Adam Smith. It is gratifying to see that the practical statesmen of the world are gradually rediscovering these essential truths. In this rediscovery of truth, we owe a debt to countries like Japan, the Republic of Korea, Nationalist China, Hong Kong, and Thailand that have most recently demonstrated how nations practicing economic freedom can outperform authoritarian countries.

I see a basis for optimism about the future in the economic experience of both the countries that have forged ahead and those that have lagged behind. What has gone wrong, after all, is not something immutable. A country can change its future for the better by changing its policies. The countries that have lagged in the economic contest have the opportunity to learn from experience and to alter their course.

In concentrating, as I have, on the power of free markets to spur economic growth, I am not unmindful of the responsibilities that the advanced industrialized countries have to assist the developing nations. We have, at times, overestimated our potential contribution. There has been a tendency to think that external technical assistance, or external capital, could of itself provide sufficient impetus to generate rapid growth all over the world.

We now know that the solutions are more complex. Nevertheless, technical assistance, capital flows, whether governmental

13

or private, and liberal trade policies on the part of the industrialized countries can contribute significantly to the process of economic development.

It is even more important that the advanced countries maintain their own economic strength if the world economy as a whole is to prosper and international trade is to flourish. Clearly, the prosperity and growth of the developing countries depend heavily on the economic well-being of the advanced countries, which provide the major export markets as well as the principal source of the capital and technology required to promote rapid economic development.

I am fully aware of the importance of the role of the United States in keeping the world economy on a sound basis. At the present time, the exercise of our responsibilities in this regard requires that we bring an end to the inflationary pressures present in our own economy. This is proving to be a difficult task. As a result of restrictive monetary and fiscal policies pursued last year, the rate of economic expansion slowed appreciably and some slack has developed in markets for labor and other resources. However, while we have succeeded in eliminating excess demand in our economy, we are still experiencing rather strong upward pressures on costs and prices. Expectations of consumers, businesses, and workers have not yet fully adjusted to the current balance of aggregate demand and supply.

The continuance of rising costs and prices in the face of a sluggish economy has been deeply disturbing to many observers. Some have concluded that success in our battle against inflation might require so restrictive a monetary policy that a liquidity crisis could develop. Concern about this has given rise to some turbulence in our financial markets in recent weeks. Let me assure you that the Federal Reserve Board is fully aware of its responsibility to prevent anxieties of this kind from leading to a scramble for liquidity. Any such development could harm the world economy, as well as our own. Fortunately, we in the United States have the legislative authority, the tools, and— I believe—also the knowledge and wisdom to enable us to deal quickly and effectively with any problems of this nature that might emerge.

While the process of getting inflation under control in the United States has been difficult, there have been scattered signs recently of moderation in the rate of advance in some major categories of prices, and also of some improvement in the trend of productivity in the manufacturing sector of our economy. I believe we will be able to extend the progress that is beginning to emerge in these areas, by pursuing stabilization policies that prevent the reemergence of excess demand later this year or in 1971. However, we must also be careful to ensure that the economic slowdown which began last fall does not become more pervasive or continue much longer. On this score, I think there is room for optimism too. Both monetary and fiscal policies have become less restrictive in recent months, and I believe we may look forward with reasonable confidence to a resumption of sustainable economic growth in the near future, as well as to a gradual diminution in the rate of advance in prices.

For a time, however, we must expect to see a continuation of cost-push inflation, with increases in wage rates and prices reflecting the excess demand that existed in the past, the effects of which have not yet fully worked their way through the economic system. There are some who think that, under the circumstances, we should abandon our traditional reliance on market forces and impose mandatory controls on wages and prices to halt inflation. I have always been strongly opposed to direct controls, since they are discriminatory and a source of great inefficiency. But I think the administration has taken a proper step in announcing the establishment of a procedure to review the economic implications of wage and price increases in key industries. In a transitional period of cost-push inflation, such as we are now experiencing, the moderate incomes policy recently announced by the President should help us to avoid an increase in unemployment and yet hasten the return to reasonable price stability.

The task of bringing inflation under control has caused, and will continue to cause, some discomfort in many sectors of our economy. The anti-inflationary program pursued in the United States has had repercussions which have even extended as far as Japan, I understand. However, I can assure you that our economy is fundamentally sound and resilient. Just as I had confidence that the lulls in Japanese growth that I observed on some of my earlier visits were only temporary, so I have confidence that economic growth and progress will be resumed in the

United States in the near future. We are still a long way from having exhausted the possibilities of improving our standard of living or increasing our productive capacity.

Man has taken a giant step forward in entering the era of interplanetary exploration. Our technology and education will continue to advance. How well the industrial countries or the less developed countries use new knowledge to better man's lot in life will depend on many things. It will depend in part on the goals that we set for ourselves. It will depend in part on our ability to live together in peace and to maintain the kind of mutually beneficial relations that have existed between Japan and the United States for nearly a quarter of a century. It will depend in important measure on the extent to which the nations that have lagged behind in the economic contest. But it will also depend in important measure on the extent to which the nations of the world recognize the great advantages of the free market system and are willing to pursue fiscal, monetary, and commercial policies that are compatible with its efficient operation.

Dedication and Hope

This is my third visit to Israel. I remember, just before my first visit here in 1958, being admonished not to come by several United States ambassadors.

The reason for the warning was plain. Israel was then in the midst of the Lebanon crisis. With tension mounting by the hour, even a professor ought to have enough sense to stay away from a country about to become involved in war. The men who told me this were seasoned diplomats; they were gravely alarmed by the state of affairs.

But when I came here, I was struck by just the opposite— not by the tension, not by the alarm, but by the coolness of the Israeli people in the midst of international anxiety.

There is an ironic saying we have in America, paraphrasing a line in a Kipling poem: "If you can keep your head while all about you are losing theirs, perhaps you do not understand the gravity of the situation."

But the fact was that the Israelis I met here—some of whom had been my students at Columbia University in years past— fully understood the gravity of the international situation. They kept the calm that is found in the eye of a hurricane.

I was struck then, as I am struck now, by what Ernest Hemingway defined as the essence of courage—"grace under pressure."

That quality of calm courage is found only in a people with a clear sense of purpose and a firm sense of duty. This simple fact must weigh heavily in every assessment by outsiders of the future of Israel.

Commencement address at Hebrew University, Jerusalem, July 6, 1970.

On another visit, I asked David Ben-Gurion how the Israelis were able to achieve so rapidly their advances in industry and commerce. As you know, many economists associate economic growth with a nation's endowment of natural resources. England's early progress was attributed to her coal, America's to her abundant minerals and vast agricultural resources. But Israel was not blessed with large mineral deposits, much of its land was barren, and even water was in short supply.

How, I therefore asked the prime minister, was Israel able to build such a strong economy in such a short time? He answered: "We did it first by dreaming, then by doing what the economists said was impossible."

Keeping in mind that gentle reminder of fallibility, I would like to speak to you today about three discoveries in seemingly different fields—in the management of economic affairs, in the management of power, and in the achievement of ideals.

You are a part of those discoveries, and the way the young people of Israel govern their lives will have an important impact on the use of those discoveries in the years ahead.

The first discovery, in the field of economic management, is this: the human element is basic in the creation of an economy that combines full employment with high productivity and relative price stability.

The great debate you read about in economics today is between those who feel that fiscal policy is all-important and those who believe that monetary policy is all-important. The two schools joust in learned debate, but both are also beginning to take account of the human element in economic affairs—that is, the dreams, fears, and hopes that so often upset the most expert calculations.

And so we are gradually discovering—or perhaps I should say rediscovering—that there is more to economic policy than the established principles of economics. When the older writers on economics entitled their treatises "political arithmetic" or "political economy" they were telling us something we have forgotten: that man's hope is a crucial element in man's fate.

What is your role in this discovery? Right now, right here in Israel, you are proving that hope is perhaps the most powerful of all economic forces. You are proving that a spirit of purpose can give meaning to human energy and overcome a lack of material resources. In this, you are not breaking any rules of economics; but you are developing new rules of political economy.

A generation ago, the only thing we had to fear was fear itself; today, the only thing we should despair of is despair. In nations all around the world, on both sides of the Iron Curtain, an enervating mood of despair is becoming fashionable, especially on the part of some young people. The cultivation of despair can do as much to undermine the strength of some economies as the cultivation of hope can do to overcome the apparent weaknesses of other economies.

This brings me to a second discovery that is being made, in a related but different field—in the exercise of power in the world.

Power traditionally has been thought of in military terms. And, of course, as you know better than most, the survival of freedom in the world as it is today would be impossible without military power.

But I do not hold with those who say that power corrupts men. Rather it is the other way around; men without morality corrupt power. And the world is making a remarkable discovery about the exercise of power: with nations, as with individual men, the most effective application of power is the power of moral example.

This, I submit, is what has made and continues to make America great. We have a dream of freedom, of equal opportunity, and of human dignity. It is true, of course, that our reach exceeds our grasp, but by striving to make our way of life better and to help other nations enrich their freedom, we set a moral example that is one of the greatest sources of our power. We are criticized so much around the world because people expect so much of America; I would never trade away those high expectations for mere approval.

And this, too, is what makes Israel a "great power" in her own right. The power of her example in dignifying life, in conquering disease, and in extending technical assistance to other poor nations, can never be underestimated. I know that President Nixon feels this deeply. Not long ago, in discussing why America supports Israel, he put it this way: "Americans admire a people who can scratch a desert and produce a garden. The

19

Israelis have shown qualities that Americans identify with: guts, patriotism, idealism, a passion for freedom. I have seen it. I know."

The young people of Israel, born to this noble example, have a special responsibility both to their own nation and to the world to preserve and enhance those qualities. You must continue to show the world that you know the difference between bravery and bravado. You must continue to show the world how dearly you hold the moral precepts of brotherhood. You must continue to show the world your readiness to seek peace and progress for yourselves and for your neighbors.

The example of Israel is nowhere more vivid than in the field of education. You have the privilege of being graduated today from one of the great universities of the world. But what impresses the world is not so much your fine educational facilities or the magnificence of Mount Scopus where you began to build this university, but the fact that education in Israel permeates the very existence of her people.

You do not "go to school" in Israel; in a sense, this whole land—every home, factory, kibbutz, or even army camp—is a school. Education is an exciting part of life. The mistake that others sometimes make, and that I trust you will never make, is to treat education as a chore instead of a joy; to treat graduation as an end of education rather than as a beginning.

You consider yourselves pioneers in many things, and rightly so, but I suggest that there is a discovery you are making that you may not be aware of: that a passion for learning diffused throughout a society is the surest road to the achievement of its ideals.

The President of the United States likes to say: "When you're through learning, you're through." And he's right—the strength of a nation, like the strength of an individual, depends on its ability to learn how to change and to grow.

Perhaps the greatest thing that can be said about the people of Israel is that in fighting for the life of your nation, you have stimulated the life of the mind.

Today I have been speaking of three discoveries that are being made in the world, and of your part in them in the years ahead.

In creating a lasting prosperity, the human element is at last being recognized as of fundamental importance.

In exercising power in the world, the power of moral example can be far greater than material riches or equipment.

In achieving ideals, a reverence for learning and education is indispensable.

As you take leave of the university, as you graduate into a new life of the mind, may each of you ask yourself this: What am I doing to increase the sum of hope in this world? What am I doing to nourish the sense of purpose that founded this nation and made it strong? What am I doing to teach someone else what I have learned?

In asking questions like these, you will come to new discoveries, you will rise to new challenges, and you will justify the faith of your fathers and the admiration of millions of free men all around the world.

I am deeply honored to join the fellowship of this graduating class and I salute you: Shalom.

The Relevance of Adam Smith
to Today's Problems

During the past quarter century, economists have been devoting much of their energy to studies of the process of economic growth. Some have concentrated on the interplay of social, cultural, political, and economic forces that shape the destiny of developing nations. Others have sought to determine along empirical lines what part of the economic growth of industrialized countries may be attributed to improvements in education, what part to increases in the stock of capital, what part to scientific research, improvements of technology, and other factors. Still other economists have developed formal mathematical models to gain insight into the dynamics of a growing economy. The formidable literature generated by this research could be aptly assembled under the title of Adam Smith's treatise: *An Inquiry into the Nature and Causes of the Wealth of Nations.*

In thinking about what I might say here today, I was led to reread passages of that celebrated work and to reflect once again on the legacy of Adam Smith to the field of economics. *The Wealth of Nations* is universally recognized as the first major exposition of modern economic thought. Adam Smith himself is commonly regarded as the father of political economy. Yet it is a striking fact that the principles underlying the growth of national wealth and income, which was the central theme of his book, remained for many years a subordinate issue in the great works on economics.

Address at the Adam Smith Symposium, Kirkcaldy, Scotland, June 5, 1973.

The Wealth of Nations was, first and foremost, a theory of production. Smith's main interest was in the means by which a nation could use its resources of labor and capital most effectively, thereby increasing its output and improving the lot of its people. He examined in considerable detail also the principles underlying the distribution of output. But while this was a subsidiary theme of *The Wealth of Nations*, it became the primary concern of the classical economists—David Ricardo, John Stuart Mill, Alfred Marshall, and others. About 150 years elapsed before economists again developed any substantial interest in the determinants of national output or national income; but it is hardly an exaggeration to assert that this has now become the central subject of scientific economics. Schumpeter, Mitchell, Robertson, Keynes, Kuznets, Roy Harrod, to name but a few of the great economists of recent times, have concentrated on this vital theme.

The contribution of Adam Smith to the formal body of economic theory is of towering proportions. Yet, it is less significant to the history of mankind than his influence on the ways in which individual nations, both large and small, have organized their economic activities. Smith proposed a bold new venture in national policy—the organization of economic life on the principle of free enterprise. He believed that governmental regulations were stifling economic growth in Great Britain and the rest of Europe; and that the abundant energies of people, particularly the British, would be released if these barriers to progress were swept away.

The importance of Smith's revolutionary ideas to the course of economic development in Great Britain and other parts of the Western world can be best appreciated by recalling the historical setting in which *The Wealth of Nations* appeared.

The economic policies and practices of England, France, and other European countries between the sixteenth and eighteenth centuries were governed by a loose body of principles known as mercantilism. In its popular conception, mercantilist doctrine is identified with protective measures for seeking a favorable balance of trade and an abundant supply of the precious metals. This characterization is correct as far as it goes, but it is incomplete. In fact, the mercantilist principles expounded in 1767 by another great Scotsman, Sir James Steuart, and widely practiced in England during the preceding two centuries, revolved around a system of governmental regulation of nearly every aspect of economic life—industrial output, agriculture, domestic and foreign trade, occupational choice, apprenticeship, prices, wages, labor mobility, and so forth. The direction of economic activity was considered to be the task of statesmen, who alone could guide the activities of businesses and individuals in ways that promote the national interest.

Mercantilism rendered service in its time by weakening some local monopolies and increasing the mobility of resources within a nation. It was nevertheless a crude economic and social philosophy, as it still is in its modern recrudescences. Smith recognized vividly its practical consequences—an economy of limited enterprise, a vital people caught in a web of governmental controls, a nation missing its opportunity for innovation and greatness. The way out seemed entirely clear to him. Governments everywhere had to stop interfering with the economic decisions of individuals and businesses, so that free enterprise could become the great organizing principle of economic life.

The mercantilist form of economic organization, Smith reasoned, lacked a number of ingredients essential to satisfactory growth of the wealth of nations—ingredients that free enterprise would forthwith supply. Of these, three stood out in importance in his mind.

First, economic rewards had to be commensurate with the market value of the work that individuals performed and the risks they took in investing their capital. Smith believed—as did the mercantilists—that self-interest was a dominant force in human behavior. But he perceived a truth that had escaped the mercantilists—namely, that a system of free enterprise could successfully harness individual motives to achieve national economic objectives.

Second, achievement of the progress of which a country was capable required active competition, including competition from abroad. Active competition, Smith believed, would lead to greater specialization of labor; it would encourage commercial application of technical and managerial knowledge; and, more important still, it would stimulate greater industry among businessmen and workers alike.

Third, a pricing mechanism was needed to allocate resources among competing uses, in accordance with the wants of consumers. Free markets, Smith argued, generate price and wage adjustments which result in a use of resources that is consistent with the prevailing pattern of consumer and business demands, and thus solve problems that governmental rules cannot handle.

This was an exciting new doctrine of enormous significance for economic and social organization in the European states, and also for the emerging nations of North America. Under the influence of the revolution in commerce and industry that got under way during the eighteenth century, many businessmen and artisans had found the intricate governmental regulations of their conduct needlessly burdensome, and they not infrequently reacted by ignoring or circumventing them. Smith's philosophy of free enterprise thus appeared at a time when political leaders as well as men engaged in commerce were ready to reexamine accepted doctrines. The lucidity and dignity of Smith's prose, the authority of his scholarship, and the cogency of his reasoning hastened the appeal of his work to intellectuals and the new merchant class. Before many years passed, *The Wealth of Nations* became the most influential guide to economic reform in his own country. Adam Smith's influence, however, did not stop there.

If my reading of history is anywhere near the mark, developments over the past two centuries have demonstrated beyond serious doubt the essential validity of Smith's theory of production. Where free enterprise has flourished, nations have prospered and standards of living have risen—often dramatically. Where detailed governmental regulation has repressed individual initiative and stifled competition, economic growth has been hampered and the well-being of the people has generally suffered.

The outstanding example of economic progress under a system of free markets is provided by the United States. The standard of living enjoyed by the people of my country has been, and still is, the envy of the world. The rate of economic growth in many countries has of late exceeded that of the United States, and thus the disparity of living standards—at least among the industrial nations of the world—has been shrinking. This is a heartening development. Yet, the fact is that per capita output in the United States is still far above that of any other country. For example, the gross national product per person in the United States is some 20 percent higher than in Sweden or Canada—the two closest nations in terms of per capita output—and it is about twice as high as in the more advanced socialist countries, such as the Soviet Union and Czechoslovakia. You may recall that Premier Khrushchev predicted in the late 1950s that the per capita output of the Soviet Union would equal or surpass that of the United States by 1970. This forecast proved to be an idle boast by a political leader who had not yet arrived at a mature understanding of the mainsprings of economic progress.

The standard of living that we enjoy in the United States reflects more than our system of economic organization. Rapid development of the American economy was fostered also by our rich endowment of natural resources and our vast expanse of fertile lands. Our free institutions and opportunities for self-advancement attracted to our shores millions of venturesome individuals from all over the world. The people who came were industrious and highly motivated, and they often brought with them useful technical skills and educational accomplishments. However, other countries also have been blessed with rich natural resources and with people of unusual educational and technical achievements, and yet have not managed to find the path to rapid economic development.

The key to the economic progress of the United States, I believe, is therefore to be found in our institutions, which by and large have permitted anyone in our midst to choose his occupation freely, to work for himself or for an employer of his choice, to produce whatever he chose, to benefit from the fruits of his individual effort, and to spend or to save or to invest as he deemed proper.

Under the economic system that has flourished in the United States, the natural thing for individuals and businesses to do is to plan for the future, so as to be in a position to take advantage of the opportunities that continually become available in a growing and prosperous economy. This feature of a free enterprise system, and its crucial role in fostering economic development, is seldom appreciated by advocates of centralized planning. Planning for economic growth in the United States and other free enterprise economies—unlike that of socialist nations—is a mass activity pursued by literally millions of producing and consuming units, each looking to a better future and striving to attain it. Over the years, our business firms have become accustomed to planning their investments in plant and equipment, their inventories, their advertising programs, their labor policies, their financing requirements. More important still, they now plan on a vast scale the development of new products and new methods of production by conducting extensive research and development programs. Our families, meanwhile, have remained eager to provide for a better life in the future, and therefore find themselves planning for a new home, for a good education for their children, and for reasonable comforts in the years of their retirement. Americans work hard to realize their goals, and they are enterprising enough to search out or to create new opportunities.

The present condition of the economy of the United States thus provides impressive evidence of the essential truth of Smith's theory of production. Individual initiative, properly compensated, has been the dynamic force behind the growth of a mighty nation. And market forces, operating in a competitive environment, have served to harmonize the plans of millions of economic units, thereby fostering the national welfare.

The validity of Smith's views has been reaffirmed time and again during the past two or three decades. By the end of World War II, for example, a large part of the industrial plant of Germany had been destroyed and the confidence of its people shattered by the collapse of the German nation and its division into two separate political entities. The postwar recovery of the economy of West Germany, operating under conditions of free enterprise, has nevertheless been spectacular. Its per capita output is now among the highest in the world, and its products are exported to every corner of the globe. East Germany, on the other hand, installed a centrally managed system, and its economy floundered for a number of years. Economic growth in East Germany appears to have perked up of late, but its per capita output is still well below that of West Germany.

The postwar record of economic progress in countries such as Israel and Japan, which encourage individual initiative and private enterprise, is even more striking. In a mere quarter of a century, the Israelis have managed to transform a desert into a flourishing modern nation. Japan is also poorly endowed with natural resources and its large population is crowded into a small area; its economy has nevertheless grown swiftly. Currently, the production of Japan is exceeded only by that of the United States and the Soviet Union. Since 1960, the real gross national product of Japan has more than tripled, and it is still rising much faster than in any other major industrial country.

The Japanese economic miracle has received universal acclaim. The achievements of other Asian countries that give large scope to free enterprise—Thailand, South Korea, Taiwan, Singapore, and Hong Kong—are not as widely known. Yet, all these countries experienced average yearly increases in real per capita output ranging from 5 to over 8 percent during the decade of the 1960s.

The Crown Colony of Hong Kong might indeed serve as a monument to Adam Smith, for nowhere in the modern world have his economic principles been followed more closely. You may recall that Smith, in his discussion of the benefits of foreign trade, noted that a nation would be most likely to profit from foreign commerce if its trading partners were rich, industrious, and commercial nations. Lacking geographical neighbors that fit this description, Hong Kong took advantage of advances in transportation and communication that have made it possible to trade profitably on a worldwide basis. In 1972, over three-fourths of Hong Kong's exports—largely manufactured goods—went to Europe and North America. And the value of its total exports apparently exceeded that of mainland China, whose population is perhaps 200 times as large as that of Hong Kong.

In Latin America, the highest rate of economic growth of any nation at the present time is enjoyed by Brazil, whose economic system has moved closer in recent years to the principles of Adam Smith. Decisions as to the direction of investment are now left largely to the business community; foreign investments are encouraged; individuals are free to choose the line of work that best suits their talents and to enjoy the rewards accorded by the market to successful performance. This system of economic organization, aided by the great natural and human resources of Brazil, is producing excellent results. The rate of growth of Brazilian production has been 9 percent or more in each of the past five years; last year, in fact, real output in that country rose more than 11 percent.

Lively competition, individual incentives, and a pricing mechanism to allocate resources are as important to the growth of national wealth now as they were in the Great Britain of the eighteenth century. That fact, I believe, is gaining recognition beyond the boundaries of what we loosely call the Free World. In recent years, the socialist countries of Eastern Europe have begun to reconsider their earlier policy of guiding the course of their complex economies through central planning and detailed regulation of most aspects of economic life. They have begun to ponder whether the production of some unwanted goods or obsolete machines might not reflect the failure of prices to signal changes in consumer or business demands; whether more rapid technological progress might be encouraged by providing industrial managers with stronger incentives for taking risks; whether workers would increase their productivity if more opportunities became available to improve their own lot and that of their families through greater individual effort.

In most of these countries, pockets of free enterprise have indeed remained, and they have provided the socialist authorities with some dramatic examples of the vitality of Adam Smith's theory of production. In the Soviet Union, for example, individuals are allowed to cultivate small agricultural plots and to retain or sell the produce they raise. Yields per acre on these small pieces of land are typically far higher than on the huge and highly mechanized collective farms. In 1962, for example, small private farms constituted only 3 percent of the total acreage cultivated in the Soviet Union, but they accounted for a decisive part of the meats, milk, eggs, vegetables, and fruit produced and consumed in the country—in fact, for over a third of the country's total agricultural production. The Soviet people have literally been kept alive by free enterprise in their household agriculture, and the significance of this fact cannot have escaped their attention entirely.

In some if not all socialist countries, doctrinaire adherence to centralized planning and regimentation of economic life is gradually being displaced by a more flexible administration of the economic system. Wider scope for decision making is being given to individual factory managers; monetary incentives related to economic performance are becoming more common; a larger role is being assigned to prices in the allocation of resources. Notable examples of this trend may be found in Yugoslavia and Hungary, where significant efforts have been made in recent years to accelerate economic development by moving toward a more flexible, less centrally directed form of economic organization. In the Soviet Union, also, a reform of the industrial structure is currently under way, aiming among other things at decentralization of research and development programs.

In the developing nations, too, a trend is evident towards wider acceptance of Adam Smith's theory of economic development. A decade or two ago, many of these countries were seeking to rush headlong into heavy industry, bypassing the development of agriculture and light industry for which their resource base and their technical skills were better suited. Barriers to imports were created to speed industrial development, while one industry after another was saddled with restrictions and regulations that made competition in world markets extremely difficult. Political leaders in these countries had become so fascinated with the thought of rapid industrialization that they not infrequently ended up by creating industrial temples rather than efficient and commercially profitable enterprises.

Some costly lessons have been learned, and some ancient truths rediscovered, from this experience. Of late, developing countries have been reconsidering the benefits of agriculture and light industry as paths to economic progress. More of the developing countries are now encouraging private foreign investment, and practically every nation is seeking ways to raise productivity, open new markets, and foster a spirit of enterprise among its people.

Policy makers across the world thus keep coming back to the principles enunciated by Adam Smith some two hundred years ago. A contemporary reader of *The Wealth of Nations* cannot escape being impressed with the vigor of Smith's analysis and its relevance to the world of today. Yet, he will also be struck, I believe, by the fact that nations are nowadays concerned with economic problems that were hardly foreseen in his great treatise on political economy.

While Adam Smith was at work on *The Wealth of Nations*, another enterprising Scotsman, James Watt, was still struggling to perfect the steam engine. Today we split the atom to augment the supply of electricity, and we send men on fantastic voyages to the moon. With the progress of science, the proliferation of industry, and the spread of urbanization, the interdependence of economic activities has greatly increased. Opportunities for conflict between private and public interests have therefore grown in importance. Adam Smith, to be sure, was not unaware that such conflicts could occur. Contrary to a widespread impression, he put fences around free enterprise—for example, by arguing in behalf of certain restrictions on free trade, by recognizing the need for governmental maintenance of roads, harbors, and similar public works, and even by accepting statutory ceilings on interest rates as a contribution to the general welfare. Adam Smith, however, had no need to concern himself with pollution of air or water, or with urban blight, or with depletion of energy sources, or with insistent political pressures for better education, improved health care, more recreational facilities, and a host of other things that have led to extensive governmental involvement in the economic life of industrialized nations.

The business cycle of modern times, especially in nations that practice free enterprise, has given special impetus to the enlargement of governmental responsibilities. Experience over many years had demonstrated that active competition serves to coordinate individual plans and thus enables markets for specific commodities to function, on the whole, in satisfactory fashion. However, experience also taught us that while competition is a good cure for overproduction in a specific market, it is a very inadequate cure when a shortage of demand develops simultaneously in many markets. In such a case, business activity as a whole will slump, the flow of incomes will be checked, and unemployment will spread; in short, the nation will experience a business recession. On the other hand, when demand becomes excessive in many markets simultaneously, the general level of prices will rise and this too will bring economic troubles.

In recent decades, therefore, governments have sought to stimulate the general level of economic activity at certain times, and to restrict it at other times, by a flexible use of their monetary and fiscal policies. Of late, a new phenomenon—a disconcerting rise in the price level even in the absence of excess aggregate demand—has troubled various industrial countries. This development has led some governments to intervene directly in wage and price decisions in the hope of achieving simultaneously both full employment and general price stability.

We thus face problems today with which Adam Smith did not concern himself. Economic life keeps changing, and each generation must face anew the central problem with which he dealt so boldly—that is, how best to draw the line between private and governmental activities in the interest of augmenting the general welfare. As we go about this task, we cannot be blind to the imperfections of market processes or to the abuses of market power by business firms or labor organizations. But we also cannot afford to neglect Adam Smith's warning, of which recent experience provides ample illustration, that governments not infrequently create new problems, besides wasting resources that could have been put to effective use by private citizens or business firms.

In the course of my career, both as a student and as a public official, I have found it necessary to revise my ideas about the proper role of government in specific economic matters. Experience is a demanding teacher, and my respect for it has led me at times to favor governmental actions that I abhorred in my youth. My confidence in the basic advantages of free enterprise remains, however, unshaken. I continue to believe, as Adam Smith argued so cogently, that when a nation's economic activity is organized on the basis of free enterprise, men and women will by and large employ their talents in ways that enrich and strengthen the nation's economy. More important still, it is only by avoiding excessive concentration of power in the hands of government that we can preserve our individual liberties and have the opportunity to seek personal fulfillment with full dignity.

The Significance of
Our Productivity Lag

It is a pleasure for me to join this commencement assemblage in paying tribute to the graduating class of the University of South Carolina.

Those of you graduating today are part of a great tradition. The first graduate went forth from Carolina's classrooms when Thomas Jefferson was President of the United States. And many of the students who have followed since then—some of whose names commemorate the buildings in which you have lived and studied—have made notable contributions both to this region and to the country at large. I trust that in the years ahead—in whatever careers you pursue—you will never cease to draw inspiration from the achievements of those in whose footsteps you follow.

In considering what I might appropriately say to you today, I found my thoughts turning repeatedly to the remarkable transformation that our nation's economy has undergone since the time this institution was founded. The broad outlines of that transformation—from simple agrarianism to the complexities of our modern industrial state—are well known to all. So, too, is the remarkable record of material gain that has flowed to our people in the process.

What may perhaps be less fully appreciated is that the material progress we have made as a nation—and which has long been the marvel of the world—was by no means an inevitable occurrence, despite our endowment of natural resources. Nor is it something whose extension we dare take for granted. I believe,

Commencement address at the University of South Carolina, May 14, 1977.

35

rather, that the bounty that is ours came about chiefly because we have had the wisdom throughout most of our history to foster an environment in which the latent energies of our people had generous scope for realization. Ours has been a society in which men and women, no matter what the circumstances of their birth, have known that there were ultimately no boundaries to what might be achieved with effort and ingenuity. That faith—and the spirit of independence and drive it has fostered—has been the essential dynamic force in the economic life of our nation.

In the language economists are prone to use in describing material gains, what we have had in America is an astonishing record of productivity achievement. Our environment of enterprise and the rewards it has offered have prodded us to great effort. Historically, we have been an industrious and an inventive people. We have striven for self-improvement and the betterment of our families; and we have been willing, both individually and collectively, to sacrifice and scrimp when investment opportunities beckoned. We have, moreover, been imaginative and persistent in devising better ways of doing things and in applying new technologies in the organization of our productive activities.

The consequences of all this in terms of the efficiency of performance of the individual American worker have been striking. It is, indeed, our impressive historical record of upward climb in output per hour worked that is the foundation of our economic strength. To be sure, the aggregate income and wealth of our nation have grown with the passage of time partly because our work force has grown in size. But that has been far less important as a source of output gain than some of you may realize. Overwhelmingly, what has been critical—to the extent of accounting for about two-thirds of the rise in national output over the span of our history—has been the advance in labor productivity, the simple fact that an hour of labor progressively has yielded more and more output.

I focus on this today because I think it is important for you to have an awareness that our country's productivity growth has exhibited a slowing in recent years, both absolutely and relative to that of other countries. You should recognize this as a matter of great concern to you personally and to the future of the nation. Indeed, largely because of the slowing of the underlying rate of productivity growth—to a pace a third less rapid in the last ten years than in the 1950s and early 1960s—we can no longer boast of having the highest per capita standard of living in the world.

Far more is at stake, of course, than the issue of international prestige. As a nation, we can consume no more than we produce, so that unless productivity growth reaccelerates, our citizens inevitably will enjoy less rapid gains in living standards in the future than has been customary historically. It requires little imagination to foresee that troublesome tensions could arise from that situation as competing groups in our society endeavor to secure a larger share for themselves of production gains that are disappointing in the aggregate. Also of great significance is the fact that without a reacceleration of productivity growth we shall find ourselves increasingly cramped in our public life in channeling resources to the solution of domestic and international problems.

These are powerful reasons for trying to understand the causes of the productivity weakening that has recently occurred. A good deal of scholarly effort has in fact been devoted precisely to that end. However, we still cannot be sure how much of the slowdown in productivity growth reflects transitory as distinct from more basic causes.

One cause of slower productivity growth in recent years that is presumably of a temporary nature has been an increase in the proportion of relatively inexperienced workers in our labor force. This reflects several influences: first, a greatly enlarged stream of young people entering labor markets in the late 1960s and early 1970s as a delayed consequence of the very high fertility rates that followed World War II; second, the increasing tendency for adult women—many lacking recent work experience—to seek employment; and third, the prevailing trend toward early retirement. As the younger workers and adult women gain in job experience, however, the depressant effect on productivity growth of the shift in the age and sex composition of the labor force will no longer be operative. Indeed, a reversal may already be in progress.

A more complicated issue to assess—but one that likewise involves the potential for a favorable turn—concerns the way in which our nation's capital stock grows in relation to the labor force. In recent years, the exceptionally rapid rate of labor-force growth has not been matched by a corresponding acceleration in capital formation. In fact, even apart from the slump in capital investment during the recent recession and the disappointing recovery in capital spending since then, the growth of this country's stock of capital has tended to be slower for some time than in the earlier postwar period. This combination of circumstances —rapid labor-force increase and a slowing in the pace of capital formation—has meant that progress in equipping our work force with increasing amounts of capital equipment has proceeded much less rapidly than in the 1950s and the 1960s. That unquestionably has been detrimental to the maintenance of productivity gains at their historical pace. Demographic influences, however, are gradually becoming somewhat less awesome. Within the next few years, the growth rate of the labor force is likely to decline appreciably, reflecting the lower fertility rates that followed the earlier postwar bulge. In that situation, the challenge of achieving an accelerated pace of capital formation relative to labor supply will become less formidable—provided, of course, that we are successful in maintaining a climate of enterprise that is conducive to capital spending by business firms.

Despite these two potentially favorable influences—that is, the trend emerging toward restoration of a more experienced work force and the definite possibility that faster growth may resume in the capital stock per worker—complacency about future productivity developments is by no means warranted.

I say this because the productivity slump which we have been experiencing is only partially explained in terms of the changing experience of our labor force and the amount of capital our workers have been equipped with. Careful study of those two factors still leaves a substantial part of the recent productivity slowing unexplained. Other adverse influences apparently have been at work as well.

My own judgment is that we have been undergoing a change in our societal values and attitudes that has contributed significantly to poorer job performance in recent years. I advance that as a hypothesis only, not as an established fact. It is a hypothesis, however, for which there is regrettably a considerable body of supportive evidence.

Testimony to a lessened sense of industriousness on the part of our work force is certainly present, it seems to me, in this country's record of job absenteeism. The number of people who simply do not show up for work on any given day, especially before and after weekends, has been rising in recent years and has assumed worrisome proportions. In a typical week last year, almost five million workers had unscheduled absences from their jobs for a day or more either because of reported illness or for other personal reasons. Last year's absenteeism involved the loss of more than 100 million hours of working time per week, giving rise, one can be sure, to a great deal of unnecessary cost and inefficiency in the operations of our businesses—ranging from disruption of production schedules to overstaffing by employers as a defensive measure. No one would deny, of course, that many unscheduled absences are justified by illness or personal or family emergencies. But there is evidence that absenteeism has risen faster in recent years than the number of employed individuals, and this suggests that decided changes have been under way in our country in the basic work attitudes of employees.

The high and rising incidence of absenteeism would be easier to understand if workers in this country enjoyed less paid time off than they do. Significantly, however, the average factory worker now gets nine paid holidays each year and many workers get more. There has been an impressive liberalization throughout the postwar period, moreover, in the amount of time employees can take as paid vacation. Indicative of the trend is the fact that more than two-thirds of factory workers with twenty-five years service now get a full month's vacation, whereas fifteen years ago only about one in five enjoyed such generous vacations.

Employers, in short, are increasingly remunerating workers for time during which no work is performed. At present about 7 percent of total payroll costs incurred by the average employer in this country goes to pay for time that employees are not explicitly on the job. And the full costs of paying for nonworking time would be much larger if there were any meaningful way of measuring the extraordinary number of hours spent on coffee breaks, wash-up time, retirement parties, and other social rites that have increasingly become a part of our working lives.

Against this background, is there really any wonder that many of our producers find it difficult to compete internationally and that so many of the products in our homes and garages bear foreign names?

These developments relating to work attitudes and the amount of leisure time we are opting for as a society are a relatively neglected aspect, I believe, of scholarly investigation into the causes of the slowing in our productivity growth. I think they must be brought into sharper focus to facilitate wider public understanding of what is at stake. It is not at all clear that people actually perceive that lessened work effort inevitably must be reflected in the material benefits we as a people can enjoy. That linkage was inescapably evident earlier in our history—when, to a much greater degree than is now the case, men and women could literally see what their individual effort yielded in consumable products; but the linkage has been blurred as our productive and distributive mechanisms have grown in complexity.

I trust it is clear that these matters are by no means of remote concern to young people such as you who are now embarking on careers. Indeed, I would call your attention to the fact that during your lifetimes the degree of productivity growth achieved by the work force, will, if anything, be more important than it is now, simply because of the changing ratio of the working to the nonworking portions of our population. Reflective of the longer lifespan people are enjoying and the trend toward lower birth rates, we are now experiencing a rapid expansion in the elderly portion of our population. A relatively heavy burden will thus fall on the employed portion of the population to produce goods and services not just for themselves, but also for the swelling numbers of people who will be beyond retirement age. That prospect emphatically underscores the importance of re-achieving and maintaining strong productivity growth.

I urge you to think about the implications of that challenge and to consider carefully the interest you have in helping to foster a renewed spirit of industriousness in this nation. The future is yours to do with it what you will. I hope you will choose wisely.

The Need for Better Profits

It is a pleasure for me to be here on the campus of Gonzaga University to participate in this celebration of Founder's Day. I am also pleased to be able to join you in honoring a great teacher of economics, Dr. Graue. It is eminently fitting that Dr. Graue's contribution to economic understanding should be noted today not only by festivity but also by serious economic discussion.

In consonance with that, I would like to address a feature of our current economic environment which, as long as it persists, could well prove an insurmountable barrier to the achievement of full employment in our country. I refer to the fact that the profits being earned by American business are at an unsatisfactory level.

It is both striking and disturbing, I believe, that profits get relatively little attention these days from economists. I have the impression that the economics profession has almost forgotten that ours is still predominantly a profit-motivated economy in which, to a very large extent, whatever happens—or doesn't happen—depends on perceived profit opportunities. Certainly, the preoccupation in the nation's capital tends to be with other matters. The slightest hint, for example, of emerging trouble for the economy will promptly unloose a flood of fiscal and monetary proposals, virtually all predicated on the notion that what is crucial is governmental manipulation of aggregate demand. Seldom does anyone pause to ask what should be a

Address at Gonzaga University's 1977 Founder's Day, Spokane, Washington, October 26, 1977.

compellingly obvious question—namely, whether lack of confidence in profit opportunities on the part of our profit-oriented businessmen and investors may not be the essential cause of difficulty.

My own judgment is that a deep-rooted concern about prospective profits has in fact become a critical conditioner of economic performance in our country. If I am right in thinking so, actions taken in Washington to enlarge the already huge budget deficit in the interest of more consumer spending are likely to be of little sustained benefit in reducing the level of unemployment. That was a principal reason why I felt no lasting benefit could flow from the fifty-dollar rebate that was under consideration early this year.

If poor profitability is adversely affecting economic performance, we should expect business firms to exercise great caution in embarking on capital-investment projects. No businessman is likely to add to his plant or equipment if the promise of a decent return is not present. The current expansion of the overall economy, while otherwise generally satisfactory, has been marked by notably weaker investment spending than was characteristic of previous recoveries. In the two-and-a-half years of this expansion, real capital outlays have increased only half as much as they did, on average, over like periods in the previous five expansions. The shortfall has been especially marked in the case of major long-lived industrial construction projects, and it has occurred even in industries—such as paper and basic chemicals—in which the rate of utilization of industrial capacity is well advanced.

Unless the willingness of businessmen to invest in new plant and equipment increases decisively, the expansion of economic activity now under way will continue to lack balance. And that, I need hardly add, will make it more uncertain whether the expansion is going to continue at a sufficient pace to bring unemployment down significantly, or—for that matter—whether the expansion itself will long continue.

The weakness of profits in recent years is not the only cause of investment hesitancy, but it is unquestionably a very important cause. To be sure, many people have a contrary impression about the general level or the trend of profits. In fact, the most commonly cited profits figures—the so-called book profits that businesses report to their stockholders—have risen spectacularly in the last few years, and in total are currently running just about double their level a decade ago. But these raw profit figures are misleading and they should never be taken at face value.

In actuality—as the more sophisticated observers of corporate finances know—raw profit numbers have become virtually meaningless as a guide to corporate affairs because of the way in which inflation distorts the calculation of profits. Under historical cost accounting—the method used widely for inventory valuation and universally for capital-asset valuation—the true costs of producing goods in an ongoing business are far from fully captured. Rather, they are significantly understated with respect to both the drawdown of materials from inventory and the consumption of capital assets. And when costs are understated on an accounting basis, profits of course are overstated; that is to say, the reported total of profits contains an element of inflationary fluff that in no sense enlarges a firm's ability to pay dividends or add to retained earnings.

The practical consequence of the inflationary fluff on a company's fortunes is decidedly negative, since taxes have to be paid on the "phantom" portion of profits. Quite obviously, this has lessened the ability of corporations to add to their capital investment without borrowing. The tax drain has become very large in recent years because of the enormous understatement of costs. For 1976, for example, the Commerce Department estimates that the replacement cost of inventories used up by nonfinancial corporations exceeded by $14 billion the materials expenses claimed for tax purposes. More striking still is the Department's estimate for last year of the amount by which depreciation charges based on historical cost fell short of the replacement cost of the capital assets consumed. That estimate came to nearly $36 billion, making the combined understatement of costs from these two sources $50 billion in 1976.

The huge understatement of costs that arises because of inflation cannot be ignored by anyone seriously concerned with corporate earnings. Once account is taken of the distortions wrought by inflation—and when an offsetting adjustment is also made to allow for the changes over time in Treasury depreciation rules—we find that the level of corporate profits was overstated in 1976 by about $30 billion, and that this resulted in an over-payment of some $10 to $12 billion in income taxes. True economic profits of corporations are thus very different from reported book profits.

Just how poor the trend of profits has recently been is clearly indicated by the fact that in each year from 1968 through 1975 the after-tax "economic profits" of nonfinancial corporations from domestic operations were, in the aggregate, consistently below the levels reached during 1965–1967. A new high level of these profits was indeed reached during 1976, but even that achievement is decidedly unimpressive when profits are expressed as a rate of return on the amount of equity capital in use. So far in the inflation-riddled 1970s, the after-tax rate of return on stockholders' equity has averaged only about 3¼ percent when the tangible assets portion of equity capital is valued, as it should be, on a replacement cost basis. That figure is lower by two percentage points than the average rate of return for the 1950s and 1960s. Despite a sizable recovery from the recent recession, the rate of return on the equity investment in our corporations appears to be running currently at a level not significantly different from the depressed average so far this decade.

Anyone who wonders why capital spending has been so halting or why stock prices have behaved so poorly for so long would be well advised to study this dismal record of what American business has been earning. Historically, there has been an impressively close correlation between the rate of return on stockholders' equity and the rate of real investment. The linkage between the rate of return on equity and the behavior of equity prices is looser, but it still suggests that professional investment managers are no longer being deceived by the inflationary fluff in profit numbers. The stock market, by and large, has not been behaving capriciously; instead it has been telegraphing us a message of fundamental importance.

At any given point in time, investment activity and stock market behavior are conditioned, of course, by much more than current profit readings. What is ultimately decisive in determining the behavior of investors and businessmen is not the rate of return currently earned on past investments but rather expectations about future earnings. Very often current earnings are an excellent proxy for expectations about future earnings; some-times they are not. My judgment is that businessmen and in-vestors at present have a sense of doubt and concern about the future that is even greater than would be justified by the low level of true economic profits.

One telling piece of evidence that this is so is the pro-nounced hesitancy of businessmen in going forward with capital-spending projects that involve the acquisition of long-lived assets. The investment recovery that we have experienced so far in this cyclical expansion has been heavily concentrated in rela-tively short-lived capital goods that promise quick returns—trucks, office equipment, and light machinery, for example. Major investment projects that cannot be expected to provide payback for many years encounter serious delays in getting management's approval. Indeed, the decline of industrial construction that set in during the recent recession continued through the first quarter of this year—two years after general economic recovery got under way—and has not yet turned around decisively enough to establish a clear trend.

Many businessmen have a deep sense of uncertainty about what the longer future holds and, as a consequence, are dis-counting expected future earnings more heavily than they ordi-narily would in their investment calculations. The special degree of risk that businessmen see overhanging new undertakings means that they often will not proceed with a project unless the prospect exists for a higher-than-normal rate of return. This is not only skewing investment toward short-lived assets; it is also fostering an interest in mergers and acquisitions—something that does not require waiting out new construction undertakings. There has been a noticeable pickup in merger activity recently, but such activity generates neither additional jobs nor additional capacity for our nation's economy.

The reasons why businessmen appear to be assigning special risk premiums to major investment undertakings are complex, and I certainly cannot deal with them exhaustively today. But I would like at least to touch on the conditioning influences that seem most important—beyond, of course, the critical fact that current corporate earnings, properly reckoned, are discourag-ingly low.

My frequent discussions with businessmen leave little doubt in my mind that a strong residue of caution in businessmen's thinking has carried over from the recession of 1974–1975. I think it is fair to say that the present generation of business managers had developed an inordinate degree of faith in government's ability to manage and sustain economic expansion. When they discovered that that faith was not justified, the experience was sobering—particularly for the not inconsiderable number of businessmen who had imprudently expanded debt in the froth of the earlier prosperity. Moreover, the lingering sense of unease produced by the severity of the recession has been deepened by the sluggishness of the subsequent recovery in much of the world economy outside the United States. In contrast to the widely shared conviction of just a few years ago that the business cycle had been mastered, a surprising number of businessmen are now seized by concern that the world economy may have entered a downphase of some long cycle. One factor sparking such speculation is apprehension that the quantum jump in energy prices may be affecting the world's growth potential to a more serious extent than was originally thought likely.

More troublesome still, the specter of serious inflation continues to haunt the entire business community. The fear that inflation will not be effectively controlled is indeed a key reason for the high-risk premiums that businessmen nowadays typically assign to major investment undertakings. Increasingly, businessmen understand the severity of the burden they are carrying on account of the taxation of "phantom" profits. They also have learned the hard way—from the frenetic conditions of 1973–1974 —that inflation is totally inimical to a healthy business environment. Having little basis for projecting how inflation will affect their enterprises and fearful that government may in time resort to direct controls once again, they feel bewildered in attempting to judge their future costs or their future selling prices. Because of that, they yearn for some solid piece of evidence that inflation will be tamed. They are troubled because no such evidence is yet at hand.

Added to these concerns is the fact that businessmen have had great difficulty in evaluating the implications of the major policy initiatives that are being considered this year. Businessmen cannot at this juncture confidently judge what kinds of energy will be available in the years ahead. Nor do they yet have any firm basis for assessing what kinds of tax incentives or disincentives may apply to particular energy uses. They are concerned that innovations in social security financing now under consideration may end the traditional rule under which employer and employee taxes have been the same and, as a consequence, lead to multibillion dollar increases in the social security levies they have to pay. They suspect, moreover—as do many others—that the revamping of welfare programs will prove much more expensive than is now being estimated and that still additional taxes on businesses will be imposed as a means of financing reform. And the daily rumors about impending tax reform, among which ending of preferential treatment of capital gains is frequently emphasized, have contributed to a mood of unease in both corporate board rooms and the stock exchanges. So too has the expectation that a serious campaign for a costly undertaking in national health insurance may start next year.

I strongly suspect that the ability of businessmen to assimilate new policy proposals into their planning framework has now been stretched pretty far. In fact, I seldom talk with a businessman these days who does not, in one way or another, voice concern about his inability to make meaningful projections of corporate costs and earnings for the years immediately ahead.

The implications of the matters on which I have been dwelling—the behavior of profits and the state of mind of the business community—appear to have escaped a good many people. Economic analysts who insist, for instance, that capital spending will automatically catch fire as capacity margins diminish are, in my judgment, thinking too mechanically. Much will depend on the process by which the economy reaches more intensive utilization of resources—especially on government's role in that process.

I also think that analysts endeavoring to assess capital-spending prospects—and indeed prospects for the economy generally—may be neglecting a sensitive cyclical development. I refer to the fact that, whereas prices charged by business generally advanced more rapidly than did the costs incurred by business in the early stages of this expansion, that is no longer the case. This, of course, means that profits per unit of output have stopped rising and may indeed have begun to fall—a development typical of the more advanced stage of business cycle expansions and one that is certainly not conducive to vigorous capital-investment activity. I know enough about business cycle behavior to avoid at this time the inference that a sustained profits squeeze is emerging. We have here, nevertheless, an incipient imbalance in the economic situation that ought to concern us. And it is one more compelling reason to ask if national policy does not need to be more explicitly oriented to the strengthening of profitability and the encouragement of capital formation.

The last time business investment in fixed capital was as weak as it has been since 1973 was in the late 1950s and early 1960s. I believe there are some policy lessons we can profitably draw from that period. There was a great deal of concern at that time that a phase of deep-seated economic malaise had set in, with worry voiced that sluggishness in business investment might well prevent the economy from attaining full employment. The parallels with today—both in objective fact and in assessment—are close in many respects, the major differences being that profit rates were not as low then, nor was inflation comparably troublesome.

A bold policy approach—predicated on the need for stimulation of capital investment—was then developed, with one of President Kennedy's early messages to Congress calling for enactment of an innovative tax device, namely, the investment tax credit. The Revenue Act of 1962 brought the tax credit into being. That same year witnessed a reinforcement of investment incentives in the form of significant liberalization of Treasury depreciation rules. The investment-oriented thrust of policy was followed, moreover, by recommendations for broadly based income tax reductions for both businesses and individuals, and they ultimately were embodied in the Revenue Act of 1964. Taken together, those actions of the early 1960s were sensitively responsive to conditions that have many similarities to the situation in which we now find ourselves. And what is particularly worth recalling, those actions soon had the consequence of strengthening dramatically both investment activity and the general economy.

If we were able to launch a policy response now that was just as unambiguously positive in its implications for profitability, I for one would have little doubt about our economy's capacity to shake off its malaise. As every recent study of our nation's investment needs has emphasized, we are confronted with an enormous capital-formation challenge for the years ahead. If we have the good sense to create hospitable conditions for saving and investing, I truly believe ours could become an age of sustained progress in employment and well-being.

The doubts and uncertainties that now prevail in the business and investing community reflect, in large part, irritation or annoyance at what is viewed as governmental myopia. They must not be interpreted as being indicative of business timidity. That enormous vitality and dynamism still exist in our business system is attested by the extraordinary fact that, despite the weakness of profits in recent years and the cumulating anxieties about the future, our economy has actually generated nearly seven million jobs since the spring of 1975—nearly all of them, I should add, in private industry.

The practicality of so many initiatives in this administration's first year is arguable, but the President's leadership also bespeaks a seriousness of purpose that in the end may bring lasting benefits to our nation. We have been through a year of animated policy debates—a year, I think, of useful growth in the perception of how plausible but divergent objectives can be practically blended. The basic reform this country now needs is the creation of an environment with many new job opportunities for our people. I expect the dust of controversy to settle and that constructive legislation will follow.

I do not mean to suggest that encouragement of investment through a bold tax policy is all that is needed. Such encouragement is vital, to be sure, and it will undoubtedly make a difference in the willingness of businessmen to invest in new plant and equipment. But the effort at eliminating the high risk that now attaches to investment must be of broader reach. It must go to the array of concerns of the business community about energy policy, about environmental codes, about governmental regulations at large, and—above all—about inflation.

I cannot overstate the importance of unwinding the inflation that is continuing to plague our economy. There is a paramount need for avoiding new cost-raising measures by government, of which the recently legislated increase of the minimum wage is only the most recent very troublesome example. Fiscal and monetary policies need to be conducted in ways that will quiet rather than heighten inflationary expectations. On the fiscal side, this means that great caution will have to be observed both in giving up tax revenues and in program initiatives entailing new expenditures. As a practical matter, expenditures on some existing programs may therefore have to give way. We simply dare not take steps that would result in any appreciable enlargement of our already swollen budget deficit. That could only excite unease in the business and financial community.

On the monetary side, I want to assure you that we at the Federal Reserve fully appreciate the critical linkage between money creation and inflation. We have no intention of letting the money supply grow at a rate that will add fuel to the fires of inflation. On the contrary, we are determined to bring about a gradual reduction in the rate of money expansion to a pace compatible with reasonable price stability. That cannot be done quickly because of the powerful inflationary pressures that have become embedded in our economic life over so many years; but I assure you that it will be done if the Federal Reserve retains— as I expect it will—the independence from political pressures on which the Congress has so wisely insisted across the decades. That does not mean that the Federal Reserve is preoccupied with the objective of monetary firmness. Our obligation to foster financial conditions that favor the expansion of job opportunities is clear and I assure you this is very much on our minds. We constantly keep probing for that delicate balance between too much and too little money.

The increase of short-term interest rates that has occurred since late April has served to check what would otherwise have been an explosion of the money supply. By taking measures to check the growth of money, we have demonstrated that we remain alert to the dangers of inflation. As a consequence, long-term interest rates, which nowadays are extremely sensitive to expectations of inflation, have remained substantially stable. Had we not taken steps to bring the money supply under control, I have little doubt that fears of inflation would now be running stronger, and that long-term interest rates, which play such a significant role in shaping investment decisions, would therefore now be higher than they in fact are. In that event, of course, the continuance of economic expansion would be less secure.

We at the Federal Reserve always welcome advice on how best to proceed. Ours, however, is the responsibility to act in the monetary area, and we intend to exercise that responsibility in ways that promote the long-run as well as the immediate interests of this nation.

Investing in Physical and Human Capital

I am truly delighted to be here this morning. Back last spring when Dick Shinn invited me to be a speaker on this occasion, I promptly accepted. I knew, first of all, that being here would afford me the pleasure of seeing old friends. I also knew that I could count on an audience seriously concerned with the economic problems that confront our nation. That, indeed, is the strong tradition of the entities from which this council has been formed. As a former trustee of a life insurance company and as a former participant in the work of the National Bureau of Economic Research, I know something firsthand of your industry's record of sustained and generous support of scholarly research relating to economics and finance. Against such a background of considerations, your chairman's offer to me was one I could hardly refuse.

I want to use my time at this rostrum today to share some thoughts with you about the troubles our economy is experiencing in reaching a satisfactory level of jobs and in purging itself of inflation. I make no pretense of being able to advance quick solutions for the problems we are living with. But I do have convictions about some steps that ought to be taken—and others that ought to be shunned—if we are eventually to extricate ourselves from our present condition. In my judgment, inadequacy of investment in plant and equipment—and also in human capital—is the most important reason why the ongoing economic

Address at the annual meeting of the American Council of Life Insurance, New York City, November 29, 1977.

recovery has been somewhat disappointing; it also is a factor in explaining why so little headway is now being recorded in lowering the basic inflation rate.

In characterizing the present recovery as disappointing, I do not want to be misunderstood. In view of the disabilities our economy accumulated over a long span of years, it would have been extremely difficult—no matter how skillful policy making had been—to achieve a recovery that was dramatically better than we have actually experienced. It is a statistical fact that this recovery has been of roughly average vigor compared with previous expansions since World War II. Indeed, it has been impressively better than average by the yardstick of increases in employment.

Still, there is ample reason for the sense of disappointment that so many people feel. Partly because of the unusual severity of the last recession, and partly also because of the accelerated expansion of our nation's labor force, the recovery of our economy since early 1975, while of substantial scope, has left us with a disturbingly large total of unemployment. As you well know, the national unemployment rate is currently about 7 percent, and it has exhibited a stickiness at that level for the last half year. Large segments of our work force, moreover, have been unusually hard hit. Young people and nonwhites especially have faced formidable difficulties in the search for jobs. The unemployment rate for blacks—approximating 14 percent at present—has shown no real improvement during this economic expansion, and the unemployment rate for black teenagers has soared to the dismaying level of nearly 40 percent. Clearly, we are a long way from satisfactory conditions in our labor markets.

I need hardly add that recent price behavior also has been disappointing. During the recession period, inflation did slow considerably from its puffed-up double-digit pace. During the last two years, however, despite considerable slack in both product and labor markets, the basic rate of inflation appears to have settled at an annual rate of about 6 percent. This reflects the fact that businesses have been granting annual compensation increments of between 8 and 9 percent on average, while experiencing productivity gains that recently have not averaged much above 2 percent.

The picture of economic performance before us is thus

blemished by having in it both too much unemployment and too much inflation. I know of no one who would take exception to that assessment. Where differences arise, of course, is with respect to remedial action.

Throughout most of the past thirty or forty years, the dominant view in this country—as in much of the rest of the world—has been that a condition of significant slack in the economy requires aggressive pursuit of fiscal and monetary ease; in other words, the government would have to run a sizable budget deficit by spending more or taxing less, and such a fiscal policy would need to be accommodated or reinforced by liberal supplies of money and credit. In this philosophic approach the kind of fiscal stimulus to be employed came to be viewed as much less important than its size. Giving the economy an adequate push and repeating the push again and again if necessary—that was the crucial imperative of economic policy.

This simplified Keynesian mode of thinking consistently tended to overlook structural rigidities in our economy. It also proceeded on the mistaken assumption that upward pressures on the price level would come into play only when high rates of resource utilization were achieved. Despite these blemishes of thought, Keynesian-type remedies worked reasonably well as long as they were applied in moderation. But their very success led to overdoing. With caution thrown to the winds in the mid-sixties, a relentless inflation has since then engulfed our economy. As a result, fears or expectations of inflation have become a vital fact that must now be reckoned with.

In this new economic environment, Keynesian-type remedies do not work as effectively as they once did. Many people have learned that larger governmental deficits and aggressive monetary ease are often forerunners of a new wave of inflation. Hence, when expectations of inflation mount, consumers are nowadays apt to save more rather than less, and such behavior obviously tends to offset the stimulating impulses that stem from a liberal fiscal policy. The like tends to be true of business behavior. Many, if not most, businessmen have learned that inflation inevitably confuses the calculation of costs, that in our present institutional setting it is generally destructive of profits, and that it sooner or later throws the economy out of balance and thereby leads to recession. Thus our economy is no longer working as it once did, and this paramount fact is now better understood than it was five years ago or even one year ago.

Nevertheless, mechanical Keynesianism still retains a strong grip on the thinking of many opinion makers in our country and abroad. Let the Federal Reserve, for example, move to restrain a burst of money growth—as it has felt compelled to do during the past half year—and such action triggers a torrent of protest. Much of the protest is predicated on the simple proposition that any rise of interest rates in the context of a less than fully employed economy jeopardizes continuance of economic expansion. The consideration that unimpeded money growth—if allowed to proceed under recent conditions—would greatly heighten expectations of inflation has been virtually ignored by the critics. Yet with such a heightening of inflationary expectations, long-term interest rates—which have become extremely sensitive to inflationary psychology—would surely have moved upward, in contrast to their actual behavior in remaining essentially stable. I need hardly add before this audience that long-term interest rates are far more important to the proper functioning of our economy—especially for homebuilding and capital formation generally—than are short-term rates.

The same attitudes that trigger protest whenever interest rates go up are also continuing to color thinking as to what constitutes appropriate fiscal policy. Let there be, for instance, a show of hesitancy in the expansion of the economy and proposals immediately come forth in great number urging stimulative governmental action. Only rarely is there any careful effort to tailor recommendations to identified specific weaknesses of economic performance. The overriding concern rather is with enlarging aggregate demand for goods and services by the quickest possible means. That, of course, was the genesis of last winter's fifty-dollar rebate scheme; and for a while at least, mechanical Keynesianism again inspired a good deal of thinking this autumn about how to keep economic recovery going next year.

I submit that our country will not succeed in making much headway against the problems that our economy is burdened with until we shed such conventional thinking about stabilization policies. Fortunately, I believe we are moving in that direction. I do not underestimate, however, the distance that yet needs to be travelled.

The way in which we as a nation deal with this problem of investment inadequacy will tell us whether policy making is in fact evolving constructively. As you in the audience know well, spending by American business on capital goods has been weak in this recovery relative to that in previous expansions. This weakness is all the more glaring when one takes into consideration the fact that a significant portion of capital spending is now devoted to governmentally mandated pollution-control and safety equipment that in no way enlarges industrial capacity. Moreover, recent business investment in capital goods has been disproportionately concentrated in relatively short-lived assets such as trucks, office equipment, and light machinery. Businesses have shown marked reluctance to undertake major investment projects where payback cannot be expected for many years. This failure of investment to show greater vigor has cost our economy many hundreds of thousands of jobs.

For a considerable while, the conventional explanation for the weak showing of investment activity was the low rate of utilization of industrial capacity. The counsel was not to fret, that capital investment will be reenergized as aggregate demand grows. However, as we moved up the scale of capacity utilization, investment in major, long-lived investment projects has continued to be characterized by a good deal of caution. My own view—which I have spelled out on previous occasions—is that businessmen's hesitancy in initiating major investment projects is fundamentally grounded in a deep sense of uncertainty about how the economic environment is likely to evolve over the next few years. That uncertainty—coupled with what has been a record of poor profitability in recent years—is the real barrier, I believe, to more normal investment activity.

To the extent that is true, indiscriminate federal injections of purchasing power into the economy would do little to end business reluctance to invest in major projects. To achieve a substantial lift in capital formation, specific attention to the shortcomings of the business environment is needed—particularly, to uncertainty about governmental policy concerning taxes, inflation, energy, and environmental controls. The need to reduce business taxes has become especially acute: first, in order to offset impending increases in social security and energy taxes; and second, to neutralize the massive overpayment of income taxes that stems from applying standard accounting rules to our inflation-ridden economy. Fortunately, perception of all these needs has been growing.

I believe that President Carter fully appreciates the importance of substantially lessening the psychological and financial obstacles to business investment. The like is true of many influential members of the Congress. I therefore expect that economic policy generally—and both tax and energy policy specifically— soon will take on a more constructive character. Over the next several months, I anticipate that decisions in Washington will at last reduce uncertainty, improve the state of business confidence, and encourage capital formation. Even now, there are some indications that investment in heavy machinery and in industrial construction projects is beginning to revive, and this tendency is practically bound to be reinforced by the more constructive turn of economic policy that now appears to be emerging.

The need for a stronger trend of business investment is important both for short-range and longer-term reasons. So far, the driving force of economic recovery has been supplied overwhelmingly by consumer spending and homebuilding. The outlook remains favorable for continued expansion in these activities, but it would not be at all surprising if further gains moderated. The consumer saving rate has become rather low and cannot reasonably be expected to drift downward; and the rate of housing starts has attained a level suggesting that additional gains in the coming year are likely to be modest. Thus, if the rate of overall economic growth is to be strong enough to reestablish a declining pattern in unemployment, it is vital that investment activity take on new vigor.

And there are other compelling reasons for fostering an environment favorable to capital formation. Historically, the enrichment of our labor force with a greater quantity and improved quality of capital goods has been a major source of productivity gains in our country and, consequently, of advances in "real" income per worker. One of the worrisome features of the lag in capital spending of recent years is that it has come at a time when growth in the labor force was accelerating. The combination of these trends has resulted in drastically slowing the secular updrift in the amount of fixed capital available per worker. Whereas in the 1950s and 1960s the ratio of capital stock to the work force increased by more than 2 percent a year, it rose by only about 1 percent in the early part of this decade and has actually slipped somewhat in the last two years. It should not be surprising that the slowing in the growth of capital investment has been accompanied by a slowing of productivity gains; output per man-hour has risen a third less rapidly over the last ten years than in the 1950s and early 1960s. By revitalizing the process of capital formation, productivity gains are likely to improve again and thus help to reduce the cost pressures that keep driving prices upward.

The imbalance that has been developing between capital formation and labor force growth has one other troublesome implication that needs to be brought into sharp focus. At present, the issue of potential capacity shortages does not arouse much interest, since capacity margins generally are quite comfortable. But when one bears in mind the long lead times in bringing major capital projects to completion, the emergence of a serious mismatch between industrial capacity and labor supply within the next several years is not difficult to visualize; that is to say, the practical limits of capacity utilization could be reached before unemployment is reduced to an acceptable level. That may well occur if we do not generate enough growth in industrial capacity to match the growth of our burgeoning labor force. In short, the case for substantially enlarged business spending on plant and equipment has become very powerful. Since this is coming to be increasingly understood and since fairly clear avenues for a governmental contribution to a better investment climate beckon, I am optimistic that the general economic outlook will indeed brighten.

I wish I could be equally sanguine that we will deal appropriately with the barriers that stand in the way of job opportunities for so many of our citizens. To the extent, of course, that encouragement of capital formation helps to produce a more balanced and stronger expansion of the economy, employment will be stimulated. But even with additional momentum imparted to the expansion, it is doubtful that the unemployment rate will drop over the next few years to a reading that would be commonly regarded as acceptable. The reason for skepticism is that a formidable array of structural factors is now impeding the smooth functioning of our labor markets—much more so than was the case ten or twenty years ago.

The most prominent of these is the recent upsurge in the growth of the labor force—a phenomenon dominated by sharply increasing participation of adult women. I mentioned earlier the substantial increase in employment since the recession trough of March 1975. In fact, the growth of jobs since then—totaling almost 7 million—has been larger, in percentage as well as in absolute terms, than during the comparable phase of any of the economic expansions since World War II. However, the increase in the labor force also has been exceptionally large in the course of this expansion—amounting to more than 6 million persons. Consequently, the reduction in overall unemployment has been quite limited.

The greatly increased participation of women in the labor force that has developed in recent years marks a revolution in the role of women in our society. The pressure of inflation on household budgets has spurred many women to seek supplementary family income, but it is clear that fundamental changes in social attitudes toward family life and careers for women have also played a large role. In March 1975, women of age twenty-five or over participating in the labor force constituted 43 percent of the adult female population. If this percentage had remained unchanged, the adult female labor force would now be lower by about 1.6 million. The large "extra" influx of female job seekers has, of course, taxed the absorptive capabilities of the labor market. So, too, have the large additions of young people seeking gainful employment—a reflection of the high birth rates of the 1950s and also of the rising rate of participation by young people in the labor force.

Both young people and adult women newly entering the labor market tend to have unemployment rates higher than average, in large part because they often lack relevant work experience. Their increasing role in the labor force has thus imparted a significant upward tilt to the overall unemployment rate compared, say, with the situation twenty years ago. That upward tilt has been reinforced by a number of other developments. The liberalization of both unemployment insurance and welfare programs has clearly increased the potential for extended idleness. The very fact that we have become a more affluent people also has made it possible for many individuals to be more selective in their search for work. Evidence has grown, too, that minimum wage legislation has become an increasingly significant deterrent to the employment of young people. And the reporting of unemployment has been influenced to some degree by the fact that being unemployed is sometimes a requisite in establishing eligibility for welfare benefits.

The combined effect of these and lesser structural influences cannot be gauged precisely. There is, nevertheless, fairly common agreement among careful analysts that an unemployment rate of something like 5 or 5½ percent would now be the economic equivalent of a 4 percent rate, say, two decades ago. This does not mean that we need permanently reconcile ourselves to such a level of unemployment; but it should caution us, as we strive to bring the unemployment rate down, that we are likely to experience labor market tautness and resulting inflationary stresses at a much higher level of joblessness than in the past.

In time, of course, some part of the upward bias now affecting the unemployment rate should automatically lessen. Growth in the younger-age component of the labor force can be expected to taper off in the next few years, reflecting the decline in birth rates that started in the 1960s. A lessened influx of young people into the job market should ease competition for youth-type jobs. And as the proportion of adult women with work experience increases, the incidence of unemployment among them should also gradually diminish. Such ameliorative tendencies, however, are likely to impinge slowly on the overall unemployment rate, and particularly stubborn obstacles to lowering black joblessness could well persist. The rush of white adult females into the labor force appears to have been responsible for some crowding out of less educated black workers, both male and female. And still another kind of competition may now be affecting younger black workers—that stemming from the sizable decline in the college enrollment rate of white youths since the late 1960s.

In view of the complex forces that have recently come into play in our job markets, an overall unemployment rate well above that which used to be regarded as normal remains a prospect for a considerable time ahead—in the absence, that is, of effective countering strategies. A persistently high unemployment rate would, of course, entail great wastage of economic potential for the nation, and—what is of greater consequence— it would destroy all hope of a decent place in life for hundreds of thousands of citizens. The need to address the structural influences that overhang our labor markets has become especially urgent for young people and black workers. The jobless rates of about 40 percent for black teenagers and of more than 20 percent for blacks between the ages of twenty and twenty-four express a tragic failure of our economic society. Unless we deal with that phase of unemployment constructively, whatever else may be done by way of trying to arrest and reverse urban deterioration is going to make little difference.

I have long argued, as some of you know, that a major impediment to job opportunities for unskilled workers is governmental interference with wage determination. However well-intentioned such action may be, our government has inflicted grievous injury to disadvantaged members of the labor force by mandating ever higher wage minima. An employer's decision to hire or not hire a particular individual depends critically on the relation between the wage of the employee and his likely productivity. When government raises the cost of hiring workers, as has just been done under a new minimum wage statute, no compensating increase takes place in their productivity; hence it becomes more difficult for some workers to retain their jobs and for others, particularly young people and other low-skill workers, to find jobs.

Despite widespread infatuation with raising wage minima, the perversity of such legislation is gradually being recognized. It is noteworthy that a proposal for a special subminimum youth wage lost by only one vote this year in the House of Representatives. That is the closest we have come to a sensible departure from our mistaken course. If this whole issue is not reopened in the next session of Congress, it would be desirable, at the very least, to seek legislation for a pilot experiment with a youth differential in, say, a half dozen cities with a view to demonstrating actual consequences of a lower minimum wage for young people. At the same time, and for much the same reasons, I would urge attention to the harmful results, especially for young people and blacks, of the wage floors mandated by the Davis-Bacon Act and the Walsh-Healy Act, which deal respectively with federally financed or assisted construction projects and with work performed on manufacturing and supply contracts of the federal government.

We need to understand that widespread access to jobs—especially for young people—is the surest way a society has of facilitating sound investment in human capital. Normally, the time for learning skills is when one is young. To the extent that meaningful work experience is blocked for young people, they can hardly be expected to become useful, productive citizens. Our legacy of missed training and of failure to acquire basic work habits will plague this country for literally decades ahead. The past cannot be undone, but that is all the more reason to prevent further human wastage by opening more channels to jobs that afford useful learning opportunities. Public service jobs that fail to teach transferable skills, as is often the case, merely disguise the problem. So, too, do income-maintenance welfare programs. Again, I wish to avoid misunderstanding. I happen to favor public service jobs that provide useful training, and I certainly do not oppose thoughtfully structured income-maintenance efforts for the needy. I do believe, however, that we must guard against social attitudes in which either course is seen—in the case of young people especially—as a tolerably acceptable alternative to entry into the mainstream of the job market.

Governmentally mandated wage minima are by no means the only institutional obstacle to the assimilation of young people and minorities into the active work force. Sooner or later—if only as an anti-inflationary step—we will have to come to grips with other artificial restrictions to employment opportunities that have developed in our country. In particular, attention needs to be directed to governmental licensing and certification requirements that limit entry to various occupations. It is hard to see, for instance, economic or social justification for the extremely high cost of becoming an owner-operator of a taxicab in this and other cities. Nor is it easy to justify the licensing requirements that complicate entry to trades that range from barbering to plumbing. Such licensing is at times merely a form of disguised monopoly that makes it difficult for people, especially members of minorities, to enter fields that otherwise would accommodate many additional workers.

The opening up of job opportunities for young people

and minorities clearly needs to be reinforced by improved education in primary and secondary schools. Despite the rapid closing in recent years of the wide educational gap that used to exist between whites and blacks, educators generally agree that the quality of black education is still markedly inferior. Diplomas and credentials alone mean little. What is critical on graduation is what has been learned that is useful for job performance. Too often, the knowledge acquired does not enable the graduate to be of much value in labor markets. Too often, habits important to employers—such as punctuality, a sense of responsibility, and personal neatness—have not yet been acquired. All this is an extremely important aspect of our failure as a nation to invest wisely in human capital.

I lack the practical knowledge to comment at any length on the enormous challenge of improving inner-city schools. But I do know that here and there schools of excellence exist within inner cities, thereby demonstrating—among other things—that great financial cost is not a requisite condition for good schooling. It is promising that a good deal of scholarly examination of these schools is now under way, so that in time their procedures can be emulated elsewhere.

The approach I have suggested for dealing with youth and minority unemployment involves proceeding on a number of different fronts. I am convinced that there simply is no grandiose scheme by which our economy's complex problems of structural unemployment are going to be solved. I realize it is tempting to think that very rapid expansion of demand through monetary and fiscal stimuli would pull many of those who are now sidelined in idleness into the mainstream of the nation's economic life. And, for a while, it is possible that an effect of that kind would occur in some measure. But experience of recent years should by now have driven home the truth that such policies cause inflationary pressures that are inimical to sustained prosperity. Temporary benefits conferred on young people and minorities would only leave a legacy of bitterness once the distortions of inflationary stress caused the bubble of prosperity to burst, as I have no doubt would again be the case.

I well realize that, despite my neglect of numerous problems, including the plight of many older citizens, I have ranged this morning over a wide terrain. I hope that in so doing I have not blurred my central thesis. That is simply that our nation urgently needs to enlarge its investment in both physical and human capital: first, to solidify the ongoing recovery of production and employment; second, to put our economy on a track that will carry us to sustainable conditions of improved economic health in which all of our citizens will have a decent chance to share.

Among other benefits, accelerated investment in physical and human capital will materially aid our economy in making headway against the scourge of inflation. The prospect of reducing the pressure of costs on selling prices will brighten as improvements in productivity strengthen. A vital key to that achievement is more and more modern capital equipment per worker together with a better trained work force. And the act of unblocking job avenues for workers, while politically difficult, will in time not only serve to reduce unemployment; it will do so without releasing inflationary waves that are bound to follow from excessive fiscal or monetary ease.

In closing, I would like to make just one further point. You in this audience have tremendous capability—through this council, your companies, and as individuals—to make a difference in the battle for a healthier economy. I well remember the impressive effort your industry made years ago to counter the insidious theory that a little inflation is a healthy thing. I know you are continuing your educational endeavors. But I would urge you to stretch your energies and to share even more fully with your policyholders—a multitude almost coterminous with the public at large—the special insights that you have accumulated into the economic and social damage caused by inflation and unemployment. Widespread understanding of economic problems has become crucial to the vitality of our democracy. Your industry has a proud record in improving economic knowledge, and I am confident you will continue to build on it.

Blessings of a Free Society

Thank you very much, Mr. Joseph. This has been a very warm and friendly evening. I've loved every part of it. I even found Mr. Epstein's listing of contributors instructive. In fact, I've told my colleagues in Washington over the years that if they want to solve the nation's budgetary problem, or if they want to solve the problem of prices and wages, they ought to come to a meeting of UJA or the ADL and learn the technique of achieving real success.

I listened with a sense of humility to the kind words spoken by your national chairman, Mr. Joseph. As I stand before you this evening, I also find myself in a mood of reverence for the distinguished men who previously received the award which is mine this evening. I need hardly add that I accept this award with a feeling of some pride.

I've listened with real care to the numerous reasons that Mr. Joseph listed why I am being honored this evening in such a unique way. I sensed an element of exaggeration in what Mr. Joseph had to say, and yet I cannot dismiss his words completely. I see no way of denying that in this world of ours, I have achieved over the years a measure of success. Therefore, if you will permit me, I would like to reflect on the reasons for whatever success I have achieved in the course of my career.

I can say quite honestly a few things in my own behalf. First, I've been lucky. I've enjoyed good health throughout my life, and while I am approaching seventy-four, I still may have

Address at a meeting of the Anti-Defamation League of B'nai B'rith, Palm Beach, Florida, February 2, 1978.

more energy than most members of my staff at the Federal Reserve. Second, I think I can fairly say that I have a moderately good mind—and I can even say I use my mind at times. Third, I am accustomed to working diligently—in good measure because I enjoy working. And fourth, I can also say in my behalf that I respect a fair number of the laws laid down in the books of Moses, also the laws laid down by the later prophets, and even some of the laws written by our own Congress.

To these virtues or qualities I readily confess. And yet the qualities that I have just attributed to myself—good health, some intellectual power, habits of industry, a respect for law and morality—are by no means unique. Millions of people in this world—in Latin America, the Soviet Union, on the African continent—have all these virtues and more in abundance. Yet, they lead lives of spiritual poverty, lives marked by fear, lives marred by failure to express their yearning for truth or for excellence. My heart goes out to all these people—especially to the hundreds of thousands of Jews in the Soviet Union who, being kept in bondage, are denied the opportunity to find spiritual peace and self-fulfillment in Israel.

It is clear to me, therefore, as I reflect on my own life, that whatever success I have been able to achieve is due fundamentally to the fact that it has been my good fortune to be a citizen of a country whose people have had the opportunity to acquire a decent education, whose people have had the freedom to seek truth and to express it as they see fit, whose people have had the opportunity to put to work such special talents as they may have and to utilize these talents for themselves, their families, and their country.

In short, it has been my great privilege to be an American. This is a privilege that I, along with millions of other of our adopted citizens, may appreciate even more keenly than do our native born citizens.

But as a student of history, I also know that the freedom and opportunity with which the American people are blessed cannot be taken for granted. The Anti-Defamation League, under whose auspices we meet this evening, did not come into existence because brotherly love, because respect for human rights, because regard for human dignity were universal attributes of the American people. On the contrary, the founders of ADL, as men of experience and practical wisdom, were well aware of the fragility of human nature. They were well aware of the messages of bigotry and hate that from time to time kept stirring in our land—sometimes against Jews or Catholics, sometimes against Italians or Poles or Hungarians, and frequently against people with black or yellow skins.

The founders of ADL were particularly aware of the long and troubled history of the Jewish people, who despite their gift of the Torah and their ancestral search for a life of holiness, had suffered calumny, discrimination, even torture on account of their faith. The founders of ADL understood well the weakness of human nature. They knew that what had happened before could happen again, as it indeed did on such a tragic scale during the Nazi holocaust. The founders of ADL therefore set for themselves the objective of communicating to their fellow Americans a better understanding of the character of the Jewish people. But they did not stop there. The founders of ADL went on to declare that the ultimate purpose of the Anti-Defamation League was to do what it can to assure justice and fair treatment to all citizens alike.

These principles of ADL were articulated with eloquence in the year of its founding, 1913, the very year it so happened that my family emigrated to this blessed land. Thus, my own life as an American and the life of ADL have been virtually coterminous.

During these sixty-odd years that have elapsed, I have witnessed tremendous strides in our country toward justice and toward fair treatment of all of our citizens. When I began my university teaching in the mid-twenties, I was one of a very tiny group of Jews who had attained that privilege. Anti-Semitism was still rife in our country, and it was still widespread during the 1930s. But after the end of World War II, anti-Semitism rapidly diminished, and it now has practically disappeared in our universities and in our colleges.

What has happened in our colleges and universities has also happened in many lines of business, in the professions, and in government. Since 1946, when the Employment Act became law, we have had eleven chairmen of the President's Council of Economic Advisers; five of these eleven have been members of the Jewish faith.

The decline of anti-Semitism in our country—also the remarkable advance of our black people and of Mexican-Americans
in their struggle for civil rights—did not happen by accident.
These fruits of our evolving democracy are attributable to the
civilized impulses, to the generous nature, to the energy of our
nation's churchmen, legislators, and educators. Foremost among
these educators has been the Anti-Defamation League. Because
of its vision, because of its humane spirit, because of its vigilance,
because of its energy, because of its perseverance, I, among millions of others, have had the freedom and the opportunity to
achieve the professional success that has come my way.

Thus, what personal qualities I have—and I have no intention this evening to minimize my personal qualities since I may
soon be unemployed—would have counted for little had I not
had the good fortune to become a citizen of this wonderful
land of opportunity—a land whose cultivation of democratic
values has been protected and richly expanded by the courageous
leadership of the Anti-Defamation League.

What has been true in my case has been true of many
millions of others—Jews and Christians, black men and white
men, immigrants and native citizens. So, in accepting ADL's
award, I feel that I am doing so symbolically in the name of
countless Americans, and if I may, I want to express to ADL
my gratitude for what it has done in behalf of these millions.

Let us always keep in mind, nevertheless, that the objectives
of justice and fair treatment for all our citizens which ADL
has been championing so persistently have thus far been only
approximated in our land. They certainly have not yet been fully
attained in our country, to say nothing of much of the rest of
the world. Moreover, in view of the waywardness of human
nature, the enormous strides that we have made towards true
democracy in our land cannot safely be counted on to inform
the lives of our people in the indefinite future. To assure the
retention and enlargement of our democratic achievements, we
need to keep alive and to nourish the educational efforts in behalf
of human decency—efforts which the ADL has been conducting
with such great energy and with such unique understanding of
the nature of man.

But that is not all. In order to extend justice and end
discrimination in our land, we need also a strong economy—an

economy that provides an abundance of meaningful jobs for all those who are able, willing, and seeking gainful employment. One of the clearest lessons of our history and that of other countries is that bigotry, class hatred, and discrimination have the best chance to thrive when a nation's economy becomes depressed and the ranks of its unemployed multiply. A healthy and strong economy is therefore essential to our way of life so that justice and fair treatment to all citizens alike may be preserved and indeed enlarged in our country.

Ours is a progressive country, but I regret to say that persistence of a high rate of inflation during recent years has cast a cloud on the future of our economy. Inflation, I regret to say, is sapping our nation's strength. Inflation is causing hardship to elderly citizens dependent on an income fixed in dollars, but each of which is constantly shrinking in purchasing power. Inflation is eroding the value of our bank deposits and the life insurance we have arranged to protect our families. Inflation is weakening the willingness of our people to save for the future.

Also, inflation is confusing the accounts kept by our business firms of their costs, their revenues, and their profits. Inflation is keeping the level of interest rates far higher than it would otherwise be, since lenders expect to be repaid in cheaper dollars. Inflation is causing a depression in stock exchange values on which the fortunes of many millions of Americans depend. Inflation is causing uncertainty in the business and financial world, since our businessmen now have no good way of judging what their costs of production may be in the future, or what prices they may be able to charge, or what profits, if any, will accrue to them when they undertake risky investments.

And worst of all, inflation is causing doubts to spread among the American people about themselves, about their government, about their country, and thus is weakening our nation's will to improve the economy and to strengthen our democratic way of life.

I am often asked whether it is possible to check inflation within the constraints imposed by national politics. I have no hesitation in answering this question in the affirmative. But what is required first and foremost is better understanding on the part of the American people of the evils of inflation, so that their national leaders may muster their inner courage with some assurance of popular support.

The federal government is fully capable of leading our country out of the inflationary morass. The government could, for example, cut back on our huge and persistent budget deficits. Again, instead of raising the pay of federal employees by 7 percent—as the government did last October and may do again this year—the increase could be limited to 3 percent or 4 percent, thus setting an example for American businessmen and their employees. Again, the President might cut his own salary by some 10 percent and invite all presidential appointees and perhaps Congressmen to do likewise, thus dramatizing his leadership in unwinding the inflation that is plaguing our country.

To give one more example, the federal government could actively encourage every factory, every office, every mining establishment, every shop to establish a productivity council consisting of management and labor representatives, so that ways might be devised to increase output per hour and thus reduce the upward pressure of labor costs on prices.

The federal government can certainly check the depreciation of the dollar that has been under way in our foreign exchange markets, a development that is putting new upward pressure on our price levels. Among other things, our government could adopt, at long last, an energy policy that will encourage the rapid development of new sources of supply, as well as lead to some conservation of oil. And certainly our government could adopt a tax policy that would lead to more productivity-enhancing investments in our country, not only by American businesses but also by foreign capitalists.

In short, ladies and gentlemen, inflation is a disease that can be conquered, but it will be conquered only when the will to do so becomes strong enough. Contrary to a widespread opinion, this disease could be conquered even as we expand job opportunities for our people. I have in mind in particular the main sufferers of unemployment—our young people and our young black citizens. Not only have we neglected their education, but we have also erected numerous impediments that stand in the way of their job opportunities—impediments such as our federal and state minimum wage laws, impediments such as the membership limitations imposed by many of our craft unions, impediments such as the licensing and certification requirements for trades that range from plumbing to barbering.

Since the spring of 1975, total employment in our country has grown at an extraordinary pace, in fact, at an unprecedented rate. Despite the influx of millions of women into the job market, total unemployment has dropped from a rate of about 9 percent to a current rate of about 6½ percent. But not all citizens have shared in the expansion of jobs and incomes that has taken place in our country.

Unemployment among black teenagers is now running at a rate of about 40 percent; unemployment among these black teenagers is, in fact, even higher today than it was at the bottom of the recession. Ours is a wonderful country which has brought blessings of freedom and opportunity to most of its people. But as a nation with a conscience, disciplined by practical sense, we have no greater priority in thinking of the future than to bring young unemployed people—particularly our black brothers— into the mainstream of our nation's economic life.

In pronouncing this basic truth, I am simply endorsing the noble purpose of the Anti-Defamation League—to secure justice and fair treatment to all citizens alike and to put an end forever to unjust and unfair discrimination.

In closing these remarks, may I thank once again the officers of ADL for thinking of me today. And may I also thank this large and distinguished audience in joining me in expressing gratitude to the Anti-Defamation League for remembering what Israel has meant to our Judeo-Christian civilization and for enlarging the freedom and the opportunity for self-advancement of the entire American people.

The Future of the
Free Enterprise System

Prediction of the economic future has always been a hazardous task. Noting this fact, a distinguished economic historian, Werner Sombart, once remarked that "it is precisely the most gifted men who have made the most fundamental mistakes" in predicting the economic future. While I am by no means sure that "gifted men" are more prone to misjudge the future than are ordinary mortals, there is ample evidence that judgments of the future even by the ablest economists have often been mistaken.

Karl Marx, who revolutionized economic and political thinking over much of the world, provides an outstanding example.

Marx believed that certain tendencies inherent in capitalism would ultimately lead to its destruction. In his vision, small business firms would gradually disappear as capitalism evolved. The concentration of production in a diminishing number of large enterprises would be accompanied by concentration of wealth in fewer and fewer hands. The middle class would thus be destroyed and the masses proletarized. Inadequate consumption would lead to recurring epidemics of overproduction, and depressions of increasing severity would follow. As the misery of the proletariat deepened, resistance to capitalist exploitation would intensify and become more militant. With such powerful tendencies at work, the capitalist order was bound to collapse;

Address at the Seidman Distinguished Award in Political Economy dinner, Southwestern at Memphis, Memphis, Tennessee, September 21, 1978.

it was only a matter of time when the capitalists would be expropriated and all instruments of production socialized.

Thus, according to Marx's theory, the failure of capitalism in its later stages to meet even elementary economic needs of the working masses would inevitably lead, although not without intense struggle, to the replacement of free enterprise by a socialistically planned regime.

In our own century, another great economist, Joseph Schumpeter, brilliantly challenged Marx's analysis. Schumpeter saw in capitalism a highly efficient engine of mass production and mass consumption. In his view the capitalist spirit expresses itself characteristically through innovation—that is, developing new commodities, devising new technologies, harnessing new sources of supply, devising new market strategies, forming new types of organization. The competition of new products and new ways of doing business against old products and customary procedures—that is the essence of the capitalist process. This competition of the new against the old is what really matters in the business world; it has been continuing at a rapid pace, and it accounts for the vast improvement in living standards wherever capitalism has flourished. Indeed, not only economic improvement, but the major achievements of modern times in the sciences and arts are, directly or indirectly, the products of capitalism.

Being a student of business cycles, Schumpeter was well aware of recurring business slumps and their spells of unemployment. But he regarded recessions as temporary phenomena that paved the way, so to speak, to more effective utilization of resources and therefore to still higher standards of living. He went on to argue, nevertheless, that the great economic and cultural achievements of modern capitalism did not assure its future; on the contrary, the very success of capitalism would eventually cause its replacement by a socialist civilization. He thus accepted Marx's conclusion but not the analysis on which it was based.

According to Schumpeter, capitalism would be destroyed by factors growing out of its own inner processes. As business corporations became larger, they would become bureaucratic and impersonal. The entrepreneurial function of innovating would be largely assumed by trained specialists. Increasing affluence would provide both the means and the will to expand social programs and thus lead to a growing role of government. The intellectual class created and nourished by capitalism would become increasingly hostile to its institutions. Animosity toward free enterprise would be exploited by government officials seeking additional power for themselves. The general public would fail to support free enterprise because the issues debated in the public arena are much too complex and often involve long-range considerations that go beyond popular concern. Even businessmen would become increasingly willing to accept the teachings of their detractors. In this social and political environment, capitalist enterprises would in time be undermined and finally replaced by socialism.

Thus, Schumpeter arrived at precisely the same conclusion as Karl Marx. But whereas Marx attributed the eventual coming of socialism to the failure of capitalism, Schumpeter attributed it to the outstanding success of capitalism.

When we turn from the theories of Marx and Schumpeter to recorded experience, several facts immediately stand out. First, we find that the nations practicing socialism in Marx's and Schumpeter's sense had either banished free enterprise under external military pressure, as in the case of Eastern Europe, or had undergone an internal revolution without ever developing a significant degree of free enterprise, as in the case of the Soviet Union and mainland China.

Second, we find that greater economic success has been generally achieved in nations that extensively practice free enterprise than in nations where it is prohibited or severely limited. The economic performance of the United States, West Germany, and France has been more impressive than that of the Soviet Union or East Germany or Poland. Likewise, the economic performance of Japan, Taiwan, or Brazil has clearly surpassed that of India, Sri Lanka, or Egypt.

Third, although Marx's analysis continues to appeal to many intellectuals, his elaborate theoretical structure has been discredited by experience. Instead of bringing economic misery to the masses, capitalism has produced vast improvements in their economic condition. True, socialism has triumphed in some countries, but the triumph was achieved in a far different way than Marx had envisaged. On the other hand, Schumpeter's theory that capitalism would eventually be destroyed by its very success in improving the lot of people cannot be dismissed so readily. His prognosis may or may not turn out to be valid. But there is no denying that much of what has happened in recent decades in countries that boast of practicing free enterprise fits rather closely his theoretical model.

Let me speak more specifically about one prominent feature of Schumpeter's analysis—namely, the expanding role of government in economic life. The broad trend of American economic development has been toward increasing emphasis on the service industries, and the government has become the channel through which much of the public's demand for services is satisfied. As our economy has undergone industrialization and urbanization, there has been a steady increase in the interdependence of people—that is, in their reliance on the wisdom and enterprise, and also in their exposure to the folly and indolence, of their neighbors. In such an environment, social and economic problems often arise that cannot be adequately handled by private enterprise and governmental activities therefore tend to expand.

The spread of political democracy has accentuated the trend toward seeking governmental solutions of economic and social problems. With more people in the lower income groups taking advantage of the right to vote and with advocates of all sorts active in legislative halls, demands on the government have been mounting—to eliminate or regulate private monopoly, to conserve natural resources, to strengthen trade unions, to raise minimum wages, to protect the environment, to improve housing conditions, to protect unwary consumers, to subsidize agriculture or other industries, and so on and on.

The range of governmental activities has thus been steadily expanding and so too has the cost. In 1929 governmental expenditure—that is, the combined total of federal, state, and local spending—amounted to 11 percent of the dollar value of our nation's entire production of goods and services. The corresponding figure rose to 20 percent in 1940, 23 percent in 1950, 30 percent in 1960, 35 percent in 1970, and 37 percent in 1977.

The sharply rising trend of governmental spending has, of course, involved a steady increase in the fraction of the nation's labor force that works directly or indirectly for the government. But our government affects the economy not only by employing people or by purchasing supplies and equipment from private industry. In addition, vast sums of money are transferred by the government to individuals not involved in current production—that is, beneficiaries of public retirement funds, unemployment insurance, medicare, aid to veterans, food stamps, and so forth. And our government also affects the economy by guaranteeing a variety of private loans and by regulating numerous industrial, commercial, and financial practices.

All these activities, particularly transfer payments and governmental regulation, have grown by leaps and bounds in recent years. Transfer payments, which were merely 3 percent as large as the nation's total wage and salary bill in 1930, rose to 11 percent by 1965 and reached 21 percent in 1977. The *Federal Register*, which records governmental regulations, ran to 3,400 pages in 1937, but swelled to about 10,000 pages in 1953 and to 65,000 pages in 1977. At least ninety federal agencies are now involved in issuing governmental regulations. Funds allocated for regulation in this year's federal budget amount to $4.5 billion—more than twice the expenditure in 1974. This figure, of course, omits the expenditures on regulation by our state and local governments. And it omits also the enormous costs of compliance imposed on private industry. According to a recent investigation by the Center for the Study of American Business at Washington University, these compliance costs amounted to $63 billion in 1976.

The proliferation and increasing cost of governmental activities in our country have resulted in a growing burden of taxation—higher income taxes, higher sales taxes, higher property taxes, higher social security taxes. Even so, the willingness of our government to raise revenue by taxation has fallen distinctly short of its propensity to spend.

Since 1950 the federal budget has been in balance in only five years. Since 1970 a deficit has occurred in every year. Budget deficits have thus become a chronic condition of federal finance; they have been incurred in years when business conditions were poor and also when business was booming. Not only that, but the deficits have been mounting in size. In the fiscal year now ending, the deficit is likely to exceed $60 billion when "off-budget" outlays are included in the total—as they indeed should be. Instead of vanishing or diminishing as the economy improves, which was once accepted practice, the deficit has been increasing in the course of the current economic expansion.

The persistence of substantial deficits in our federal finances is mainly responsible for the serious inflation that got under way in our country in the mid-sixties. Let us never forget the simple fact that when the government runs a budget deficit, it pumps more money into the pocketbooks of people than it takes out of their pocketbooks. That is the way a serious inflation is typically started and later nourished. And when the deficit increases at a time of economic expansion, as it has been doing lately, we should not be surprised to find the rate of inflation quickening. Of course, other factors—particularly, money creation by our central bank and the power wielded by trade unions—have played their part in the inflationary process.

The growing intervention of government in economic affairs that has taken place in the United States has been matched or exceeded by similar developments in other countries that we think of as continuing to practice free enterprise. The causes of this increasing penetration of government into the economic life of individual countries have been broadly similar—namely, industrialization and urbanization, increasing interdependence of people, faster communication through radio and television, rising expectations of people, wider participation of citizens in the political arena, and increasing reliance on government for the solution of economic and social problems.

The degree of government participation in economic life has thus been increasing in every industrial country outside the Socialist sphere. To cite some examples: government expenditure in the United Kingdom amounted to 34 percent of the gross domestic product in 1962 and to 44 percent in 1975. Corresponding figures in the case of West Germany are 34 and 42 percent; in the case of France, 36 and 40 percent; in the case of Canada, 29 and 41 percent; in the case of Australia, 24 and 32 percent. A similar trend appears also in Japan; but it is worth noting that governmental spending amounted to only 23 percent of the gross domestic product of Japan in 1975—a substantially lower figure than in any other major industrial country.

And just as the rapid expansion of governmental activities in the United States has been accompanied by persistent budget deficits, that too has happened in other industrial countries. Indeed, loose governmental finance and rapid inflation have often been practiced more intensively outside the United States, and they have recently become characteristic features of major economies that still boast of free enterprise.

The worldwide inflation that has been under way since the late 1960s has become a serious threat to the free enterprise system. The fact that inflation masks underlying economic realities makes it all the more insidious. For example, the trend of retail trade and housing starts began to weaken in the United States early in 1973, but many members of the business community paid little attention to that ominous development. Nor did they recognize that standard accounting practices, which rely on historical costs in reckoning inventories and capital consumption, were resulting in enormous overstatements of their profits. Caught up in the euphoria of inflation, they built up inventories out of all proportion to actual or prospective sales, and thus set the stage for the subsequent sharp decline of production and employment. What happened in the United States was paralleled in greater or lesser degree in European industrial countries and in Japan.

The corrosive effects of inflation go far beyond the distortion of businessmen's perspective. Inflation erodes the purchasing power of everyone's money income. Inflation weakens the willingness of many people to save for the future. Inflation drives up the level of interest rates. And once businessmen become aware of the illusory element in profits, inflation adds to uncertainty about the future. In an inflation-ridden environment, businessmen have no good way of judging what their costs of production may turn out to be, or what prices they may be able to charge, or what profits, if any, will accrue when they undertake new investments. The risk premium that attaches to calculations of prospective profits from new investments therefore goes up. This discourages business capital investment and hampers the improvement of productivity.

Nor is that all. As the effects of inflation spread across the economy, they in time weaken the capital market. The classical view that inflation tends to favor business profits and therefore higher stock prices no longer fits today's world of powerful trade unions, high interest rates, and a governmental bias toward consumption. Recent experience in the United States and in other countries has demonstrated that persistent inflation adversely affects stock prices as well as bond prices. Even now, despite the recent upsurge in stock prices, the Dow-Jones industrial average is below the level reached in 1965; and in view of the huge rise in the general price level since then, the stock market has obviously suffered a severe depression.

As a result of the disappointing performance of the stock exchanges, the interest of investors in equity securities has greatly diminished during recent years. Some wealthy individuals, seeking a refuge from inflation, have turned to investing in works of art, or in real estate, or in foreign currencies, gold or other commodities. Many members of the middle class, being similarly disillusioned with equities, have sought an inflation hedge by purchasing a home or an extra house when they already owned one. But the many millions who lack financial sophistication, and even some who possess it, have found no better way to protect themselves against the ravages of inflation than to let cash pile up in the form of bank deposits or other liquid assets—with the result that the purchasing power of their monetary savings has generally kept eroding.

Many professional money managers, likewise discouraged by the behavior of common stock prices, have found solace in the high yields that have become available on corporate and government bonds. And they have also displayed some tendency to shorten the maturity of their investments, so that they could shift to higher-yield securities if faster inflation served to raise interest rates another notch or two in the future. With institutional as well as individual investors switching from common stocks to other investments, brokerage firms and investment advisory services have suffered reverses. Numerous firms of this type have closed down their operations or sold out to more enterprising members of their industry. These in turn have reacted to the declining interest in equities by becoming department stores of finance—that is, by offering to their troubled customers stock options, commodity futures, municipal bond funds, money market funds, tax shelters, and so on, in addition to the more traditional services. Adjustments of this type have enabled some brokerage and advisory firms to survive and even to prosper.

But what matters most for the future of our economy is the erosion of investor interest in equity issues. In 1965 corporate shares constituted over 43 percent of all financial assets of American households; by 1977 they were down to 25 percent. Between 1970 and 1975 the number of individual shareowners in our country fell from about 31 million to 25 million. More significant still, this decline was concentrated among young and middle-aged people. Net purchases of equity issues by private pension funds have also slumped in recent years. So-called "equity kickers," once a prominent feature of loans placed by insurance firms, have practically vanished. As a result of this declining interest in equities, the supply of venture capital has drastically diminished in our country. Public issues by small firms have dwindled and we rarely hear nowadays of the formation of new high-technology companies.

If the skepticism about equities that has marked recent years continues in the future, it will become difficult even for some well-established corporations to finance their long-term investment projects. This difficulty will be accentuated if internally generated funds continue to provide a reduced share of total financing needs—as has been the case during the past decade of high inflation. Furthermore, if business firms are forced to rely more heavily on short-term funds, the corporate economy will become more vulnerable to financial strains in the future. In such an environment a business recession could be even more disruptive than the recession we recently experienced.

In short, the changes wrought by inflation have already weakened the framework of our economic system. They threaten to do so to a greater degree if the inflationary bias of the economy is extended. I judge from the sluggishness of stock exchanges in other major industrial countries during the past decade that, with the exception of Japan, their experience has been similar to that of the United States. If inflationary trends should persist, the economies of these countries will also face a very uncertain future.

Serious as these longer-range economic consequences of inflation appear to be, there is even greater reason for concern about its impact on social and political institutions. Inflation has capricious effects on the distribution of income and wealth among a nation's families and businesses. Inflation eventually leads to recession and extensive unemployment, and such adversities are generally followed by new measures of governmental intervention. Inflation robs people who in their desire to be self-reliant have set aside funds for the education of their children or their own retirement. Inflation hits many of the poor and elderly especially hard. More ominous still, by causing disillusionment and breeding discontent, inflation excites doubts among people about themselves, about their government, and about the free enterprise system itself.

Such anxieties tend to spread from one country to another. In particular, when the value of our own dollar depreciates in foreign exchange markets, as has happened again during the past two years, confidence in the international economy as well as in our own tends to weaken. The ultimate consequence of persistent inflation may therefore be a decline in both the scope and the efficiency of free enterprise on a worldwide scale.

At the beginning of this address, I reviewed the theories of capitalist evolution by Marx and Schumpeter. It is interesting to observe that while Marx visualized numerous developments that would weaken capitalism, persistent inflation was not among them. Nor was this threat to our free enterprise system foreseen by Schumpeter in the early editions of his *Capitalism, Socialism and Democracy*. Nor, for that matter, was it foreseen by Keynes; both he and his early followers were concerned about vanishing investment opportunities and unemployment, not about inflation. These failures of economic vision counsel humility in any judgments about the future; and yet I keep wondering whether the inflationary development that Schumpeter had failed to foresee may not be reinforcing the very processes on which he dwelt so provocatively.

Ours is still a dynamic and prosperous economy, but the prosperity around us has become uneasy and even joyless to many thoughtful citizens. Inflation is certainly our nation's main economic problem, but it is by no means the only economic problem. Unlike earlier times, when we were troubled either by inflation or by unemployment, we have experienced in recent times a disconcerting rise of the general price level even when unemployment was extensive. And our social economy has been beset by other problems—among them a growing burden of taxes, excessive governmental regulation, excessive power of labor, restrictive business practices, depressed business profits, deteriorating central-city areas, decline of the work ethic, and widespread crime. Not all of these ills can be ascribed to inflation. And yet this factor has had a more ramifying influence on our economy than may appear at first glance.

I have already observed that inflation ultimately leads to recession. In turn, extensive unemployment creates an environment that is favorable to new or larger welfare programs and other increases in governmental spending—increases that often outlast the recession. Again, it is at least partly because of inflation that workers, particularly when they are well organized, can achieve increases in wages that far exceed improvements in productivity. It is at least partly because of inflation that the statutory minimum wage keeps rising—thereby causing unemployment among young people and breeding crime. It is at least partly because of inflation that many of our cities have suffered physical and cultural deterioration. And, needless to add, the poverty that persists in the midst of our plenty is in no small degree attributable to inflation.

The burden of taxes has also risen because of inflation. Although deficits at the federal level of government have become our way of life, taxes have increased along with expenditures. Indeed, federal revenues fell below 90 percent of federal expenditures in only seven years since 1946. Since our individual income tax is highly progressive, the tax burden on workers goes up, just as if Congress had legislated higher taxes, even when real wages remain constant—that is, when wages in dollars simply keep pace with increases in the consumer price level. The corporate income tax, to be sure, is essentially proportional; but under conventional accounting techniques, inflation creates phantom profits on which corporations have been paying many billions of dollars in taxes. And the consequences of inflation for the capital gains tax have been still more drastic. A recent study by Professor Martin Feldstein of Harvard indicates that in 1973 individuals paid taxes on more than $4.5 billion of capital gains from corporate shares; but when the costs of the shares are adjusted for increases in the general price level, it turns out that these individuals actually experienced a real capital loss of nearly $1 billion.

Human nature inevitably takes its toll. If intense effort or large financial risks are no longer compensated by the possibility of earning large rewards, the effort and the risks will be less readily undertaken. That is the condition toward which we have been generally moving. And it is precisely because a grim future may eventually become our lot and that of other nations still enjoying freedom that big government and the disease of inflation that comes in its train must be resisted by an alert citizenry. This need is now more widely appreciated than at any time since World War II, but it is not yet understood widely enough.

There are some faint flickerings, however, that the American people are becoming less passive about the dangers facing our nation. The recent tax revolt of California citizens may be a symptom of a general awakening of the middle class. Of late, many politicians have been vying with one another in proclaiming inflation as our number one problem. Trade unions have been unable to persuade Congress this year that their market power needs strengthening. Much is heard these days in congressional halls about the importance of reducing business taxes. A move to cut back rather than increase the tax on capital gains has won widespread support. And of late we have even witnessed some minor reductions within the still swelling total of federal expenditures.

These are interesting and promising events. As yet, they are much too tenuous and uncertain to justify extrapolation. They nevertheless suggest that the time may be right for a serious attack on the inflation that has been plaguing our country. That will not be an easy task, but it will be even harder if we hesitate or delay. Once an economy has become engulfed by expectations of inflation, economic policy makers no longer have very good choices. Still, much can in time be accomplished with determined leadership.

Restrictive monetary and fiscal policies, if pushed far enough, are always capable of bringing inflation under control; they might, however, also unsettle the economy by bringing on extensive unemployment. To minimize that risk, it would be wise to supplement monetary and fiscal policies with carefully selected structural policies. A prescription for a balanced attack on the inflation problem might therefore run as follows in today's environment: first, that the Federal Reserve continue its present moderately restrictive monetary policy without interference by the Congress or the White House; second, that the budget for next year permit a substantial cut in the federal deficit and that the move toward budgetary balance be completed within the following two years; third, that this and next year's increase in the salaries of federal employees be scaled down to one-half the figure suggested by wage comparability studies; fourth, that the President cut his own salary by, say, 10 percent and call on all presidential appointees and members of Congress to do likewise; fifth, that the President reinforce these examples for the nation by calling on top corporate executives to refrain from any increase in their compensation over the next two years; sixth, that a national center be promptly established for encouraging the organization of productivity councils across the nation, factory by factory and shop by shop, with a view to cooperation by management and labor in raising output per man-hour; seventh, that we make a start towards blunting the cost-raising measures that we have allowed to flourish—such as tariffs, import quotas, farm price supports, and minimum wage laws, and that we also postpone the target dates that have been set for environmental and safety regulations.

In the course of my remarks this evening I have dwelt on the corrosive influence of inflation because I consider this the greatest danger to our free enterprise system. I am convinced that inflation is a disease that can be brought under control; but that will happen only when the will to do so becomes strong enough. In our country there is a powerful political constituency behind each of the government's spending programs, behind every tariff and import quota, behind every regulation that protects a particular group from the pressures of competition. We have powerful political constituencies in favor of perennially easy credit. We have powerful political constituencies in favor of other public or private arrangements that benefit some groups but raise prices to everyone. Our urgent need now is for a nationwide constituency that will fight for the paramount interest that we as a people have in a dollar of stable purchasing power.

Other nations—notably, Germany, Switzerland, and Japan—have demonstrated that inflation can be unwound. Even Great Britain has recently succeeded in reducing its inflation rate sharply. If we and other inflation-ridden nations succeed in curbing inflation within the framework of our basic institutions, we may yet experience a true economic renaissance in the Western world. On the other hand, if the present worldwide inflation continues, a command economy may eventually be the bitter fruit of this generation's complacency and neglect. It is the duty of each of us to do what we can to prevent this from happening.

PART TWO

Inflation and Unemployment

Inflation: The Fundamental Challenge to Stabilization Policies

We have gathered together as representatives of government and the banking industry to discuss our problems, experiences, and concerns about financial affairs. Each of our countries has specific problems that are peculiar to the character of its own economy. In nearly all of our countries, however, the fundamental challenge to current stabilization policies is the persistence of inflationary pressures.

What I should like to convey to you today is the following simple message: although the forces making for inflation in modern society are strong and pervasive, these forces need not prevail. Stabilization policies can be formulated and executed in a way that will permit our economies to enjoy the benefits of prosperity without inflation. I do not minimize the difficulties of meeting this challenge, but I am convinced that success is possible.

We are living now in an inflationary climate. In the United States periods of strong upward price pressures over the past quarter century have been episodic. Interspersed between them have been years of relative price stability. But the period since 1964 has witnessed stronger and more widespread cost and price pressures than in the previous inflationary outbreak of the mid-1950s. And the current episode of inflation has lasted longer than any other since the end of World War II.

In most other industrial countries, price performance over the past two decades has been poorer than in the United States.

Remarks before the Seventeenth Annual Monetary Conference of the American Bankers Association, Hot Springs, Virginia, May 18, 1970.

However, after 1964 the American price level began to move up briskly and our inflation from 1966 to 1969 tended to outpace that in Europe. More recently, we see an acceleration of cost and price pressures in Europe and Japan.

In these circumstances, it should not be surprising that so many businessmen and consumers believe that inflation is inevitable. This has happened before. During the 1950s, the notion that creeping inflation was endemic to a modern economy was widely held in the United States. Yet the period from 1958 through 1964 was marked by reasonable price stability. We in government therefore have a responsibility, I feel, to make it convincingly clear to everyone that inflation is not an economic necessity and that it will not be accepted as an inevitable course of events.

I believe there are grounds for optimism about our ability to achieve and maintain reasonable price stability, and to do so without incurring excessive costs in terms of unemployment and lost output. I reach that conclusion from long exposure to the inflationary problem in the United States. The basic sources of inflation in all of our economies are similar, however, and what we can learn from American experience may also be applicable elsewhere.

What are the sources of the inflationary bias that is presently troubling us? On a first view, the root of the difficulty seems to be the broadening of the social aspirations that have been shaping our national economic policies, and especially the commitment to maintain high levels of employment and rapid economic growth. For several decades, the primary concern of economic stabilization policies was to avoid substantial or prolonged declines in the level of economic activity—declines of the sort that had plagued industrialized economies for a century or more. As we gained experience in moderating business downturns, our standards of economic performance became more exacting. Now, we are not prepared to accept more than brief departures of our economic growth rate from its full employment path.

Improvements in our ability to control cyclical fluctuations in business activity have also emboldened us to search for ways to increase the potential growth rate of our economies—through better education and training of the labor force, through larger investment in public facilities, and through stimuli to private investment in fixed capital. In this effort, too, we have achieved some measure of success. In the short run, however, I suspect that these policies have added more to aggregate demand than to aggregate supply.

Another source of inflationary pressure in recent years has been the rise of government expenditures for social welfare. The consequences for the federal budget in the United States have been dramatic. Since fiscal year 1965, federal expenditures for health, income security, veterans' benefits, education and manpower, and community development and housing have more than doubled. And as we look to the future, we must expect substantial further increases in the level of government expenditures to help halt the decay of our central cities, to bring air and water pollution under control, to provide added financial assistance to beleaguered state and local governments, to finance basic research in areas where private incentives are insufficient, to provide better housing for the less privileged, better medical services to the indigent and the aged, improved job training—in short, for the host of things our people have come to expect their government to provide.

The present worldwide inflationary trend may thus be ascribed to the humanitarian impulses that have reached such full expression in our times. This explanation, however, encompasses only part of the truth. As every economist knows, the growth of aggregate demand that has been generated by our social aspirations could, in principle, have always been offset by monetary and tax policies, supplemented by more selectivity in public expenditures.

The present worldwide inflationary trend must, therefore, also be recognized as evidence of the shortcomings of economic stabilization policy. Serious inflationary problems are always traceable to excessively expansionist monetary and fiscal policies or to the failure of such policies to offset the effects of excessively exuberant demand in the private sector. This, however, is something that admits of correction.

The reason for my optimism about the prospects for long-run improvement of our price performance is a deep faith in the learning process. True, we have made many mistakes in the formulation and administration of our national economic policies, and we will doubtless make some mistakes in the future. But we can also learn from past experience how to distinguish the paths that need to be taken from those that must be shunned if we are to win the ever-recurring bouts with the threat of inflation.

Let us consider briefly the experience with stabilization policy in the United States, drawing on the record of the past few years by way of illustration. These years offer, I believe, lessons that we cannot afford to ignore.

One of the serious economic blunders of recent years was the failure to alter the course of fiscal and monetary policies when early warnings of inflation began to flash. Late in 1964, signs of growing pressure on our nation's resources were already multiplying and these signs became stronger and more widespread in the first half of 1965. With the economy moving rapidly toward full employment, the time had come for backing away from the stimulative policies pursued in the earlier years of the 1960s. But precisely the opposite course was taken—both fiscal and monetary policies became substantially more stimulative during 1965.

In my judgment, the fateful policies of 1965 stemmed only in part from the inadequacies of economic forecasting. It is true that attention had been diverted from the problems of inflation by the experience of the previous five or six years, when much slack existed both in industrial plants and the labor market and the price level moved within a narrow range. By the late summer of 1965, however, it was entirely clear that storm clouds were gathering on the economic horizon. The unemployment rate had moved close to the 4 percent target, while the rate of utilization of industrial capacity—which was already high— still kept rising. Yet, despite the strains under which industry was already operating, the economy was called upon to shoulder a much enlarged military burden in Vietnam without any change in monetary or fiscal policy. Monetary policy continued on its expansionist track during the latter half of 1965 and fiscal restraints of material consequence were postponed much longer.

The mistakes of stabilization policy in 1965 reflected an unwillingness to face up promptly to the urgent need for restrictive actions on the fiscal and monetary front. It was soon found, however, that by eschewing an ounce of prevention, a pound of cure had become necessary. Inflationary forces gathered such momentum that it took stern measures in subsequent years to eliminate excess demand.

Another deficiency in the formulation of stabilization policies in the United States has been our tendency to rely too heavily on monetary restriction as a device to curb inflation, rather than on a balanced program of fiscal and monetary restraints. There are several reasons why excessive reliance on monetary restraint is unsound.

First, severely restrictive monetary policies distort the structure of production. General monetary controls, despite their seeming impartiality, have highly uneven effects on different sectors of the economy. On the one hand, monetary restraint has relatively slight impact on consumer spending or on the investments of large businesses. On the other hand, the homebuilding industry, state and local construction, real estate firms, and other small businesses are likely to be seriously handicapped in their operations. When restrictive monetary policies are pursued vigorously over a prolonged period, these sectors may be so adversely affected that the consequences become socially and economically intolerable, and political pressures mount to ease up on the monetary brakes.

Second, the effects of monetary restraint on spending often occur with relatively long lags. The initial actions of a central bank to moderate the pace of expansion in money and credit may come at a time when liquidity positions are relatively ample in the commercial banking system and elsewhere in the economy. Loan commitments to businesses by banks and life insurance companies may be sizable, and other financial institutions may have committed large sums to the mortgage market based on expected inflows of funds. For a time, therefore, the effects on spending of the slower rate of expansion of bank reserves will be cushioned. Moreover, the length of lags in the response of spending will vary from one period of monetary stringency to another, depending on the state of liquidity, the expectations of the business and financial community, and a variety of other factors.

Primary reliance on monetary policy to restrain inflation thus places a high premium on accurate forecasting of both the strength of private demand and the temporal effects of monetary restraint on spending. Because the lags tend to be long, there are serious risks that a stabilization program emphasizing monetary restraint will have its major effects on spending at a point in time when excess demand has passed its peak. The consequence may then be an excessive slowdown of total spending and a need to move quickly and aggressively toward stimulative policies to prevent a recession. Such a stop-and-go process may well lead to a subsequent renewal of inflationary pressures of yet greater intensity.

Something like this happened, I believe, in 1966 and early 1967. The monetary brakes began to be applied with considerable force in the spring of 1966, and they began to take their greatest toll in spending in the fall months of that year. By that time, the adverse structural effects of excessive monetary restraint had become obvious to everyone, and some modest fiscal action was taken to help slow the economy. Just about that time, however, the rate of consumer spending relative to income declined rather sharply. With the expansion of total final demand for goods and services tapering off, monetary policy then moved aggressively toward ease to ward off a threat of recession. As things turned out, the adjustment proved to be mild and short-lived, and by the latter half of 1967 we found ourselves in an aggravated condition of economic overheating.

We need to recognize, of course, that there is considerable uncertainty also about the effects of fiscal policy on the performance of the economy. The direct effects of changes in federal expenditures or tax rates on private incomes and spending are themselves often difficult to predict. But the overall impact of fiscal policy must also take into account the effects of budgetary changes on interest rates and hence on private spending. Our knowledge about these effects is sketchy. Much will depend, of course, on the precise nature of the actions taken and on the state of private expectations at the time.

In recent years, we have tended to overestimate our knowledge of economic processes, and how they are influenced by monetary and fiscal policies. We have, for example, adopted temporary increases in taxes as though we knew with reasonable certainty that the economic situation a year hence would warrant their removal. The economic impact of such taxes has been considered without due regard to our limited understanding of the effects of temporary taxes on consumer and business spending decisions. Furthermore, growth rates of the major monetary aggregates have been permitted to vary over an extremely wide range, notwithstanding our hazy perception of the timing and magnitude of the economic effects of such variations. There has been much loose talk of "fine tuning," when the state of knowledge permits us to predict only within a fairly broad band the course of economic development and the results of policy actions.

Improvement in the formulation and implementation of stabilization policies requires full recognition of the great uncertainties with which we must live. This means that we need to adopt a cautious approach to large changes in the intensity of monetary and fiscal policies—avoiding extreme courses of action unless the evidence clearly indicates that exceptional policy moves are needed. Furthermore, the uncertainties inherent in the use of any single instrument of policy suggest that the prudent course is to adopt a balanced program that relies on prompt adaptations of fiscal as well as monetary policy.

Let me turn now more specifically to the current inflationary problem in the United States, and suggest what these lessons of recent experience seem to imply for the course of monetary and fiscal actions.

First, I want to note that we have made much more progress than is generally realized in getting the inflationary forces of recent years under control. The excess demand that bedeviled our economy during the past four or five years has been eliminated. In recent months, total real output has declined somewhat. Industrial production has dropped faster and is now about 2½ percent below its peak last summer. Demand for labor has moderated, the unemployment rate has increased, and the degree of unused industrial capacity has also risen.

Throughout this phase of economic sluggishness, there has been a risk that the decline in industrial output would intensify and spread across the economy, with the business slowdown taking on the characteristics of a recession. Thus far, the pervasive and cumulative characteristics of a recession have not developed—largely, I believe, because of the continuing strength of business investment in fixed capital. It seems highly probable, moreover, that the business slowdown will not extend much further, and that before long we will be enjoying a resumption of growth in industrial output and employment. If that proves to be the case, the success we will have had in slowing aggregate demand without precipitating a recession will have been a notable achievement.

We have been less successful than we would have liked in moderating the advance of prices, and also less successful than we might have expected on the basis of past experience. But there are some signs of progress in that area, too. After seasonal adjustment, the rate of increase in consumer prices slowed in February and again in March. The level of wholesale prices remained unchanged in April for the first time in a year and a half, as prices of some agricultural products fell sharply. The price rise for industrial commodities in March and April was the smallest since last July.

It is clear, nonetheless, that the average rate of price increase during recent months is far too high. The question might be raised, therefore, whether our current inflationary illness could be cured more quickly with a shock treatment designed to rid the patient, once and for all, of the troublesome disease.

Such a prescription would, I believe, be unsound as well as unacceptable. The inflationary developments we are now experiencing do not reflect the present state of balance between aggregate demand and supply. Rather, they are the aftermath of economic overheating that existed earlier and which is still having lagged effects on wage rates, on other costs, and hence on prices. We are in a transitional period of cost-push inflation, and we therefore need to adjust our policies to the special character of the inflationary pressures that we are now experiencing.

An effort to offset, through monetary and fiscal restraints, all of the upward push that rising costs are now exerting on prices would be most unwise. Such an effort would restrict aggregate demand so severely as to increase greatly the risks of a very serious business recession. If that happened, the outcries of an enraged citizenry would probably soon force the government to move rapidly and aggressively toward fiscal and monetary ease, and our hopes for getting the inflationary problem under control would then be shattered.

It would be an equally serious mistake, however, for the central bank to supply money and credit in sufficient quantities to permit businesses simply to pass on all cost increases to their customers. Readiness to validate the pressures of costs on prices, through generous provision of money and bank credit, would greatly increase the probability of a later resurgence of excess demand. This, too, must be avoided.

The right course for monetary policy is, I believe, a cautious approach that avoids both of these extremes. In recent months the major monetary aggregates have been following a path of moderate expansion—a path that provides added insurance that the current economic slowdown will not cumulate, but at the same time is consistent with avoidance of excess demand later this year and on into 1971. The adequacy of growth in supplies of money and credit to finance increases in real output and employment will, of course, depend heavily on the movement of costs and prices. As I noted a moment ago, it would be inappropriate for the central bank simply to validate the effects of all cost increases on prices. Consequently, the longer inflationary wage settlements and pricing decisions continue, the larger may be the shortfall of economic growth from its potential.

In the months ahead, we may be witnessing economic developments that will test patience—with costs and prices continuing to advance despite the slack that exists in markets for goods and for productive services. It seems likely that we will hear an increasing number of suggestions that additional steps need to be taken to moderate the rise in wage rates and the advance of prices—steps that could involve the government more directly in the operations of the private economy.

Other countries that have depended on specific wage-price policies—or incomes policies, as they are frequently called—have achieved relatively little success, and the same can also be said of our own experiment during the sixties. Nevertheless, we should not close our minds to the possibility that an incomes policy, provided it stopped well short of direct price and wage controls and was used merely as a supplement to overall fiscal and monetary measures, might speed us through this transitional period of cost-push inflation. I recognize that an incomes policy may not have a lasting effect on the structure of costs and prices if its use is restricted to a transitional period of cost-push inflation. Moreover, it seems clear to me that an incomes policy applied over a long period would be completely impractical. Even with these reservations, however, there may be a useful—albeit a very modest—role for an incomes policy to play in shortening the period between suppression of excess demand and restoration of reasonable price stability.

Of course, primary reliance in the battle against inflation must always be placed on policies that impinge on aggregate demand. It is of fundamental importance that monetary and fiscal policy work together, in this regard, in the months ahead. If the tempo of economic activity picks up later this year, as may now be reasonably anticipated, the task of ensuring that this recovery does not become too brisk—thereby threatening a reemergence of excess demand—should not fall on monetary policy alone. Fiscal policy must do its share.

The budget set forth by the administration in January called for a small surplus for fiscal 1971. Since January, there have been some modifications in the projected course of federal expenditures as a result of actions taken by the Congress and the administration. Thus far, the most significant change in projected expenditures has come from the acceleration of the federal pay raise, which added a little over $1 billion to expenditures in the current fiscal year, and a like amount to prospective outlays in fiscal 1971.

During prior periods of economic slack, a small change of this kind in the outlook for federal expenditures would have created scarcely a ripple in financial markets. In recent weeks, however, reactions in financial markets have been dramatic. Interest rates have increased sharply, with yields in the long-term markets rising above the peaks of late last year. A number of factors have been responsible for this change in market expectations, but concern about federal expenditures appears to have been the catalytic agent. Participants in financial markets greeted the news of the pay raise as if it were the first in a series of steps that would let down the bars on federal spending, and recent developments in Indochina have intensified this feeling.

Perhaps these reactions are just one more evidence of the strength of the inflationary fears and expectations still present in our economy. However, the public is also mindful that promises of fiscal restraint emanating from the Executive and the Congress have, time and again, been unfulfilled. We must not permit that to happen in the year ahead.

At this juncture of history, the business and financial public is deeply concerned that the federal budgetary process may have gotten out of hand in recent years. There is some basis for this concern. Reforms of the federal budgetary process are, I believe, essential to long-run improvement in conducting our stabilization policies and our battle against inflation.

For the long run, there are a number of budgetary reforms that will be needed to keep federal expenditures under control. Ultimately, I think the concept of zero-base budgeting will have to be adopted in order to weed out expenditures on outmoded programs whose costs have long since exceeded their benefits. In other words, we need to have each year a careful review by the Budget Bureau and the Congress of the total spending proposed on each program, not just the proposed increases in spending.

Progress toward this objective of zero-base budgeting might be speeded by personnel rotation among the major divisions of the Budget Bureau, so that a fresh point of view would be brought to bear on the budget requests of the various departments of government. But for the immediate future, the single most constructive step that could be taken would be a legislative ceiling on federal expenditures for the coming fiscal year. This ceiling should be tight enough to give reasonable assurance that federal expenditures for fiscal 1971 do not rise appreciably above the level projected in the budget last January. Alternatively, if expenditures threaten to rise significantly above that level, taxes should be provided to cover the excess.

In conclusion, I believe that the prospects for a return to reasonable price stability are brighter than is generally recognized. Excess demand in our economy has been eliminated. After a long period of overheating, the first signs of moderation in price behavior—though halting and slow—have begun to appear. It seems probable, moreover, that economic recovery, as it develops, will proceed satisfactorily and yet not strain our physical capacities.

The sources of long-run inflationary bias in the United States, as elsewhere in the world will, of course, continue to operate. But by applying sensible monetary and fiscal policies, we can check the inflationary tendencies that emanate from the pursuit of our social and economic goals. The clearest lesson of the past few years is that delay in coping with inflationary pressures merely compounds the difficulties that need to be faced later. Fortunately, this basic fact is now more widely recognized in the United States and in other industrial countries than it was ten or even five years ago.

The Basis for Lasting Prosperity

Nearly three years ago, in a talk here in Los Angeles, I pointed out that once an economy becomes engulfed by inflation, economic policy makers no longer have any good choices. To regain a lasting prosperity, a nation must have the good sense and fortitude to come to grips with inflation. There is, however, no painless way of getting rid of the injustices, inefficiency, and international complications that normally accompany an inflation.

Events of the past several years have lent poignancy to these simple truths. Recent experience has demonstrated once again that the transition from an overheated economy to an economy of stable markets is a difficult process. Elimination of excess demand was an essential first step to the restoration of stability, but this step has brought with it a period of sluggish economic activity, slow income growth, and rising unemployment. And while we have made some progress in moderating the rate of inflation, our people are still seeing the real value of their wages and savings eroded by rising prices.

The struggle to bring inflationary forces under control, and to return our labor and capital resources to reasonably full employment, is still going on. I am convinced, however, that corrective adjustments in the private sector over the past twelve to eighteen months are creating, in conjunction with governmental stabilization policies, the foundation on which a prolonged and stable prosperity can be constructed.

Address in the Pepperdine College Great Issues Series, Los Angeles, California, December 7, 1970.

103

A cardinal fact about the current economic situation, and one that promises well for our nation's future, is that the imprudent policies and practices pursued by the business and financial community during the latter half of the 1960s are being replaced by more sober and realistic economic judgments. In my remarks to you today, I want first to review some of the key developments that lead me to this conclusion. Then I shall turn to the tasks that must still be faced in order to enhance the prospects for an early resumption of growth in production and employment in an environment of reasonably stable prices.

The current inflation got under way in 1964. Perhaps the best single barometer of the extent to which it served to distort economic decisions and undermine the stability of the economy is found in the behavior of financial markets during the late 1960s. In 1968, well over 3 billion shares of stock exchanged hands on the New York Stock Exchange—about two and one-half times the volume of five years earlier. The prices of many stocks shot upward with little reference to actual or potential earnings. During the two years 1967 and 1968, the average price of a share of stock listed on the New York Exchange rose 40 percent, while earnings of the listed companies rose only 12 percent. On the American Exchange the average share price rose during the same two years more than 140 percent on an earnings base that increased just 7 percent.

A major source of the speculative ardor came from some parts of the mutual fund industry. Long-term investment in stocks of companies with proven earnings records became an outmoded concept for the new breed of "go-go" funds. The "smart money" was to go into issues of technologically oriented firms—no matter how they were meeting the test of profitability, or into the corporate conglomerates—no matter how eccentric their character.

This mood of speculative exuberance strongly reinforced the upsurge of corporate mergers which occurred during the middle years of the 1960s. No doubt many of these mergers could be justified on grounds of efficiency. But the financial history of mergers—including some of the great conglomerates— suggests that many businessmen became so preoccupied with acquiring new companies and promoting the conglomerate image that they lost sight of the primary business objective of seeking larger profits through improved technology, marketing, and management. When talented corporate executives devote their finest hours to arranging speculative maneuvers, the productivity of their businesses inevitably suffers and so too does the nation's productivity.

These speculative excesses had to end, and it is fortunate that they ended before bringing disaster to our nation. Equity values are now being appraised more realistically than a year or two ago. Investors are now more attentive to high quality stocks. Indeed, many of them have discovered or rediscovered that even bonds and time deposits are a fit use of their funds. Not a few of those responsible for the frantic search for "performance stocks" have shifted to other activities or joined the ranks of the unemployed; so also have numbers of security analysts and stock brokers. With speculation giving way to longer-term investment, the stock market is now channeling risk capital to business firms more efficiently.

A searching reappraisal of the economic philosophy of mergers is also under way. Merger activity has slowed materially since mid-1969. To some degree this is a response to the growing concern in governmental circles over the dangers that may inhere in large concentrations of economic power. But it stems mainly from the fact that businessmen are recognizing that time and energy can usually be spent more productively in searching for ways to increase the economic efficiency of their firm than in a scramble for corporate acquisitions.

Businessmen are also reconsidering the wisdom of financial practices that distorted their balance sheets during the late 1960s. In the manufacturing sector, the ratio of debt to equity— which had been approximately stable during the previous decade —began rising in 1964 and was half again as large by 1970. Liquid asset holdings of corporate businesses were trimmed to the bone. On the average, the ratio of prime liquid assets to current liabilities fell by nearly half during those six years. In permitting such a drastic decline in liquidity, many of our corporations openly courted trouble.

Perhaps the most ominous source of instability produced by these financial practices was the huge expansion of the commercial paper market. The volume of commercial paper issued by nonfinancial businesses increased eightfold between the end of

1964 and mid-1970, as an increasing number of firms—some of them with questionable credit standings—began to tap this market. The hazards inherent in the spreading reliance on commercial paper were taken much too lightly. After all, the relations between the buyer and seller of commercial paper are by their very nature distant and impersonal—unlike the close working relationship that normally develops between a bank and its business customers. The buyer—typically an industrial enterprise—rarely has the facilities or the experience to carry out a full investigation of the risks attaching to commercial paper. Moreover, the buyer regards his investment as temporary—to be withdrawn when cash is needed or when questions arise about the quality of the paper. The issuer, therefore, faces considerable uncertainty as to the amount of his maturing obligations that may be renewed on any given day. The risks facing the individual issuer and buyer inevitably pose a problem also for the nation's financial system, since the difficulties experienced by any large issuer of commercial paper may quickly spread to others.

These familiar truths were lost sight of in the inflationary aura of the late 1960s. It took the developments of last summer, when the threat of financial crisis hung for a time over the commercial paper market, to remind the business community that time-honored principles of sound finance are still relevant.

As a result of that experience and the testing of financial markets generally during the past two years, corporate financial policies are now more constructive than in the recent past. This year, new stock issues have continued at a high level—even in the face of unreceptive markets—as corporations have sought to stem the rise in debt-equity ratios. Of late, borrowing by corporations has been concentrated in long-term debt issues, and their rate of accumulation of liquid assets has risen. Liquidity positions of industrial and commercial firms are thus improving, though it will take some time yet to rectify fully the mistakes of the past.

These efforts to restore sound business finances are not without costs to the nation. For example, long-term interest rates, while below their peaks at the end of last year or last spring, are still at unusually high levels because of this year's extraordinary volume of new capital issues. But there can be no doubt that substantial adjustments in the financial practices of our nation's businesses were essential if the basis for a lasting and stable prosperity was to be reestablished.

By and large, our major financial institutions conducted themselves with prudence during the years when lax practices were spreading in financial markets. There were, however, some individual institutions that overextended loan commitments relative to their resources, others that reduced liquidity to unduly low levels, still others that permitted a gradual deterioration in the quality of loan portfolios, and even a few that used funds of depositors to speculate in long-term municipal securities. Fortunately, such institutions were distinctly in the minority. When the chips were down, our major financial institutions proved to be strong and resilient. And they are stronger today. As monetary policy has eased, the liquidity of commercial banks has been increasing. Even so, loan applications are being screened with greater care. The emphasis on investment quality has also increased at other financial institutions, as is evidenced by the recent wide spread between the yields of high and lower grade bonds.

These corrective adjustments in private financial practices have materially improved the prospects for maintaining order and stability in financial markets. But no less important to the establishment of a solid base for a stable and lasting prosperity have been the developments this year in the management of the industrial and commercial aspects of business enterprise.

During the latter half of the 1960s, business profit margins came under severe pressure. The ratio of profits after taxes to income originating in corporations had experienced a prolonged rise during the period of price stability in the early 1960s. But this vital ratio declined rather steadily from the last quarter of 1965 and this year reached its lowest point of the entire postwar period.

Until the autumn of 1969 or thereabouts, the decline in profit margins was widely ignored. This is one of the great perils of inflation. Underlying economic developments tend to be masked by rising prices and the state of euphoria that comes to pervade the business community. Though profit margins were falling and the cost of external funds was rising to astonishing levels, the upward surge of investment in business fixed capital continued. True, much of this investment was undertaken in the interest of economizing on labor costs. Simultaneously, however, serious efforts to bring operating costs under control became more and more rare, labor hoarding developed on a large scale, huge wage increases were granted with little resistance, and some business investments were undertaken in the expectation that inflationary developments would one way or another validate almost any business judgment. While the toll in economic efficiency taken by these loose managerial practices cannot be measured with precision, some notion of its significance can be gained by observing changes in the growth rate of productivity.

From 1947 through 1966, the average rate of advance in output per man-hour in the private sector of the economy was about 3 percent per year. In 1967, the rate of advance slowed to under 2 percent, and gains in productivity ceased altogether from about the middle of 1968 through the first quarter of this year. The loss of output and the erosion of savings that resulted from this slowdown in productivity growth are frightfully high.

The elimination of excess demand, which the government's anti-inflationary policies brought about, is now forcing business firms to mend their ways. Decisions with regard to production and investment are no longer being made on the assumption that price advances will rectify all but the most imprudent business judgments. In the present environment of intense competition in product markets, business firms are weighing carefully the expected rate of return on capital outlays and the costs of financing. The rate of investment in plant and equipment has therefore flattened out, and advance indicators suggest that business fixed investment will remain moderate in 1971.

Business attitudes toward cost controls have of late also changed dramatically. A cost-cutting process that is more widespread and more intense than at any time in the postwar period is now under way in the business world. Advertising expenditures are being curtailed, unprofitable lines of production discontinued, less efficient offices closed, and research and development expenditures critically reappraised. Layers of superfluous executive and supervisory personnel that were built up over a long period of lax managerial practices are being eliminated. Reductions in employment have occurred among all classes of workers—blue collar, white collar, and professional workers alike. Indeed, employment of so-called nonproduction workers in manufacturing has shown a decline since March that is unparalleled in the postwar period.

Because of these vigorous efforts to cut costs, the growth of productivity has resumed, after two years of stagnation. In the second quarter of this year, output per man-hour in the private nonfarm economy rose at a 4 percent annual rate, and the rate advanced to 5 percent in the third quarter. These productivity gains have served as a sharp brake on the rise in unit labor costs, despite continued rapid increases in wage rates.

In my judgment, these widespread changes in business and financial practices are evidence that genuine progress is being made in the long and arduous task of bringing inflationary forces under control. We may now look forward with some confidence to a future when decisions in the business and financial community will be made more rationally, when managerial talents will be concentrated more intensively on efficiency in processes of production, and when participants in financial markets will avoid the speculative excesses of the recent past.

Let me invite your attention next to the role that government policies have played this year in fostering these and related adjustments in private policies and practices.

The fundamental objective of monetary and fiscal policies this year has been to maintain a climate in which inflationary pressures would continue to moderate, while providing sufficient stimulus to guard against cumulative weakness in economic activity. Inflationary expectations of businessmen and consumers had to be dampened; the American people had to be convinced that the government had no intention of letting inflation run rampant. But it was equally important to follow policies that would help to cushion declines in industrial production stemming from cutbacks in defense and reduced output of business equipment, and to set the economy on a course that would release the latent forces of expansion in our homebuilding industry and in state and local government construction. I believe we have found this middle course for both fiscal and monetary policy.

A substantial reduction in the degree of fiscal restraint has been accomplished this year with the phasing out of the income tax surcharge and the increase in social security benefits. These sources of stimulus provided support for consumer disposable incomes and spending at a time when manufacturing employment was declining and the length of the workweek was being cut back.

I do not like, but I am also not deeply troubled by, the deficit in the federal budget during the current fiscal year. If the deficit had originated in a new explosion of governmental spending, I would fear its inflationary consequences. This, however, is not the present case. The deficit in fiscal 1971—though it will prove appreciably larger than originally anticipated—reflects in very large part the shortfall of revenues that has accompanied the recent sluggishness of economic activity. The federal budget is thus cushioning the slowdown in the economy without releasing a new inflationary wave. The President's determination to keep spending under control is heartening, particularly his plea last July for a rigid legislative ceiling on expenditures that would apply to both the Executive and the Congress. However, pressures for much larger spending in fiscal 1972 are mounting and pose a threat to present fiscal policy.

Monetary policy this year has also demonstrated, I believe, that it could find a middle course between the policy of extreme restraint followed in 1969 and the policies of aggressive ease pursued in some earlier years. Interest rates have come down, and liquidity positions of banks, other financial institutions, and nonfinancial businesses have been rebuilt—though not by amounts that threaten a reemergence of excess aggregate demand. A more tranquil atmosphere now prevails in financial markets. Market participants have come to realize that temporary stresses and strains in financial markets could be alleviated without resort to excessive rates of monetary expansion. Growth of the money supply thus far this year—averaging about a 5½ percent annual rate—has been rather high by historical standards. This is not, however, an excessive rate for a period in which precautionary demands for liquidity have at times been quite strong.

The precautionary demands for liquidity that were in evidence earlier in 1970 reflected to a large degree the business and financial uncertainties on which I have already commented. It was the clear duty of the nation's central bank to accommodate such demands. Of particular importance were the actions of the Federal Reserve in connection with the commercial paper market last June. This market, following the announcement on Sunday,

June 21, of the Penn Central's petition for relief under the Bankruptcy Act, posed a serious threat to financial stability. The firm in question had large amounts of maturing commercial paper that could not be renewed, and it could not obtain credit elsewhere. The danger existed that a wave of fear would pass through the financial community, engulf other issuers of commercial paper, and cast doubt on a wide range of other securities.

By Monday, June 22—the first business day following announcement of the bankruptcy petition—the Federal Reserve had already taken the virtually unprecedented step of advising the larger banks across the country that the discount window would be available to help the banks meet unusual borrowing requirements of firms that could not roll over their maturing commercial paper. In addition, the Board of Governors reviewed its regulations governing ceiling rates of interest on certificates of deposit, and on June 23 announced a suspension of ceilings in the maturity range in which most large certificates of deposit are sold. This action gave banks the freedom to bid for funds in the market and make loans available to necessitous borrowers.

As a result of these prompt actions, a sigh of relief passed through the financial and business communities. The actions, in themselves, did not provide automatic solutions to the many problems that arose in the ensuing days and weeks. But the financial community was reassured that the Federal Reserve understood the seriousness of the situation, and that it would stand ready to use its intellectual and financial resources, as well as its instruments of monetary policy, to assist the financial markets through any period of stress. Confidence was thus bolstered, with the country's large banks playing their part by mobilizing available funds to meet the needs of sound borrowers caught temporarily in a liquidity squeeze.

The role that confidence plays as a cornerstone of the foundation for prosperity cannot, I think, be overstressed. Much has been done over recent months by private businesses and by the government to strengthen this foundation. If we ask what tasks still lie ahead, the answer I believe must be: full restoration of confidence among consumers and businessmen that inflationary pressures will continue to moderate, while the awaited recovery in production and employment becomes a reality.

The implications of this answer for the general course of

monetary and fiscal policies over the near term seem to me clear. The thrust of monetary and fiscal policies must be sufficiently stimulative to assure a satisfactory recovery in production and employment. But we must be careful to avoid excessive monetary expansion or unduly stimulative fiscal policies. Past experience indicates that efforts to regain our full output potential overnight would almost surely be self-defeating. The improvements in productivity that we have struggled so hard to achieve would be lost if we found ourselves engulfed once again in the inflationary excesses that inevitably occur in an overheated economy.

As I look back on the latter years of the 1960s, and consider the havoc wrought by the inflation of that period, I am convinced that we as a people need to assign greater prominence to the goal of price stability in the hierarchy of stabilization objectives. I have recommended on earlier occasions that the Employment Act of 1946 be amended to include explicit reference to the objective of general price stability. Such a change in that law will not, of course, assure better economic policies. But it would call the nation's attention dramatically to the vital role of reasonable price stability in the maintenance of our national economic health.

At the present time, governmental efforts to achieve price stability continue to be thwarted by the continuance of wage increases substantially in excess of productivity gains. Unfortunately, the corrective adjustments in wage settlements that are needed to bring inflationary forces under control have yet to occur. The inflation that we are still experiencing is no longer due to excess demand. It rests rather on the upward push of costs—mainly, sharply rising wage rates.

Wage increases have not moderated. The average rate of increase of labor compensation per hour has been about 7 percent this year—roughly the same as last year. Moreover, wage costs under new collective bargaining contracts have actually been accelerating despite the rise in unemployment. In the third quarter of this year, major collective bargaining agreements called for annual increases in wage rates averaging 10 percent over the life of the contract. Negotiated settlements in the construction industry during the same three months provided for wage increases averaging 16 percent over the life of the contract, and

22 percent in the first year of the contract. Nor is the end of this explosive round of wage increases yet in sight. Next year, contracts expire in such major industries as steel, aluminum, copper, and cans. If contracts in those industries are patterned on recent agreements in the construction industry—or, for that matter, in the trucking and automobile industries—heavy upward pressures on prices will continue.

I fully understand the frustration of workers who have seen inflation erode the real value of past wage increases. But it is clearly in the interest of labor to recognize that economic recovery as well as the battle against inflation will be impeded by wage settlements that greatly exceed probable productivity gains.

In a society such as ours, which rightly values full employment, monetary and fiscal tools are inadequate for dealing with sources of price inflation such as are plaguing us now—that is, pressures on costs arising from excessive wage increases. As the experience of our neighbors to the north indicates, inflationary wage settlements may continue for extended periods even in the face of rising unemployment. In Canada, unemployment has been moving up since early 1966. New wage settlements in major industries, however, averaged in the 7 to 8 percent range until the spring of 1969, then rose still further. This year, with unemployment moving above 6½ percent, negotiated settlements have been in the 8 to 9 percent range.

Many of our citizens, including some respected labor leaders, are troubled by the failure of collective bargaining settlements in the United States to respond to the anti-inflationary measures adopted to date. They have come to the conclusion, as I have, that it would be desirable to supplement our monetary and fiscal policies with an incomes policy, in the hope of thus shortening the period between suppression of excess demand and the restoration of reasonable relations of wages, productivity, and prices.

To make significant progress in slowing the rise in wages and prices, we should consider the scope of an incomes policy quite broadly. The essence of incomes policies is that they are market-oriented; in other words, their aim is to change the structure and functioning of commodity and labor markets in ways that reduce upward pressures on costs and prices.

The additional anti-inflationary measures announced by the

President last Friday will make a constructive contribution to that end. The actions to increase the supply of oil will dampen the mounting cost of fuels, and the recommendations made by the President to improve the structure of collective bargaining in the construction industry strike at the heart of a serious source of our current inflationary problem.

I would hope that every citizen will support the President's stern warning to business and labor to exercise restraint in pricing and wage demands. A full measure of success in the effort to restore our nation's economic health is, I believe, within our grasp, once we as a people demonstrate a greater concern for the public interest in our private decisions.

If further steps should prove necessary to reduce upward pressures on costs and prices, numerous other measures might be taken to improve the functioning of our markets. For example, liberalization of import quotas on oil and other commodities would serve this purpose. So also would a more vigorous enforcement of the antitrust laws, or an expansion of federal training programs to increase the supply of skilled workers where wages are rising with exceptional rapidity, or the creation on a nationwide scale of local productivity councils to seek ways of increasing efficiency, or a more aggressive pace in establishing computerized job banks, or the liberalization of depreciation allowances to stimulate plant modernization, or suspension of the Davis-Bacon Act to help restore order in the construction trades, or modification of the minimum wage laws in the interest of improving job opportunities for teenagers, or the establishment of national building codes to break down barriers to the adoption of modern production techniques in the construction industry, or compulsory arbitration of labor disputes in industries that vitally involve the public interest, and so on. We might bring under an incomes policy, also, the establishment of a high-level price and wage review board which, while lacking enforcement power, would have broad authority to investigate, advise, and recommend on price and wage changes.

Such additional measures as may be required can, of course, be determined best by the President and the Congress. What I see clearly is the need for our nation to recognize that we are dealing, practically speaking, with a new problem—namely, persistent inflation in the face of substantial unemployment—and that the classical remedies may not work well enough or fast enough in this case. Monetary and fiscal policies can readily cope with inflation alone or with recession alone; but, within the limits of our national patience, they cannot by themselves now be counted on to restore full employment, without at the same time releasing a new wave of inflation. We therefore need to explore with an open mind what steps beyond monetary and fiscal policies may need to be taken by government to strengthen confidence of consumers and businessmen in the nation's future.

In the past two years we have come a long way, I believe, towards the creation of a foundation for a lasting and stable prosperity. Confidence has been restored in financial markets. Businesses have turned away from the imprudent practices of the past. Productivity gains have resumed. Our balance of trade has improved. The stage has been set for a recovery in production and employment—a recovery in which our needs for housing and public construction can be more fully met.

To make this foundation firm, however, we must find ways to bring an end to the pressures of costs on prices. There are no easy choices open to us to accomplish this objective. But that, as I indicated at the outset, is the tough legacy of inflation.

The Economy in Mid-1971

I am pleased to meet with you again today to report the views of the Board of Governors of the Federal Reserve System regarding the state of the economy at mid-year.

Since I last appeared before this committee on February 19, it has become evident that a cyclical recovery of our economy has commenced. Indicators of future business activity, which were already rising in the latter part of 1970, have strengthened further. Comprehensive measures of current activity—such as the physical volume of industrial production, total employment, retail sales adjusted for price changes, and total real output of good and services—have shown moderate improvement as the year has progressed. We are confident that this recovery process will continue and broaden in the months to come.

Nonetheless, some of the economic problems that have troubled us as a people over the recent past are still much in evidence. Large increases in wages and prices persist in the face of extensive unemployment of labor and capital. The international balance of payments remains unsatisfactory; indeed, our fragile export surplus has disappeared in recent months. In financial markets, interest rates are responding to fears of continued high rates of inflation by moving up again despite rapid monetary expansion. And while business profits have improved somewhat, they remain exceptionally low.

The cost-push inflation we are experiencing, and the widespread concern over continued rapid inflation, are a grave obsta-

Statement before the Joint Economic Committee of the U.S. Congress, July 23, 1971.

cle to the full economic improvement we all ardently seek. As long as inflation persists, consumers are likely to remain rather conservative in their spending plans, fearing the possibility of budgetary overcommitment. As long as inflation persists, businessmen are likely to remain cautious in their investment policies, apprehensive that profit margins may erode despite higher prices. As long as inflation persists, financial investors will remain reluctant to commit funds to long-term securities unless they are compensated by a higher interest rate. Expectations of inflation thus permeate the gamut of private decisions to spend and invest, and this is restraining the private efforts needed for vigorous and sustained economic recovery.

A year or two ago it was generally expected that extensive slack in resource use, such as we have been experiencing, would lead to significant moderation in the inflationary spiral. This has not happened, either here or abroad. The rules of economics are not working in quite the way they used to. Despite extensive unemployment in our country, wage rate increases have not moderated. Despite much idle industrial capacity, commodity prices continue to rise rapidly. And the experience of other industrial countries, particularly Canada and Great Britain, shouts warnings that even a long stretch of high and rising unemployment may not suffice to check the inflationary process.

I shall return to the causes and implications of this new rigidity in our economic structure at a later point. Let me turn first, however, to a brief review of economic developments during the first half of 1971, and to the supportive role that public policy has played—and will continue to play—in the evolving economic recovery.

The performance of the economy during the first half of 1971 is not easy to interpret because many crosscurrents are always present in the vicinity of a cyclical turning point. In addition, the rebound from the extended auto strike last fall, and the accumulation of steel inventories in anticipation of a possible strike this summer, have been distorting the underlying trend.

Abstracting from these transitory influences, the record of the first half of 1971 is one of gradual, but quickening, recovery. Late last year, only the construction industry exhibited significant strength, as the sharp recovery in residential building that began in the spring was joined by renewed expansion in the construction programs of state and local governments. Early this year consumer spending began to improve, with increases of sales spreading to a wide variety of consumer items. The sales of retailers other than automobile dealers rose at about a 10 percent annual rate in the second quarter—considerably more than normal and well above the rise in consumer goods prices. Recently, activity in our factories has also been stepped up, especially in consumer goods lines. The index of industrial production, adjusted to exclude autos and steel, rose at a 6 percent annual rate between March and June.

The improving trend of business is being supported by a faster rate of growth in personal incomes. During the three months from March through May, total personal income rose at an annual rate of 8 percent, compared with a 6 percent rate over the previous six months. Governmental transfer payments, which have been contributing to recent income growth, were particularly large during June when the retroactive increase in social security benefits was paid. The flow of private wage and salary payments has also quickened, in response to some gain in man-hours worked as well as to continued large increases in wage rates. And while employers have not yet reentered the labor market for appreciable numbers of new employees, further business improvement should soon lead to faster employment growth also.

Inventory investment promises to supply an added source of economic impetus in the months ahead, after allowance for a probable rundown in steel stockpiles. Thus far in the recovery, there has been little accumulation of inventories, apart from the restocking by automobile dealers and strike-hedge buying by steel merchants and users. But with business sales rising, and the ratio of inventories to output and to sales declining in many lines, we are coming closer to the time when needs for larger inventories—of raw materials, work in process, and finished goods—will begin to express themselves. The adjustment of stocks to higher levels of activity will in turn generate further increases in output, employment, and incomes. This is a common element in cyclical recoveries, and I judge that we are approaching that point in the current recovery process.

There are grounds for concern, nonetheless, with regard to

some features of the recovery now under way. First, there is little evidence as yet of any material strengthening in consumer or business confidence. Recent surveys of consumer attitudes show only modest improvement, while uneasiness appears to persist among many businessmen and investors regarding the effects of continuing rapid increases in labor costs on future profitability. Confidence is likely to strengthen with the passage of time, as sales and employment conditions improve. But there is a danger that hesitation and uncertainty will continue on an extensive scale until significant progress is made in moderating inflation. Greater success in the battle against inflation is probably the most important single prerequisite of more rapid and enduring economic expansion.

Second, our international competitive position appears to have deteriorated. In the first five months of 1971, imports spurted and our normal trade surplus vanished. This is a distressingly poor performance in an economy experiencing substantial underutilization of its resources of labor and capital. The problem is dramatized by the success of foreign manufacturers in capturing a rapidly expanding share of our automobile market. In the past six months, sales of foreign models have accounted for 16 percent of total U.S. sales and, in addition, close to one-tenth of the American models sold were produced in Canada. It may be tempting to react to foreign competition by imposing added restrictions and quotas on imports, but such a policy would not serve our national interests. The constructive course is to bring inflation under control and to stimulate our businessmen to increase their penetration of the expanding markets abroad and to compete more effectively with foreign producers in our domestic markets. I would favor consideration of new government incentives toward this end.

Third, there is as yet no evidence of resurgence in business capital spending programs. New orders for capital equipment show little—if any—recovery from the 1970 lows when allowance is made for rising prices. Construction contract footage for commercial and industrial buildings remains far below earlier highs. Official surveys of business spending plans for plant and equipment show no increase, even in dollar terms, for the remainder of this year. The hesitation in business investment may reflect the sizable amounts of unused capacity that presently exist. But it also results, I believe, from low business profits and uncertainty about the profit outlook. History indicates rather clearly that a vigorous, sustained economic recovery requires a strengthening trend in business capital investment.

We need to encourage business firms to undertake new capital investment; and I strongly supported, therefore, the liberalization of depreciation allowances recently adopted by the Treasury. I have also endorsed the general proposition that an investment tax credit be adopted permanently. At the moment, however, I am doubtful about the wisdom of restoring the investment tax credit—or of taking other stimulative fiscal actions—in view of the state of the federal budget. In the fiscal year just ended, the budget deficit was in excess of $20 billion. It will remain very large in fiscal 1972. Many influential citizens in the business and financial community view this situation with alarm, so that these large budget deficits have become an important psychological factor contributing both to inflationary expectations and to high interest rates.

A large part of the budget deficit is, of course, attributable to the shortfall in tax receipts stemming from sluggishness in the economy. Some expenditures, notably on unemployment insurance and welfare, have risen for this same reason. Even taking these factors into account, however, the federal budget is more stimulative now than a year or two ago. The President submitted in January a moderately expansive budget for fiscal 1972, and since then the net effect of congressional actions has been to make it more stimulative. Social security benefits have been liberalized, retroactive to the first of the year, and the scheduled increase in social security taxes postponed for a year. The public service employment bill has become law, and it appears probable that the military pay raise bill will be larger than the budget proposals. These and other actions, along with increases in the so-called uncontrollable items in the budget, as Chairman Mc-Cracken reported to you, have served to raise estimated expenditures $5 billion above those originally proposed for fiscal 1972, and to reduce estimated receipts by some $2 billion.

I would not want to rule out additional fiscal stimulus if the recovery in the economy should prove to be well below normal proportions, particularly if such a move were preceded or accompanied by a more effective incomes policy. But I would urge caution at the present time. Once confidence becomes stronger, we may find that there is enough fiscal stimulus already at work. And in any case, the fear of inflation is much too great, and its potential effect on private behavior too negative, to run the risk of taking new fiscal actions that would now seem imprudent.

Let me turn next to monetary policy, and to the substantial contribution it has made to stimulating economic activity over the past year.

The shift toward monetary expansion early in 1970 was rather promptly followed by a resurgence in bank deposits and in the flow of funds to other financial intermediaries. As financial institutions rebuilt their liquidity, they became more eager lenders, the availability of credit increased greatly, and interest rates declined. As a result, housing starts rebounded and state and local government construction began to rise more briskly. More receptive credit markets also enabled our business corporations to issue new securities in record volume, thereby rebuilding their liquidity and putting themselves in a financial position to expand production and the capital investment that they may wish to carry forward later on.

Late last year, as this committee knows, there was a marked decline in the rate of expansion of the narrowly defined money supply—that is, currency plus demand deposits. In these circumstances, a brief period of more rapid expansion in the money supply to compensate for the fourth quarter shortfall seemed appropriate. The System, consequently, provided bank reserves liberally over the winter months, and interest rates—partly reflecting the increased supply of reserves—declined sharply further. Expansion of the narrowly defined money supply rose to a 9 percent annual rate during the first quarter of this year; but the average growth rate for the fourth and first quarters combined, being little more than 6 percent, remained very close to the earlier trend in 1970.

This March and April, the Federal Reserve System faced a dilemma. Information available at that time suggested that high rates of monetary growth might well persist under existing conditions in the money market. Interest rates, however, were already displaying a tendency to rise, and vigorous action to restrain monetary growth might have raised them sharply further. In view of the delicate state of the economic recovery, which was just getting under way, it seemed desirable to prevent the possible adverse effects of sharply higher interest rates on expenditure plans and public psychology. The Federal Open Market Committee decided, therefore, to move very cautiously toward restraining the growth of the monetary aggregates.

With the benefit of hindsight, I now feel that stronger action was warranted this spring. For, as matters turned out, we experienced even faster monetary growth in the second quarter than had been anticipated, while interest rates also moved substantially higher. Present estimates indicate that the narrowly defined money supply rose at an annual rate of 11 percent in the second quarter. However, growth in a more broadly defined money supply—that is, currency, plus demand deposits, plus commercial bank time deposits other than large denomination CDs—receded from an annual rate of 18 percent in the first quarter to a rate of 13 percent in the next three months. It is worth noting also that bank credit expansion has been considerably more restrained than growth in any of the measures of the money supply. Total bank credit rose at a 12 percent annual rate during the first quarter and then dropped to a 7 percent rate in the second.

It may be that the recent high growth rates in money balances, besides being a lagged response to the lower interest rates of this past winter, reflect some of the uncertainties of the general public about the economic situation. To the extent that this is true, the inclination to hold unusually large money balances should subside as economic recovery becomes more evident. In any event, it is clear that recent monetary growth rates are higher than is necessary or desirable over any length of time to sustain healthy economic expansion. The Federal Reserve has, therefore, already taken some steps to reduce the growth rate of bank reserves and thereby promote a more moderate rate of monetary expansion.

These actions are partly responsible for the recent rise in interest rates—particularly interest rates on very short-term market securities. But it should be kept carefully in mind that the rise in interest rates since March has occurred despite rapid rates of monetary growth and continuing large flows of savings funds to depository institutions. Factors other than monetary policy must therefore be primarily responsible for the upturn in interest rates this spring; they include, in addition to indications that a business recovery is developing, the prospect of very large Treasury financing needs, deepening concern about the unrelenting character of cost-push inflation, some apprehension over international financial developments, and not a little anticipatory borrowing in the capital market on top of that currently needed. The fear of inflation appears to have been especially important in the recent behavior of our money and capital markets, and a reversal of psychology may well be required to achieve a significant downward adjustment of interest rates.

The rise in short-term interest rates during recent months had the effect of putting the Federal Reserve discount rate, which had been reduced in a series of actions to 4¾ percent last February, well below the rates at which funds could be obtained by banks in the open market. The effect of this discrepancy in rates was to encourage member bank borrowing from the Reserve Banks—borrowing which was rising rapidly and thereby providing reserves to support continued high rates of monetary expansion.

Accordingly, as you know, the Board last week approved increases in Federal Reserve Bank discount rates to 5 percent by a unanimous vote of the five Board members present at the meeting. I participated by telephone in the discussion leading to this action, and I want you to know that I supported it fully. Our hope is that the higher discount rate will serve to moderate the demand for discounting at the Federal Reserve, that it will help prevent excessive growth of the monetary aggregates, and also impart a degree of stability to interest rate expectations.

I continue to feel that the country needs lower interest rates, and that lower rates—especially on mortgages and state and local government securities—would contribute to a more vigorous economic recovery. But I am not hopeful that substantially lower interest rates can be achieved—until we as a nation make steady and meaningful progress in solving our inflation problem.

The inflation we are confronted with has become deeply rooted since its beginnings in 1965. The forces of excess demand that originally led to price inflation disappeared well over a year ago. Nevertheless, strong and stubborn inflationary forces, emanating from rising costs, linger on. I wish I could report that we are making substantial progress in dampening the inflationary spiral. I cannot do so. Neither the behavior of prices nor the pattern of wage increases as yet provides evidence of any significant moderation in the advance of costs and prices. If growth in productivity accelerates with a quickening economy, some real moderation may well develop in the months ahead. Even so, the residual rate of inflation may well run above the characteristic level of previous cyclical upswings.

Let me cite some of the evidence that leads me to this view. Thus far in 1971, prices of newly produced goods and services in the private economy are still rising, on the average, at about a 5 percent annual rate—or at essentially the same rate as in 1969 and 1970. The rate of advance of consumer prices did diminish conspicuously during the first five months of 1971, but most of this improvement is attributable to the decline in mortgage interest rates. The wholesale price index for all commodities has increased at an annual rate of 5 percent thus far this year, or twice last year's rate. Wholesale prices of industrial commodities, moreover, have accelerated from a 3½ percent increase last year to a 4 percent rate thus far in 1971.

Much the same picture emerges from a review of changes in wages and salaries—by far the most important component of business costs. Wages in the private nonfarm economy, adjusted for changes in industrial composition and for overtime work, rose at about a 7 percent annual rate in the first half of 1971—slightly more than in 1970 or 1969. This sustained sharp rise in wages during a period of substantial economic slack contrasts markedly with our experience in earlier recessions, when the rate of advance in wages typically dropped sharply or actually ceased.

Nor is the picture more encouraging when one inspects the trend of new agreements reached in major collective bargaining settlements—agreements which tend to establish wage trends throughout industry. The wage increases agreed to, for example, in the automobile, can and aluminum settlements, and most recently by AT&T, amount to 12 percent or more for the first year. The full extent of the increase contracted for later years is not yet known, since it will depend in part on the speed of future advances in the consumer price index.

It is important to inquire into the reasons for this unusual behavior of wages and salaries. The answer is doubtless complex, involving a myriad of structural, psychological, and social changes. Ironically, our national commitment to high employment and economic prosperity, and our relative success in achieving these objectives, accounts for part of the problem. For a general expectation has developed on the part of both business and labor that recessions, if they occur at all, will prove brief and mild; and this expectation has influenced both the strength of wage demands and the willingness of management to accept them.

A second factor contributing materially to the sustained character of wage rate increases in the current situation is the intensity and duration of the previous phase of excess demand. Consumer prices have been rising steadily since 1965—much of the time at an accelerating rate. Continued substantial increases are now widely anticipated over the months and years ahead. In such an environment, workers naturally seek wage increases sufficiently large to compensate for the effects of past inflation on their real incomes, and to give some protection against future price advances—besides providing for a measure of improvement in living standards. Thoughtful employers are bound to have some sympathy with these efforts, all the more so when they reckon—as they now generally do—that cost increases can probably be passed on to buyers grown accustomed to inflation.

Other factors too have been at work. The increased militancy of workers, whether union or nonunion and whether in private or public service, has probably led to wider and faster diffusion of excessive wage rate increases through the economy. I cannot help but wonder, also, whether our recent experience with wage settlements in unionized industries may not reflect a gradual shift in the balance of power at the bargaining table.

Labor seems to have become more insistent, more vigorous, and more confident in pursuing its demands, while resistance of businessmen to these demands appears to have weakened—perhaps because they fear the loss of market position that would be caused by a long strike or because they believe that their competitors too will give in to similar wage demands. More recently, the balance of power—so important to the outcome of wage bargaining—may have been influenced by expansion in the public welfare programs which can be called upon to help sustain a striking employee and his family, valid though these programs may be on social grounds. And the hand of labor may have been strengthened also by the evident success that public sector employees have had in recent years in winning large wage increases, frequently with the use of illegal strikes against the government.

In my judgment, and in the judgment of the Board as a whole, the present inflation in the midst of substantial unemployment poses a problem that traditional monetary and fiscal remedies cannot solve as quickly as the national interest demands. That is what has led me, on various occasions, to urge additional governmental actions involving wages and prices— actions that would serve, by moderating the inflationary trend, to free the American economy from the hestitations that are now restraining its great energy.

There has been some progress in this area over the past year or two. The President deserves credit for his efforts to deal with the special supply-demand problems that had developed in the lumber and petroleum industries, and for bringing together labor and business leaders in the steel industry for a discussion of basic economic issues at the outset of the current wage negotiations. The Construction Industry Stabilization Committee, formed earlier this spring, appears to be having some success in moderating the staggering trend of wage settlements in that industry. The periodic Inflation Alerts serve a useful function in stimulating public discussion of areas in which wage or price decisions do not seem to conform to economic fundamentals. And the National Commission on Productivity may yet provide the basis for important improvements in the cost trends of our economy.

In the Board's judgment, these efforts need to be carried further—perhaps much further. The problem of cost-push inflation, in which escalating wages lead to escalating prices in a never-ending circle, is the most difficult economic issue of our time. It needs to be given top priority by our business and labor leaders as well as by the government. There is much good will and statesmanship in the ranks of business and labor, and it would be wise for the government to draw upon it more fully.

The New Committee on Interest and Dividends

I appreciate the opportunity to participate in your discussion of H.R. 11309. This bill, besides extending the Economic Stabilization Act, brings interest rates and dividends under its umbrella of potential controls. I therefore appear before you in my capacity as Chairman of the new Committee on Interest and Dividends.

Let me say, at the outset, that the most urgent economic task facing our nation is to make a success of the stabilization program initiated by the President on August 15.

The current price and wage freeze is a major step in breaking the hold of inflation on our country. The freeze must be followed by effective restraints on the upward movement of wages and prices, so that a solid foundation may be laid for the early restoration of general price stability under free market conditions.

This high objective will require unreserved, continuing support of business, labor, and the population as a whole. It will require the support of sound fiscal and monetary measures. And it will entail the extension and amendment of the Economic Stabilization Act to assure continuity of the new policy.

As Phase II of the wage and price policy gets under way, one of our major assets is the wide public acceptance of Phase I. If this early success is sustained, which I consider likely, confidence will grow that full prosperity can be attained without inflation. Under those conditions, we can expect business and con-

---

Statement before the Committee on Banking and Currency, House of Representatives, November 1, 1971.

sumer spending to continue to increase; we can expect wage demands to moderate; and we can expect further reduction of the inflation premium built into interest rates.

Before turning to the mission of the Committee on Interest and Dividends and its relationship to Phase II, I should like to make a few broad observations on the economic setting which launched our nation on its stabilization policy of mid-August.

Over the past two years, strong cost and price pressures had persisted in the face of rather sluggish demand for goods and services, a high rate of excess plant capacity, and more extensive unemployment than the American people will long accept. In part, the cost pressures stemmed from efforts by workers and their trade unions to compensate for the eroding impact of past price increases on their real earnings. But they also reflected the efforts of labor to anticipate future price increases. Both labor and management came to expect that inflation would persist, and that it might become our way of life. In this environment, labor typically demanded large wage increases, and business firms typically met these demands in the belief that higher costs could be passed on in the form of higher prices.

As the pace of inflation quickened, expectations of continuing inflation began to dominate economic decision making. Between mid-1970 and mid-1971, average hourly compensation of workers in the private economy rose from 7 to 8 percent. Major collective bargaining contracts negotiated over the same period called for first-year increases averaging 11 percent, while increases over the life of the contracts—without considering future advances under cost-of-living escalators—were to average over 8 percent per year.

Wage increases of this magnitude outstripped productivity gains by a wide margin, and made price advances inevitable. Even so, profit margins shrank, and during 1970 reached the lowest level experienced in the post–World War II period. The declining trend in profits, of course, intensified pressure on business firms to raise their prices.

The wage-price spiral that had developed threatened our economic recovery, which rested much too heavily on residential building. Businessmen showed little enthusiasm for new capital investment. Consumers were likewise cautious in their buying and permitted their savings to mount. Moreover, foreign producers had become more successful, both here and abroad, in competing against domestically produced goods. In consequence, our balance of trade swung into a virtually unprecedented deficit, and this too affected adversely our domestic production and employment.

Inflationary expectations were also tending to retard declines in long-term interest rates. The easing of monetary policy that began in early 1970 led to a very sharp decline in short-term interest rates. For example, the three-month Treasury bill rate dropped from 8 percent to about 3¼ percent by March 1971, its most recent low. Over roughly the same period, yields on high-grade new corporate bond issues declined from 8½ percent to only around 7 percent. The unusually wide spread that developed between long and short interest rates reflected in large part the inflation premium that buyers of long-term securities demanded and borrowers were willing to pay.

Monetary and fiscal policies, meanwhile, had gone about as far as was prudent in the circumstances. The money supply was growing rapidly. Banks and other financial institutions were amply supplied with funds. The deficit in the federal budget was already large and still increasing. The liquidity of business firms was largely restored. In this situation, additional stimulative efforts would have run the serious risk of augmenting inflationary fears, thereby threatening more hestitation by business and consumers, still higher long-term interest rates, higher prices, and further deterioration of the balance of payments.

In this state of our national economy, more and more thoughtful citizens became convinced that an incomes policy was temporarily needed to speed the transition from rapid inflation to general price stability. Properly executed, such a policy could change the psychological climate, help to rein in the wage-price spiral, squeeze some of the inflation premium out of interest rates, and improve the state of confidence sufficiently to lead consumers and business firms to spend more freely out of the income, savings, and credit available to them. Thus the nation was in a mood to respond favorably when President Nixon announced his new wage-price policy, as a part of a comprehensive plan for orderly economic growth, embracing also taxes, expenditures, and our international trade and payments balance.

It is, of course, too early to speak with certainty about the degree to which the new economic program has changed the economic climate. But the available information suggests that during the period of the freeze it has been working in the right direction.

The freeze appears to have effectively halted the spiral of prices and wages. Average hourly earnings in the private sector of the economy leveled off in September. Wholesale prices actually declined. And the consumer price index, which moderated to an annual rate of rise of 2½ percent, would probably have shown even greater improvement with more precise measurement techniques.

The new mood of confidence in our nation's ability to control inflation has also led to reductions in interest rates. Since mid-August long-term market interest rates have come down three-fourths to one percentage point, while short-term market rates have declined about one-half to three-fourths of a percentage point.

In the meantime, signs of improvement in economic activity have been gradually gaining. Figures for September show a good expansion in retail sales, with automobile sales particularly strong. Industrial production rose. And employment increased sharply, with gains widespread among various industries. Contracts for commercial and industrial construction spurted. However, orders for business capital equipment have thus far remained sluggish.

Once the economic recovery gathers momentum, we can expect the nation's unemployment problem to be substantially alleviated. To assure this outcome, we must maintain and extend the psychological and real benefits gained during the past two or three months.

The period of the freeze will soon be followed by a more flexible program of wage and price restraints. The objective of policy is to bring the rate of increase in the general price level down to 2 to 3 percent by the end of 1972. This would represent a cutting in half of the recent inflation rate, and would be a major accomplishment.

This objective must not be compromised. If we succeed, our economy will be once again on a path leading to noninflationary growth, and we may therefore look forward to a bright economic future. If, however, we fail, our economy will suffer grievously—not only next year but also in later years.

The actual outcome will depend crucially on the practical wisdom of the new Pay Board and Price Commission. They will be subject to many pressures for wage and price adjustments on equity grounds, for reasons of catch-up or comparability. These may be particularly intense in the period immediately following the outright freeze. Still, over the longer run, as the wage-price program of Phase II takes hold, it is essential to our nation's future that overall wage and price adjustments be contained within the reasonable limits set by the President and his Cost of Living Council.

Let me turn now more directly to the subject of interest rates and the role of the Committee on Interest and Dividends. Since inflation has exercised a significant influence on interest rates in recent years, it seems clear that the future of interest rates will depend heavily on the success of the wage and price program. If telling progress is made in curbing advances in the price level, as can be reasonably expected, the inflation premium built into the interest rate structure over the past few years will be appreciably reduced. However, this premium will not be eliminated immediately; the inflationary attitudes that developed over the past half-dozen years will retreat only gradually as success in the struggle against inflation is demonstrated.

As I noted earlier, we have already experienced some reduction of interest rates in consequence of the initial reaction of borrowers and lenders to the new economic program. Further declines in the months ahead are probable if wage and price pressures are visibly curbed. Once businessmen come to believe that interest rates are not destined to move ever higher in the future, long-term credit demands from corporations—which have been very large in the past year and a half—are likely to abate. When key market interest rates—such as corporate bond yields —continue to decline, the downward pressure exerted on the rate structure can be expected to work through to other, less volatile areas, such as the rates charged by lenders on mortgage and consumer loans.

We have to recognize, however, that as the pace of economic recovery accelerates, new demand pressures on interest rates will be generated. As one looks across the history of business cycles, it is clear that interest rate movements have accompanied fluctuations in aggregate economic activity. Although the movements of interest rates and economic activity have not corresponded exactly in either timing or amplitude, it is reasonable to expect that economic expansion will—sooner or later—begin to generate credit demands in excess of supply, just as economic contraction in time dampens the demand for credit relative to the available supply.

The interest rate fluctuations that correspond to such demand-supply imbalances serve an essential economic purpose. For example, when the demand for goods and services races ahead of existing supplies, increases in interest rates help to limit the expansion of credit and thus check the upward pressure on product and labor markets.

In a period of strong economic activity, if all the credit desired were supplied at unchanged interest rates, the overall demand for goods and services would inevitably exceed the nation's capacity to produce. In such conditions, inflation could perhaps be suppressed for a time by rigid economic controls; but—if history over the centuries is any guide—I doubt if anything in the world could prevent the eventual riot of inflation. Nor would we control interest rates in the end. Once it became clear that inflation was footloose, higher and higher premiums would be attached to the interest rates on which investors insisted and which borrowers were willing to pay. It is no accident that interest rates on six-month business promissory notes have run to over 20 percent in Argentina and over 40 percent in Brazil during the past few years.

The new economic policy, as I have already explained, is capable of releasing powerful psychological forces that will tend to drive interest rates to lower levels. The outlook for interest rates over the next year or so nevertheless remains uncertain. We cannot be sure how quickly or to what extent the inflation premium on interest rates will be reduced. If economic recovery gains momentum and the Phase II program succeeds in holding down wage and price increases, opposite forces will be at work in the money and capital markets. On the one hand, the demand for credit on the part of the private sector will be larger, thereby tending to raise interest rates. On the other hand, inflationary expectations will become weaker, thereby tending to lower interest rates. We are moving into a period for which there is no historical precedent, and little basis for gauging exactly how credit markets will adapt to the new circumstances.

The Committee on Interest and Dividends will need to tread cautiously in these circumstances. It cannot ignore market conditions, for it would then run the risk of thwarting the overriding national objective of economic recovery and sustained noninflationary growth. At the same time, the committee can and should undertake surveillance of interest rates, particularly those that most directly affect the American family, in order to determine if they are unduly sticky—that is to say, by way of example, whether they are adjusting appropriately to whatever declines occur in the more flexible and competitive market interest rates.

In evaluating the role of the committee, it should be recognized that credit markets are among the most competitive in our entire economy. Large financial institutions are, of course, a fact of modern economic life; but no single institution, or small group of them, is capable of dominating the market for credit, partly because there are so many of both the large and small institutions. Moreover, the money and capital markets in the various parts of our country are closely connected. In this age of the automobile and telephone, most borrowers can readily move from one financial institution in their vicinity to another, or—in the case of large, nationally known borrowers—from virtually any bank or insurance company in the nation to any other or from any of these institutions to the open market. In turn, many financial institutions can shift their lending from one market to another, depending on the rate of return available to them. The same is true of savers.

The result is that the level of interest rates is highly responsive to changes in the underlying demand-supply conditions for credit. The structure of interest rates is also responsive. When interest rates in one part of the market decline, interest rates in other parts of the market generally follow along, although sizable variations in interest rate spreads are not uncommon.

The price flexibility that is so characteristic of financial markets is rarely found in product markets and practically never occurs in labor markets. These latter markets are subject to all sorts of rigidities. Competition is less pervasive. Some of

135

our industries are dominated by a few large firms. Large segments of the labor market are fenced off from effective competition by trade unions or governmental regulation. Even in the absence of unions, employee demands derive support from the impracticability, in most cases, of assembling a substitute labor force. Most product and labor markets are thus less sensitive than is the world of finance to changes in underlying demand and supply conditions.

To illustrate these differences, we need only recall the substantial decline in interest rates, particularly short-term rates, that occurred from early 1970 to mid-1971. During this period, wholesale prices, consumer prices, and wage rates continued to rise sharply, despite substantial unemployment and sluggish demand for the products of industry. Clearly, interest rates responded with promptness and vigor to basic market conditions. This cannot be said of wages or most product prices.

However, it is important to recognize that not all credit markets are equally competitive or responsive, and that some types of interest rates move sluggishly. These rates are often termed "administered rates" or "conventional rates," but they are not administered in the sense of being determined by a small group that is insensitive to the surrounding financial environment. Rather, they are rates for which a continuous, impersonal process of bidding in the open market, such as characterizes U.S. government securities and corporate bonds, does not exist.

The so-called administered rates—for example, on residential mortgages, for consumer credit, and on loans to businesses and farmers—generally fluctuate over a narrower range than market rates. These sluggish rates involve such factors as longer-term customer relationships or substantial costs of administration. Hence, they also generally lag behind the market; that is, they may not move until it seems clear that market rates have established a new trend and are not just going through an erratic or episodic fluctuation.

It is at this point that the new committee can make its contribution. The main role of the committee, as I see it, should be to speed up the adjustment of traditionally sluggish interest rates to movements in market rates. This may be especially important in the year ahead, when we expect a further reduction in the inflation premium on interest rates. When and as rates in the open market move downward, administered rates should move more and with shorter lags than they have in the past.

For the present, the committee intends to concentrate on those interest rates that most directly affect the American family, including residential mortgage and consumer credit rates. But it is not unmindful of other areas of sluggishness, and will therefore watch the behavior of rates charged by a variety of institutions to a broad range of customers.

In recent years, some of the "administered" or "conventional" interest rates have tended to show greater flexibility. For example, the prime loan rate charged by banks was reduced eleven times between March 1970 and March 1971, declining from 8½ to 5¼ percent. It subsequently rose moderately, and most recently, as you know, has again declined. Major banks have been relying increasingly on the money market as a source of funds, and interest-rate changes in the money market consequently have a greater influence on key bank lending rates. Moreover, the business customers of commercial banks have become more and more aware of the open market as a source of funds; this, too, has increased the flexibility of bank lending rates. Recently, a few banks have indicated that they intend to tie the prime rate to one or another of the open market rates.

Mortgage rates are also becoming more sensitive to competitive conditions. The periodic auctions by the Federal National Mortgage Association provide a means by which lenders can gauge more promptly the extent to which supply and demand pressures in the broad capital market are affecting the mortgage market. And the information on interest rates that will be gathered by the Committee on Interest and Dividends, once it is disseminated throughout the country, should likewise help to increase the sensitivity of a wide variety of sticky rates to underlying conditions.

In evaluating interest rate developments, the committee does not intend to try to hold particular rates at levels that are not competitive. If, in the face of accelerating credit demands, an attempt were made to keep some interest rates down through the use of rate ceilings, lenders would tend to withdraw from the affected markets. They would place their funds in other activities where the returns that could be earned were not controlled, including the equity markets. Or they would send their money abroad. Or some individuals, trust funds, and so forth would lend their funds directly to borrowers within their reach, bypassing the financial institutions and the organized security markets that play such a major role in our economy by mobilizing capital for the use of all borrowers, small and large alike.

Let us never forget that while a legislature may impose an interest ceiling, it has no way of compelling the owner of investable funds to lend them out to anyone. Indeed, the threat posed by ceilings might in itself be sufficient to keep lenders from committing resources to areas that may eventually become subject to rigid ceilings.

Of course, some banks or other financial institutions could be expected, whether because of custom or legal restriction, to continue lending in markets subject to interest ceilings that are below the free market level. But the supply of credit to such markets would then be reduced, so that the still active lenders would be forced to ration their short supplies of credit by some means other than interest rates. In such a situation, they could also be expected to use various nonrate devices—such as compensating balances, cash payments similar to points on a mortgage, special fees, or equity kickers—that would serve to enhance the return on their money. The result would surely be an erosion of freely functioning credit markets as we now know them, and the substitution of less efficient, less equitable processes of allocating the supplies of credit that remained available. Arbitrary attempts to control interest rates, either in selected areas or for the economy as a whole, must be rejected as inefficient, inequitable and, in the end, unworkable for all concerned.

True, some interest rates are now legally prevented from moving in ways that accord with underlying demand and supply conditions. Interest-rate or usury ceilings apply, for example, to rates on consumer and conventional mortgage loans in most states, to rates on state and local securities in some jurisdictions, and to rates on federally underwritten mortgages. In the past such ceilings have limited the flow of credit to these areas in periods of rising market interest rates; they represent a type of impediment that it would be well to avoid in the future.

The legislation before your committee empowers the president "to stabilize interest rates and dividends at levels consonant with orderly economic growth." This language has the great advantage—should mandatory controls be required—of not implying fixed ceilings; instead, it recognizes that interest-rate levels must be appropriate to orderly economic growth, and thus leaves room for essential flexibility.

Let me hasten to add that the President's Executive Order, dated October 15, directs the committee to undertake a voluntary program; that is, to "formulate and execute a program for obtaining voluntary restraints on interest rates and dividends." I am confident that this objective can be achieved without resorting to mandatory controls.

Since August 15, indeed over the past year and a half, interest rate developments have been generally salutary. However, not all interest rates have responded fully to market developments, and some have hardly moved at all. The committee will seek to encourage downward adjustment of these rates, and it would certainly frown upon any premature upward move of rates that had previously been sluggish in moving down. There is every reason to believe that banks and other lenders will cooperate in our program on a voluntary basis, just as business corporations have fully accepted on a voluntary basis the need to hold dividend payments unchanged during the period of the freeze.

Nevertheless, the legislation before you does provide standby authority to control interest rates and dividends in the unlikely event that the voluntary program proves unsuccessful. The authority is comparable to that already granted the president with respect to prices, rents, wages, and salaries. "Stabilization" of interest rates in the legislative context refers, of course, to the regulation of particular interest rates. It does not relate to general fiscal and monetary policies, which must continue to play a vital independent role in our economic stabilization efforts.

I need add only a word here about dividends, which represent a less troublesome problem than interest rates in the context of a wage-price program. In general, the committee believes that increases in dividends during the Phase II period should be limited in such fashion that expansion of dividend income will be equitably related to increases in the incomes of wage earners. Some exceptions may, of course, be necessary to facilitate the raising of capital for expansion, particularly by small businesses.

The details of the voluntary program with respect to dividends have not yet been worked out. Meanwhile, the committee has asked that dividends be maintained at levels that accord with the guidelines of the Cost of Living Council.

As I have said earlier, success in reducing the inflation premium built into interest rates will depend, ultimately, on the strength of our national will. It will depend on our ability to restrain the growth in average wage rates to a pace that is appropriately related to national productivity gains. It also will depend on reasonable price restraints. The full support and cooperation of business, labor, and the general public will be required in order to reach the objective of cutting the inflation rate in half by the end of 1972.

It is highly important to bear in mind that the whole program of restraint on wages and prices represents a temporary effort aimed at speeding the return to noninflationary conditions in a free economy. This goal requires that we conduct fiscal and monetary policies so as to avoid setting in motion forces that would lead to excessive aggregate demand on our resources and trigger still another round of inflation. Only if all of the policy instruments available to the government are working in harmony can the present anti-inflation policy succeed. Only then will interest rates move down to the more normal levels that we would all like to see.

Finally, let me say that it would be wise to use the opportunity granted us by Phase II to ponder dispassionately why our economy has become so prone to inflation, and why the fires of inflation, once started, are so difficult to extinguish. Has the structure of our economy changed so as to impart an increasing bias toward inflation? Are business or labor groups abusing their economic power to a larger degree than they did ten, twenty, or thirty years ago? If so, to what degree are our laws or regulations responsible for such abuses? Why did the normal growth of productivity come to a virtual halt toward the end of the 1960s? How can our governmental training programs, on which vast sums are being expended, be made more effective? What contribution can local productivity councils make to improvements in industrial efficiency? How can the advantages of computerized job banks be effectively harnessed? These are a few of the questions that we need to ask and try to resolve in order to help assure that the controls of Phase II, once dismantled, will not be needed again in our lifetime.

The Problem of Inflation

Substantial progress has been achieved during the past several decades in understanding the forces of economic instability and in devising policies for coping with them. Severe depressions in economic activity, which earlier generations knew and feared, are no longer a serious threat. And although recessions are still troublesome, their amplitude has diminished and they occur less frequently than they did earlier.

Our very success in limiting declines in business activity has become, however, a major source of the stubborn inflationary problem of our times. As recent experience has demonstrated once again, inflation damages the national economy. Confidence of businessmen and consumers in the economic future is shaken; productive efficiency falters, export trades languish, interest rates soar, financial markets become unruly, and social and political frictions multiply. We in the United States can have little hope of sustaining vigorous economic growth, or using our resources with maximum efficiency, or restoring equilibrium in our international accounts, or attaining a more salutary distribution of personal incomes unless the powerful forces that have been pushing up costs and prices are subdued.

The current inflationary problem has no close parallel in economic history. In the past, inflation in the United States was associated with military outlays during wars or with investment booms in peacetime. Once these episodes passed, the price level typically declined, and many years often elapsed

Address before the joint meeting of the American Economic Association and the American Finance Association, Toronto, Canada, December 29, 1972.

before prices returned to their previous peak. In the economic environment of earlier times, business and consumer decisions were therefore influenced far more by expectations concerning short-term movements in prices than by their long-term trend.

Over the past quarter century, a rather different pattern of wage and price behavior has emerged. Prices of many individual commodities still demonstrate a capability of declining when demand weakens. The average level of prices, however, hardly ever declines. Wage rates have become still more inflexible. Wage reductions are nowadays rare even in ailing businesses, and the average level of wages seems to rise inexorably across the industrial range.

The hard fact is that market forces no longer can be counted on to check the upward course of wages and prices even when the aggregate demand for goods and services declines in the course of a business recession. During the recession of 1970 and the weak recovery of early 1971, the pace of wage increases did not at all abate as unemployment rose, and there was only fragmentary evidence of a slowing in price increases. The rate of inflation was almost as high in the first half of 1971, when unemployment averaged 6 percent of the labor force, as it was in 1969, when the unemployment rate averaged 3½ percent.

The implications of these facts are not yet fully perceived. Cost-push inflation, while a comparatively new phenomenon on the American scene, has been altering the economic environment in fundamental ways. For when prices are pulled up by expanding demands in times of prosperity, and are also pushed up by rising costs during slack periods, decisions of the economic community are apt to be dominated by expectations of inflation.

Thus, many businessmen have come to believe in recent years that the trend of production costs will be inevitably upward, and their resistance to higher prices—whether of labor, or materials, or equipment—has therefore diminished. Labor leaders and workers now tend to reason that in order to achieve a gain in real income, they must bargain for wage increases that allow for advances in the price level as well as for the expected improvement in productivity. When individuals and families set aside funds for the future, they tend to do so in full awareness that some part of their accumulated savings is likely to be eroded by rising prices. Lenders in their turn, expecting to be paid back in cheaper dollars, tend to hold out for higher interest rates. These new patterns of thought are an ominous development.

I do not wish to minimize the substantial progress that has been made since August 1971 in suppressing inflationary forces, and in altering public attitudes about the inevitability of inflation. The shock therapy applied by the President in the summer, of last year has had lasting benefits. The pace of business activity strengthened almost immediately after the announcement of the New Economic Policy, and it has gathered momentum over the past year. Moreover, inflation has been cut from an annual rate of about 5 percent in the first half of 1971 to about 3 percent toward the end of this year. That improvement reflects the widespread support by the American public, including the trade unions, of the recent controls on wages and prices. It must be recognized, however, that the controls were aided by continued slack in resource and product markets and by a pronounced rise in output per man-hour.

Next year further progress in moderating inflation will be more difficult to achieve. The backlog of unused resources has been gradually declining, and there is good reason to expect less unemployment and fuller utilization of plant capacity as 1973 unfolds. Market forces may thus be exerting upward pressure on wage rates and prices at a time when productivity gains will probably be diminishing. If major collective bargaining agreements next year call for pay increases that appreciably exceed the growth of productivity, the upward pressure on costs and prices will intensify.

Extension of the benefits from the recent hard-won decline in the pace of inflation thus hangs in the balance. A further reduction during 1973 in the rate of increase in wages and prices is essential if the inflationary trend that has so long plagued our economy is to be brought to a halt in the near future. If that does not happen and cost and price pressures intensify next year, the nation's economic future may be adversely affected for a long time to come.

In fact, the outcome of our struggle with inflation is likely to have worldwide repercussions. If we continue to make progress in solving the inflation problem, our success will bring new hope to other countries of the Western world where inflationary trends stem in large measure from the same sources as ours.

Almost the entire world is at present suffering from inflation, and in many countries—for example, Canada, France, the United Kingdom, West Germany, and the Netherlands—the pace of inflation is more serious than in the United States.

In Canada, unemployment has been rising since 1966, but it has had little visible effect on wage rates. Actually, during the third quarter of 1972, the Canadian unemployment rate reached 6.7 percent—the highest quarterly figure in many years; yet, new settlements in unionized industries still provided for annual wage increases on the order of 8 percent. Prior to the recent freeze, wages in the United Kingdom were rising at a rate of 10 percent or more, in defiance of an unemployment rate that had gone up over a number of years and was still abnormally high.

These countries have discovered, as we in the United States have, that wage rates and prices no longer respond as they once did to the play of market forces.

As I have already noted, a major cause of the inflationary bias in modern industrialized nations is their relative success in maintaining prosperity. Governments, moreover, have taken numerous steps to relieve burdens of economic dislocation. In the United States, for example, the unemployment insurance system has been greatly strengthened since the end of World War II: compensation payments have increased, their duration has lengthened, and their coverage has been extended to a wider range of industries. Social security benefits have also expanded materially, thus easing the burdens of retirement or job loss for older workers, and welfare programs have proliferated.

Protection from the hardships of economic displacement has been extended by government to business firms as well. The rigors of competitive enterprise are nowadays blunted by import quotas, tariffs, price maintenance laws, and other forms of governmental regulation; subsidy programs sustain the incomes of farmers; small businesses and homebuilders are provided special credit facilities and other assistance; and even large firms of national reputation look to the federal government for sustenance in times of trouble.

Thus, in today's economic environment, workers who become unemployed can normally look forward to being rehired soon in the same line of activity, if not by the same firm. The unemployment benefits to which they are entitled blunt their incentive to seek work in an alternative line or to accept a job at a lower wage. Similarly, business firms caught with rising inventories when sales turn down are less likely to cut prices to clear the shelves—as they once did. Experience has taught them that, in all probability, demand will turn up again shortly, and that stocks of materials and finished goods—once depleted—nearly always have to be replaced at higher cost.

Institutional features of our labor and product markets reinforce these wage and price tendencies. Excessive wage increases tend to spread faster and more widely than they used to, partly because workmen have become more sensitive to wage developments elsewhere, partly also because employers have found—or come to believe—that a stable work force can best be maintained in a prosperous economy by emulating wage settlements in unionized industries. In not a few of our businesses, price competition has given way to rivalry through advertising, entertaining customers, and other forms of salesmanship. Trade unions at times place higher priority on the size of wage increases than on the employment of their members, and their strength at the bargaining table has certainly increased. The spread in recent years of trade unions to the public sector has occasioned some illegal strikes which ended with the union demands, however extreme, being largely met. The apparent helplessness of governments to deal with the problem has encouraged other trade unions to exercise their latent power more boldly. And their ability to impose long and costly strikes has been enhanced by the stronger financial position of American families, besides the unemployment compensation, food stamps, and other welfare benefits that are not infrequently available to strikers.

In view of these conditions, general price stability would be difficult to achieve even if economic stabilization policies could prevent altogether the emergence of excess aggregate demand. But neither the United States nor any other Western nation has come close to that degree of precision. In fact, excess aggregate demand has become rather commonplace. In country after country, stabilization efforts have been thwarted by governmental budgets that got out of control, and central banks

ten felt compelled to finance huge budgetary deficits by
reation.

ere are those who believe that the hard struggle to rid
our economy of inflation is not worthwhile and that it would be
better to devise ways of adjusting to inflation than to continue
fighting it. On this view, social security payments, insurance
contracts, bank deposits, and other contractual arrangements
should be written with escalator clauses so as to minimize the
distortions and hardships that inflation causes.

This is a counsel of despair. Those who are hurt most by
inflation are nearly always the poor, the elderly, the less educated—those in our society most in need of shelter from economic
adversity. I doubt if there is any practical way of redesigning
economic contracts to deal with this problem satisfactorily. In
any event, if a nation with our traditions attempted to make it
easy to live with inflation, rather than resist its corrosive influence, we would slowly but steadily lose the sense of discipline
needed to pursue governmental policies with an eye to the permanent welfare of our people.

The only responsible course open to us, I believe, is to fight
inflation tenaciously and with all the weapons at our command.
Let me note, however, that there is no way to turn back the
clock and restore the environment of a bygone era. We can no
longer cope with inflation by letting recessions run their course;
or by accepting a higher average level of unemployment; or by
neglecting programs whose aim it is to halt the decay of our
central cities, or to provide better medical care for the aged, or
to create larger opportunities for the poor.

A modern democracy cannot ignore the legitimate aspirations of its citizens, and there is no need to do so. The rising
aspirations of our people are consistent with general price stability if we only have the will and the good sense to pursue an
appropriate public policy. Our needs are, first, to restore order
in the federal budget and strengthen the stabilizing role of fiscal
policy; second, to pursue monetary policies that are consistent
with orderly economic expansion and return to a stable price
level; third, to continue for a while longer effective controls over
many, but by no means all, wage bargains and prices; and fourth,
to reduce or remove existing impediments to a more competitive
determination of wages and prices.

The single most important need at the present time is to curb the explosive growth that has marked federal spending in recent years. Some shock therapy may be needed here, such as a freeze or near freeze for a year or two of federal expenditures. The President is struggling to hold budgetary outlays to $250 billion in the current fiscal year. Even if he succeeds, as I trust he will, federal spending will still have more than doubled during the past eight years, and it will still exceed last year's outlays by $18 billion.

Contrary to a widespread impression, this burst of federal spending reflects only in small part the Vietnam war. The fundamental cause has been political indulgence of the theory that most social and economic problems can be solved by quick and large expenditures of federal money. We have tried to meet the need for better schooling of the young, for upgrading the skills of the labor force, for expanding the production of low-income housing, for improving the nation's health, for ending urban blight, for purifying our water and air, and for other national objectives, by constantly excogitating new programs and getting the Treasury to finance them on a liberal scale before they have been tested. The result has been that we have hastily piled one social program on another, so that they now literally number in the hundreds and defy understanding—beyond the obvious fact that they have disappointed our expectations and frustrated our fiscal calculations. In view of this experience, a tax increase— even if that were immediately attainable—would hardly be a suitable alternative to tightened expenditure controls.

Significant progress in curtailing the future growth of federal spending will require major reforms of a budgetary process that has long been badly outdated. The executive establishment does not yet have adequate devices for evaluating the benefits of individual programs relative to their cost, such as would be needed in zero-base budgeting. More serious still, the Congress continues to consider individual appropriation bills in isolation, without regard to any controlling total. Consequently, there is little incentive or opportunity to compare the contribution of alternative programs to the public welfare, or to consider systematically whether the nation would be better off if the resources now absorbed by government were larger or smaller.

Recognizing the need to focus on the overall budget, the

149

Congress wisely decided this October to reexamine its procedures. A logical first step would be to establish a Joint Congressional Committee on Expenditures and Revenues. Such a committee would review and evaluate the budget proposed by the administration each January for the next fiscal year. It would seek to determine whether the proposed total of expenditures was in keeping with the nation's needs and capabilities, whether new sources of revenue would be required or if some taxes could be lowered, thus returning resources to the private sector. Determinations of this character would serve as a useful guide to the individual committees of the Congress, and so too would projections of the growth of revenues and expenditures over the next three to five years, given existing federal programs and new initiatives under consideration.

Besides such a joint committee, formal Congressional procedures for controlling total expenditures are needed. Legislative budgets merit fuller and more careful consideration than they have yet received. For example, the Congress might act on a single comprehensive appropriation bill instead of the dozen or so bills that it now handles. Another procedure might be to legislate an overall budget total, with outlays specified for a limited number of major categories, before turning to the appropriations process. Then, if any individual appropriation bill involved expenditures exceeding the limit already established for that category, a two-thirds vote in the House and the Senate might be required to enact that appropriation.

Alternatively, the Congress could impose a rigid ceiling on total expenditures, and require the Executive to adjust outlays on individual categories so that they would be consistent with the ceiling. Such an approach was considered by the Ninety-second Congress, but rejected because of concern that too much power over the purse strings would be ceded to the president. There is some justification for that view. But it should be noted that a ceiling also limits the ability of the president to spend as much as he might desire, and that restrictions might be placed on his power to readjust spending priorities. A vigilant Congress could, I believe, take steps to ensure that Congressional control over the direction of spending would not be weakened by a legislative budget ceiling.

Formal and systematic control over federal expenditures

would, as I have already suggested, do a good deal to eliminate recurring bouts with excess aggregate demand. But there are times when overheating of the economy originates in the private sector. At such times, better fiscal tools are needed to curb private spending. In a recent report to the Congress, the Federal Reserve Board argued that it would be wise to enlarge the role of fiscal policy in short-run economic stabilization, and that a promising way of doing this would be to vary the investment tax credit in the light of business cycle developments.

To facilitate timely adjustments, without which stabilization policy cannot be effective, the president might be given the authority to initiate changes in the investment tax credit. At the same time, Congress could retain its traditional control over taxes and act as a full partner in making the needed adjustments. For example, the president might be permitted to change the tax credit within a specified range, say between zero and 10 or 15 percent, subject to modification or disapproval within sixty days by either house of Congress.

Experience since 1966 suggests that variation in the rate of the investment tax credit would influence significantly the behavior of business investment over the course of the business cycle. Such a fiscal tool would therefore reduce the burden on monetary policy, and make possible some improvement in the management of aggregate demand.

There has been a tendency throughout the postwar period—both in the United States and in other countries—to rely heavily on monetary policy to adjust to shifts in private spending propensities, and even to expect monetary policy to offset the impact of unwanted fiscal stimulus. It is difficult, however, to maintain adequate control over aggregate demand when primary reliance is placed on monetary policy, first, because its effects occur with variable lags, second, because its influence on economic activity is disproportionately large in particular industries such as housing. If improved fiscal instruments were used side by side with monetary policy to influence total spending, the chances of avoiding excessive bursts of aggregate demand, with their inevitable inflationary consequences, would be greatly enhanced. Furthermore, undesired effects on the structure of real output would be reduced, greater stability could prevail in financial markets, and the monetary managers could focus more consistently on maintaining a course conducive to sustainable economic growth and reasonable price stability over the longer run.

This conception of the role of monetary policy has guided our thinking at the Federal Reserve over the past several years. During this period, more careful attention has been given to the monetary aggregates because we recognize that excessive amounts of money and credit might inadvertently be supplied in a period of rising credit demands if attention were focused primarily on interest rates. We recognize, however, that changes in the cost and availability of credit affect the nation's economic activity, and we therefore cannot neglect the condition of financial markets.

Monetary policy since early 1970, when judged by any of the major monetary aggregates, has favored moderate economic expansion. During the past three years, the narrowly defined money stock—that is, currency plus demand deposits—has grown at an annual rate of about 6 percent. Defined more broadly, so as to include also consumer-type time and savings deposits of commercial banks, the stock of money has grown at an average annual rate of 10 percent. Between the third quarter of 1971 and the third quarter of this year, the narrowly defined money stock increased 5.6 percent. This was well below the growth rate of total real output, and far below the increase in the current dollar value of output.

Monetary policy has thus provided the funds needed for a good expansion in production and employment, and it has done so without fostering a condition of excess aggregate demand. We at the Federal Reserve expect to continue a policy of supporting economic growth, but we are firmly resolved to do this without releasing a new wave of inflation.

Responsible monetary and fiscal policies are clearly essential for coping with the current inflationary problem. However, as the incomes policy initiated in August of last year has demonstrated, efforts to influence wages and prices directly can play a constructive role when cost-push inflation reaches serious proportions. The energy released by the New Economic Policy has been abundantly evident to businessmen, workers, and consumers. True, the control program did not bring inflation to a halt, but any such expectation would have been unrealistic.

There are those who believe that the time is at hand to abandon the experiment with controls and to rely entirely on monetary and fiscal restraint to restore a stable price level. This prescription has great intellectual appeal; unfortunately, it is impractical.

If some form of effective control over wages and prices were not retained in 1973, major collective bargaining settlements and business efforts to increase profits could reinforce the pressures on costs and prices that normally come into play when the economy is advancing briskly, and thus generate a new wave of inflation. If monetary and fiscal policies became sufficiently restrictive to deal with the situation by choking off growth in aggregate demand, the cost in terms of rising unemployment, lost output, and shattered confidence would be enormous. As a practical matter, I see no alternative but to pursue for a while longer the experiment with direct controls. I trust, at the same time, that reasonable steps will be taken to reduce the distortions and inequities that are beginning to accumulate.

But the greater need in the year ahead will be to use the breathing spell afforded by the control program to seek ways to improve the functioning of our labor and product markets, so that wage rates and prices become more responsive to the balance between market demand and supply.

There has been much discussion recently of the need for structural reform—by some, because they see evidence of abuse of economic power by large business firms; by others, because they see trade unions forcing up wage rates well beyond productivity gains and raising costs otherwise through restrictive work practices; by still others, because they see a multiplicity of governmental regulations that restrict productivity and impede the workings of competition. While opinions may differ as to which of these several areas merits primary attention, I believe that informed observers of the current economic scene would agree that structural reforms are needed in all of these areas in the interest of weakening the built-in forces of inflation. In any event, given the realities of political life, genuine progress is likely only if we move on all fronts simultaneously.

It will take courage for the Congress and the Executive to deal with the issues of structural reform in forthright fashion. The ground to be covered is difficult and enormous. We need to reassess the adequacy of our laws directed against monopolistic practices of business, the enforcement of these laws, the power of trade unions at the bargaining table, restrictions on entry into business or the professions, the restrictive practices of trade unions, the subsidies to farmers, the federal minimum wage (particularly for teenagers), restrictions on the activities of financial institutions, the welfare system, import quotas, tariffs, and other legislation that impedes the competitive process. We need also to reevaluate our extensive manpower training programs and the feeble effort to establish computerized job banks, for it is clear that our labor market policies have thus far failed to contribute sufficiently to the objective of expanding employment and yet avoiding the inflationary effects that monetary and fiscal policies so often tend to generate.

There is no quick or easy path to meaningful structural reform. But I see no real alternative if our national aspiration for prosperity without inflation is to be realized, while free enterprise and individual choice are being preserved.

In conclusion, let me remind you that in August of last year, confidence of our citizens was at ebb tide. The measures then taken created hope that our government had the will to halt inflation and move the nation's economy forward. It is time now to take the further steps needed to consolidate the progress already achieved. In the measure that we succeed we will not only protect our domestic prosperity, but we will also facilitate the rebuilding of the international monetary system and the economic growth of our sister nations around the world.

Some Problems of Central Banking

The advent of the 1970s has not diminished the range or difficulty of the problems that central bankers face. In the international area, relationships among economies have been undergoing rapid change, and our governments are now actively seeking to develop new international rules to guide their future conduct in the spheres of money and trade. As central bankers, we have inevitably become involved in efforts to achieve urgently needed reforms of the international monetary system. We have also had to wrestle anew with problems of recession, economic overheating, and the stubborn persistence of inflation.

Today, I want to focus my remarks on the problem of achieving greater stability in the performance of our domestic economies. There is no more crucial need for the stability and welfare of our economies than to find more effective methods for dealing with inflation and its causes. Restoration of international financial order also depends heavily on our handling of this problem. The policies that are needed to halt inflation, without at the same time plunging our nations into economic stagnation or recession, extend beyond the normal province of central banking. Skillful management of monetary matters nevertheless remains an indispensable ingredient in reaching the objective of noninflationary growth that we all seek.

Since the end of World War II, our economies have developed a disconcerting bias toward inflation. A variety of influences—social, political, and institutional—have been at work

Address before the 1973 International Monetary Conference, Paris, France, June 6, 1973.

here. But there can be no doubt that the speed and vigor with which governments tend to deal with recession, their considerable success in this endeavor, and their reluctance to act with similar decisiveness to curb economic booms, have contributed materially to the worldwide upward trend of the price level and the persistence of inflationary expectations.

Monetary and fiscal policies for managing aggregate demand now bear, and must continue to bear, the main responsibility for regulating the overall performance of our national economies. At times, the level or pace of total economic activity will continue to call for restraining policies, and at other times there will be need for stimulus. But I must caution that experience suggests that we will need to embark on policies of active stimulation with greater care, unless we subdue the natural inclination to stay too long with such policies. The ability and the will to make timely shifts in the thrust of fiscal and monetary policies are of the utmost importance if these policy instruments are to play a more constructive contracyclical role.

We need also to recognize that skillful, timely, and flexible use of demand management policies may not suffice to achieve satisfactory economic performance. To be sure, total spending in the economy can be slowed through monetary and fiscal measures. But under the institutional conditions that now prevail in many of our countries, shifts in these policies have a much stronger and more prompt effect on real output and employment than on the pace of inflation. The persistence of rapid advances of wages and prices in the United States and other countries, even during recent periods of recession, has led me to conclude that governmental power to restrain directly the advance of prices and money incomes constitutes a necessary addition to our arsenal of economic stabilization weapons, to be used occasionally—but nevertheless vigorously—when needed.

There is another difficulty in relying exclusively on broad monetary and fiscal policies for combating cyclical fluctuations. Overall restraint, it is true, will in time slow any exuberant expansion. It may not, however, curb sufficiently or in timely fashion the sectors of demand that are leading to economic imbalance, and thereby set the stage for later economic trouble. Overall restraints that are sufficient to curb expansion in aggregate economic activity may do so by inducing sizable declines promptly in some areas, such as housing, and yet have slight effect for some time in other areas, such as business investment. This is particularly likely to be the case when reliance is placed mainly on monetary policy, and hence on sharp changes in credit conditions, for purposes of economic stabilization.

Throughout business cycle history, the major force making for economic instability has been the rather large fluctuations characteristic of business investment. At times, of course, the spending and taxing policies of government have been a source of economic trouble, especially in connection with wars and their financing. On occasion, also, large changes in the spending propensities of consumers have played their part in carrying aggregate activity to unsustainably high, or unacceptably low, levels. But it is in the pronounced changes of the investment plans of business firms, with respect both to their fixed capital and inventories, that much of the cyclical instability of advanced industrial economies has originated.

Business investment is, of course, vital to the growth in productivity, and the improvement in material welfare, to which all nations aspire. Over the long run, incentives to invest therefore need to be enhanced. But it would be far better if a high average level of investment could be achieved without the sizable fluctuations that have characterized the past. The general economy would benefit from a reduction of this source of instability. Business enterprises would also benefit from a more regular pace of investment, since they would thus avoid a concentration of expenditures at times when financing costs are high, when the capabilities of suppliers are strained, and when delivery and installation dates become more uncertain.

In view of our continuing problems in achieving economic stability, we must persist in the search for new and more refined tools of stabilization policy. Ideally, these measures should be of the kind that can be introduced or removed quickly and that will affect private spending decisions rather promptly. Many countries have recognized this need, and we at the Federal Reserve have sought to profit from their experience and studies, as well as from our own research.

Last year, for example, the Federal Reserve Board completed a study of ways in which the housing industry could be provided a degree of insulation from the fluctuations brought on

by sharp changes in credit conditions. One of our major con-
clusions was that more stability in residential construction would
require less instability in business investment. Toward this end,
we proposed that consideration be given to the use of a variable
investment tax credit. When contracts or orders for new plant
and equipment are advancing too rapidly, the tax credit could be
reduced, and when such investment is lagging, the tax credit
could be raised; thus providing a direct cost incentive for moderating cyclical movements in this area.

I continue to believe that the concept of a variable tax incentive to business investment has merit. Because of our need in
the United States to encourage greater productivity, however, I
would now recommend that the tax credit remain in effect continuously and that it at no time drop to zero. It could vary,
perhaps, between 3 or 4 percent and 15 percent, depending on
economic conditions. It would be important also to retain a
decisive role for the Congress in determining the specific rate of
tax credit. This could be done by empowering the president to
initiate changes in the investment tax credit, but making it subject to veto or approval—and perhaps also some modification—
by the Congress within a forty-five or sixty day period.

In recent months, the Federal Reserve has faced the problem of dealing with a rapidly escalating demand for bank credit,
even though the monetary aggregates, by and large, have grown
at a moderate pace. The upsurge in bank credit has been associated mainly with the demand for business loans, and it has
been largely accommodated by the banks through the issuance
of certificates of deposit in the money market. Accordingly, the
Board in mid-May announced a new restrictive action aimed
specifically at this development. Since May 16, any further increase in bank issues of large certificates of deposit or similar
money market instruments, over a base of $10 million or the
amount then outstanding, whichever is larger, is to be subject
to an additional reserve requirement, presently set at three percentage points. At the same time, any additional funds obtained
abroad by U.S. banks for domestic purposes became subject to
reserve requirements on a comparable basis, and the remaining
interest rate ceilings on large certificates of deposit were suspended.

The new marginal reserve requirement will raise the cost
incurred by banks in obtaining additional funds through the

money market for the financing of loan expansion. Banks doing so will have the use of only 92 percent of the proceeds, rather than the 95 percent that they had before. The purpose of the marginal reserve requirement is to restrain bank lending to business on a market-oriented basis, so that rationing of funds by the banks to their large business customers may be accomplished through higher costs, rather than by the imposition of arbitrary and inflexible interest rate controls. We expect that the result will be to moderate the willingness of banks to accommodate their customers through this source of financing. If it fails to do so sufficiently, we are prepared to consider additional actions that will limit further the availability of the funds that banks have at their disposal.

I have urged bankers in the United States to discipline the pace at which they are extending credit, in the interest both of our economy's present need and of sound banking practice. I repeat that appeal today. In doing so, I recognize that earnest efforts by commercial banks to moderate their rate of credit accommodation will not, by itself, be a sufficient remedy. It is no less important that our business leaders recognize the need to limit their investment plans for the time being, and thus restrict their requirements for external finance, whether from the banks or the money and securities markets. Moderation in the growth of bank credit will be of little avail if the result is merely to augment open-market financing of an unsustainable increase in business spending.

In times like these, it is also necessary that public expenditure in the United States be restrained to the maximum extent feasible. It is necessary that our government seek strenuously to achieve balance, or actual surplus, in its income relative to its expenditure. And as far as the Federal Reserve is concerned, it is more necessary than ever that we keep monetary expansion down to a moderate pace, while we at the same time avoid the kind of constriction in credit markets that could lead to recession and the certainty of large stimulative measures later on. We must avoid serious overheating of the American economy now, and we must try to curb our inflation through methods that will not add to future economic instability. With reasonable cooperation by all leading groups in our society, I am confident that we can achieve these goals. This is of critical importance to the United States and also to the world at large.

The Menace of Inflation

It is a pleasure to be with you today here in the heartland of America. As graduates of this college, you are launching your careers at a challenging but troubled time. Confidence in established institutions, particularly in our government, is at a low ebb. And hopes for the future of our economy have been shaken by the debilitating effects of inflation on the nation's businesses, workers, and consumers.

Inflation is not a new problem for the United States, nor is it confined to our country. Inflationary forces are now rampant in every major industrial nation of the world. Inflation is raging also in the less developed countries, and apparently in socialist countries as well as in those that practice free enterprise.

The gravity of our current inflationary problem can hardly be overestimated. Except for a brief period at the end of World War II, prices in the United States have of late been rising faster than in any other peacetime period of our history. If past experience is any guide, the future of our country is in jeopardy. No country that I know of has been able to maintain widespread economic prosperity once inflation got out of hand. And the unhappy consequences are by no means solely of an economic character. If long continued, inflation at anything like the present rate would threaten the very foundations of our society.

I want to discuss briefly with you today the sources of our inflationary problem, the havoc being wrought in the economy,

Commencement address at Illinois College, Jacksonville, Illinois, May 26, 1974.

and the steps that must be taken to regain general price stability and thus strengthen confidence in our nation's future.

A large part of the recent upsurge in prices has been due to special factors. In most years, economic trends of individual nations tend to diverge. But during 1973 a business cycle boom occurred simultaneously in the United States and in every other major industrial country. With production rising rapidly across the world, prices of labor, materials, and finished products were bid up everywhere.

To make matters worse, disappointing crop harvests in a number of countries in 1972 forced a sharp run-up in the prices of food last year. The manipulation of petroleum supplies and prices by oil-exporting countries gave another dramatic push to the general price level last autumn and early this year. The influence of these factors is still being felt in consumer markets.

Recently, our price level has also reacted strongly to the removal of wage and price controls—a painful but essential adjustment in the return to free markets.

These special factors, however, do not account for all of our inflation. For many years, our economy and that of other nations has had a serious underlying bias toward inflation which has simply been magnified by the special influences that I have mentioned.

Ironically, the roots of that bias lie chiefly in the rising aspirations of people everywhere. We are a nation in a hurry for more and more of what we consider the good things of life. I do not question that yearning. Properly directed, it can be a powerful force for human betterment. Difficulties arise, however, when people in general seek to reach their goals by means of shortcuts; and that is what has happened.

Of late, individuals have come to depend less and less on their own initiative, and more on government, to achieve their economic objectives. The public nowadays expects the government to maintain prosperous economic conditions, to limit such declines in employment as may occasionally occur, to ease the burden of job loss or illness or retirement, to sustain the incomes of farmers, homebuilders, and so on. These are laudable objectives, and we and other nations have moved a considerable distance toward their realization. Unfortunately, in the process of doing so, governmental budgets have gotten out of control, wages and prices have become less responsive to the discipline of market forces, and inflation has emerged as the most dangerous economic ailment of our time.

The awesome imbalance of the federal budget is probably the contributory factor to inflation that you have heard the most about. In the past five years, total federal expenditures have increased about 50 percent. In that time span, the cumulative budget deficit of the federal government, including government-sponsored enterprises, has totaled more than $100 billion. In financing this deficit, and also in meeting huge demands for credit by businesses and consumers, tremendous pressures have been placed on our credit mechanisms and the supply of money has grown at a rate inconsistent with price stability.

I am sure that each of you in this graduating class is aware of some of the troublesome consequences of inflation. The prices of virtually everything you buy have been rising and are still going up. For the typical American worker, the increase in weekly earnings during the past year, while sizable in dollars, has been wiped out by inflation. In fact, the real weekly take-home pay of the average worker is now below what it was a year ago. Moreover, the real value of accumulated savings deposits has also declined, and the pressure of rising prices on family budgets has led to a worrisome increase in delinquency rates on home mortgages and consumer loans.

Many consumers have responded to these developments by postponing or canceling plans for buying homes, autos, and other big-ticket items. Sales of new autos began to decline in the spring of 1973, and so too did sales of furniture and appliances, mobile homes, and newly built dwellings. The weakness in consumer markets, largely engendered by inflation, slowed our economic growth rate last year some months before the effects of the oil shortage began to be felt.

Actually, the sales of some of our nation's leading business firms have been on the wane for a year or more. Their costs, meanwhile, have continued to soar with increasing wage rates and sharply rising prices of materials.

The effect on business profits was ignored for a time because accountants typically reckon the value of inventories—and also the value of machinery and equipment used up in production—at original cost, rather than at current inflated prices.

These accounting practices create an illusory element in profits—an element that is not available for distribution to stockholders in view of the need to replace inventories, plant, and equipment at appreciably higher prices. Worse still, the illusory part of profits is subject to the income tax, thus aggravating the deterioration in profits. This result is especially unfortunate because of the shortage of industrial capacity that now exists in key sectors of our economy—particularly in the basic materials area.

By early this year, a confrontation with economic reality could no longer be put off. Major business corporations found that the volume of investable funds generated internally was not increasing fast enough to finance the rising costs of new plant and equipment, or of the materials and supplies needed to rebuild inventories. Businesses began to scramble for borrowed funds at commercial banks and in the public markets for money and capital. Our financial markets have therefore come under severe strain. Interest rates have risen sharply; savings flows have been diverted from mortgage lending institutions; security dealers have experienced losses; prices of common stocks have declined; the liquidity of some enterprises has been called into question; and tensions of a financial nature have spilled over into international markets.

Concerned as we all are about the economic consequences of inflation, there is even greater reason for concern about the impact on our social and political institutions. We must not risk the social stresses that persistent inflation breeds. Because of its capricious effects on the income and wealth of a nation's families and businesses, inflation inevitably causes disillusionment and discontent. It robs millions of citizens who in their desire to be self-reliant have set aside funds for the education of their children or their own retirement, and it hits many of the poor and elderly especially hard.

In recent weeks, governments have fallen in several major countries, in part because the citizens of those countries had lost confidence in the ability of their leaders to cope with the problem of inflation. Among our own people, the distortions and injustices wrought by inflation have contributed materially to distrust of government officials and of government policies, and even to some loss of confidence in our free enterprise system. Discontent bred by inflation can provoke profoundly disturbing social and political change, as the history of other nations teaches. I do not believe I exaggerate in saying that the ultimate consequence of inflation could well be a significant decline of economic and political freedom for the American people.

There are those who believe that the struggle to curb inflation will not succeed and who conclude that it would be better to adjust to inflation rather than to fight it. On this view, contractual payments of all sorts—wages, salaries, social security benefits, interest on bank loans and deposits, and so on—should be written with escalator clauses so as to minimize the distortions and injustices that inflation normally causes.

This is a well-meaning proposal, but it is neither sound nor practical. For one thing, there are hundreds of billions of dollars of outstanding contracts—on mortgages, public and private bonds, insurance policies, and the like—that as a practical matter could not be renegotiated. Even with regard to new undertakings, the obstacles to achieving satisfactory escalator arrangements in our free and complex economy, where people differ so much in financial sophistication, seem insuperable. More important still, by making it easier for many people to live with inflation, escalator arrangements would gravely weaken the discipline that is needed to conduct business and government affairs prudently and efficiently. Universal escalation, I am therefore convinced, is an illusory and dangerous quest. The responsible course is to fight inflation with all the energy we can muster and with all the weapons at our command.

One essential ingredient in this struggle is continued resistance to swift growth in money and credit. The Federal Reserve System, I assure you, is firmly committed to this task. We intend to encourage sufficient growth in supplies of money and credit to finance orderly economic expansion. But we are not going to be a willing party to the accommodation of rampant inflation.

As this year's experience has again indicated, a serious effort to moderate the growth of money and credit during a period of burgeoning credit demand results in higher interest rates— particularly on short-term loans. Troublesome though this rise in interest rates may be, it must for a time be tolerated. For, if monetary policy sought to prevent a rise in interest rates when credit demands were booming, money and credit would expand

165

explosively, with devastating effects on the price level. Any such policy would in the end be futile, even as far as interest rates are concerned, because these rates would soon reflect the rise in the price level and therefore go up all the more. We must not let that happen.

But I cannot emphasize too strongly that monetary policy alone cannot solve our stubborn inflationary problem. We must work simultaneously at lessening the powerful underlying bias toward inflation that stems from excessive total demands on our limited resources. This means, among other things, that the federal budget has to be handled more responsibly than it has been in the past.

Incredible though it may seem, the Congress has been operating over the years without any semblance of a rational budget plan. The committees that consider spending operate independently of the committees that consider taxes, and appropriations themselves are treated in more than a dozen different bills annually. All of this means that the federal budget never really gets considered as a whole—a fact which helps explain why it is so often in deficit.

Fortunately, after many years of advocacy by concerned citizens and legislators, this glaring deficiency in the congressional budget process is about to be remedied. Bills that would integrate spending and taxing decisions have passed both the House and the Senate. This is a most encouraging development, and we may confidently expect final action soon by the Congress on this landmark legislation.

Procedural changes, however, will mean little unless the political will exists to exploit the changes fully. And this can happen only if the American people understand better the nature of the inflation we have been experiencing and demand appropriate action by their elected representatives.

As you leave this hall today, I urge you to give continuing thought and study to the problem of inflation. If it persists, it will affect your personal lives profoundly. Where possible, I urge you to assume a leadership role in getting people everywhere interested in understanding inflation and in doing something about it. In the great "town hall" tradition of America, much can be accomplished if people organize themselves—in their offices, trade unions, factories, social clubs, and churches—

to probe beneath the superficial explanations of inflation that are the gossip of everyday life. Productivity councils in local communities and enterprises, established for the purpose of improving efficiency and cutting costs, can be directly helpful in restraining inflation.

While I am on the subject of what individuals can do to be helpful, let me note the need for rediscovery of the art of careful budgeting of family expenditures. In some of our businesses, price competition has atrophied as a mode of economic behavior, in part because many of our families no longer exercise much discipline in their spending. We have become a nation of impulse shoppers, of gadget buyers. We give less thought than we should to choosing among the thousands of commodities and services available in our markets. And many of us no longer practice comparative price shopping—not even for big-ticket items. Careful spending habits are not only in the best interest of every family; they could contribute powerfully to a new emphasis on price competition in consumer markets.

I do not expect that the path back to reasonable price stability can be traveled quickly. Indeed, our government will need to take numerous steps to reduce the inflationary bias of our economy besides those I have emphasized. The forces of competition in labor and product markets need to be strengthened—perhaps by establishing wage and price review boards to minimize abuses of economic power, certainly through more vigorous enforcement of the antitrust laws, besides elimination of barriers to entry in skilled occupations, reduction of barriers to imports from abroad, and modification of minimum wage laws to improve job opportunities for teenagers. Impediments to increased production that still remain in farming, construction work, and other industries need to be removed. And greater incentives should be provided for enlarging our capacity to produce industrial materials, energy, and other products in short supply.

But if inflation cannot be ended quickly, neither can it be eliminated without cost. Some industries will inevitably operate for a time at lower rates of production than they would prefer. Government cannot—and should not—try to compensate fully for all such occurrences. Such a policy would involve negating with one hand what was being attempted with the other.

167

But government does have a proper ameliorative role to play in areas, such as housing, where the incidence of credit restraint has been disproportionately heavy. The special burden that has fallen on homebuilding should be lightened, as is the intent of the housing aids which the administration recently announced. And my personal judgment is that it would be advisable, too, for government to be prepared, if need be, to expand the roster of public service jobs. This particular means of easing especially troublesome situations of unemployment will not add permanently to governmental costs. And in any event, it would conflict much less with basic anti-inflation objectives than would the conventional alternative of general monetary or fiscal stimulus. A cut in personal income taxes, for instance, would serve to perpetuate budget deficits. Not only that, it might prove of little aid to the particular industries or localities that are now experiencing economic difficulty. Much the same would be true of a monetary policy that permitted rapid growth of money and credit. There is no justification for such fateful steps at this time.

In concluding, I would simply repeat my central message: there is no easy way out of the inflationary morass into which we have allowed ourselves to sink through negligence and imperfect vision. But I am confident that we will succeed if the American people become more alert to the challenge. I hope that the members of this graduating class will join with other citizens across the country in a great national crusade to put an end to inflation and restore the conditions essential to a stable prosperity—a prosperity whose benefits can be enjoyed by all our people. This objective is within our means and is essential to our nation's future.

Key Issues of Monetary Policy

I am pleased to appear before this committee today to discuss the six questions posed by Chairman Patman's letter of June 19, 1974. The several areas addressed by these questions are of great interest, particularly to professional economists. My comments on them convey the basic thinking of the Board of Governors, and will—I believe—be responsive to the committee's needs.

I must, however, go beyond a narrow or technical interpretation of these questions. Rapidly rising prices, rapidly rising wages, rapidly rising interest rates—these are the burning economic issues of our time. My testimony today will seek to identify the sources of this menacing inflationary problem and to outline the course that public policy must take to restore price stability.

The first question raised by Chairman Patman concerns the reliability of the trade-off between inflation and unemployment—the so-called Phillips curve—as a guide for monetary policy. The discovery some years ago of a statistical correlation between the rate of inflation and the rate of unemployment seemed to offer a straightforward choice to policy makers. These early studies—using data first for the British economy, later for the United States and other economies—suggested that unemployment could be reduced if a nation were willing to put up with more inflation, and that advances in the general price

Statement before the Committee on Banking and Currency, House of Representatives, July 30, 1974.

level could be slowed down if a higher rate of unemployment were tolerated.

Further research and subsequent developments have indicated, however, that simple statistical correlations of this kind are misleading. The forces affecting economic activity and prices in a modern economy are far too complex to be described by a simple mathematical equation.

We found in 1970 and early 1971, for example, that increases in wage rates and prices may continue—and even accelerate—in the face of rising unemployment and declining real output. The experience of the United States in this regard was not unique; similar developments occurred at about the same time in Canada and the United Kingdom.

We have also come to recognize that public policies that create excess aggregate demand, and thereby drive up wage rates and prices, will not result in any lasting reduction in unemployment. On the contrary, such policies—if long continued—lead ultimately to galloping inflation, to loss of confidence in the future, and to economic stagnation.

The central objective of monetary and fiscal policies should be to foster lasting prosperity—a prosperity in which men and women looking for work are able to find work; a prosperity in which incomes and savings are protected against inflation; a prosperity that can be enjoyed by all. Of late, such a prosperity has eluded us, because we have not yet found a way to bring an end to inflation.

Let me turn to your second question, concerning the benefits and risks involved in the Federal Reserve accommodating increases of the general price level that originate in supply shortfalls and other special events.

Prices in the United States have been affected heavily in the past several years by a variety of special factors. Disappointing harvests in 1972—both here and abroad—caused a sharp run-up of food prices in 1973. Beginning in the fall of last year, the manipulation of petroleum shipments and prices by oil-exporting countries led to huge increases in the price of gasoline, heating oil, and related products.

Furthermore, a worldwide boom in economic activity during 1972 and 1973 led to a bidding up of prices everywhere. In the United States, larger foreign orders for industrial materials, component parts, and capital equipment added to growing domestic demands. Pressures became particularly intense in the major materials industries—such as steel, aluminum, cement, paper—in which expansion of capacity had been limited in earlier years by low profits and environmental controls.

The impact of worldwide inflation was especially severe in the United States because of the decline in the exchange value of the dollar relative to other currencies. Besides stimulating our export trade, and thereby reinforcing the pressures of domestic demand on available resources, devaluation raised the dollar prices of imported products, and these effects spread through our markets.

More recently, the removal of controls over wages and prices has led to sharp upward adjustments in both our labor and commodity markets.

It has at times been suggested that monetary policy could have prevented these special factors from affecting significantly the average level of wholesale and consumer prices. That may well be true, but the cost of such a policy should not be underestimated. Last year, about 60 percent of the rise in consumer prices was accounted for by food and fuel; for wholesale prices, the proportion was even higher. To achieve stability in the average price level, it would therefore have been necessary to bring down very sharply the prices of other goods and services.

Prices of many commodities—particularly farm products and industrial raw materials—are established in highly competitive markets and are therefore capable of declining as well as rising. The prices of many other commodities and services that make up the gross national product, however, are nowadays rather inflexible in a downward direction, in large part because of the persistent upward push of labor costs and imperfect business competition. For these commodities, significant price declines could be achieved only by drastically restrictive policies—policies that would lead to widespread bankruptcies and mass unemployment. A monetary policy that sought to offset completely the effects on the average price level of the rising cost of food, petroleum products, and other commodities whose prices were so heavily influenced during the past two years by special factors, would clearly have been undesirable.

Nevertheless, monetary policy must not permit sufficient

growth in money and credit supplies to accommodate all of the price increases that are directly or indirectly attributable to special factors. The rise in the price of petroleum, for example, has increased the costs of energy, plastics, petroleum-based chemicals, and other materials. Business firms will endeavor to pass these higher costs through to consumers. Workers, too, will bargain for larger wage increases, in order to compensate for declines in their real incomes. To the extent that wage increases outrun gains in productivity, business costs—and ultimately consumer prices—are driven up. Thus, in addition to their direct effects on prices, special factors may have large and widespread secondary effects on the price level.

A monetary policy that accommodated all of these price increases could result in an endless cost-price spiral and a serious worsening of an already grave inflationary problem. The appropriate course for monetary policy is the middle ground. The price rigidities characteristic of modern industrialized economies must be recognized, but a full pass-through of all the price effects stemming from special factors must not be permitted.

The middle course of policy we have adopted has resulted in a growth rate of the narrowly defined money supply—currency and demand deposits—of about 6 percent during the past twelve months. This rate of growth is still too high for stability of average prices over the longer term. But moderation in the growth rate of money and credit supplies must be achieved gradually to avoid upsetting effects on the real economy. This is particularly true now, when price-cost relations are seriously distorted.

I turn now to Chairman Patman's third question, which relates to the positive elements and the risks involved in monetizing deficit spending. The simple fact is that financing federal deficits by printing money involves risks, and the risks are grave.

Fortunately, since 1951 monetary policy in this country has not been conducted with an eye to providing a ready market for Treasury securities, or for financing federal deficits. Considerations of this kind were an objective of Federal Reserve policy during World War II, when Treasury borrowing proceeded on an unprecedented scale in relation to the size of our economy. I doubt if such a policy was warranted even under wartime circumstances, and its continuation in the years immediately after the war was a very serious mistake. It led to excessive increases in borrowing by private firms, consumers, and state and local governments, and thus fueled the subsequent inflation.

The dangers inherent in this situation became acutely evident during the Korean War, when federal deficits once again threatened. With the aid of prodding by the Congress, particularly by Senator Douglas, the Federal Reserve and the Treasury resolved their disagreements, and monetary policy returned to its traditional role of regulating the supply of money and credit in the interest of economic stability. Since then, the Treasury has financed its deficits at prevailing market interest rates in competition with other borrowers.

During periods of large Treasury financings, the Federal Reserve follows the practice of maintaining "even-keel" in the money market—that is, we refrain from taking overt actions that market participants might interpret as a change in monetary policy. On some occasions, therefore, the maintenance of "even-keel" has delayed the timing of changes in monetary policy. Treasury financing operations thus pose problems for monetary policy, particularly when they are large and frequent.

Federal deficit financing becomes a major source of economic and financial instability when it occurs during periods of high economic activity, as it has in recent years. The huge federal deficits of the past decade have added enormously to aggregate demand for goods and services, and have thus been directly responsible for upward pressures on the price level. Heavy borrowing by the federal sector has also been an important contributing factor to the persistent rise in interest rates, and to the strains that have at times developed in money and capital markets. Worse still, continuation of budget deficits has tended to undermine the confidence of the public in the capacity of our government to deal with inflation.

If the present inflationary problem is to be solved, and interest rates brought down to reasonable levels, the federal budget must be brought into better balance. This is the most important single step that could be taken to restore the confidence of people in their own and our nation's economic future.

Let me turn, next, to the committee's fourth question, dealing with the benefits and risks of the Federal Reserve's fighting money market fires.

As this committee well knows, the cardinal aim of monetary policy is maintenance of a financial environment in which our national objectives of full employment and price stability can be realized. For the most part, this responsibility is best achieved by striving for appropriate growth rates of the monetary aggregates, and letting financial markets take care of themselves.

The appropriate monetary growth rates will vary with economic conditions. They are apt to be higher during periods of economic weakness, when aggregate spending is in need of stimulus, than when the economy is booming and inflationary tendencies threaten economic stability. Special circumstances may, however, call for monetary growth rates that deviate from this general rule. For example, as noted in my response to the second question, the special factors giving rise to extraordinary price pressures during the past year or two have required toleration of a monetary growth rate that has been relatively high by historical standards.

There are times when responsibility for maintaining financial and economic stability requires the Federal Reserve to focus attention primarily on factors other than growth in the money supply or bank credit. The oldest and most traditional function of a central bank is to act as a lender of last resort—that is, to provide liquidity when dislocation of financial markets threatens serious damage to the economy. Acting in this capacity, the Federal Reserve in the summer of 1970 warded off a developing liquidity crisis in the commercial paper market. This year, difficulties encountered by a large commercial bank led to rumors of widespread illiquidity of the commercial banking system. These concerns were reduced by timely Federal Reserve action at the discount window.

It so happens that in neither of these instances did the Federal Reserve's intervention result in a significant deviation of the monetary aggregates from desired growth rates. But let there be no mistake about our determination to deal with financial troubles. In the future, as in the past, we will surely not stand aloof and permit a crisis to develop out of devotion to this or that preconceived growth rate of the money supply.

The responsibility of the Federal Reserve for conditions in

the money and capital markets goes beyond its historic function to act as lender of last resort. Monetary policies need to be implemented, I believe, in ways that avoid large and erratic fluctuations in interest rates and money market conditions.

From one month to the next, the public's demand for money is subject to variations that are usually of a short-run nature. For example, a large tax refund, a retroactive increase in social security benefit payments, or a sizable disbursement by the Treasury of revenue-sharing funds may produce a temporary bulge in the demand for cash balances. If the Federal Reserve tried to maintain a rigid monetary growth rate in the face of such developments, interest rates could fluctuate widely, and to no good end. The costs of financial intermediation would be increased, and the course of monetary policy might be misinterpreted. To avoid these harmful effects, the Federal Reserve seeks to achieve desired growth rates of money and credit over relatively long periods. Experience over the past two decades suggests that even an abnormally large or abnormally small rate of growth of the money stock over a period of six months or so has a negligible effect on the course of the economy—provided it is subsequently offset.

We recognize, of course, that too much attention to preventing short-run fluctuations in interest rates could inadvertently cause the growth rate of money or credit to drift away from what is appropriate for the longer run. To guard against this possibility, the Federal Reserve in early 1972 introduced a new set of procedures for implementing monetary policy. These procedures focus more attention on provision of bank reserves through open market operations at a pace consistent with desired growth rates of monetary and banking aggregates.

The new procedures have been helpful, but numerous problems of monetary control still remain. For example, a substantial part of the money supply is in the form of deposits at nonmember banks. As a consequence of this and other factors, there is considerable slippage between the supply of bank reserves controlled by the Federal Reserve and the nation's money supply. Monetary control is therefore less precise than it could or should be. I would once again urge the Congress to correct this defect by extending the Federal Reserve's power over reserve requirements to all commercial banks.

175

Let me turn next to Chairman Patman's fifth question, which deals with the relationship that interest rates, the money supply, and the rate of inflation bear to one another.

Most interest rates in the United States are now at the highest levels in our history. There are some who believe that restrictive monetary and credit policies are responsible for this state of affairs. This view is erroneous. The basic reason why interest rates have risen to their present level is the accelerating pace of price advances over the past decade, so that we now find ourselves in the midst of a two-digit inflation.

Historical evidence—from other countries as well as our own—indicates beyond any doubt that inflation and high interest rates go together. The reasons are not hard to understand. In most countries throughout the Western world, inflationary expectations have become deeply imbedded in the calculations of lenders and borrowers. Lenders now reckon that loans will probably be repaid in dollars of lesser value, and they therefore hold out for nominal rates of interest high enough to assure them a reasonable real rate of return. Borrowers, on their part, are less resistant to rising costs of credit when they anticipate repayment in cheaper dollars.

Interest rates at anything like present levels are deplorable. They cause hardships to individuals and pose a threat to the viability of some of our industries and financial institutions. But we cannot realistically expect any lasting decline in the level of interest rates until inflation is brought under control.

History also indicates that high rates of inflation are typically accompanied by high growth rates in supplies of money and credit. But inflationary tendencies and monetary expansion are not as closely related as is sometimes imagined. For example, the econometric model of the St. Louis Federal Reserve Bank, which assigns a major role to growth of the money stock in movements of the general price level, has seriously underestimated the rate of inflation since the beginning of 1973. Simulations of the model, using the actual growth rates of the money supply since the first quarter of 1972, suggest that the rate of inflation during the past two quarters should have been a mere 3½ percent. Apparently, special factors—such as I mentioned previously—have been at work.

Inflationary processes are characterized by rising turnover

rates of the existing stock of money as well as by relatively high rates of monetary expansion. Recent experience in the United States illustrates this fact. Over the past ten years, the average annual increase in the money stock has been about 6 percent—a higher rate than in the previous decade. Since 1964, however, the income velocity of money—that is, the ratio of gross national product to the money stock—has risen at an average annual rate of about 2½ percent, thus contributing importantly to the inflationary problem.

The role of more rapid monetary turnover rates in inflationary processes warns against assuming any simple causal relation between monetary expansion and the rate of inflation either during long or short periods. Excessive increases in money and credit can be an initiating source of excess demand and a soaring price level. But the initiating force may primarily lie elsewhere, as has been the case in the inflation from which this country is now suffering.

The current inflationary problem emerged in the middle 1960s when our government was pursuing a dangerously expansive fiscal policy. Massive tax reductions occurred in 1964 and the first half of 1965, and they were immediately followed by an explosion of federal spending. The propensity of federal expenditures to outrun the growth of revenues has continued into the 1970s. In the last five fiscal years, total federal debt—including the obligations of the federal credit agencies—has risen by more than $100 billion, a larger increase than in the previous twenty-four fiscal years.

Our underlying inflationary problem, I believe, stems in very large part from loose fiscal policies, but it has been greatly aggravated during the past year or two by the special factors mentioned earlier. From a purely theoretical point of view, it would have been possible for monetary policy to offset the influence that lax fiscal policies and the special factors have exerted on the general level of prices. One may therefore argue that relatively high rates of monetary expansion have been a permissive factor in the accelerated pace of inflation. I have no quarrel with this view. But an effort to use harsh policies of monetary restraint to offset the exceptionally powerful inflationary forces of recent years would have caused serious financial disorder and economic dislocation. That would not have been a sensible course for monetary policy.

The last question put to me deals with how monetary policy should be used to check inflation and bring interest rates down to reasonable levels.

The principal objective of monetary policy since late 1972 has been to combat the inflationary forces threatening our economy. To this end, supplies of money and credit have been restricted at a time when credit demands were booming. Inevitably, therefore, interest rates have risen. This unhappy consequence has led some observers to conclude that restrictive monetary policies are counterproductive—because rising interest rates are an added cost to businesses and thus may result in still higher prices.

There is a grain of truth in this argument, but no more than that. For most businesses, interest costs are only a small fraction of total operating expenses. The direct effects of a restrictive monetary policy on costs and prices are therefore small. The indirect effects of a restrictive monetary policy on prices are far more important. When growth in supplies of money and credit is restrained, some business firms and consumers are discouraged by the high cost of credit from carrying through their plans to spend; others find it more difficult to obtain credit and therefore trim their spending; still others, reckoning that monetary restraint will cool off aggregate demand, curtail their outlays for goods and services even though they do not depend on the credit markets for spendable funds. In all these ways, a restrictive monetary policy helps to moderate aggregate spending and thus to reduce inflationary pressures.

In order to bring interest rates down to reasonable levels, we shall need to stay with a moderately restrictive monetary policy long enough to let the fires of inflation burn themselves out.

Progress can still be made this year in slowing the rate of price increase, and it is urgent that we do so. Inflation has been having debilitating effects on the purchasing power of consumers, on the efficiency of business enterprises, and on the condition of financial markets. The patience of the American people is wearing thin. Our social and political institutions cannot indefinitely withstand a continuation of the current inflationary spiral.

We must face squarely the magnitude of the task that lies ahead. A return to price stability will require a national commitment to fight inflation this year and in the years to come. Monetary policy must play a key role in this endeavor, and we in the Federal Reserve recognize that fact. We are determined to reduce over time the rate of monetary and credit expansion to a pace consistent with a stable price level.

Monetary policy, however, should not be relied upon exclusively in the fight against inflation. Fiscal restraint is also urgently needed. Strenuous efforts should be made to pare federal budget expenditures, thus eliminating the deficit that seems likely in fiscal 1975. The Congress should resist any temptation to stimulate economic activity by a general tax cut or a new public works program. There may be justification for assistance to particular industries—such as housing—that are especially hard hit by a policy of monetary restraint. An expanded public service employment program may also be needed if unemployment rises further. But government should not try to compensate fully for all the inconvenience or actual hardship that may ensue from its struggle against inflation. Public policy must not negate with one hand what it is doing with the other.

There are other actions that may be of some help in speeding the return to general price stability. For example, limited intervention in wage and price developments in pacesetting industries may result in considerable improvement of wage and price performance. I would urge the Congress to reestablish the Cost of Living Council and to empower it, as the need arises, to appoint ad hoc review boards that could delay wage and price increases in key industries, hold hearings, make recommendations, monitor results, issue reports, and thus bring the force of public opinion to bear on wage and price changes that appear to involve an abuse of economic power. Encouragement to capital investment by revising the structure of tax revenues may also be helpful, as would other efforts to enlarge our supply potential. For example, minimum wage laws could be modified to increase job opportunities for teenagers, and reforms are still needed to eliminate restrictive policies in the private sector—such as featherbedding and outdated building codes.

A national effort to end inflation requires explicit recognition of general price stability as a primary objective of public policy. This might best be done promptly through a concurrent resolution by the Congress, to be followed later by an appropriate amendment to the Employment Act of 1946. Such actions would heighten the resolve of the Congress and the Executive to weigh carefully the inflationary implications of all new programs and policies, including those that add to private costs as well as those that raise federal expenditures. And they would signal to our people, and to nations around the world, that the United States firmly intends to restore the conditions essential to a stable and lasting prosperity.

Jobs and Prices

Thank you very much, Mr. President.

I am not going to take full advantage of the opportunity you are giving me. If I took equal time, you and this fine audience might have to listen to me for a full hour or two.

But, I do want to take a few minutes and comment on the inflation problem and on the role of monetary policy.

I listened very carefully to every speaker this morning. I was encouraged by the fact that everyone showed full understanding of the gravity of the inflation problem that our nation is now facing. I learned one thing more, namely, that the Federal Reserve will not necessarily win a popularity contest.

Now, the job of the Federal Reserve System is not to be popular. Our job is to use all of our energy, all of the ability and knowledge that we can muster, to help protect the jobs of American workers and the integrity of their money.

In doing our job we operate in an environment that is made by others—by the Congress, by trade unions, by business firms, by the general public. Now, there are some facts of life that the Federal Reserve Board must take account of if it is to serve the public with good conscience. The Federal Reserve has to make some hard decisions if only because hard decisions are being avoided by others. I want to call your attention to some hard facts of life.

We are in the midst of an inflation which has been gathering force over the past decade. This inflation has now reached

Remarks at the Summit Conference on Inflation, Washington, D.C., September 27, 1974.

a stage where it is endangering our economic and political future.

As a result of this inflation, first of all, our nation's capacity to produce has suffered a setback. Despite sluggish economic conditions for some months now, shortages of materials, component parts, and equipment remain acute in many of our essential industries.

Secondly, as a result of inflation, consumer purchasing power is being eroded. During the past year, the take-home pay of the typical worker has declined from 4 to 5 percent in what it will buy.

In the third place, as a result of the inflation, the real value of the savings deposits, pension reserves, and life insurance policies of the American public has diminished.

Fourth, as a result of the inflation, corporate profits derived from domestic operations have eroded—a fact that is concealed by accounting techniques that were devised originally for inflation-free times.

Fifth, as a result of the inflation, financial markets have been experiencing strains and stresses. Interest rates have soared. Some financial and industrial firms have found it more difficult to refund maturing debt or to raise needed funds in the money and capital markets. The savings flow to thrift institutions has sharply diminished and stock prices have been badly depressed.

In short, as a result of the inflation, much of the planning that American business firms and households customarily do has been upset and the driving force of economic expansion has been blunted.

It should not be surprising, therefore, that the physical performance of the economy has stagnated in recent months, and that unemployment is now larger than it was last fall. We cannot realistically expect a resurgence of economic activity until confidence in our nation's economy is restored.

The most important requirement for rebuilding confidence, I believe, is hard evidence that we are making progress in checking the disease of inflation.

In view of the protracted character and the growing intensity of inflation, the Federal Reserve has been striving for some time to hold down the growth of money and credit.

I received a good deal of advice this morning, all of which

suggested that the monetary spigot should be opened up. I was told to let the money supply expand more rapidly so that interest rates could come down. If that advice were followed, the inflation would become much more intense and interest rates, as they always do in such circumstances, would go higher and higher and soon be a good deal above their present level.

Rapid monetary expansion in the present inflationary environment would add fuel to the fires of inflation and thus worsen our economic troubles.

Now, we at the Federal Reserve have tried to apply the monetary brakes firmly enough to get results, but we have also been mindful of the need to allow the supply of money and credit to keep expanding moderately. The overall supply of money and credit has continued to grow this year but at a slower pace than before.

However, the demand for money and credit has been much greater than the supply. As a result of the huge demand for borrowed funds, credit markets have become tight and interest rates have risen to an extraordinarily high level.

These high interest rates have imposed a heavy burden on businesses and families across the nation. Homebuilding in particular has been hard hit by the developments in the money market. Soaring interest rates, outflows of deposits from thrift institutions, and the consequent decline in availability of mortgage credit have greatly aggravated the condition of the homebuilding industry, which was already suffering from sharply rising construction costs, from erosion in the purchasing power of consumer incomes, and from the overbuilding of the last two years.

It may now be, however, that tensions in financial markets are beginning to ease. With continued moderation in current demands for goods and services, shortages and imbalances in our factories and shops are diminishing. And the Federal Reserve in recent months has been successful, as I have already suggested, in limiting the growth of money and credit to reasonably appropriate dimensions.

We have, therefore, been able recently to take actions that have reduced somewhat the pressures exerted on the banking system. Short-term market interest rates have responded to this relaxation and have declined from their early July peaks.

Long-term market interest rates have stabilized, albeit at very high levels, and they can surely be expected to fall back once some progress is made in curbing inflation. Mortgage interest rates and other institutionally determined rates traditionally lag behind market rates, and they, too, will respond to progress in curbing inflation.

The recent movements of interest rates are encouraging, but we cannot count on any very substantial reduction until borrowers and lenders in the market are convinced that the Federal Reserve is no longer pursuing a lonely struggle against inflation.

Monetary policy is much too blunt an instrument to be relied upon exclusively in what needs to be a national crusade to bring inflation under control.

It is of vital importance that fiscal policy actively join in the battle. Frugality in public expenditures, and a budget that is tilted toward surpluses instead of deficits, can make an enormous contribution to curbing inflation and to lowering interest rates.

A policy of monitoring wages and prices, but relying on voluntary cooperation, can also play a modest, but useful, role in curbing inflationary excesses. I am hopeful that the newly established Council on Wage and Price Stability will help to point the way to anti-inflationary conduct on the part of business, labor, and the consuming public alike.

Programs that seek to enlarge our nation's productive capacity and to intensify the forces of competition can be very helpful in combating inflation over a longer period of time. In this connection let me stress the need to devise effective measures for improving the productivity of our labor force, which has been lagging badly of late.

Greater output potential and increased productivity per worker are essential to achieving a better life for all of our people.

In closing, I want to assert once again and to assure you that the Federal Reserve will persevere in pursuing monetary policies that are necessary to curb our rampant inflation.

We also intend to keep the supply of money and credit moving upward, so that the needs of the economy may be met.

Further, we fully recognize our responsibilities as the nation's lender of last resort, and we will not hesitate to come to the assistance of financial institutions that are caught in a temporary liquidity squeeze.

I can assure you all that there will be no credit crunch in our country.

Immediate and Long-Range
Economic Problems

I am pleased to meet with the Joint Economic Committee once again to present the views of the Board of Governors on the condition of the national economy.

Our nation today is suffering from a serious economic recession. It is also in the midst of an inflation that is threatening the very fabric of our society.

Public policy is thus confronted with a grave and profoundly difficult problem. There is an immediate need for measures to cushion the recession. Yet, we cannot ignore the longer-run implications of our actions for the rate of inflation or for the other adverse trends that in recent years have hampered the nation's economic performance.

Let me turn, first, to the immediate economic situation and then move to some of our longer-range economic problems.

Since last fall, general business activity has deteriorated. The decline in the real gross national product in the fourth quarter was unusually large. Reductions in production and employment over recent months have been about as rapid as at any time in the postwar period. Cutbacks in activity have been especially sharp in the auto industry, but they have been substantial also in the production of other consumer goods, business equipment, construction products, and industrial materials.

Total employment increased during the first ten months of 1974; but there has been a marked decline in recent months, and unemployment has risen sharply. Overtime work has also been

Statement before the Joint Economic Committee, U.S. Congress, February 7, 1975.

reduced and an increasing number of workers have been able to find only part-time employment.

As so often happens in a recession, consumer demands for autos, furniture, household appliances, and other durable goods have declined sharply. Sales of domestic-type autos in January—although up from December—were at an annual rate of only 6.6 million units, nearly one-fourth below last summer's pace. Weakness in consumer demand has extended also to clothing and other nondurable goods. Total retail sales expressed in current dollars fell more than 3 percent from the third to the fourth quarter of last year, and the decline in real terms was even larger. Actually, the physical volume of retail trade has been moving on a downward trend since the spring of 1973.

Residential construction was notably weak throughout 1974. New housing starts in December were at an annual rate of only 870,000 units, the lowest rate since 1966. However, conditions in the mortgage credit markets are rapidly improving, and there has been some tendency for new building permits to stabilize recently. Thus, we may reasonably expect some upturn in home-building before very long.

Business capital spending, on the other hand, will probably decline this year in real terms—although dollar outlays may be rising moderately further. Of late, business firms have been canceling or postponing plans for construction of new facilities and for the purchase of new machinery and equipment. This has resulted in a drop of new orders for capital equipment, and of contracts for commercial and industrial construction.

The decline in final sales during recent months has been unusually large—when we allow for the advance in prices—so that inventories continued to pile up despite substantial cutbacks in production. However, business firms are working strenuously to cut back excess stocks—through further curtailments of output, special promotions, and price concessions—and it appears that we are now moving into a period of inventory liquidation. This adjustment of inventories will have a temporary depressing effect on production and employment, but it is an essential pre-condition for an upturn in business activity later on.

As the economy weakened during the course of 1974, the behavior of prices began to reflect it. Sensitive prices of industrial raw materials started to decline in the spring of last year.

Last fall, the effects of declining business activity began to show up in wholesale prices of intermediate materials, supplies, and components, and later on in prices of finished goods. In December, wholesale prices of industrial commodities were unchanged, agricultural prices declined, and the overall wholesale price index turned down.

The rise in consumer prices has also slowed, partly because the run-up in prices of energy items associated with the rise in the cost of imported crude oil has been tapering off. There have also been substantial price concessions by automobile dealers and other retailers to help stimulate sales and thus bring inventories down.

It would be premature to conclude, however, that the menace of inflation is, or soon will be, behind us. Agricultural products are still in short supply, in large part because of a series of disappointing crop harvests both here and abroad. Also, in some sectors of the economy, such as the service area, prices are continuing to respond to past increases in costs. A major source of inflationary pressure now is the run-up of wage rates. Recent increases in wages greatly exceed the long-run growth trend of productivity. To make matters worse, productivity has declined substantially over the past year, and unit labor costs consequently rose by almost 15 percent in 1974.

Other industrial countries have also been beset by the dual problem of recession and inflation. With the notable exception of Germany, the rate of inflation in other industrial nations has been about the same or higher than in the United States. Most major countries also experienced a leveling off or decline in employment and output last year, and these tendencies were increasingly apparent as the year progressed.

Despite the weakening in economic activity around the world, our export markets held up well last year. Merchandise exports increased considerably, even after allowance for the rise in prices. Our trade balance would have improved, had it not been for the higher price of imported oil, which moved it into substantial deficit. And the exchange value of the dollar has slipped in recent months, due in some measure to capital flows caused by the sharper decline of market interest rates here than abroad.

Mainly because of higher oil prices, most oil-importing

countries have had large current account deficits during the past year, and some have experienced difficulty in obtaining needed financing. For poorer countries, financing problems have become particularly acute. Recent international understandings to extend the oil facility of the International Monetary Fund, to increase Fund quotas, and to create a $25 billion safety net among member countries of the Organization for Economic Cooperation and Development will help to cope with the international financial problems of 1975. But new strains could develop in international financial markets. Private banking systems handled a huge volume of international financing last year, and it is unlikely that they can repeat this performance in 1975.

Both here and in other industrial countries, monetary policy has responded to the weakening in economic activity by encouraging easier conditions in financial markets. In the United States, that easing has proceeded somewhat faster than has generally been the case abroad. Federal Reserve open market operations began to be more accommodative last summer, and short-term market interest rates began to move down from the exceptionally high levels reached in July. As the year progressed, evidence accumulated that economic activity was weakening and that advances in commodity prices were beginning to moderate. Open market operations were, therefore, steadily directed towards a more ample provision of reserves to the banking system.

More recently, open market policy has been reinforced by other monetary instruments. The discount rate was reduced on three occasions—in early December, early January, and again this week—from 8 percent to 6¾ percent. Reductions in member bank reserve requirements were also ordered—in September, November, and January, releasing a total of nearly $2½ billion of reserves and thus helping to improve the liquidity position of the banking system.

Since last July, these policy actions—together with weaker demands for credit by businesses and consumers—have resulted in a sharp decline of short-term market interest rates. Downward movements have continued in recent weeks, even though Treasury financing needs have grown and market participants have begun to anticipate massive federal deficits that, unhappily, are now in prospect.

Long-term interest rates have also declined, but much less than short-term rates. Lenders are still demanding a sizable inflationary premium to supply long-term funds. Moreover, corporations have issued in recent months exceptionally large amounts of long-term bonds—in part reflecting their need to lengthen debt and thereby improve their liquidity position. Demands for long-term capital by state and local governments have also been well sustained.

The beneficial effects of easier conditions in financial markets are not all registered in the movement of interest rates. For example, member banks responded initially to the greater availability of reserves by repaying their borrowings from the Federal Reserve and by taking other steps that improved their liquidity. Banks became overextended during the 1971–1974 credit expansion, and an improvement of their financial position was needed to lay the basis for subsequent expansion of lending. Reductions in the prime rate of interest, therefore, have lagged behind the decline in open-market rates, as banks encouraged businesses to meet their credit needs in the open market.

Growth of the monetary aggregates has reflected this cautious behavior on the part of banks. Despite a series of expansive monetary actions, the narrowly defined money stock (M_1) grew at an annual rate of only $1\frac{1}{2}$ percent in the third quarter of 1974 and $4\frac{1}{4}$ percent in the fourth quarter. In January of this year, moreover, a decline occurred in M_1, probably because demands for bank credit were unusually weak during the month.

Broader measures of money have shown more strength than has M_1. With interest rates declining, net inflows of consumer-type time and savings deposits at banks and at nonbank thrift institutions have improved markedly. Growth in M_2—which includes consumer-type time and savings deposits at commercial banks—rose at an annual rate of about 7 percent in the fourth quarter, compared with a $4\frac{1}{2}$ percent rate in the third. Expansion in M_3—a still broader measure of money that includes also deposits at nonbank thrift institutions—showed similar acceleration. Furthermore, the volume of large denomination certificates of deposit and other liquid instruments bought by major investors has continued to increase at a brisk pace.

Enlarged inflows of deposits to savings and loan associations have permitted these suppliers of home mortgage funds to reduce their borrowing and to replenish liquid assets, thereby laying the base for renewed expansion in mortgage lending. The full benefits of these developments will not be felt for some time, but the improved deposit inflows have already had an effect on mortgage interest rates. Rates on new conventional home mortgages have declined by almost a full percentage point from the peaks of early autumn, and lenders are also more active now in seeking out borrowers.

In short, financial conditions have eased in a variety of ways over recent months. The liquidity of banks and other thrift institutions has improved; short-term interest rates have dropped sharply; a large volume of long-term securities has been successfully marketed; uncertainties afflicting financial markets earlier last year have diminished; and stock prices of late have been rising again.

Despite this marked improvement in financial markets, some further decline in economic activity has to be expected. Consumer willingness to spend is likely to be held back by the effects of widespread unemployment on personal incomes; business spending for fixed capital and inventories will be adversely influenced by the deterioration in sales, profits, and internal cash flows; even residential construction activity may remain depressed for a short time in view of the continuing decline in housing starts.

Evidence is accumulating, however, that the corrective forces needed to lay the basis for economic recovery are already under way. Price rebates on autos and other products are helping to stimulate sales. Consumer incomes are being sustained by enlarged unemployment compensation as well as an expanded public service employment program. The adjustments in financial markets to which I have referred should be of major benefit in supplying funds for housing and for other purposes. And the upturn in the stock market is serving to improve the state of confidence.

For their part, businessmen have responded to declining sales and profits by making strenuous efforts to work off excessive inventories, by concentrating production in more efficient plants, and by economizing on labor and materials. In the manufacturing sector, productivity actually improved somewhat during the last quarter of 1974, despite a sharp decline in output. This is a most encouraging development.

Thus, while business activity is likely to slide off further in the months immediately ahead, there is reason to expect an upturn later this year. The stimulative fiscal actions proposed by the President would serve to increase the likelihood of a turn-around in the course of the economy. The personal tax rebate, if enacted promptly, should have a stimulative effect on spending by late spring or summer, and the effects on business capital expenditures of a liberalized investment tax credit should soon follow. The resulting expansion in investment would help to provide more jobs later this year, and would also contribute to moderating inflation over the longer-run by improving the capacity and efficiency of our industrial plant.

I cannot stress strongly enough the importance of measures to increase productivity at our nation's business enterprises. This is the first of several longer-range problems to which I want to direct the committee's attention.

For some time now, the trend of productivity in the private nonfarm economy has tended to flatten out. During the past decade, the average annual increase in output per manhour was less than 2 percent, compared with nearly 3 percent in the previous ten years. Within the past decade, the rate of improvement in productivity has diminished also. This development has a significant bearing on the living standards of our people, and also on the impact that rising wage rates have on costs of production and prices.

The unsatisfactory record of productivity improvement stems in large part from inadequate investment by business firms in new plant and equipment. Business profits have fallen increasingly short of the amounts needed to finance the growth and modernization of our nation's industrial plant. Environmental and safety regulations, while desirable in their own right, have often delayed fulfillment of capital spending plans and at times have forced adoption of less efficient methods of production. Productivity improvement has also been hampered by changes in the attitude of the labor force and some laxity in management. Workers nowadays are well trained, but many of them work with less energy than they should, and absenteeism has become a more serious problem.

193

These changed attitudes toward work are to some degree the outgrowth of a second disturbing trend in our economy—namely, the fact that taxes have progressively reduced the rewards for working, while government at the same time has increased the share of national output going to persons who are not productively employed. Twenty-five years ago, a typical worker with three dependents gave up about 1 percent of his gross weekly earnings in federal income and social security taxes. Since then, that fraction has risen steadily and reached 13 percent in 1974.

Any large increase in the absorption of private incomes by government poses a threat to individual incentives—all the more so when taxes are levied on persons who work and produce, and the funds are then transferred to others who remain idle. Over the past twenty-five years, transfer payments by all governmental units—in such forms as public welfare, social security benefits, unemployment insurance, and other public assistance— have risen about twice as fast as total wages and salaries. These transfer payments now amount to almost one-fifth of the aggregate of wage and salary disbursements, and the fraction is steadily increasing. A society as affluent as ours can ill afford to neglect the poor, the elderly, the unemployed, or other disadvantaged persons. But neither can it afford to neglect the fundamental precept that there must be adequate rewards to stimulate individual effort.

Besides weakening individual enterprise, massive increases in governmental expenditures—for social welfare, defense, and whatnot—have been a major cause of intensifying inflationary pressures. This is the third of the longer-run problems that our nation must confront. Inflation has been a problem in this country through most of the postwar period; however, the upward march of prices began to accelerate during the middle 1960s, when our government embarked on a highly expansionary fiscal policy. Since 1965, total federal expenditures have risen about 50 percent faster than the gross national product; budget deficits have become chronic; interest rates have soared to unprecedented heights; expectations of rising prices have gotten built into wages and other contracts; and inflation has emerged as the most dangerous economic ailment of our time.

There can be little doubt that inflation is the principal cause of the decline in economic activity in which we now find ourselves. The havoc wrought in our economy by inflation, however, goes well beyond the immediate loss of production and employment. Because of its capricious incidence on income and wealth, inflation has caused disillusionment and discontent among our citizens. And because of its distorting effects on business decisions, inflation has brought into question the liquidity of some major business and financial institutions.

There is no easy way out of the inflationary morass into which we have allowed ourselves to sink. Unwinding from an inflationary process built up over a decade will take time, and will cause further hardships for our people. But defeat of inflationary forces must remain a major goal of public policy. We cannot realistically expect to regain lasting prosperity until businesses and consumers glimpse some end to the inflation that has been damaging our economy.

Lasting prosperity will also require steps to reverse the deterioration in corporate profits that has taken place over the past decade or more. This is another longer-run problem of major importance.

The condition of business profits is widely misunderstood. Profits are thought by some observers to be ample, or even overabundant. The fact is, however, that profit margins of nonfinancial businesses have been declining rather steadily for many years, and profits in the aggregate have been far too low in recent years to supply the financing needed for a vigorous expansion in capital investment.

The major source of confusion about the recent behavior of corporate profits is not hard to find. Last year, the estimated pre-tax profits of all nonfinancial corporations from their domestic operations were 16 percent higher than in 1973 and 46 percent higher than in 1972. The dominant factor in this rise, however, was an enormous increase in inventory profits—an element of earnings that is illusory. It stems from the fact that the accounting practices of many corporations still do not allow for the fact that inventories used up in production must be replaced at higher prices during a period of inflation. As a consequence, costs of operation have been understated, and fictitious profits have been created that are being taxed by the federal government.

Excluding this illusory inventory profit, the after-tax domestic profits of nonfinancial corporations did not rise last year. On the contrary, they declined by 20 percent, and were smaller than eight or ten years earlier—when the dollar value of the output of these corporations was about half what it is today.

Last year, in fact, the after-tax profits of nonfinancial business corporations—adjusted for inventory gains—were no larger than the amount of dividends these firms paid to their stockholders. Worse still, when allowance is made for the fact that depreciation schedules for fixed capital are also based on historical costs—rather than replacement costs—and thus contribute yet another illusory element to book profits, these firms actually paid out more in dividends to their stockholders than they earned from current production.

As I noted earlier, this slump in corporate profits is a major reason why business capital investment has been impeded and why the rate of productivity improvement has been sluggish. But there has been another ominous consequence of deteriorating business profits—namely, some decline in the financial strength of our nation's business firms. This is the fifth long-run problem to which the committee's attention should be directed.

Years ago, when their profit positions were more adequate, our nation's major business corporations financed much of their capital investment from internal sources rather than from borrowed funds. However, dependence on borrowed funds has been rising steadily for more than a decade. In the past five years, funds borrowed in the money and capital markets by all nonfinancial corporations averaged nearly 70 percent of the amount raised internally, and in 1974 their borrowings appear to have exceeded their internal funds.

This growing reliance on borrowed money has brought with it a steep rise in the amount of debt owed by business firms relative to their equity positions. In 1950, total liabilities of manufacturing corporations amounted to less than half of the book value of stockholders' equity. Today, the magnitudes of debt and equity for manufacturing corporations are almost equal. Moreover, a large part of the indebtedness piled up by business firms has been in the form of short-term debts, and these in turn have grown much more rapidly than holdings of current assets.

The liquidity position of nonfinancial businesses has thus been weakened.

These are disturbing trends. The balance sheets of many of our business corporations have become distorted by the need to finance capital investment from external sources. Moreover, the issuance of new stock has been inhibited by unreceptive markets and by tax considerations. The consequence has been that margins of equity have been significantly reduced, and many large businesses no longer have the resiliency they once had to resist economic and financial adversity.

The sixth longer-range problem of major concern to the nation is the foreign exchange value of the dollar. Actually, the dollar began weakening many years before its formal devaluation in 1971. Earlier, there had been an enormous rise in the dollar holdings of foreign central banks, because our balance of payments was in deficit for a prolonged period. Capital outflows—some of them speculative—were large, and they were not offset by surpluses in our current account because costs and prices in the United States were rising rapidly. The devaluation of 1971 and also that of 1973 were thus a consequence of trends that had been under way for many years.

Following the second devaluation in 1973, the foreign exchange value of the dollar has fluctuated fairly widely, but without much net change. Such fluctuations make it more difficult for foreign traders and investors to make rational plans for the future. We must bear this in mind, and also the fact that any appreciable decline in the external value of the dollar would add to our domestic inflationary problem. The Federal Reserve and other central banks can and occasionally do intervene to smooth out movements in exchange rates. But a substantially greater degree of exchange rate stability will not be achieved until underlying economic and financial conditions have been put in better order.

Let me now turn, in conclusion, to the implications for public policy of our immediate and longer-range economic difficulties. The most urgent need at the present time is for measures to cushion recessionary forces. But great care must be taken to avoid aggravating the underlying inflationary forces that have produced our present problems.

Action to reduce income taxes temporarily is an appropriate

197

course at the present time. Because of inflation, many individuals have moved into higher tax brackets, even though their real incomes have declined or remained unchanged. Unless personal tax rates are reduced, that trend will continue, and the automatic budgetary stabilizers we normally count on to moderate recessionary tendencies will therefore not function effectively. Also, action is needed to reduce business taxes in view of the serious deterioration in corporate profits and the taxing of illusory profits by the federal government.

The President's fiscal program recognizes the need to deal with the current recession and yet avoid releasing a new wave of inflation. Both the tax rebate to individuals and the increase in the investment tax credit will provide a temporary boost to aggregate demand without adding to federal deficits over the longer run. Moreover, increases in federal expenditures are to be limited in several ways—by postponing new program initiatives apart from the energy area, by various rescissions and deferrals of spending for existing programs, and by ceilings on increases in social security benefits and on federal pensions and salaries. Even so, federal expenditures should be scrutinized with special care in an effort to hold spending well below the levels projected in the President's budget message. Such a step would improve the prospects for moderating the rate of inflation, and would also bolster the confidence of our people by indicating the clear intent of the Congress to stick to a course of fiscal prudence.

These same considerations must guide the course of monetary policy in the months ahead. The Federal Reserve intends to encourage recovery by providing for an adequate expansion in supplies of money and bank credit. Relatively soon, growth in the monetary aggregates—including the narrowly defined money supply—should strengthen. Let me assure this committee, however, that we have no intention of permitting an explosion in money and credit no matter how large private or public financing demands may become. Such a reckless course of action might hold short-term interest rates down for a time, but it would before long plunge our economy into deeper trouble.

This committee would be well advised to focus a large part of its attention on the course of public policy needed to cope with the serious longer-range problems facing the nation. The issues at stake are large and complex, and solutions will not be readily found. Besides a major national program to deal with the critical problem of energy—which I have not discussed—it seems clear that efforts to gain a better measure of discipline in federal finances have become a matter of great urgency. Ways must be found to curb the ever increasing share of the national income absorbed by governmental programs—especially programs that transfer funds from persons who work to those who are not productively employed. Ways must be found also to strengthen business profits and the state of business finances, and to increase the incentives for expansion of productive capacity and for modernization of our nation's industrial plant.

Above all, ways must be found to bring an end to inflation, and thus lay the basis for a lasting prosperity at home and a strengthening of our position in international markets. Our people are weary of inflation; they are confused and disturbed by the huge budget deficits that are in the making this fiscal year and next; and they are anxiously awaiting evidence that their government can and will take the necessary steps to restore economic and financial stability.

The Current Recession
in Perspective

I am glad to meet with this distinguished group of business and
financial journalists in a leisurely setting. As a policy maker,
I feel I have much in common with the members of your profession. Both you and I must be alert to every twist and nuance
of the changing economic scene. Both you and I must keep busy
searching the business skies for some clues to the economic
future. I find this aspect of my work exciting and intriguing,
as I am sure you do. But it does involve a certain risk for
both of us.

Sharing—as we do—the problem of continually meeting
deadlines, we are in danger of becoming so preoccupied with
the very short run that we fail to see economic events in perspective. For that very reason, I have wanted to take advantage
of your invitation, so that we might ponder together the historical developments which have brought our economy to its
present condition. This is a large and highly important subject.
I cannot hope to do full justice to it on the present occasion.
Nevertheless, I shall make a start this evening.

As you are well aware, these past few years have been trying
times for the American people. Not only have we lived through
the agony of Vietnam and Watergate, but some of us have even
begun to wonder whether our dream of full employment, a stable
price level, and a rising standard of living for all our people is
beyond fulfillment.

Address at the twelfth annual meeting of the Society of American Business
Writers, Washington, D.C., May 6, 1975.

Early last year, economic expansion began to falter in our country, as it did in other countries around the world. At the same time, the pace of the inflation that had been building for more than a decade accelerated sharply further. As the year advanced, it became increasingly clear that our economy was moving into a recession.

During the past two quarters, the real gross national product has declined by 5 percent, and the level of industrial production is now 12 or 13 percent below last September. The unemployment rate has risen swiftly, and so also has the idle capacity in our major industries. The decline in business activity since last fall has been the steepest of the postwar period, and yet the advance of the price level—while considerably slower than last year—is continuing at a disconcerting pace.

No business cycle movement can be comprehended solely in terms of the events that occur within that cycle or the one preceding it. The economic currents of today are heavily influenced by longer-range developments—such as changes in economic and financial institutions, the course of public policy, and the attitudes and work habits of people. By examining the historical background of recent economic troubles, we should be able to arrive at a better understanding of where we now are.

The current recession is best viewed, and I believe it will be so regarded by historians, as the culminating phase of a long economic cycle.

There have been numerous long cycles in the past—that is, units of experience combining two or more ordinary business cycles. One such long cycle ran its course from 1908 to 1921, another from 1921 to 1933. And if we go back to the nineteenth century, we encounter long cycles from 1879 to 1894 and from 1894 to 1908. These long cycles differ in innumerable ways from one another. But they also have some features in common— in particular, each culminates in an economic decline of more than average intensity.

The beginning of the long cycle that now appears to be approaching its natural end may be dated as early as 1958, but it is perhaps best to date its start in 1961. The upward movement of economic activity which began in that year was checked briefly in 1967 and interrupted more significantly in 1970. Although these interruptions were watched with concern and some anxiety by practicing economists and other interested citizens, they will be passed over lightly by economic historians concerned with large events.

The reason is not hard to see. Putting aside monthly and quarterly data, and looking only at annual figures, we find that total employment rose every year from 1961 through 1973. So also did disposable personal income and personal consumption expenditures—both viewed on a per capita basis, and in real terms. This sustained upward trend of the economy came to an end in 1974.

The successive phases of the long upswing from 1961 to 1974 provide a useful perspective on our current problems. Some years ago, in my work at the National Bureau of Economic Research, I observed a pattern in past long upswings—an initial stage that may be called the "industrial phase" followed by what is best described as the "speculative phase." The imbalances that develop in this latter phase lead inevitably to the final downturn. The events of the past fifteen years conform rather closely to this pattern.

The period from 1961 through 1964 may be regarded as the industrial phase of the long upswing. Productivity grew rapidly—increasing in the private nonfarm sector at an annual rate of 3.6 percent between the final quarters of 1960 and 1964, or well above the average rate of the preceding decade. Unit labor costs were then remarkably stable, and so too was the general price level. Real wages and profits rose strongly. During this period of sustained economic expansion, unemployment fell from about 7 percent of the labor force to 5 percent, while the rate of use of industrial capacity rose substantially.

The second—or speculative—phase of the long upswing began around 1965 and continued through much of 1974. This ten-year period was marked by a succession of major, inter-related, and partly overlapping speculative waves that in varying degrees gripped other leading industrial countries as well as the United States.

The first speculative movement involved corporate mergers and acquisitions. In the euphoria of what some commentators have called the "go-go" years, rapid growth of earnings per share of common stock became the overriding goal of many business managers. Other yardsticks of corporate performance—

such as the rate of return on new investments—were neglected, and so too were the serious risks of increased leveraging of common stock.

The aggregate volume of large corporate acquisitions, which for some years had been running at about $2 billion per year, jumped to $3 billion in 1965, to $8 billion in 1967, to $12½ billion in 1968, and then tapered off. This was the great era of conglomerates, when a variety of unrelated businesses were brought together under a single corporate management. Entrepreneurs who displayed special skill in such maneuvers were hailed as financial geniuses—until their newly built empires began to crumble. Being preoccupied with corporate acquisitions and their conglomerate image, many businessmen lost sight of the traditional business objective of seeking larger profits through better technology, aggressive marketing, and improved management. The productivity of their businesses suffered, and so too did the nation's productivity.

The spectacular merger movement of the late 1960s was reinforced, and to a degree made possible, by the speculative movement that developed in the market for common stocks. The volume of trading on the New York Stock Exchange doubled between 1966 and 1971, and for a time trading volume on the American Exchange rose even faster. The prices of many stocks shot up with little regard to actual or potential earnings. During the two years 1967 and 1968, the average price of a share of common stock listed on the New York Exchange rose 40 percent, while earnings per share of the listed companies rose less than 2 percent. On the American Exchange, the average price per share rose during the same years more than 140 percent on an earnings base that again was virtually unchanged.

Much of this speculative ardor came from a section of the mutual fund industry. For the new breed of "performance funds," long-term investment in the shares of established companies with proven earnings became an outmoded concept. In their quest for quick capital gains, these institutions displayed a penchant for risky investments and aggressive trading. In 1965, a typical mutual fund turned over about one-fifth of its common stock portfolio; by 1969, that fraction had risen to nearly one-half. As Wall Street then had it, the "smart money" went into issues of technologically oriented firms or into corporate conglomerates

—no matter how well or poorly they met the test of profitability.

Speculation in equities was cooled for a time by the stock market decline of 1969–1970, but then it resumed again and took on new forms. Money managers began to channel a preponderant part of their funds into the stocks of large and well-known firms—apparently with the thought that earnings of those companies were impervious to the vicissitudes of economic life. A huge disparity was thereby created between the price-earnings ratios of the "favored fifty" and those of other corporations. Share prices of these "favored" companies were, of course, especially hard hit in the subsequent shakeout of the stock market.

Speculation in common stocks was not confined to the United States. From the late 1960s until about 1973, nearly every major stock exchange in the world experienced a large run-up in share prices, only to be followed by a drastic decline. Indeed, speculation reached a more feverish pace in some countries than in the United States. On the Tokyo stock exchange, for example, both share prices and the trading volume actually doubled in the twelve months between January 1972 and January 1973, and then suffered a sharp reversal.

The third speculative wave that nourished the long upswing of our national economy occurred in the real estate market. Homebuilding fluctuated around a horizontal trend during the 1960s. The vacancy rate in rental housing was at a high level from 1960 to 1965, then fell steadily until the end of the decade, and thus helped pave the way for a new housing boom. Between January of 1970 and January of 1973, the volume of new housing starts doubled. Since then, homebuilding has plunged, and in some sections of the nation it has virtually come to a halt. Failures of construction firms and unemployment among construction workers have reached depression levels. These unhappy developments stem in large measure from the excesses of the housing boom that got under way in 1970.

Inflationary expectations clearly played a substantial role in bolstering the demand for houses. But the boom was fostered also by an array of governmental policies designed to stimulate activity in the housing sector. These governmental measures, however well intentioned, gave little heed to basic supply conditions in the industry or to the underlying demand for housing.

In response to easy credit and federal subsidies, merchant builders moved ahead energetically, put up one-family homes well ahead of demand, and thus permitted the inventory of unsold homes to double between 1970 and 1973. Speculative activity was even more intense in the multifamily sector—that is, in apartments built for renting, and particularly in condominiums and cooperatives, which accounted for a fourth of the completions of multifamily structures by the first half of 1974.

The boom in housing was financed by a huge expansion of mortgage credit and construction loans. Real estate investment trusts played an exceptionally large role in supplying high-risk construction loans for condominiums, recreational developments, and other speculative activities. The growth of real estate trusts was extraordinary by any yardstick. Their assets, amounting to less than $700 million in 1968, soared to upwards of $20 billion by 1973. Unsound practices accompanied this rapid growth and, as a result, many real estate trusts now face difficult financial problems.

The speculative boom in real estate was not confined to residential structures. It extended to speculation in land, to widespread building of shopping centers, and to construction of office buildings. By 1972, the vacancy rate in office buildings reached 13 percent, but this type of construction still kept climbing.

The real estate boom in the United States during the early 1970s had its parallel in other countries. Speculation in land and properties became rampant in the United Kingdom. In 1972 alone, new house prices rose 47 percent on the average. The amount of credit absorbed in real estate ventures rose so rapidly that the Bank of England felt forced to place special controls on bank lending for such purposes. And in Germany, the boom in residential construction during 1971–1973 left an inventory of about a quarter million unsold units—more than a third of a peak year's output—that now overhang the market.

It is in the nature of speculative movements to spread from one country or market to another. Just as the speculative wave in real estate was beginning to taper off in 1973, a new wave of speculation got under way—this time in inventories. That was the fourth and final speculative episode of the long economic upswing from 1961 to 1974. It involved massive stocking up of raw materials, machinery, parts, and other supplies in the United States and in other industrial countries.

The inventory speculation of 1973 and 1974 was the outgrowth of a boom in business activity that had raised its head by 1972 in virtually every industrial country of the world. The synchronism of economic expansion in these countries was partly coincidental, but the expansion that stemmed from ordinary business cycle developments was reinforced by the adoption of stimulative economic policies almost everywhere. As a result, production increased rapidly around the world, and led to a burgeoning demand for raw materials, machine tools, component parts, and capital equipment—goods for which our country is a major source of supply. The pressure of rising world demand was reinforced in our markets by the devaluation of the dollar, which greatly improved our competitive position in international trade.

By the beginning of 1973, as business firms attempted to meet intense demands from both domestic and foreign customers, serious bottlenecks and shortages had begun to develop in numerous industries—especially those producing steel, nonferrous metals, paper, chemicals, and other raw materials. In this environment of scarcities, the rise in prices of industrial commodities quickened both here and abroad. The dramatic advance of food prices in 1973, and later in energy prices, greatly compounded the worldwide inflationary problem. In our country, these price pressures were suppressed for a time by price and wage controls, but the general price level exploded when controls were phased out in late 1973 and early 1974.

One of the unfortunate consequences of inflation is that it masks underlying economic realities. As early as the spring of 1973, a perceptible weakening could be detected in the trend of consumer buying in this country. The business community, however, paid little attention to this ominous development. The escalating pace of inflation fostered expectations of still higher prices and persistent shortages in the years ahead, so that intensive stockpiling of commodities continued. Inventories increased out of all proportion to actual or prospective sales. In fact, the ratio of inventories to sales, expressed in physical terms, had risen by the summer of 1974 to the highest figure for any business cycle expansion since 1957—another year when a severe recession got under way.

In summary, the period from 1965 to 1974 was marked by a succession of interrelated, partly overlapping, speculative waves—first, in buying up of existing businesses; then, in the stock market; next, in markets for real estate; and finally, in markets for industrial materials and other commodities.

A prolonged speculative boom of this kind can seldom be traced to a single causal factor. In this instance, however, a dominant source of the problem appears to have been the lack of discipline in governmental finances.

The industrial phase of the long upswing drew to a close in late 1964 or early 1965. By then, the level of real output was very close to the limits imposed by our nation's physical capacity to produce. By then, the level of wholesale prices was already moving out of its groove of stability. Nevertheless, our government did nothing to moderate the pace of expansion of aggregate monetary demand. On the contrary, it actually embarked on a much more expansive fiscal policy. The tax reductions of 1964 were followed in 1965 by fresh tax reductions and by a huge wave of spending both for new social programs and for the war in Vietnam. These misadventures of fiscal policy doomed the economy to serious trouble, but we were slow to recognize this. Indeed, substantial tax reductions occurred again in 1969 and 1971, and they too were followed by massive increases of expenditures.

Deficits therefore mounted, and they persisted year in and year out. Over the last ten complete fiscal years—that is, from 1965 through 1974—the federal debt held by the public, including obligations of federal credit agencies, rose by more than 50 percent. The large and persistent deficits added little to our nation's capacity to produce, but they added substantially to aggregate monetary demand for goods and services. They were thus directly responsible for much of the accelerating inflation of the past decade.

Monetary and credit policies were not without some fault. As every student of economics knows, inflation cannot continue indefinitely without an accommodating increase in supplies of money and credit. It is very difficult, however, for a central bank to maintain good control of money and credit when heavy governmental borrowing drives up interest rates, and when the public is unwilling to face squarely the long-run dangers inherent in excessively stimulative economic policies.

To make matters worse, laxity in our national economic policies spilled over into private markets. The "new economics," of which less is now heard than before, held out the possibility, if not the actual promise, of perpetual prosperity. Many businessmen and financiers came to view the business cycle as dead, and to expect the federal government to bail out almost any enterprise that ran into financial trouble. All too frequently, therefore, the canons of financial prudence that had been developed through hard experience were set aside.

Many of our business corporations courted trouble by permitting sharp reductions in their equity cushions or their liquidity. In the manufacturing sector, the ratio of debt to equity—which had been stable in the previous decade—began rising in 1964 and nearly doubled by the end of 1974. Moreover, a large part of the indebtedness piled up by business firms was in the form of short-term obligations, and these in turn grew much more rapidly than holdings of current assets.

Similar trends developed in some segments of commercial banking. Large money-market banks came to rely more heavily on volatile short-term funds to finance their business customers, and at times they increased their loan commitments to businesses beyond prudent limits. A few bank managers, too, began to concern themselves excessively with maximizing short-run profits, so that the prices quoted for their common stock would move higher. Capital ratios of many banks deteriorated; questionable loans were extended at home and abroad; insufficient attention was given here and there to the risks of dealing in foreign exchange markets; and too much bank credit went into the financing of speculative real estate ventures.

A variety of loose practices also crept into state and local government finance. Faced with rapidly expanding demands for services and limited sources of revenue, some governmental units resorted to extensive short-term borrowing and employed dubious accounting devices to conceal their budget deficits. Statutory debt limits were circumvented through the creation of special public authorities to finance the construction of housing, schools, and health facilities. Some of these authorities issued so-called "moral obligation" bonds, which investors in many instances regarded as the equivalent of "full faith and credit" obligations. The novel financial devices seemed innocuous at the time, but they have recently become a source of serious concern to investors in municipal securities.

A nation cannot realistically expect prosperous economic conditions to continue very long when the federal government fails to heed the warning signs of accelerating inflation, when many of its business leaders spend their finest hours arranging financial maneuvers, and when aggressive trade unions push up wage rates far beyond productivity gains. After 1965, the strength of the American economy was gradually sapped by these ominous trends. Productivity in the private nonfarm sector, which had grown at an annual rate of 3.6 percent from 1961 through 1964, slowed to a 2.2 percent rate of advance from 1964 to 1969, then to 1.5 percent from 1969 to 1974. Expansion in the physical volume of national output likewise declined during successive quinquennia. The rate of inflation, meanwhile, kept accelerating.

With the pace of inflation quickening, seeds of the current recession were thus sown across the economy. Rising prices eroded the purchasing power of workers' incomes and savings. Corporate profits diminished—a fact that businessmen were slow to recognize because of faulty accounting techniques. New dwellings were built on a scale that greatly exceeded the underlying demand. Inventories of commodities piled up, often at a fantastic pace, as businessmen reacted to gathering fears of shortages. Credit demands, both public and private, soared and interest rates rose to unprecedented heights.

These basic maladjustments are now being worked out of the economic system by recession—a process that entails enormous human and financial costs. Our country has gone a considerable distance in developing policies to alleviate economic hardships, and these policies have been strengthened recently. Nevertheless, the recession has wrought great damage to the lives and fortunes of many of our people.

This recession has cut deeply into economic activities. It must not, however, be viewed as being merely a pathological phenomenon. Since we permitted inflation to get out of control, the recession is now performing a painful—but also an unavoidable—function.

First, it is correcting the imbalances that developed between the production and sales of many items, also between orders and inventories, between capital investment and consumer spending, and between the trend of costs and prices.

Second, business managers are responding to the recession by moving energetically to improve efficiency—by concentrating production in more modern and efficient installations, by eliminating wasteful expenditures, by stimulating employees to work more diligently, and by working harder themselves.

Third, the recession is improving the condition of financial markets. Interest rates have moved to lower levels as a result of declining credit demands and of the Federal Reserve's efforts to bolster the growth of money and credit. Commercial banks have taken advantage of the reduced demand for loans to repay their borrowings from Federal Reserve Banks, to reduce reliance on volatile sources of funds, and to rebuild liquid assets. The rapidly rising inflow of deposits to thrift institutions has likewise permitted a reduction of indebtedness and addition to their liquid assets.

Fourth, the recession is wringing inflation out of the economic system. Wholesale prices of late have moved down, and the rise of consumer prices has also slowed. Although general price stability is not yet in sight, a welcome element of price competition has at long last been restored to our markets.

These and related business developments are paving the way for recovery in economic activity. No one can foresee with confidence when the recovery will begin. The history of our country indicates clearly, however, that the culminating downward phase of a long cycle need not be of protracted duration.

Signs are multiplying, in fact, that an upturn in economic activity may not be far away. For example, employment rose in April after six successive months of decline. The length of the workweek also stabilized last month. The rate of layoffs in manufacturing is now turning down, and some firms have been recalling workers who formerly lost their jobs. Sales of goods at retail—apart from autos—have risen further. Business and consumer confidence has been improving. And prospects for an early upturn in economic activity have been strengthened by passage of the Tax Reduction Act of 1975.

Our nation stands at present at a crossroads in its history. With the long and costly cycle in business activity apparently approaching its end, the critical task now is to build a solid foundation for our nation's economic future. We will accomplish that only if we understand and benefit from the lessons of recent experience.

Since World War II, a consensus has been building in this country that the primary task of economic policy is to maintain full employment and promote maximum economic growth. We have pursued these goals by being ever ready to stimulate the economy through increased federal spending, lower taxes, or monetary ease. Neglect of inflation, and of longer-run economic and financial problems, has thus crept insidiously into public policy making. Our government has become accustomed to respond with alacrity to any hint of weakness in economic activity, but to react sluggishly, and sometimes not at all, to signs of excess demand and developing inflationary pressures.

The thinking of many of our prominent economists has encouraged this bias in our economic policies. During the 1950s and 1960s, they frequently argued that "creeping inflation" was a small price to pay for full employment. Some even suggested that a little inflation was a good thing—that it energized the economic system and thus promoted rapid economic growth.

This is a dangerous doctrine. While inflation may begin slowly in an economy operating at high pressure, it inevitably gathers momentum. A state of euphoria then tends to develop, economic decision making becomes distorted, managerial and financial practices deteriorate, speculation becomes rampant, industrial and financial imbalances pile up, and the strength of the national economy is slowly but surely sapped. That is the harsh truth that the history of business cycles teaches.

To emphasize this truth, I should now like to offer this distinguished group of journalists a bit of professional advice. Since few of you are reluctant to pass along hints as to how I should do my job, I have decided to suggest to you what the really big economic news story of 1975 is likely to be.

The story has to do with the drama now unfolding on

Capitol Hill in the implementation of the Budget Control Act adopted last year. If I am right in thinking that our present economic difficulties are largely traceable to the chronic bias of the federal budget toward deficits, there can be no doubt about the importance of what is now being attempted. No major democracy that I know of has had a more deficient legislative budget process than the United States—with revenue decisions separated from spending decisions and the latter handled in piecemeal fashion. Budgets in this country have just happened. They certainly have not been planned.

We are now attempting to change that by adopting integrated congressional decisions on revenues and expenditures. My advice to you journalists is to follow this new effort closely. It has a significance for our nation that may carry far into the future. But nothing can be taken for granted here. We have tried budgetary reform once before under the Legislative Reorganization Act of 1946, and it failed. It failed partly because of the challenge to cherished committee prerogatives, partly also because Congress as a whole balked at accepting so much self-discipline. I would urge you to study the history of that earlier effort and to watch the present undertaking for telltale signs of similar faltering.

The potential gain for our nation from budget reform is enormous even in this first year of "dry run." If, in fact, the work of the new budget committees produces in the Congress a deeper understanding of the impossibility of safely undertaking all the ventures being urged by individual legislators, a constructive beginning toward a healthier economic environment will have been made. On the other hand, if the new budget procedures are scuttled, or if they are used with little regard to curbing the bias toward large-sized federal deficits, there ultimately may be little anyone can do to prevent galloping inflation and social upheaval.

I am inclined to be optimistic about the outcome. More and more of our people are becoming concerned about the longer-range consequences of federal financial policies. Perspective on our nation's economic problems is gradually being gained by our citizens and their congressional representatives. A healthy impatience with inflation is growing. You journalists are becoming more actively involved in the educational process. I therefore remain hopeful that we shall practice greater foresight in dealing with our nation's economic problems than we have in the recent past, and that we will thus build a better future for ourselves and our children in the process.

The Real Issues of Inflation and Unemployment

I am pleased to be here at the University of Georgia and to have the opportunity to address this distinguished audience. Tomorrow promises to be an exciting day for you, and you will need all the rest you can muster. I shall therefore not waste many words as I share with you my concern about our nation's future.

Our country is now engaged in a fateful debate. There are many who declare that unemployment is a far more serious problem than inflation, and that monetary and fiscal policies must become more stimulative during the coming year even if inflation quickens in the process. I embrace the goal of full employment, and I shall suggest ways to achieve it. But I totally reject the argument of those who keep urging faster creation of money and still larger governmental deficits. Such policies would only bring us additional trouble; they cannot take us to the desired goal.

The American economy has recently begun to emerge from the deepest decline of business activity in the postwar period. During the course of the recession, which began in late 1973, the physical volume of our total output of goods and services declined by 8 percent. The production of factories, mines, and power plants fell even more—by 14 percent. As the overall level of economic activity receded, the demand for labor rapidly diminished and unemployment doubled, reaching an intolerable 9 percent of the labor force this May.

Address at the Blue Key Honor Society annual awards dinner, University of Georgia, Athens, Georgia, September 19, 1975.

The basic cause of the recession was our nation's failure to deal effectively with the inflation that got under way in the mid-sixties and soon became a dominant feature of our economic life. As wage and price increases quickened, seeds of trouble were sown across the economy. With abundant credit readily available, the construction of new homes, condominiums, and office buildings proceeded on a scale that exceeded the underlying demand. Rapidly rising prices eroded the purchasing power of workers' incomes and savings. Managerial practices of business enterprises became lax and productivity languished, while corporate profits—properly reckoned—kept falling. Inventories of raw materials and other supplies piled up as businessmen reacted to fears of shortages and still higher prices. Credit demands, both public and private, soared and interest rates rose to unprecedented heights. The banking system became overextended, the quality of loans tended to deteriorate, and the capital position of many banks was weakened.

During the past year many of these basic maladjustments have been worked out of the economic system by a painful process that could have been avoided if inflation had not gotten out of control. As the demand for goods and services slackened last winter, business managers began to focus more attention on efficiency and cost controls. Prices of industrial materials fell substantially, price increases at later stages of processing became less extensive, and in many instances business firms offered price concessions to clear their shelves. With the rate of inflation moderating, confidence of the general public was bolstered, and consumer spending strengthened. Business firms were thus able to liquidate a good part of their excess inventories in a rather brief period. Meanwhile, as the demand for credit diminished, tensions in financial markets were relieved, and the liquidity position of both banks and business firms generally improved.

These self-corrective forces internal to the business cycle were aided by fiscal and monetary policies that sought to cushion the effects of economic adversity and to provide some stimulus to economic recovery. On the fiscal side, public employment programs were expanded, unemployment insurance was liberalized, and both personal and corporate income taxes were reduced. On the monetary side, easier credit conditions were fostered, resulting in lower interest rates and a rebuilding of liquidity across the economy.

With the base for economic recovery thus established, business activity has recently begun to improve. Production of goods and services turned up during the second quarter and is continuing to advance. The demand for labor has also improved. Both the number of individuals at work and the length of the workweek are rising again, and unemployment has declined three months in a row. Retail sales have risen further, and of late residential construction has joined the recovery process.

Along with these favorable developments, however, some ominous signs have emerged. Despite an occasional pause, inflation once again may be accelerating. By the second quarter of this year, the annual rate of increase in the general price level was down to 5½ percent—about half the rate of inflation registered in the same period a year earlier. But over the summer, prices began to rise more briskly.

This behavior of prices is particularly worrisome in view of the large degree of slack that now exists in most of our nation's industries. Price increases in various depressed industries— aluminum, steel, autos, industrial chemicals, among others—are a clear warning that our long-range problem of inflation is unsolved and therefore remains a threat to sustained economic recovery.

History suggests that at this early stage of a business upturn, confidence in the economic future should be strengthening steadily. A significant revival of confidence is indeed under way, but it is being hampered by widespread concern that a fresh outburst of double-digit inflation may before long bring on another recession. By now, thoughtful Americans are well aware of the profoundly disruptive consequences of inflation for our economy. They also recognize that these consequences are not solely of an economic character. Inflation has capricious effects on the income and wealth of a nation's families, and this inevitably causes disillusionment and discontent. Social and political frictions tend to multiply, and the very foundations of a society may be endangered. This has become evident in other nations around the world, where governments have toppled as a result of the social havoc wrought by inflation.

If we in the United States wish to enjoy the fruits of a

prosperous economy and to preserve our democratic institutions, we must come to grips squarely with the inflation that has been troubling our nation throughout much of the postwar period, and most grievously during the past decade.

A first step in this process is to recognize the true character of the problem. Our long-run problem of inflation has its roots in the structure of our economic institutions and in the financial policies of our government. All too frequently, this basic fact is clouded by external events that influence the rate of inflation— such as a crop shortfall that results in higher farm prices, or the action of a foreign cartel that raises oil prices. The truth is that, for many years now, the economies of the United States and many other countries have developed a serious underlying bias toward inflation. This tendency has simply been magnified by the special influences that occasionally arise.

A major cause of this inflationary bias is the relative success that modern industrial nations have had in moderating the swings of the business cycle. Before World War II, cyclical declines of business activity in our country were typically longer and more severe than they have been during the past thirty years. In the environment then prevailing, the price level typically declined in the course of a business recession, and many months or years elapsed before prices returned to their previous peak.

In recent decades, a new pattern of wage and price behavior has emerged. Prices of many individual commodities still demonstrate a tendency to decline when demand weakens. The average level of prices, however, hardly ever declines. Wage rates have become even more inflexible. Wage reductions are nowadays rare even in severely depressed industries and the average level of wage rates continues to rise inexorably in the face of widespread unemployment.

These developments have profoundly altered the economic environment. When prices are pulled up by expanding demand in a time of prosperity, and are also pushed up by rising costs during a slack period, the decisions of the economic community are sure to be influenced, and may in fact be dominated, by expectations of continuing inflation.

Thus, many businessmen have come to believe that the trend of production costs will be inevitably upward, and their resistance to higher prices—whether of labor, or materials, or equipment—has therefore diminished. Labor leaders and workers now tend to reason that in order to achieve a gain in real income, they must bargain for wage increases that allow for advances in the price level as well as for such improvements as may occur in productivity. Lenders in their turn expect to be paid back in cheaper dollars, and therefore tend to hold out for higher interest rates. They are able to do so because the resistance of borrowers to high interest rates is weakened by their anticipation of rising prices.

These patterns of thought are closely linked to the emphasis that governments everywhere have placed on rapid economic growth throughout the postwar period. Western democracies, including our own, have tended to move promptly to check economic recession, but they have moved hesitantly in checking inflation. Western governments have also become more diligent in seeking ways to relieve the burdens of adversity facing their peoples. In the process they have all moved a considerable distance towards the welfare state.

In the United States, for example, the unemployment insurance system has been greatly liberalized. Benefits now run to as many as sixty-five weeks, and in some cases provide individuals with after-tax incomes almost as large as their earnings from prior employment. Social security benefits too have been expanded materially, thus facilitating retirement or easing the burden of job loss for older workers. Welfare programs have been established for a large part of the population, and now include food stamps, school lunches, medicare and medicaid, public housing, and many other forms of assistance.

Protection from economic hardship has been extended by our government to business firms as well. The rigors of competitive enterprise are nowadays eased by import quotas, tariffs, price maintenance laws, and other forms of governmental regulation. Farmers, homebuilders, small businesses, and other groups are provided special credit facilities and other assistance. And even large firms of national reputation look to the federal government for sustenance when they get into trouble.

Many, perhaps most, of these governmental programs have highly commendable objectives, but they have been pursued without adequate regard for their cost or method of financing.

Governmental budgets—at the federal, state, and local levels—have mounted and at times, as in the case of New York City, have literally gotten out of control. In the past ten years, federal expenditures have increased by 175 percent. Over that interval, the fiscal deficit of the federal government, including government-sponsored enterprises, has totalled over $200 billion. In the current fiscal year alone, we are likely to add another $80 billion or more to that total. In financing these large and continuing deficits, pressure has been placed on our credit mechanisms, and the supply of money has frequently grown at a rate inconsistent with general price stability.

Changes in market behavior have contributed to the inflationary bias of our economy. In many businesses, price competition has given way to other forms of rivalry—advertising, changes in product design, and "hard-sell" salesmanship. In labor markets, when an excessive wage increase occurs, it is apt to spread faster and more widely than before, partly because workmen have become more sensitive to wage developments elsewhere, partly also because many employers have found that a stable work force can be best maintained by emulating wage settlements in unionized industries. For their part, trade unions at times seem to attach higher priority to wage increases than to the jobs of their members. Moreover, the spread of trade unions to the rapidly expanding public sector has fostered during recent years numerous strikes, some of them clearly illegal, and they have often resulted in acceptance of union demands, however extreme. Needless to say, the apparent helplessness of governments to deal with this problem has encouraged other trade unions to exercise their latent market power more boldly.

The growth of our foreign trade and of capital movements to and from the United States has also increased the susceptibility of the American economy to inflationary trends. National economies around the world are now more closely interrelated, so that inflationary developments in one country are quickly communicated to others and become mutually reinforcing. Moreover, the adoption of a flexible exchange rate system—though beneficial in dealing with large-scale adjustments of international payments, such as those arising from the sharp rise in oil prices—may have made the Western world more prone to inflation by weakening the discipline of the balance of payments. Furthermore, since prices nowadays are more flexible upwards than downwards, any sizable decline in the foreign exchange value of the dollar is apt to have larger and more lasting effects on our price level than any offsetting appreciation of the dollar.

The long-run upward trend of prices in this country thus stems fundamentally from the financial policies of our government and the changing character of our economic institutions. This trend has been accentuated by new cultural values and standards, as is evidenced by pressures for wage increases every year, more holidays, longer vacations, and more liberal coffee breaks. The upward trend of prices has also been accentuated by the failure of business firms to invest sufficiently in the modernization and improvement of industrial plant. In recent years, the United States has been devoting a smaller part of its economic resources to business capital expenditures than any other major industrial nation in the world. All things considered, we should not be surprised that the rate of improvement in output per man-hour has weakened over the past fifteen years, or that rapidly rising money wages have overwhelmed productivity gains and boosted unit labor costs of production.

Whatever may have been true in the past, there is no longer a meaningful trade-off between unemployment and inflation. In the current environment, a rapidly rising level of consumer prices will not lead to the creation of new jobs. On the contrary, it will lead to hesitation and sluggish buying, as the increase of the personal savings rate in practically every industrial nation during these recent years of rapid inflation indicates. In general, stimulative financial policies have considerable merit when unemployment is extensive and inflation weak or absent; but such policies do not work well once inflation has come to dominate the thinking of a nation's consumers and businessmen. To be sure, highly expansionary monetary and fiscal policies might, for a short time, provide some additional thrust to economic activity. But inflation would inevitably accelerate—a development that would create even more difficult economic problems than we have encountered over the past year.

Conventional thinking about stabilization policies is inadequate and out of date. We must now seek ways of bringing unemployment down without becoming engulfed by a new wave of inflation. The areas that need to be explored are many and difficult, and we may not find quickly the answers we seek. But if we are to have any chance of ridding our economy of its inflationary bias, we must at least be willing to reopen our economic minds. In the time remaining this evening, I shall briefly sketch several broad lines of attack on the dual problem of unemployment and inflation that seem promising to me.

First, governmental efforts are long overdue to encourage improvements in productivity through larger investment in modern plant and equipment. This objective would be promoted by overhauling the structure of federal taxation, so as to increase incentives for business capital spending and for equity investments in American enterprises.

Second, we must face up to the fact that environmental and safety regulations have in recent years played a troublesome role in escalating costs and prices and in holding up industrial construction across our land. I am concerned, as are all thoughtful citizens, with the need to protect the environment and to improve in other ways the quality of life. I am also concerned, however, about the dampening effect of excessive governmental regulations on business activity. Progress towards full employment and price stability would be measurably improved, I believe, by stretching out the timetables for achieving our environmental and safety goals.

Third, a vigorous search should be made for ways to enhance price competition among our nation's business enterprises. We need to gather the courage to reassess laws directed against restraint of trade by business firms and to improve the enforcement of these laws. We also need to reassess the highly complex governmental regulations affecting transportation, the effects on consumer prices of remaining fair trade laws, the monopoly of first-class mail by the Postal Service, and the many other laws and practices that impede the competitive process.

Fourth, in any serious search for noninflationary measures to reduce unemployment, governmental policies that affect labor markets have to be reviewed. For example, the federal minimum wage law is still pricing many teenagers out of the job market. The Davis-Bacon Act continues to escalate construction costs and damage the depressed construction industry. Programs for unemployment compensation now provide benefits on such a generous scale that they may be blunting incentives to work. Even in today's environment, with about 8 percent of the labor force unemployed, there are numerous job vacancies—perhaps because job seekers are unaware of the opportunities, or because the skills of the unemployed are not suitable, or for other reasons. Surely, better results could be achieved with more effective job banks, more realistic training programs, and other labor market policies.

I believe that the ultimate objective of labor market policies should be to eliminate all involuntary unemployment. This is not a radical or impractical goal. It rests on the simple but often neglected fact that work is far better than the dole, both for the jobless individual and for the nation. A wise government will always strive to create an environment that is conducive to high employment in the private sector. Nevertheless, there may be no way to reach the goal of full employment short of making the government an employer of last resort. This could be done by offering public employment—for example, in hospitals, schools, public parks, or the like—to anyone who is willing to work at a rate of pay somewhat below the federal minimum wage.

With proper administration, these public service workers would be engaged in productive labor, not leaf-raking or other make-work. To be sure, such a program would not reach those who are voluntarily unemployed, but there is also no compelling reason why it should do so. What it would do is to make jobs available for those who need to earn some money.

It is highly important, of course, that such a program should not become a vehicle for expanding public jobs at the expense of private industry. Those employed at the special public jobs will need to be encouraged to seek more remunerative and more attractive work. This could be accomplished by building into the program certain safeguards—perhaps through a constitutional amendment—that would limit upward adjustment in the rate of pay for these special public jobs. With such safeguards, the budgetary cost of eliminating unemployment need not be burdensome. I say this, first, because the number of individuals accepting the public service jobs would be much smaller than the number now counted as unemployed; second, because the availability of public jobs would permit sharp reduction in the scope of unemployment insurance and other governmental programs to alleviate income loss. To permit active searching for a regular job, however, unemployment insurance for a brief period—perhaps thirteen weeks or so—would still serve a useful function.

Finally, we also need to rethink the appropriate role of an incomes policy in the present environment. Lasting benefits cannot be expected from a mandatory wage and price control program, as recent experience indicates. It might actually be helpful if the Congress renounced any intention to return to mandatory controls, so that businesses and trade unions could look forward with confidence to the continuance of free markets. I still believe, however, that a modest form of incomes policy, in some cases relying on quiet governmental intervention, in others on public hearings and the mobilization of public opinion, may yet be of significant benefit in reducing abuses of private economic power and moving our nation towards the goal of full employment and a stable price level.

Structural reforms of our economy, along some such lines as I have sketched, deserve more attention this critical year from members of the Congress and from academic students of public policy than they are receiving. Economists in particular have tended to concentrate excessively on overall fiscal and monetary policies of economic stimulation. These traditional tools remain useful and even essential; but once inflationary expectations have become widespread, they must be used with great care and moderation.

This, then, is the basic message that I want to leave with you: our nation cannot now achieve the goal of full employment by pursuing fiscal and monetary policies that rekindle inflationary expectations. Inflation has weakened our economy; it is also endangering our economic and political system based on freedom. America has become enmeshed in an inflationary web, and we need to gather our moral strength and intellectual courage to extricate ourselves from it. I hope that all of you will join in this struggle for America's future.

Four Questions by a Student
of Economics

I am very pleased to join this audience in honoring the graduating class of the University of Akron. Some of you receiving a degree today will continue with your formal education; others will embark on business or professional careers. But whatever your plans for the future, our nation's economic and political condition will inevitably remain a matter of concern to you.

Recently, I received a letter from a college student named Rebecca who posed several blunt questions concerning our nation's economy. First, Rebecca asked, "What was the biggest economic setback this year?" Second, "What has been the biggest economic boost this year?" Third, "What plans are being made to get the United States out of the red?" Fourth, "What can we as citizens of the United States do to help the economic situation?"

These are thoughtful questions, and they are not easy to answer with confidence or precision. But they undoubtedly express the concerns of many of our citizens, and I want to take advantage of this occasion to share with you my attempt to answer Rebecca's earnest inquiry.

Turning to the first question, the list of candidates for the greatest economic disappointment of 1975 is regrettably quite long. During the past year, we experienced a severe recession. The physical output of our national economy declined sharply before recovery got under way. The unemployment rate rose to

Commencement address at the University of Akron, Akron, Ohio, December 14, 1975.

225

levels not seen in a long generation. Inflation continued at a disconcerting pace. The deficit in the federal government's budget exploded. Interest rates on municipal securities soared. And efforts to move our nation towards independence in the field of energy made little progress.

While all these developments have been disappointing, the persistence of inflation at a time of such widespread unemployment of labor and of capital harbors the most troublesome implications for our nation's future. True, the advance of the general price level moderated significantly during the first half of 1975. More recently, however, the upward climb of prices has begun to accelerate again. Since mid-year, wholesale prices have been rising at an annual rate of a little over 10 percent. Price markups in various depressed industries—such as aluminum, steel, and autos—convey a clear warning that our long-range problem of inflation is unsolved.

By now, many Americans are well aware of the profoundly disruptive consequences of inflation for our country. The inflation from which we continue to suffer got under way more than ten years ago and eventually became a dominant feature of our economic life. As wage and price increases quickened, seeds of trouble were sown across the economy. Rapidly rising prices eroded the purchasing power of workers' incomes and savings. Speculative fever mounted. The construction of new homes, condominiums, and office buildings proceeded on a scale that far exceeded the underlying demand. Managerial practices of business enterprises became lax and productivity languished. Corporate profits—properly reckoned—kept falling. And as businessmen reacted to fears of shortages and still higher prices, inventories of raw materials and other supplies piled up.

It is these basic maladjustments that led to the recent economic decline—the deepest since World War II. This slump has entailed enormous human and financial costs, and we have as yet only partly recovered from it. The behavior of prices in recent months is therefore very worrisome. Not only are the incomes and savings of our people still being eroded, but revival of confidence in the economic future is being hampered by fears of a fresh outburst of double-digit inflation. If such a development occurred, it would ultimately plunge us into an economic recession even more serious than the one we have just experienced.

I therefore believe that control of inflation requires a higher priority in managing our economic policies than it is as yet receiving. We cannot expect inflation to be brought under control if the federal government continues to run huge budget deficits or to permit money and credit to expand unduly. We must also face up to the hard truth that competition has become less intense in many of our private markets. If an unemployment rate of 8 or 9 percent is insufficient to bring inflation to a halt, then our economic system is no longer working as we once supposed. In the future, governmental efforts to achieve economic progress will need to encompass structural reforms as well as responsible monetary and fiscal policies.

Let me turn next to Rebecca's question concerning the most beneficial economic development this year. Once again, there is no shortage of plausible candidates. The recovery in business activity since the spring has been quite vigorous. Indeed, the rise during the third quarter in the physical volume of our national output was the largest in many a year. Since March the number of people employed has risen by 1½ million. The recovery in stock prices since the beginning of the year has been heartening to investors. The decline in interest rates from the extraordinary heights of 1974 has brought a measure of relief to business borrowers and home buyers. And the turnaround in our foreign trade from a deep deficit to a large surplus has helped to make the dollar once again a highly respected currency around the world.

These recent shifts of economic fortune deserve, and they are in fact receiving, much attention. But another and less widely noticed development—namely, rediscovery of the need for prudence in the conduct of financial affairs—is likely to prove of greater and more lasting benefit to the American people.

During the past year, we have seen the consequences of more than a decade of neglect of the principles of sound finance. Some major business corporations and many smaller ones have fallen into bankruptcy. A number of real estate investment trusts and some airlines are in serious trouble. Many individuals have lost their life's savings by making careless investments. Not a few of our nation's commercial banks face the possibility of large losses on dubious loans. And various state and local

227

government units are now finding it difficult, if not impossible, to raise new money through our financial markets.

More than any other single event, the agony of New York City has made the consequences of financial mismanagement apparent to the entire nation. A federal budget deficit in the neighborhood of $90 billion, which is in prospect for this fiscal year, may stagger the imagination; but few of our citizens can grasp its impact on their daily lives. Everyone, however, can relate to what has been happening in New York City—with thousands of municipal workers being dismissed, the number of policemen and garbage collectors dwindling, the subway fare going up, taxes rising, interest on outstanding municipal securities being scaled down, pension benefits being readjusted, and free tuition in the city's colleges placed in jeopardy.

Our country has been divided on the issue of whether, or under what conditions, federal financial assistance to New York City is justified. But those who favor federal assistance, as well as those who are opposed, agree on this much: that what happened to New York must not happen in our community or in our state. New York's dramatic encounter with bankruptcy may therefore mark a major turning point in the management of fiscal affairs in our country—certainly at the local and state levels, and perhaps at the federal level as well.

State and local governments are now busy reexamining their financial condition. Many of them are cutting back on postponable or avoidable expenditures, and raising taxes as needed. Proposals for bond issues are being appraised by the citizenry with a more critical eye. And recognition is growing across the country that the New York City crisis is just one manifestation of the lax financial practices that spread through the business, financial, and governmental sectors over the past ten to twelve years.

Fortunately, these unsound practices are now being corrected in our business firms and banks, as well as by state and local governments. This curative process is not without some pain. Capital for risky ventures is harder to obtain nowadays and it is also more costly. But this return to standards of prudent financial management has been an essential step in rebuilding the foundation for a durable prosperity.

I now come to Rebecca's third question: What plans are

there for ending the persistent stream of federal budget deficits? This concern with the need to restore order in our national fiscal affairs is shared, I believe, by the great majority of our people. To be sure, the swelling of the deficit this year reflects the deep recession of economic activity—which reduced federal revenues besides increasing outlays for unemployment benefits, welfare payments, and related programs. But the federal deficit was large even before the recession started; it has continued year after year, in both good times and bad; and it has largely resulted from inadequate attention to the consequences of excessive governmental spending.

Of late, there have been some encouraging changes in the federal budgetary process. A major reform of congressional procedures was set in motion by the Congressional Budget Act of 1974. In the past, revenue decisions by the Congress were separated from its spending decisions, and the latter were handled in piecemeal fashion. The result was that budgets just happened; they were not planned. Under the new Budget Act, Congress must assign priorities to the various outlays and set an overall limit on spending in relation to expected revenues. Hence, congressional decisions on expenditures will in the future be integrated with decisions on revenues. The discipline imposed by these new procedures offers hope, I believe, of reducing the chronic bias toward deficits in the federal budget.

So, too, does the initiative of the President in recommending that federal expenditures be cut next fiscal year by $28 billion below the level that they would otherwise reach. The basic principle underlying this expenditure proposal is sound, and I hope Congress will support it.

Once we put an end to the rapid upward spiral of federal spending, budget deficits are likely to run smaller or vanish entirely. When the government no longer pours more money into the economy than it withdraws in tax revenues, it will have removed the single most important cause of inflation in our times. Moreover, when the government no longer absorbs so large a portion of private incomes, private capital investment will tend to increase more rapidly. Improved productivity, lower product prices, and a higher standard of living will therefore be fostered.

Let me now turn to Rebecca's final and most challenging

question: What can we as citizens do to help the economic situation? This question is so difficult because our economic situation has numerous dimensions—the level of production, the extent of unemployment, the level of prices, the distribution of incomes, the profitability of investment, the state of the environment, and so on. Improvement in any one of these respects need not be accompanied by improvement in others. The question is also difficult because what any one of us can do depends on his personal situation—whether we work at home or in a business, whether we are farmers or miners, journalists or scientists. Moreover, as you well know, even experienced economists who have similar social objectives frequently disagree on what can or should be done to improve economic conditions.

Nevertheless, there are some principles of life that all of us can observe with the conviction that we will be helping our nation's economic situation.

First of all, we can curb any latent discontent or cynicism we may feel about the motives of our fellow citizens in business or government. Americans, by and large, are a moral people who have wrought economic miracles by seeking to improve themselves, their families, and their communities. We have demonstrated across the years that hope is perhaps the most powerful of all economic forces, and that a spirit of purpose can give meaning to human energy and overcome a lack of material resources.

Second, every one of us can surely improve his understanding of economic phenomena. Education is a never ending process. The intellectual excitement of the classroom need not be lost, and should not be lost, as we move on in life. The economic problems of today are profoundly challenging, and there will surely be new ones tomorrow. As citizens we need to strive for dependable knowledge of economic realities, so that we can make wiser decisions in the marketplace and in the voting booth.

Third, we can become more actively involved in the political process of our nation—by electing officials at all levels of government who demonstrate a serious and informed awareness of our economic problems, by communicating our thoughts on public issues to our representatives with the clarity of conviction, and by holding them responsible for their actions.

Fourth, we can avoid the temptation to implore the federal

government to solve every economic and social problem through the expenditure of public funds. We are a compassionate people, and I trust we will remain so. It is understandable that we attempt to muster our collective resources to aid the less fortunate among us. Yet we must take great care not to weaken the spirit of self-reliance that has been instrumental in releasing the creative and productive energies of the American people.

Fifth, we can impose discipline on our business enterprises through our daily decisions in the marketplace. The power of the consumer to force business firms to price competitively and to improve their products must never be underestimated. We as consumers can help to keep the spirit of price competition alive by shopping carefully and avoiding impulse buying.

Finally, every American can experience the satisfaction that comes from honest effort—by putting in a full day's work for a full day's pay, whether it be work in a factory, a scientific laboratory, a corporate office, a governmental agency, or wherever one may labor. "Sweet is the sleep of a laborer," so sang Ecclesiastes. Centuries later, Carlyle reminded us that "there is a perennial nobleness . . . in work," that indeed "a man perfects himself by working." The rewards of work accrue, of course, to the public at large as well as to the laborer; for the more we produce by the day or by the hour, the more surely will the standard of living of the American people improve.

The needs of the American economy today are large and compelling. Some of you graduates will approach these needs as liberals, others as conservatives. Some of you doubtless believe in free enterprise, others may aspire to a welfare state, still others may seek the nationalization of our industries. But whatever your philosophic or political attitudes may be, I hope you will recognize that your dreams of a good society have no chance of fulfillment unless our government conducts its financial affairs responsibly. This condition is essential to bringing an end to the inflation that has been raising havoc with our economic institutions; it is essential to the restoration of a lasting prosperity; it is essential also to the preservation of our democratic system.

The Worldwide Problem
of Inflation

I am pleased to join this audience in a tribute to the members of the graduating class, and also to their parents and teachers who have done so much to make this day possible.

I would like to discuss with you today the dangerous disease of inflation—which strikes me as the economic equivalent of high blood pressure. The medical profession has recently urged all of us to have our blood pressure checked. High blood pressure damages the human body and threatens the lives of those who suffer from it. Fortunately, when diagnosed promptly, it can usually be treated successfully and brought under control.

I am not a physician, but I do know something about the economic disease of inflation. The effects of inflation are pervasive. Persistent inflation saps the energies of a nation and undermines economic and political institutions. In recent years, inflation has done great damage to the economies of many countries, including our own.

Inflation is a man-made disease. If properly treated, it can be brought under control. All of us—and especially those of you who are embarking on a new career—have a vital interest in bringing an end to the forces of inflation.

During your years here at the Institute, you have lived through the worst inflation since World War II. Over the past four years alone, consumer prices in our country have risen by 35 percent—an average increase of over 8 percent a year. Of

Commencement address at the Florida Institute of Technology, Melbourne, Florida, June 11, 1976.

late, the rise has moderated—from 12 percent in 1974 to about half that rate currently. An annual advance of 6 percent in prices, however, is still very troublesome. If such a rate persisted, the price level would double every twelve years. By 1988, the purchasing power of each of your dollars would be cut in half, and twelve years later—or by the year 2000—your already shrunken dollar would be cut in half once again.

In most other countries, inflation has been proceeding at an appreciably faster pace than in the United States. On the average, consumer prices around the world rose by 15 percent in 1974, and they were still increasing at a rate of 11 percent during the past twelve months.

There is nothing inevitable about inflation, as experience in our own and other countries indicates. The overall level of prices in the United States remained relatively stable from 1952 through 1956, and again from 1960 through 1964. During the latter period, wholesale prices actually declined a little, while consumer prices increased at an average annual rate of about 1 percent. There were similar periods of relative price stability in a number of other countries—including Canada, West Germany, Belgium, Switzerland, and Japan—during the 1950s and early 1960s.

The disease of inflation will not be cured until an aroused citizenry demands corrective measures. The intellectual leadership that you in this graduating class and your counterparts around the country can provide to the public at large will play a critical role in the success of this endeavor.

Let me therefore describe briefly the characteristics of inflation, the havoc it creates in the economic body, and the course that must be pursued to regain a stable price level and a healthy economy.

The current inflation in our country began in the middle years of the 1960s. The exuberant mood that then emerged in the business community soon gave rise to a series of interrelated and partly overlapping waves of speculation. The first speculative movement involved corporate mergers and acquisitions. Entrepreneurs who displayed special skill in such maneuvers were hailed as financial geniuses—until their newly built empires began to crumble. Many businessmen were so preoccupied with corporate acquisitions that they lost sight of traditional business objectives. The productivity of their businesses suffered, and so too did the nation's productivity.

This speculative movement was reinforced, and to a degree made possible, by the speculation that developed during the late 1960s in the market for common stocks. The prices of many stocks shot up with little regard to actual or potential earnings. Speculation in common stocks, moreover, was not confined to the United States. From the late 1960s until about 1973, nearly every major stock exchange in the world experienced a large run-up in share prices, only to be followed by a drastic decline.

The third speculative wave in our country occurred in the real estate market. It involved widespread building of shopping centers, office structures, and recreational facilities, besides land speculation and an extraordinary boom in residential construction. Between January of 1970 and January of 1973, the volume of new housing starts doubled and a huge inventory of unsold homes piled up. Once a condition of overbuilding was recognized, residential construction plunged and for a time virtually came to a halt in some sections of the country.

The real estate boom in the United States also had its parallel in other countries. For example, speculation in land and properties became rampant in the United Kingdom during the early 1970s. And in Germany, the boom in residential construction during 1971–1973 led to an enormous increase in unsold housing units—and to an inevitable downturn in homebuilding.

It is in the nature of speculative movements to spread from one country or market to another. Just as the speculative wave in real estate was beginning to taper off in 1973, a new wave of speculation got under way—this time in inventories. It involved massive stocking up of raw materials, machinery, parts, and other supplies in the United States and in other industrial countries. Serious bottlenecks and shortages began to develop in numerous industries. In the resulting environment of scarcities, the rise in prices of industrial commodities quickened both here and abroad.

One of the unfortunate consequences of inflation is that it masks underlying economic realities. As early as the spring of 1973, the trend of consumer buying in this country began to weaken. Many members of the business community, however, paid little attention to this ominous development. Nor did they recognize that standard accounting practices, which had served well enough in an era of price stability, were now masking the deterioration taking place in business profits. Caught up in the euphoria of inflation, they built up inventories out of all proportion to actual or prospective sales, thus setting the stage for a subsequent sharp decline in production and employment.

The corrosive influence of inflation goes far beyond the distortion of businessmen's perspectives. Inflation erodes the purchasing power of wages. Inflation reduces the real value of the savings deposits, pensions, and life insurance policies of consumers. Inflation creates havoc in financial markets as interest rates are driven up, funds for mortgage lending diminish, and even some large and well-managed industrial firms encounter difficulty in raising funds needed for plant expansion. In short, inflation upsets much of the planning that business firms and households customarily do. The state of confidence deteriorates, and the driving force of economic expansion is blunted.

Concerned as we all are about the economic consequences of inflation, there is even greater reason for concern about its impact on our social and political institutions. We must not risk the social stresses that persistent inflation breeds. Because of its capricious effects on the income and wealth of a nation's families and businesses, inflation inevitably causes disillusionment and discontent. It robs millions of citizens who in their desire to be self-reliant have set aside funds for the education of their children or their own retirement. It hits many of the poor and elderly especially hard. And it eventually leads to business recession and extensive unemployment, such as we have just experienced to our sorrow.

In recent years, governments have toppled in Argentina, Chile, and other countries—in large part because the citizens of those countries had lost confidence in the ability of their leaders to cope with the problem of inflation. Among our own people, the distortions, injustices, and hardships wrought by inflation have contributed materially to distrust of government officials and of government policies, and even to some loss of confidence in our free enterprise system. Discontent bred by inflation can provoke profoundly disturbing social and political change, as the history of other nations teaches. I do not believe I exaggerate in saying that the ultimate consequence of inflation could well be a significant decline of economic and political freedom for the American people.

Part of the worldwide problem of inflation in recent years is attributable to special factors—such as the extraordinary rise of OPEC oil prices in 1973, and the crop shortfalls of 1972 and 1974. But the fundamental source of inflation in our country and others has been the lack of discipline in governmental finances.

The current inflation began when our government embarked on a highly expansionist fiscal policy in the middle 1960s. Large tax reductions occurred in 1964 and early 1965 and were immediately followed by an explosion of federal spending. New and substantial tax reductions occurred again in 1969 and 1971, and they too were followed by massive increases of expenditures. Over the past ten fiscal years, the public debt—including obligations of federal credit agencies—has risen by nearly $300 billion.

Deficit spending by the federal government can be justified at a time of substantial unemployment. It becomes a source of economic instability, however, when deficits persist in good times as well as bad. Actually, the federal budget has been in deficit every year but one since 1960. The huge and persistent deficits of the past decade added enormously to aggregate demand for goods and services, but they added little to our capacity to produce. They have thus been directly responsible for a substantial part of the inflation problem.

It is sometimes contended that the federal deficits of recent years have been only a minor source of economic or financial instability, since the amounts have usually been small relative to total borrowing by the private sector. This is a faulty argument. We must never confuse the power or responsibility of private citizens with the power or responsibility of government. Business firms and consumers have no way of acting in concert to prevent an inflationary expansion of credit, and their private actions may conflict with national objectives. The basic responsibility for economic stabilization lies with the federal government. Unless our government exercises that function better than it has in the past, there will be little hope for restoration of stability in the general price level.

There are some indications, I believe, that our government

has of late been taking its fiscal responsibilities more seriously. Thus, the President has recommended a very small increase in budget outlays for the forthcoming fiscal year. Moreover, the Congress has been acting constructively in the exercise of its responsibilities under the Congressional Budget Act of 1974. There is therefore some reason for hope that total federal expenditures will not continue to advance at the frightening pace of recent years.

State and local governmental budgets are also receiving closer scrutiny nowadays. The difficulties encountered by New York City have had a tempering influence on the financial practices of states and their political subdivisions—as well as on those of other economic units—across our land. The emphasis on sound finance that is now underway enhances the chances of achieving a lasting prosperity in our country. Governments abroad are also more conscious of the need to brake the growth of public expenditures in order to contain the forces of inflation.

Monetary policy too has an important role to play in the fight against inflation, and we at the Federal Reserve are well aware of that fact. We intend to see to it that enough money and credit are available to finance a good rate of economic expansion. But we firmly intend to avoid excesses that would aggravate inflation and create trouble for the future. Many central bankers abroad aspire to a similar course of policy, but some of them are unable to adhere to it because of pressures from their finance ministers or other governmental bodies. Fortunately, under our scheme of governmental organization, the Federal Reserve can make, and stick to, the hard decisions that are at times avoided by decision makers subject to the day-to-day pressures of political life.

Prudent fiscal and monetary policies are essential ingredients of a national program to restore general price stability, but they alone may not accomplish that objective within the limits of our national patience. Structural policies are also needed to help restore full employment and to aid in correcting the long-run inflationary bias in our economy.

For example, governmental efforts are long overdue to encourage improvements in productivity through larger investment in modern plant and equipment. A vigorous search should be made for ways to enhance competition among our business enterprises. Governmental policies that affect labor markets should also be reviewed. The federal minimum wage law is still pricing many teenagers out of the labor market; the Davis-Bacon Act is still escalating costs and prices in the construction industry; and governmental programs for income maintenance now provide benefits on such a generous scale that they may be blunting incentives to work.

In some countries—for example, Canada, the United Kingdom, the Netherlands—attempts are being made to hold down wage and price increases through ceilings or guidelines. In the United Kingdom, the government has recently reached an agreement with trade union leaders to grant tax reductions in return for holding wage increases to an average of about 4½ percent during the year beginning on August 1. Such a policy would involve some decline in real income for workers in the United Kingdom. It offers promise, however, of cutting the inflation rate sharply, and of relieving the downward pressures on the pound in foreign exchange markets.

In our own country, I doubt that arrangements of that kind would be practical. It is clear, however, that restraint on the part of both workers and businesses would be helpful at the present time.

The current economic recovery is now just over a year old. In some sectors of the economy, the advance of prices has already begun to quicken—even though unemployment remains extensive and a significant part of our industrial plant is still idle. If workers now began to demand large catch-up increases in wage rates or greatly enlarged fringe benefits, or if business firms began to raise prices faster than costs to increase profit margins, prospects for a gradual further abatement of inflation and a prolonged and stable prosperity would be endangered.

I am confident that we will succeed in curing the disease of inflation if the American people remain alert to the challenge. I hope that members of this graduating class will join with me and other citizens across the country in a national crusade to protect the integrity of the dollar. This objective is within our means and is essential to a future of stable prosperity in our nation.

The Effects of Inflation
on Homebuilding

Inflation affects every American and every form of enterprise. But those who are engaged in the homebuilding industry have felt the impact of inflation with especially devastating effects in recent years. Therefore, I am truly pleased to share with this audience of mortgage lenders my conviction that we as a nation are entirely capable of achieving sustained, noninflationary expansion of our economy in the future.

Since the early months of last year, homebuilding has experienced a significant revival from the drastic slump that began in 1973. The market for single-family housing has become quite active in many parts of our country, and the improvement has recently spread also to the multi-family sector.

The homebuilding industry, nevertheless, continues to face formidable problems. Extensive unemployment is retarding sales of both new and existing homes. Builders and developers are experiencing increased costs on account of zoning ordinances and delays on sewer and water hookups. Other regulations designed to maintain environmental quality are also proving costly. The rising cost of fuel and utilities is causing some hesitation among prospective homebuyers. Higher prices of gasoline, and lingering uncertainty about its availability, are tending to discourage building in outlying areas. Inflation has pushed interest rates on home mortgages to an extremely high level. On top of that, the cost of a new home has been soaring, so that a large

Address at the annual convention of the United States League of Savings Associations, New York City, November 18, 1976.

241

and increasing proportion of our citizens now find it difficult—if not impossible—to achieve the traditional American goal of owning their own home.

Inflation is not a new problem for our nation's homebuilders. Throughout the past century, if not longer, homebuilding has tended to turn down when the general price level rose and credit markets tightened. In the first two decades after World War II, inflationary pressures were still of an episodic character, as they had been in earlier years. Once excess demand for goods and services was eliminated, the price level stabilized or actually receded. At such times, interest rates generally retreated on a broad front, and activity in the homebuilding industry soon rebounded strongly.

Since the mid-sixties, however, the general level of prices has kept going up in both good times and bad. The problem of inflation has thus taken on a new and ominous character. No appreciable slowdown in the advance of wages and prices occurred during the mild recession of 1970. During the severe recession in late 1974 and early 1975, inflation did decline— from an annual rate of about 13 percent to 7 percent. In part, this slowing of inflation reflected the absence of special factors— such as the enormous increase of OPEC oil prices and the lifting of wage and price controls—that had caused prices to skyrocket in 1974. But since mid-1975, despite continued high unemployment and much idle industrial capacity, there has been little further decline in the underlying rate of inflation.

I have on other occasions discussed at length the reasons why inflation has become chronic in our country. Large and persistent deficits in the federal budget were directly responsible for the accelerating inflation of the late 1960s and early 1970s. Lack of discipline in governmental finances has thus been the dominant source of the problem. And as often happens in human affairs, laxity in national financial policies spilled over into private markets.

Many businessmen and financiers came to believe that the business cycle was dead—that governmental policies could be relied upon to keep the economy expanding indefinitely. Canons of prudent management that had been developed through years of hard experience came to be regarded as old-fashioned or were simply forgotten. Hence, many investment projects were undertaken carelessly; and liquidity positions and equity cushions were allowed to deteriorate, while debts piled up at a rapid pace. In this environment, even as the productivity of our nation's workshops languished, the resistance of business managers to demands for wage increases weakened, and trade unions used their growing power to push up wage rates far above productivity gains.

With business caution giving way to exuberance, speculative fever mounted. The first major wave of speculation, which began in 1965, resulted in numerous corporate mergers, including the formation of all sorts of conglomerates. This merger movement was reinforced, and to a degree made possible, by the speculative movement that developed in the market for common stocks. The volume of trading on the New York Stock Exchange doubled within five years, prices of many stocks shot up with little regard to actual or potential earnings, and the new breed of "performance funds" flourished.

A little later, during the early 1970s, another speculative wave engulfed the market for real estate. Merchant builders moved ahead energetically in response to easy credit and federal subsidies. Single-family homes were put up well ahead of demand, and the inventory of unsold homes doubled between 1970 and 1973. Speculative activity was even more intense in the case of apartments built for renting, and particularly in condominiums and cooperatives—which accounted for a fourth of the completions of multi-family structures by the first half of 1974. Vacancies in rental properties therefore kept increasing after 1970.

The speculative boom in real estate was not confined to residential structures. It extended to speculation in land, to building of shopping centers, and to construction of office buildings. By 1972, the vacancy rate in office buildings across the nation reached 13 percent, but this type of construction still kept climbing.

As the pace of inflation quickened, seeds of serious trouble were sown across the economy. Fearing shortages and further price increases, business firms frantically stockpiled industrial materials and other supplies during 1973 and early 1974. Interest rates climbed to unprecedented heights. Many of the major industrial corporations, and even some our nation's banks, found themselves in a somewhat precarious financial condition. The recession that inevitably followed was by far the most serious of the postwar period, and the collapse of housing production played a major role in the depth and severity of the general economic decline.

In the course of the recession, many of the imbalances that had developed among the various sectors of the economy were reduced. Determined efforts to cut costs and improve efficiency got under way. Inflationary tensions moderated, and the condition of financial markets improved.

These and related adjustments paved the way for a recovery of homebuilding and other branches of production. As conditions in financial markets eased and interest rates declined, the inflow of deposits to mortgage lenders—particularly to saving and loan associations—rose swiftly. Sales of new and existing houses increased, inventories of unsold units gradually moved down, and new housing starts began to rise. A full recovery of residential building has, however, eluded us—and it will continue to elude us until our nation makes further progress in freeing itself from the grip of inflation.

One of the most damaging results of inflation is the persistence of high interest rates. The basic reason for the high interest rates in our times—particularly on mortgages and other long-term debt contracts—is the relentless rise of the general price level since 1965. Inflationary expectations have by now become well entrenched in the calculations of both lenders and borrowers. Lenders reckon that loans may be repaid in dollars of smaller purchasing power, and they therefore tend to hold out for nominal rates of interest that are high enough to ensure a reasonable real rate of return. Borrowers, in their turn, are often less resistant to rising costs of credit, because they too anticipate repayment in cheaper currency.

The marking up of nominal rates of interest during periods of inflation is a process that is all too familiar to economic historians. Businessmen and laymen, too, have seen its recent manifestation in Great Britain and Italy, to say nothing of some Latin American countries. High interest rates are a companion of inflation, and both pose perils for the housing industry.

The underlying rate of inflation now appears to be around 6 percent, and it could well increase as our economy returns to higher levels of resource utilization. Participants in financial markets are keenly aware of this. Although fears of inflation have lessened and long-term interest rates have fallen, they still contain a sizable inflation premium. For example, home mortgage interest rates have declined by 1 to 1½ percentage points from their cyclical highs in 1974, but they still run close to 9 percent at present.

The effect of these high mortgage interest rates on the ability of potential homebuyers to meet monthly payments has been compounded by the explosion of housing prices. The median price of a new home today is close to $45,000—nearly double the level that prevailed in 1970. Over the past six years, the prices of new homes have risen almost twice as fast as the average level of consumer prices—and they are still increasing.

Other costs of homeownership have also skyrocketed. Since late 1973, the cost of fuel and utilities has risen by roughly 50 percent. In the aggregate, property taxes and other costs of home ownership—such as insurance, maintenance, and repairs—have outstripped by far the average rise of family incomes.

For a time, increasing numbers of families sought to meet their housing needs by purchasing a modestly priced mobile home. Sales of this type of dwelling rose by almost 50 percent between 1970 and 1972. Since then, the average retail price of mobile homes has nearly doubled, rising to its present level of about $13,000; the cost of buying or renting a site has also increased. For many families, the purchase of even a mobile home has become prohibitively expensive, and sales of these units are now proceeding at only a third of their volume four years ago.

The effects of inflation on homebuilding activity have been even more severe in the multi-family sector than in the markets for single-family homes. Starts of single-family houses—although still somewhat below their 1972 level—have at least shown a good recovery since early 1975. Starts of multi-family units, on the other hand, did not begin to rise until this summer, and they are still running at a level less than half that of four years ago.

Continued weakness in apartment construction partly reflects the overbuilding of condominiums and rental units in many parts of the country during the speculative boom of the early

1970s. Over the past year and a half, the demand for rental space has risen and the vacancy rate for rental units has generally declined. Nevertheless, the slump in constructing multi-family buildings has continued.

Inflation has created serious difficulties for developers and investors in the multi-family sector. In an inflationary environment, prospective construction costs are highly uncertain for a project that takes a considerable time to complete—as is the case with apartment buildings. Moreover, high interest rates on construction and mortgage loans cut deeply into profits, and investors have become apprehensive about their ability to achieve a level of net income adequate to compensate them for the risks they must incur. In recent years, rent increases have lagged behind the rising costs of operation. Since mid-1973, average rents have advanced about 15 percent, while costs of operating apartment houses increased over 25 percent.

This lag in rents reflects the relatively long-term character of many rental contracts, besides some concern that rising rents may provoke angry protests from tenants. Rent controls have also become a limiting factor. They are presently in effect in over 200 communities in which 15 percent of our urban population resides. Moreover, the fear of coming rent controls may be moderating rent increases in other areas—where rent ceilings are permitted but not yet in effect, or where rent control is now being seriously discussed.

In view of the continuing difficulties confronting the multi-family sector, commercial banks and other lenders are still cautious in committing funds to builders and developers for apartment construction, or in providing the necessary long-term financing. Moreover, real estate investment trusts, which got into trouble during the speculative boom in multi-family residential construction, still face very difficult financial problems. For the past two years they have been liquidating mortgages, and few of them are yet in any position to make sizable new loan commitments.

Of course, progress has been made over the past two years in dealing with the many problems surrounding multi-family construction. That is why activity in that sector of the home-building industry is now moving up again. Realistically, however, we cannot expect a return to boom conditions in the construction of rental buildings or condominiums in any near future, and that—I believe—is fortunate. A gradual and sustainable rise in the volume of multi-family construction will do far more for the health of the housing industry, and also for the health of our national economy, than would a resurgence of speculative exuberance.

I hope that this preference for solid and sustainable progress will guide our governmental housing policies. When unemployment is as high as it is currently, policy makers face persistent pressures to pump up activity in housing and other industries through monetary and fiscal measures. Expansionist financial policies have considerable merit as a means of reducing unemployment when the price level is relatively stable or declining. But such policies are apt to be less effective when unemployment and inflation go together—which has become our ordeal.

In practically every industrial nation around the world, the rapid inflation of the early 1970s led to larger precautionary savings, sluggish consumer buying, and a weakening of business confidence. In the present environment of deeply ingrained inflationary expectations, the results of traditional policies of economic stimulation are less predictable and less dependable than they were in earlier decades. The risk is greater now that fears of inflation will intensify and substantially weaken the intended effects of expansionist policies on business investment and consumer spending.

I have been asked recently whether a tax cut is desirable at present. For the reasons I have already suggested, and also because I anticipate a resurgence of the economy, I see no advantage in a tax cut at the present time. My mind on this subject, however, is by no means closed. Later on, I will weigh the issue carefully if economic conditions or expenditure economies seem to warrant a tax reduction. I might add that if it appeared desirable to attempt to stimulate the economy through a tax cut, among other ways, I would be inclined to favor the type of measure that President Kennedy recommended in the early 1960s —namely, a broadly based tax reduction for both individuals and businesses. Such a measure, on a responsible scale, would minimize social conflict and have the best chance of producing lasting economic benefits for our country.

In the case of the housing industry, as in other sectors of

the economy, we would be well advised to use the traditional measures of monetary and fiscal stimulation cautiously and to rely more on structural policies that can contribute to reduction of unemployment without risking a new wave of price increases or otherwise creating problems for the future. For example, much of the construction industry activity across our land is still subject to outmoded building codes and work rules that hamper productivity. The wage provisions of the Davis-Bacon Act continue to escalate construction costs. And more realistic apprenticeship programs could certainly be developed to improve the supply of skilled labor in the building trades.

We also need to reassess the consequences of the various environmental regulations adopted in recent years. These regulations have introduced long delays in obtaining approval for building projects and have otherwise run up the costs of real estate development and operation. At the federal level alone, a dozen environmental regulations may apply to any given housing project. Moreover, overlapping regulations at the federal, state, and local levels, besides causing confusion and delay, sometimes work at cross purposes.

Environmental regulations offer great promise for improving the quality of life; they are essential to human welfare in a modern society. But in our eagerness to improve the environment, we should try to avoid regulations that unnecessarily impede investment in housing and in business fixed capital. These too are essential to economic and social progress.

Structural reforms to smooth out the flow of mortgage credit would also be in the long-run interest of homebuilding. State usury laws are not now a major impediment to the flow of mortgage credit to potential home buyers. They were, however, a year or two ago, and they might again become a major obstacle in the future. We should continue to work for their removal. Further steps should also be taken to reduce the instability of savings flows to saving and loan associations and other financial institutions that supply funds for home financing.

In particular, I believe our nation would be well served by larger use of variable-rate mortgages, with attendant safeguards, so that savings institutions could raise the rates they pay on deposits during periods of rising market interest rates and thereby sustain deposit inflows. Such a development would be beneficial to small savers as well as to the mortgage market, and it would diminish the need for regulatory interest-rate ceilings on savings deposits.

It has at times been suggested that the recurring financing problems of the housing industry would be relieved, if not actually solved, by contractual arrangements that make it easier to live with inflation—such as mortgages whose principal is adjusted according to the cost of living, or savings deposits whose purchasing power is guaranteed. Such suggestions are neither sound nor practical. For one thing, there is no feasible way to renegotiate already outstanding mortgages or other long-term loan contracts. But unless that were done, the institutions that guaranteed the purchasing power of their deposits would expose themselves to intolerable risk. More important, if a nation with our traditions ever embarked on a systematic plan to make it easier to live with inflation, rather than to resist its corrosive influence, we would slowly but steadily lose the sense of discipline needed to pursue governmental policies with an eye to the permanent welfare of our people.

The single most important step our government could take to improve the long-run prospects for homebuilding activity— and for the economy at large—would be to gain better control over the forces of inflation. Restoration of reasonable stability of the general price level would lead to a sharp decline of interest rates on home mortgages. It would certainly reduce substantially the rise of construction costs, housing prices, and home maintenance and operating expenses. Residential builders would then be able to project their revenues and expenditures with greater confidence, as would also the ultimate investors providing capital for large-scale development projects. There can be little doubt that an environment of stable prices would assure a brighter future for homebuilding.

Bringing an end to inflation would be equally beneficial to other major sectors of our economy—in particular, to business capital investment. Businessmen were unprepared for the slump in sales and production that resulted in 1974 and early 1975 from an inflationary process that got out of control and undermined the strength of our economy. In the aftermath of this harsh experience, the renewal of confidence needed for a new surge of investment activity has proceeded rather slowly.

But once it becomes clear that the recent gains in the struggle against inflation are being extended, confidence in our nation's economic future is likely to deepen, and business firms should begin to move forward more boldly with long-term investment projects.

Progress in reducing inflation must therefore remain a major objective of public policy, along with reestablishment of reasonably full employment and reasonably full utilization of our industrial capacity. Actually, these policy objectives are inseparable. The experience of other countries around the world, as well as our own, indicates that lasting prosperity cannot be attained in an environment in which expectations of inflation remain intense.

The principal contribution that the Federal Reserve can now make to the achievement of our nation's basic economic objectives is to adhere to a course of moderation in monetary policy. That principle has guided our efforts to facilitate economic recovery and prevent a new wave of inflation. Firm adherence to a policy of moderation has helped to build confidence that inflation will taper off. And this in turn has made it possible for interest rates to decline even as economic activity has kept expanding.

Monetary policy alone, however, cannot solve our nation's stubborn problem of inflation. We must work also to eliminate its primary source—the persistent deficits in the federal budget. And we need to give far more attention to structural measures for lessening the powerful bias toward inflation that has been created within our economy by imperfectly functioning markets and a host of governmental regulations that impede the competitive process and run up costs for business enterprises.

As we have learned, there is no easy way out of the inflationary morass into which we have strayed through negligence and imperfect vision. But we are making progress. I am confident that we will succeed if the American people, who are alert as never before to the danger of inflation, remain steadfast. This association has in the past played a vital role in educating our citizens about the dangers of inflation and in encouraging government officials to pursue responsible financial policies. I strongly urge you to expand your educational efforts. For in the measure that we succeed in reducing inflation, we will restore the conditions essential to a stable prosperity—for the home-building industry and for the economy at large. Triumph over inflation, I believe, is well within our means.

Some Parting Thoughts

Let me say first of all that I am most appreciative of the invitation to appear before you. In making my final public appearance as Chairman of the Federal Reserve Board here at the National Press Club, I take some pride in thinking that my relations with the press over the years have been forthright and decent. I at least like to think that I have avoided the "us" and "them" mentality that so often afflicts public figures in their dealings with the press. Certainly, the press has generally treated both me and the Federal Reserve System fairly. For my part, I have found the press a vigilant ally in the endless task of contributing to public understanding of the problems before our nation.

Having spent much of my life wrestling with the subtleties and uncertainties of political economy, I am sensitively aware of the pitfalls that surround coverage of economic and financial news. I say most sincerely that I have great admiration for the professional job that the press corps does, day after day, in reporting and interpreting economic developments. To this assessment I have only one qualification, namely, that broadcast journalism still is not as effective as it might be in dealing with economic news. I recognize, of course, that the constraint of limited time slots presents formidable difficulties. In any event, written journalism, as it applies to economics, has in my judgment attained truly impressive maturity.

This luncheon is not a "good-bye," since I may be doing some things in the future that will interest you professionally.

Address at the National Press Club, Washington, D.C., January 30, 1978.

In fact, it's not beyond the realm of possibility that I may even be joining your ranks in one capacity or another. Those in town who think the time for farewell has come are mistaken. Neither a shedding of tears—nor any special rejoicing—is yet in order.

There are a few thoughts I would like to share with you on this occasion. The economy is doing very well in some respects and poorly in others. In analyzing trends, I find it helpful to distinguish between the performance of the economy in recovering from the recent recession and its performance in coping with longer-run, deeply imbedded problems.

The economic expansion that began almost three years ago still has vitality in my estimation and I see no serious risk that it will peter out soon. The upsurge in sales with which 1977 ended caused inventories to be drawn down in numerous businesses, thus creating a likelihood that overall economic activity will receive a special fillip for a while from businessmen's efforts to rebuild stocks. And with consumer activity, housing activity, and governmental activity all still exhibiting expansionary tendencies, I believe that further gains in employment and income lie ahead.

Business investment activity, to be sure, is still not showing decisive robustness. This reflects the uncertainties and unease that continue to haunt our business and financial environment. I expect, nevertheless, that the tax relief which the President has proposed for business will lead to a strengthening of investment commitments as 1978 unfolds. In saying this, I do not mean to embrace each and every aspect of the administration's tax and budgetary strategy. Many of you know my views well enough to appreciate that a tax program structured to my liking would be tilted more decisively toward the stimulation of savings and investment. I think you also know that I feel that tax reduction at this stage of economic expansion should be primarily accommodated by limiting expenditures, so that significant shrinkage in the federal budget deficit might still be achieved. But on the specific issue of tax reduction for business, I do believe that what has been proposed will help to relieve the low level of corporate profitability that has prevailed in recent times and thus constitutes an important plus for the capital-goods outlook this year and next.

So much for the bright side of the coin. The generally good record of our economy in terms of recovery from recession stands in marked contrast to a virtual absence of progress in coping with the overlay of our longer-term economic problems. I am thinking particularly, of course, of the dispiriting failure we have experienced in making headway against inflation. I am thinking also of our inability to solve the structural unemployment that is causing so many young people and blacks to be left outside the mainstream of national progress. And while most people probably think of our well-publicized balance-of-payments difficulties as being of recent origin, they too in fact are the product to a considerable extent of deep-rooted ailments that we have not dealt with effectively.

Last year witnessed no progress toward a less inflationary environment. Rather, the basic inflation rate settled in the 6 percent area, reflecting the difference between average annual pay increments of labor that are running above 8 percent and productivity gains that are averaging little more than 2 percent.

While the discrepancy between wage and productivity increases is tending at present to perpetuate inflation, it is important to recognize that the inflationary problem with which this nation is burdened did not originate with an irresponsible wage push on the part of American workers or their unions. Rather, the tragic skein of events in which we are caught is chiefly traceable to fundamental mistakes of governmental policy made in the mid-1960s. Those mistakes involved overstimulation of the economy at the very time our military involvement in Vietnam was escalating and when we were also embarking upon Great Society programs that were to become an increasingly heavy drain on the federal budget. The pressures on available resources generated in the mid-1960s started us on a path of enormous budget deficits and rapid inflation from which we have not been able to disengage ourselves. Indeed, we have continued to compound our problem by seeking to fine-tune the economy by governmental fiscal actions that, in my judgment, have weakened the private sector's dynamism and efficiency.

Events of recent years, such as major crop failures and the sharp rise in oil prices, have merely aggravated the underlying inflationary bias that our government, under both Republican and Democratic administrations, has imparted to the economy. Other

255

developments—such as the escalator arrangements sought and achieved by various economic groups— have speeded the transmission of inflationary impulses across the economy. In sum, over an extended span of time, we as a nation first created enormous upward pressures on the price structure, and we then devised elaborate arrangements that tend to perpetuate those pressures even under conditions of economic slack.

The inflation plaguing our economy may not end quickly. Government has, however, a special leadership role in the pursuit of moderate fiscal and monetary policies, in encouraging wage restraint by way of example, and in many other particulars. But private actions are critical too, ranging from more determined pursuit of productivity gains to the conduct of collective bargaining in ways that are more responsible in a broad social sense. We see nowadays too many excessive wage settlements entered into by managements and trade unions, who then band together in seeking governmental protection from the market consequences of their own actions.

The need to fight inflation is widely recognized in our country, but the will to do so is not yet strong enough. I have no doubt that the will to get on energetically with the job of unwinding the inflation will be forged someday. I only hope this will come through a growth of understanding, not from a demonstration that inflation is the mortal enemy of economic progress and our political freedom.

And just as we need a more determined approach to the challenge of inflation, so too do we need fresh initiatives for dealing with structural rigidities in the job market. The heavy incidence of unemployment among young people and blacks will not be remedied by general monetary and fiscal policies. We need, instead, specialized efforts: first, efforts to overcome serious educational deficiencies so that individual job seekers will possess greater marketable skills; second, efforts to eradicate impediments that stand in the way of job opportunities for young people and minorities even when the potential for effective job performance is present. These impediments include federal and state minimum-wage laws, restrictive practices of various craft unions in limiting membership, unnecessary licensing and certification requirements for many jobs and business undertakings, and—I must add to our shame—continuing racial discrimination.

This nation can have no greater priority than to end the tragic human wastage that we have been allowing to occur.

The disappointing aspects of economic performance are not confined to the domestic sphere. Full prosperity in this country can hardly be achieved in the absence of a healthy world economy and a stable international financial system. The recent steep decline in the value of the dollar in foreign exchange markets—precipitated in large part by our enormous trade deficit—has become a matter of serious concern.

To be sure, there are those who argue that recent exchange market developments are not worrisome. Indeed, much of conventional wisdom holds that a depreciating currency will improve a nation's trade position and, in turn, benefit its economy. Whatever merit may attach to this theory, it would serve our country poorly—particularly at the present time when such a large part of the world's economy is in a semi-stagnant condition.

The dollar, we must remember, is the currency in which the preponderance of world trade is conducted. It is also a store of value for practically every central bank, for multinational corporations, and for people of wealth and means around the world as well as for the American people. Continued uncertainty about the future value of the dollar could produce a disorderly, unsettling flight from dollar assets. It could lead to hesitation about spending or investing decisions around the world that would be inimical to prosperity—including the expansion of our exports. If the currencies of some foreign countries, especially those that depend heavily on exports, should experience significant further appreciation, their economies might well suffer. Such a development could reinforce recessionary tendencies and add to the risk of fostering protectionist sentiment around the world.

That the depreciation of the dollar has recently added to economic uncertainties both here and abroad is well understood by the administration. That is why the President has reassured the world about our country's determination to protect the integrity of the dollar. That is why the Treasury and the Federal Reserve have recently taken steps that have been helpful to the functioning of foreign exchange markets. But the technical measures so far taken cannot of themselves assure a permanently strong dollar.

To protect the integrity of the dollar, we must enact without further delay an energy policy that promises substantial reduction of our dependence on imported oil. Second, we need to institute tax policies that encourage business capital investment—including investment in this country by foreigners. Indeed, policies that make the United States a more attractive haven for foreign funds are especially important, since we cannot reasonably expect dramatic improvement over the near term in the trade portion of our international payments accounts. Finally, our international payments imbalance requires an anti-inflation strategy that promises to enhance the competitiveness of our products in international markets.

These requirements of policy will not only serve to strengthen the foreign-exchange value of the dollar and thus the entire international financial system. They are equally essential from the viewpoint of our domestic economy. An effective energy policy, a tax policy to stimulate capital investment, and a meaningful anti-inflation policy—all this, as the administration recognizes, is vital to our domestic prosperity.

Before closing, I want to comment very briefly on a matter that, to my mind, can make an enormous difference to the future of our country. I refer to the special status of the Federal Reserve System within our government structure.

Throughout the ages, national governments have had a chronic tendency to engage in activities that outstrip the taxes they are willing or able to collect—a practice that was facilitated in earlier times by clipping precious coins and in modern times by excessive printing of paper money and coercion of central banks. To afford a measure of protection against such political abuses, the authors of the Federal Reserve Act provided for an independent central bank, and their action—while at times questioned—has been confirmed time and again by the Congress. In other words, substantial independence in exercising power over money creation is not something that Federal Reserve officials have arrogated unto themselves, nor is it something that others have conferred because of a belief that central bankers have unique insight that sets them apart from other people. Rather, the ability of the Federal Reserve to act with some independence from the executive branch, and also with immunity from transient congressional pressures, was deliberately established and has been deliberately maintained by the Congress in the interest of protecting the integrity of our money.

In leaving the chairmanship of the Federal Reserve Board, I am especially pleased that President Carter has unequivocally assured the American people of his own conviction that an independent Federal Reserve serves our national interest. On that happy note, ladies and gentlemen, I will now end and turn to your questions.

PART THREE

Fiscal Responsibility

The Control of Government Expenditures

This year the Congress has devoted a great deal of attention to tax legislation. Besides aiding the fight against inflation by extending the income tax surcharge temporarily, the Congress has been heavily engaged in writing a tax reform bill that is of major significance to the American public. If the bill survives in something like its present form, some troublesome inequities under existing law will finally be corrected. However, the relative tax burden borne by individuals and corporations will also be changed, with corporate income tax liabilities gradually going up about $5 billion by 1975 and individual income taxes coming down $12 billion.

This projected shift in the tax structure will favor consumption at the expense of capital formation. Such a development will be useful in the short run by helping to cool off the business investment boom that is still under way, but it may damage prospects for the long-term growth of our economy. We surely cannot afford to take capital formation or economic progress for granted. If our economy is to grow and prosper in the future, as it both can and should, business enterprise may well need the stimulation of an improving tax climate.

In recent times, our nation has moved rapidly towards the welfare state, such as various European countries previously developed. Unlike these countries, however, we also devote an enormous part of our resources to meeting the needs of an intri-

---

Address at the annual award dinner of the Tax Foundation, New York City, December 2, 1969.

263

cate and far-flung defense system. Thus far, the prodigious productivity of American industry has made it possible to finance liberally both our defense needs and the social services of government. But in order to continue to support the growing scale of our public consumption without doing injury to private consumption, the productivity of our factories, mines, farms, construction enterprises, and service trades may have to improve more rapidly than in the past. This will not be accomplished without substantial and increasing investment in new and better tools of production. The projected shift in the structure of taxation therefore seems undesirable to me, and I trust that the President's Task Force on Business Taxation will soon point the way to better balance in our tax system.

I do not know at precisely what point the burdens of taxation will materially serve to check our nation's economic progress, but I also do not think it wise to test this issue too closely. The trend of governmental spending and taxes in the past forty years has been sharply and inexorably upward. In 1929, government expenditures at the federal, state, and local levels amounted to about 10 percent of the dollar value of the nation's production. This fraction rose to about 20 percent in 1940, to about 30 percent in 1960, and to about 35 percent this year. The broad trend of taxation has been very similar. With over a third of our nation's output already moving into the hands of the tax collector, it seems hardly prudent to contemplate any further increase in the level of taxation. And yet, unless we bring government expenditures under better control than we yet have, the modest overall reduction of tax rates that the tax reform bill projects will prove abortive and further increases in the level of taxation may become unavoidable.

As our nation's economy has grown and as our political democracy has widened, the responsibilities assumed by government have kept increasing. In fiscal year 1962, the rising curve of federal expenditures first crossed the $100 billion mark. It now appears likely that the $200 billion mark will be crossed the next fiscal year; so that we will be adding as much to the federal spending rate in a mere nine years as it took nearly two centuries to achieve previously.

The explosive increase of federal spending during this decade is commonly attributed to the defense establishment, or more simply to the war in Vietnam. The fact is, however, that civilian programs are the preponderant cause of the growth of the federal budget. When we compare the budget of 1964 with the estimates for this fiscal year, we find that total federal spending shows a rise of $74 billion, while defense outlays are larger by only $23 billion. If we go back to 1953, when the Korean war ended, and take into account state and local expenditures as well as federal, we find that defense outlays have been responsible for only about one-sixth of the vast increase in the cost of government that has occurred since then.

Thus, the basic fiscal fact is that spending for social programs now dominates our public budgets. Although the federal government's direct involvement in problems of social welfare is a recent development, it is already huge and is growing at a fast rate. This fiscal year, programs for education, manpower, health, income security, housing, community development, and crime prevention will cost over $80 billion—a sum that exceeds all the spending done by the federal government in the peak year of the Korean war. Federal aid to the poor will alone cost $27 billion this year, in contrast to $12 billion in 1964. Grants in aid to states and localities will cost about $25 billion, in contrast to $15 billion in 1967, $10 billion in 1964, and $5 billion in 1958.

This upsurge of federal spending is a response to the economic and social difficulties that afflict many of our communities—witness the slums, ghettoes, racial strife, poor public schools, teenage unemployment, drug addiction, poor health, student disorders, inadequate transportation, traffic congestion, air and water pollution, and unsafe streets and parks. The federal government has tried to solve these complex problems by spending large sums of money on projects that have often been hastily devised. Hundreds of grant-in-aid programs dealing with health, education, welfare, and other local needs were established in quick succession. Several regional commissions were established to seek better balance in economic development and social improvement. An Economic Development Administration was established to aid local communities, both urban and rural, that suffer from excessive unemployment or inadequate incomes. More recently, a Model Cities Program was established, aspiring to achieve what our best city planners can contrive. By proceeding in all these directions, we have created a costly governmental maze that involves much duplication and waste, that often hampers the constructive efforts of local officials, and—perhaps worst of all—that practically defies full understanding or evaluation.

Nowadays, many local government officials, instead of grappling with the most urgent needs of their communities, devote their finest energy to maximizing and husbanding the federal grants that happen to be available. With over 600 categorical programs of federal aid to choose from, there is plenty to keep them busy. Many of the programs involve tedious procedural steps extending over a number of months before a community can learn whether federal funds are to be granted for its proposed project. Each program is equipped with its own set of administrative requirements involving endless forms and reports. If a local official attempts to draw upon several funding sources to help finance a neighborhood project, he may be confronted with a mass of complex application forms weighing several pounds, with federal processing steps that may take well over a year to elicit a "yes" or "no" response, and with stringent requirements for hundreds of detailed reports. Further, this official will usually have to work with federal representatives scattered in a number of different cities in order to arrange the project.

I am informed by the Bureau of the Budget that one federal program requires over 100 different kinds of forms and reports; that a grant involving $1,000 may require over 30 major federal agency steps, including review by a 15-man advisory committee and headquarters approval; that a department of one state has counted 120 different reports that it is required to submit to a particular federal agency, many of them on a monthly or quarterly basis; and that there are numerous instances in which federal, state, and local governments make independent studies of the same community without one agency knowing what the other is doing, or having an opportunity to share in the results of the other studies. The mere listing of all federal requirements imposed on states and communities would be so voluminous that it has never been done.

As a result of this administrative morass, various federal programs are half smothered in paper. Employees at all levels of government are required to devote time to detailed paper work which would be better devoted to rethinking program objectives or assessing the extent to which present objectives are being met. More important, help may not reach the people who need it until months—sometimes years—after it should, with much of the money meanwhile siphoned off by the bureaucracy. To give only a few outstanding examples, neither the achievements of the compensatory education program, nor of the urban renewal and slum clearance programs, nor of the public assistance programs have come very close to the expectations of our lawmakers.

In view of the explosive growth of federal spending and the ineffectiveness or inefficiency of much of it, I am inclined to think that the need for expenditure reform may be even greater than the need for tax reform. One of the advantages of a new administration is that it can move with energy to change the direction of governmental policy. President Nixon responded to this opportunity by taking major steps to win control over federal spending. Needless to say, the rapid rise of the consumer price level has been the most troublesome economic problem facing the nation this year. In view of the inflationary pressures in our markets for goods and services, it was clearly important that the federal government curb its spending beyond the earnest move to frugality that the previous Administration made in its closing days. In all, reductions of $7½ billion from the January budget were therefore ordered by the President for this fiscal year. These reductions were widely distributed among government agencies, with $4.1 billion allocated to the Defense Department and $3.4 billion to the rest of the government. Moreover, when Congress later passed or considered legislation that foreshadowed an expenditure total well above the revised budget of $192.9 billion that the President had submitted, he firmly announced that he would try his utmost to see to it that federal finances continue to be subject to the ceiling that he had imposed. Later in the year, in order to deal with the special problem of runaway construction costs, the President ordered a cutback of 75 percent in federal construction contracts.

Administrative steps were also taken by the President to achieve greater efficiency in government spending. In March a carefully planned effort to cut red tape got under way. As a first step, the several agencies most closely concerned with human resources were directed to adopt common regional boundaries and to locate their regional offices in the same cities. Further, a review was started of the several hundred federal assistance programs, with the objective of simplifying procedure, cutting down on the paper work, and shifting responsibilities to the field so that decisions could be made both more expeditiously and by officials who are in closer touch with the local problems.

The administration has also sought legislation to correct the deficiencies of the grant-in-aid programs. In order to give local officials greater flexibility to meet their priority needs, the President has requested authority to consolidate existing grant-in-aid categories, subject to a congressional veto within sixty days. Moreover, as legislation has moved through the Congress, the administration has been alert to the opportunity of converting narrow categorical grants into block grants for broad functional areas. In line with this policy, proposals for grant consolidation were advanced in connection with legislation on hospital construction, on elementary and secondary school education, and on manpower training services, as well as through the appropriations route.

But by far the most important as well as the most dramatic step that the President has taken to reform expenditure policy is his proposal to the Congress to inaugurate a system of revenue sharing. This proposal marks a milestone in federal-state relations. It seeks to decentralize governmental power. It seeks to restore the balance that existed in earlier decades between the state capitals and the national capital. Or to be more precise, while it seeks to extend additional federal assistance to state and local government, it insists that this be done in a manner that will enable local officials to attend to urgent problems within their own jurisdictions as they deem best, without being subjected to rigid federal controls or requirements.

The leading features of the administration's revenue sharing proposals are as follows: First, in view of budgetary constraints, the revenue sharing fund will be limited in fiscal 1971 to a half billion dollars, but will subsequently grow fairly rapidly and reach $5 billion by the mid-seventies. Second, the distribution of the fund among the states will be based on a simple formula that assigns primary weight to population, but also gives some weight to tax effort. Third, the distribution within each state between the state government and the localities will be likewise based on a formula, so that each unit of government within a state will be assured a share that is proportionate to its own tax revenues. Fourth, no restriction will be placed on the use of the funds made available by the federal government; in other words, each state, county, city, or town will rely on its own judgment and use the money for education, health services, parks, law enforcement, or some other way, as it deems best.

The precise details of this revenue sharing plan grew out of detailed discussions among members of the administration, congressmen, governors, mayors, and county officials. In the course of these discussions the argument was sometimes encountered that revenue sharing may lead to fiscal irresponsibility, since local officials may be careless in using funds that they did not have to raise from their own constituents. This argument cannot be dismissed. It might in fact be decisive if the practical choice were between levying local taxes or federal taxes. By all indications, however, federal financial assistance to the states and localities will continue to grow, and the only real question is whether federal grants will lead to more or to less centralized control. In taking a definite stand for decentralization, the administration has enunciated a policy whose wisdom is now widely recognized by liberals as well as conservatives within our two major political parties.

As a result of the careful preparation of the administration's revenue sharing plan, it has already won the general approval of the Governors' Conference and also of the leading national organizations of mayors and county officials. The administration's own thinking on the subject is not rigid, and it will entertain any reasonable proposal for change that would facilitate congressional approval. In particular, the administration would welcome an enlargement of the projected revenue sharing fund, provided categorical grants were correspondingly curtailed. If that happened, revenue sharing would grow more rapidly than presently contemplated, and the decentralization of government—which has become so vital to order and efficiency in the public economy—would be speeded.

This sketch of recent progress toward federal expenditure

reform should be reassuring to responsible citizens, but it certainly leaves no room for complacency. Much of the needed legislation has yet to be passed. Many of the administrative improvements are still in an early stage and remain to be tested. The ceiling of $192.9 billion on this year's expenditure is not entirely secure. True, the curve of federal spending is now rising at a much slower pace than in recent years, but the improvement would be less impressive if the various government-sponsored financial agencies were all included in the budget. And, as far as I can judge, the growth of population, the need to improve our social and physical environment, and the widening concept of governmental responsibility will almost inevitably lead to large additions to federal as well as state and local expenditures in the future. There will therefore be a continuing need to control governmental spending, first, in order to avoid strain on our physical resources of labor and capital, second, in order to assure the continuance of a vigorous private sector, and third, in order to maintain pressure for discriminating judgment on priorities as well as for economy of execution in the public sector. These are difficult requirements and they will not be met without further significant expenditure reform.

One major step toward reform was taken last year and again this year by congressional enactment of a ceiling on expenditures. A legislative budget is a radical departure in budget making, and its significance should not be minimized by the rubbery texture of the ceiling. In the first place, the vigorous discussion surrounding the legislative ceiling has of itself served to dampen enthusiasm for larger spending. In the second place, the rubbery ceiling of today can become a rigid ceiling tomorrow. If the Congress moves in this direction, its fragmented approach to appropriations, which will doubtless continue, need no longer run up federal spending as it has commonly done in the past.

To be sure, the individual appropriation acts may imply a much larger expenditure total than had previously been legislated. In that event, the Congress would in effect say to the President: "You are the manager of our national finances. We fixed a ceiling on expenditures earlier in the year, after considering your budgetary recommendations and making our own best judgment of what the national interest requires. But there are several hundred of us; each of us is subject to heavy pressure for appropriations that seem vital to our constituents, and we find it impossible in the time at our disposal to trim individual appropriations so that they be consistent with the expenditure ceiling. In view of our inability to agree on priorities, we assign this responsibility to you; but we naturally reserve the right to challege your actions by new legislation." Such a mandate by the Congress would, of course, not make the President's job any easier; it could well lead at times to uneconomical cutbacks; and it might even mean that we will have only one-term presidents in the future. However, by enabling the members of Congress to satisfy both their conscience and their constituents, such a mandate would help powerfully to assure that total expenditure is kept under decent control.

A second reform of vital significance would be adoption of the concept of zero-base budgeting. Customarily, the officials in charge of an established program have to justify only the increase which they seek above last year's appropriation. In other words, what they are already spending is usually accepted as necessary, without examination. Substantial savings could undoubtedly be realized if both the Budget Bureau examiners and the congressional appropriations committees required every agency to make a case for its entire appropriation request each year, just as if its program or programs were entirely new. Such a budgeting procedure may be difficult to achieve, partly because it will add heavily to the burdens of budget making, and partly also because it will be resisted by those who fear that their pet programs would be jeopardized by a system that subjects every federal activity to annual scrutiny of its costs and results. However, this reform is so clearly necessary that I believe we will eventually come to it. I regard President Nixon's request of the Budget Bureau this year for a list of programs judged to be obsolete or substantially overfunded as a first step toward zero-base budgeting.

Several other reforms that I can only mention also deserve serious attention. First, earmarking of funds is often a dubious practice and should be carefully reappraised by the Congress. Second, agency heads should be subject to a presidential requirement that if they request additional funds—whether for new or old programs—after the budget has been transmitted to the Congress, they must as a rule give up an equal amount of money from their ongoing activites. Third, new programs should be typically undertaken on a pilot basis and not launched on a national scale until their promise has been reasonably tested. Fourth, the law requiring that the cost of new programs be projected five years ahead when they are first presented to the Congress should be strictly enforced. In addition, comprehensive five-year budgetary projections should be constantly maintained by the Budget Bureau for the president's guidance. Fifth, I think that it would be useful to rotate the personnel of the Budget Bureau among its major divisions, so that the key examiners can periodically shed their preconceptions or frustrations and approach with a fresh eye the financial concerns of the agencies that are newly assigned to their scrutiny.

In addition to institutional reforms such as these, effective control of public expenditures will require larger reliance on volunteer efforts for dealing with our great social ills. It will also require thorough, realistic, and penetrating study of the promises, costs, and achievements of individual governmental programs. Although federal agencies, particularly the Bureau of the Budget, need to augment their evaluative work, some doubt will always surround research that is carried out by agencies which originally advocated or subsequently supervised the programs under study. There is a great need, therefore, for expenditure studies by organizations that are independent of government and have no direct stake in any of the programs. In view of its preeminence in fiscal research and public education, the Tax Foundation is especially well equipped to organize teams of economists, accountants, political scientists, and management experts for the concrete study and evaluation of some of the major branches of federal expenditure.

I hope that the trustees of the Tax Foundation will be able to find a way of making this additional contribution to good government. If you undertake to do so, I assure you that the evaluation teams you send to Washington will receive a very warm welcome.

The Need for
New Budgetary Procedures

In a year when Congress is demonstrating a determination to reform its procedures, your committee faces a challenge worthy of its talents. You have the opportunity to enable Congress to turn its power of the purse into a truly effective instrument for stabilizing our economy. The fiscal policies of this government—its total outlays, the priorities they reflect, and their relationship to revenues—bear significantly on the lives of the people you represent. Income levels, the cost of living, the balance of international payments, and even the quality of life in this country are directly and substantially affected by the federal budget. If you can develop procedures that will enable members of Congress to vote on an overall fiscal policy that adequately reflects congressional priorities, you will revitalize representative government in this country. I am pleased to have been asked to discuss these issues with you.

Thoughtful people everywhere are aware of the need for more effective congressional review of the budget. A recent indication of this fact is Senator Mansfield's statement on February 8, 1973, disclosing that "all the new Senators of the class of 1973" had written to him and to Senator Scott urging that reform of the congressional budgetary process be given "top priority." In this letter thirteen new senators, from both political parties, fresh from election victories in states from Maine to Idaho, unanimously and "wholeheartedly" agreed that "Con-

Statement before the Joint Study Committee on Budget Control, U.S. Congress, March 6, 1973.

gress has the obligation to set priorities under which expenditures are to be authorized by this nation, and present procedures of the Congress do not in fact achieve that aim." They concluded with this perceptive comment: "The first step toward establishing priorities has to be setting a ceiling on appropriations and expenditures. This must be done first, rather than last. Unless we do this, we are not really budgeting at all."

Yet along with this awareness of the need for better budgetary procedures, there is concern and even cynicism about the prospects for achieving them. We hear speculation that the President does not really believe Congress will heed his call for a ceiling on expenditures but expects, instead, the Congress to overspend and thus become responsible for a tax increase that would then be inevitable. Congress, by it own actions, has lent some support to this pessimistic view. The early response of the House and Senate to the President's efforts to hold outlays for fiscal 1973 to $250 billion has been to pass bills requiring release of some of the impounded funds. And the Ervin bill restricting the authority to impound funds seems likely to pass the Senate soon. Thus, people are understandably concerned that Congress, in exercising its unquestioned right to determine priorities among national needs, may produce budget deficits that no one wants—not the President, not the Congress, and not the people you represent.

The problem is too acute to allow its solution to be frustrated by acrimonious debate about who is to blame. Representative Mahon recognized this in a challenging discussion of our budget problems in *Nation's Business* last April. Let me quote a few key sentences from his paper: "Who is to blame for this distressing record? The President? The Congress? The American people? I think nearly all of us are. Large segments of the population tend to demand more and more government services, and at the same time there is a demand for lower taxes."

I believe the American people understand that government spending, taxes, inflation, and interest rates are all interrelated. If they seem to favor more spending and lower taxes at the same time, it may well be because congressional procedures lead to votes on taxes and spending as though they were unrelated issues. Members are asked, in effect, to cast a number of separate votes for or against cleaner air, for or against better schools, and for or against a host of other good things government can help to provide. A vote does not occur on the question of whether expenditures for a particular category are desired strongly enough to raise taxes, or to cut back on another category. Until votes can be cast on such questions, we cannot be sure what answers people generally would give.

At present, the decision-making process that results in a unified budget being presented by the administration has no counterpart in Congress. Instead, the decisions that determine the ultimate shape of the budget are made by acting (or at times taking no action) on a large number of separate measures— 160 for fiscal 1973, as recently reported by your committee. Only after the results of these separate votes are determined can we put the pieces together and discover what kind of budget has emerged. In this process, members of Congress have no opportunity to express the wishes of their constituents on choices such as what total expenditures should be, or whether more should be spent for housing or for education or health care. Choices of this type are of greater importance to the electorate as a whole than the single proposals on which congressional votes actually occur.

Some of the choices that the Ninety-third Congress will have to make can be readily anticipated. The economy is expanding vigorously. We can look forward to a good increase in physical output and further reductions in unemployment in 1973. Thus, there is no need at this stage of the expansion for further fiscal stimulus and the administration has therefore recommended that the budget be brought into balance at full employment. Along with the new prosperity, however, we have some old problems. Persistent inflation—albeit at a somewhat diminished pace—is one of them, and the chronic deficit in our international balance of payments is another.

The recent devaluation of the dollar, combined with the Smithsonian realignment, have now placed us on the road back towards equilibrium in our balance of payments. We cannot, however, take that improvement for granted. Indeed, confidence in our own economy will be strengthened if we set a firm and definite goal for the balance of payments—namely, to end the deficit within a period of two to three years. And while devaluation will help in restoring payments equilibrium, it will also add to upward pressures on our prices at a time when both domestic and international considerations require a determined effort to restore price stability. The level of federal spending, and the way it is financed, will have an important bearing on our ability to solve these persistent problems of inflation and international imbalance.

Yet sizable deficits in the federal budget continue to plague us. The administration estimates that outlays, if held to $250 billion, will exceed revenues by $25 billion for fiscal 1973. And while the administration has recommended that the budget be brought into a position of full-employment balance for fiscal 1974, outlays are still scheduled to rise another $19 billion and the unified budget deficit is expected to be about $13 billion.

In addition to its implications for employment, price stability, and our international payments position, the budget is bound to leave its mark on interest rates. With credit demands strengthening because of the marked advance in economic activity, interest rates have been moving up. Treasury financing requirements, stemming from large budget deficits, have added to the pressures on credit markets. So far the advance in interest rates has been mainly confined to short-term credit. But our chances of continuing to avoid significant increases in long-term rates will depend heavily on whether Treasury demands for credit can be held at moderate levels.

It is clear to me that your committee fully realizes the pressing need to reestablish order in our federal finances. The question is not whether it must be done, but how. A solution requires a firm ceiling on expenditures or a tax increase, or some combination of the two. There are several reasons, I believe, for choosing a curb on spending in preference to a tax increase.

First, government expenditures—counting outlays by state and local governments as well as federal—have been rising much faster than our national production, so that an increasingly large fraction of the wealth that our citizens produce is being devoted to the support of government. In 1929, total government spending amounted to about 10 percent of the dollar value of our national output. Since then the figure has risen to 20 percent in 1940, 30 percent in 1965, and 35 percent in 1972. It is time to call a halt.

Second, the expansion in government outlays has not produced the kind of benefits the public has a right to expect. As government assumes wider responsibilities, it becomes increasingly apparent that we must have a better system of controls to screen out low-priority programs and to ensure that high-priority programs operate efficiently. The best way to get effective controls of that kind is for Congress to decide that one-third of our national output is quite enough for the tax collector.

Third, I have the impression that the American people feel that they are already carrying a sufficiently heavy tax burden and will strongly resist any increase. If that impression is correct, raising taxes may not be a realistic alternative to a ceiling on spending.

In its interim report of February 7, your committee has sketched out a tentative plan to achieve better control over expenditures, as a part of an overall plan for reviewing tax and expenditure policies. You have already accomplished much in the short time your committee has been in existence, and I find your report most encouraging.

Under this tentative plan, Congress would establish two overall spending ceilings early in the session. One would govern total outlays for the ensuing fiscal year, which stem in part from obligational authority previously enacted. The other would limit new obligational authority, which will form the basis for expenditures not only in the ensuing fiscal year but in later years as well. Each of these comprehensive ceilings would be accompanied by subceilings for major categories of expenditures, so as to reflect congressional priorities and to assist in achieving compliance with the overall ceilings.

Your report notes that earlier experiments with rubbery ceilings have failed, and that procedures must therefore be developed to assure reasonable compliance with the ceilings. Representative Findley's proposal, H. Res. 17, which would amend the rules of the House to require a two-thirds vote for passage of any bill that would exceed the previously determined ceiling for the particular category of expenditure, has much to commend it in my view, provided it is expanded to assure participation by the Senate in establishing the ceilings—as your report contemplates.

Representative Reuss has suggested a somewhat different procedure—namely, that the overall ceilings and subceilings established early in the session be treated as tentative, so that appropriations bills and other measures providing new obligational authority could be passed as now by majority vote even though they breached the ceilings. Thus, the tentative ceilings would help to guide action on individual spending measures, but adjustments would be made late in the session, in the form of a Final Budget Statute. This proposal seeks to achieve flexibility and an opportunity for late-session review, as proposed by your report, without destroying the effectiveness of the ceilings established early in the session.

I recognize that it may be too much to expect the House and Senate to agree early in the session, on the basis of limited information, on ceilings for major categories of expenditure that could be overridden only by a two-thirds vote. It may therefore be necessary to rely, as Representative Reuss has suggested, on action late in the session to set the overall ceilings and subceilings in their final form.

For the reasons I have mentioned, I would hope that where the tentative overall ceilings are exceeded, the late-session adjustment would usually take the form of reduced spending authority rather than a tax increase. But there may be circumstances where Congress should consider accepting a higher deficit than originally contemplated or financing expenditure overruns by raising taxes. The essential point, to my mind, is that Congress should take one of these courses deliberately, in full awareness of its consequences.

Moreover, if reliance is placed on a Final Budget Statute for the needed adjustments, special rules would seem to be required in order to assure that such a measure is in fact brought to the floor and acted on. Rules such as those which speed consideration of resolutions relating to reorganization plans would seem to be useful in this connection.

As an alternative approach, you may wish to consider a procedure by which Congress would adopt a joint resolution establishing overall spending ceilings as early in the session as possible, but in no event later than June 30. The resolution would set firm overall ceilings on outlays and new obligational authority for the coming year, and direct the Executive to submit within forty-five days a detailed budgetary plan for complying with these ceilings. The plan would take effect within forty-five days after its submission unless either house meanwhile passed a resolution disapproving the plan. With reasonable cooperation between the Executive and the Congress, which would of course include consultation with the House and Senate budget committees proposed in your report, such a procedure would assure that the ceilings were effective and that they also adequately reflected congressional priorities. Again, rules would be needed, analogous to those for reorganization plans, to give each house the opportunity to vote on a resolution of disapproval if it so wished.

In developing better budgeting procedures, it may be that the federal government could usefully adopt some of the techniques of the states, where budgets are subject to a relatively firm discipline. I have tried to learn something about state procedures through conversations with state officials and others familiar with the subject.

It appears that state legislatures are normally subject to a very powerful constraint—namely, elected officials of all parties recognize a balanced budget as a prerequisite to reelection. Some states permit deficits for capital expansion but a deficit on current account, even where permitted by law, poses political risks that officials are reluctant to take. The general acceptance of the need for a balanced budget enables the leadership to keep the legislature in session until it is achieved. I am not advocating that the United States Congress repair to the banner of a balanced budget at all times. But we do need a new sense of discipline—one that recognizes that a constantly stimulative fiscal policy is more apt to produce inflation than new jobs.

One important means by which the states achieve fiscal restraint is by granting considerably larger power to the governors than the Congress has granted to the president. The item veto is authorized in a number of states, and because of the shorter legislative sessions the pocket veto is a more powerful weapon. In some states the legislature is not permitted to increase spending above the level requested in the budget unless it also provides for a new source of revenue. And nearly all governors impound funds frequently. However, it appears that impounding generally involves measures such as reducing the number of state employees or stretching out construction rather than terminating programs.

Experience at the state level thus suggests that where overall outlays are subject to careful scrutiny, impounding—when it occurs—takes a form that is consistent with spending priorities established by the legislature. If the president and the Congress will work together to hold total outlays at a level reasonably related to revenues, there should be no occasion for resort to impounding on a broad scale.

Congress has made it clear that it does not wish to emulate the states by strengthening the powers of the executive branch to trim total outlays to acceptable levels. And Congress is better equipped than are the state legislatures to play a strong role in fiscal policy. But Congress can preserve and strengthen its powers only by exercising them. Procedures that produce deficits that the Congress itself does not desire invite corrective actions by the Executive.

In the long run there would seem to be no political advantage to either the Executive or the Congress in battling over budgetary prerogatives, particularly if the result is bad budgets. Let peace be declared; let Congress play a greater role in reviewing the budget, and perhaps even become involved in the preparation of the budget. Eight states have established means for doing this, generally through a board most of whose members are legislators. While the mechanisms established in these states would have to be modified for application at the federal level, perhaps some means could be found that would be mutually satisfactory to Congress and the president.

Involving the Congress in budget preparation should help to accomplish speedier action on budget proposals. Both the President's Budget Message and your committee's interim report recognize the need to reduce or eliminate the delays that have required increasing use of continuing resolutions and have frustrated efforts to make the budget a really useful management tool. For programs that operate under statutory authority that is renewed annually, enactment of the authorization bills a year in advance, as recommended in your report, would eliminate a major cause of delay in considering the related appropriations bills. Cooperation and consultation between the Executive and Congress in formulating the budget should also help to expedite its enactment.

Your report recognizes the need to provide Congress with better information about the effects of existing and proposed legislation, not only in the current year, but up to three to five years ahead. This would extend to the federal government procedures already established in some states, and should prove highly beneficial, particularly if it is buttressed by your proposal for House and Senate committees on the budget, assisted by nonpartisan, professional staffs. Indeed, the President has already taken useful steps in this direction. Thus, in his most recent budget message, he presents estimates, for individual agencies and in functional detail, of the outlays for fiscal 1975 as well as for fiscal 1973 and 1974.

Finally, I feel that any discussion of better budget procedures would be incomplete without some mention of zero-base budgeting. Traditionally, officials in charge of an established program have not been required to make a case for their entire appropriation request each year. Instead, they have had to justify only the increase they seek above last year's level. Substantial savings could undoubtedly be realized if both the administration and the Congress treated each appropriation request as if it were for a new program. Such a procedure will undoubtedly be difficult to achieve, not only because it will add heavily to the burdens of budget making, but also because it will be resisted by those who fear loss of benefits they now enjoy. But this reform is so clearly necessary that I believe we will eventually come to it, and I commend to your attention Senator Brock's bill, S. 40, which provides for zero-base budgeting for all major expenditure programs at least once in every three years.

The thoughts I have expressed today are my own, not necessarily those of the Board of Governors of the Federal Reserve System. And, needless to say, I disclaim any special expertise in regard to congressional procedures. But procedural questions at times have great substantive significance, and this is one of those occasions. I accepted your invitation because, as a concerned citizen with some knowledge of economics, I have believed for some time—and recent events have reinforced the belief—that better congressional control of the budget is absolutely essential to maintain the vitality of our economic and political system.

Reform of the Federal Budget

I deeply appreciate the privilege of addressing this graduating class, for—despite the difference in our ages—I feel that we have much in common. Both you and I have spent some years in the lively atmosphere of a university. Both you and I have been concerned with problems of economics, finance, and administration. Both you and I, as residents of this fascinating city, have had the opportunity of observing at close range the understanding, selflessness, and compassion that government officials usually bring to their daily tasks; but we have also had the disquieting experience of witnessing some abuses of governmental power.

As graduates of this School of Government and Business Administration, you are embarking on your careers at a moment in history that is fortunate in numerous respects. Our nation is again at peace, the economy is again prospering, the number of good jobs is expanding rapidly, industrial strife is at a minimum, and civil order is returning to our schools and cities. By every reasonable criterion, so it would seem, you can—and should— look forward with confidence to the future of our country and its economy. And yet, if I read the nation's mood correctly, a spirit of unease and even frustration is now widespread.

There are numerous causes of the concern and skepticism with which many Americans, especially young men and women, now view the contemporary scene. But I believe that most of

---

Commencement address at the School of Government and Business Administration, George Washington University, Washington, D.C., May 6, 1973.

these causes can be captured in two broad generalizations. First, the American people have come to feel that their lives, their fortunes, and their opportunities are increasingly beyond their control, and that they are in large part being shaped for them by their government. Second, more and more Americans have also come to feel that their government lacks either the knowledge or the competence to make good on the promises that it holds out to the people.

It is this simultaneous dependence on government and diminishing confidence in government that is at the heart of the disquiet that so many Americans are experiencing. I wish I could say that this mood will pass quickly, but I cannot do so. Building confidence in social and political institutions is inevitably a long process, and it can only be accomplished if thoughtful citizens are willing to devote their minds and energy to the task.

When I was your age, the problem that particularly concerned university students was the periodic recurrence of economic depressions that wiped out business profits, caused widespread bankruptcy, and brought mass unemployment to wage-earners. This problem no longer afflicts our society on anything like its earlier scale; and we have made even more marvelous advances in conquering disease, prolonging human life, and reducing the drudgery of physical labor. We have made progress in these fields by diligent application of thought and reason—this is, by identifying each problem, diagnosing its causes, and seeking constructive solutions. It took the best effort of many thoughtful and earnest men to solve the problems that stirred social and political unrest in the past. And it will likewise require much thoughtful and earnest effort to regain the confidence in government which is so essential to our own and our country's future.

In my own profession of economics I have seen large advances in knowledge and also substantial improvements in the application of this knowledge to public policy. I can assure you that those who participated in these developments have found the experience richly rewarding. And it is precisely because you graduates may be able to contribute to the improvement of our political processes that I want to discuss with you today one of the issues that has brought us much trouble and agony in recent years—namely, the need to achieve rational control over the federal budget.

Those who administer the affairs of government share a common problem with business executives: no private enterprise and no government can do everything at once. Both must choose among many desirable objectives, and the degree to which their efforts prove successful depends largely on their skill in concentrating available resources on those objectives that matter most. That is the very purpose of budgets. The fact that the federal budget has in recent years gotten out of control should therefore be a matter of concern to all of us. Indeed, I believe that budgetary reform has become essential to the resurgence of our democracy.

Fortunately, political leaders of every persuasion are by now convinced that Congress must change its procedures if it is to exercise effective control over the government's domestic and international policies. The old debate between free-spending "liberals" and tight-fisted "conservatives" is dying away. For the most part, liberals as well as conservatives realize that the level of federal spending, and whether it is financed by taxes or by borrowing, have a powerful effect on jobs, prices, and interest rates.

In the Employment Act of 1946 Congress declared it to be the responsibility of the federal government to "promote maximum employment, production, and purchasing power." The authors of this legislation were well aware that a stimulative fiscal policy can be useful in taking up slack in the economy, and that a restrictive fiscal policy can help to cool an economy that is overheating. Yet, despite the prosperity that our nation has generally experienced since the enactment of that statute, budget deficits have greatly outnumbered surpluses. Experience has thus demonstrated that failure to attend properly to governmental priorities leads to excessive fiscal stimulus, and that this in turn is more apt to produce inflation than jobs.

Recognizing this fact, the Congress is now seeking a way to determine an overall limit on federal outlays that will be rationally related both to expected revenues and to economic conditions. This is essential not only to achieve overall stabilization objectives, but also to enable Congress to play its expected role in determining national priorities. Early in this session of Congress, Senator Mansfield disclosed that all of the newly elected Senators had written to him and to Senator Scott urging reform of the budgetary process because "Congress has the obligation to set priorities . . . and present procedures do not in fact achieve that aim." Their unanimous conclusion was that the "first step toward establishing priorities has to be setting a ceiling on appropriations and expenditures;" and that unless this is done at an early stage of each session, the Congress is "not really budgeting at all."

The budget that the president recommends to Congress at the beginning of each session is the product of a systematic process aiming to establish an overall limit on outlays and to determine priorities within that limit. This process, however, has no counterpart in the Congress. Instead, congressional decisions that determine the ultimate shape of the budget are taken by acting separately—or at times by taking no action—on a hundred or more entirely independent measures. It is only after separate votes have been taken on housing, education, defense, welfare, and whatnot that we can put the pieces together and discover what kind of a budget has emerged.

Thus, members of Congress now vote for or against cleaner air, for or against better schools, and for or against a host of other good things that government can help to provide. But they have no opportunity to vote on what total outlays should be, or whether an appropriation for a particular purpose is needed badly enough to raise taxes or to make offsetting reductions in other appropriations. Yet choices of this type are far more important to the electorate as a whole than the single proposals on which congressional voting takes place.

This fragmented consideration of the elements that make up the budget is largely responsible for an almost uninterrupted succession of deficits. Since 1960, we have had a deficit in every year except 1969. Some of these deficits have occurred because of efforts to use the federal budget as a means of stimulating a lagging economy, but for the most part we have allowed deficits to happen without plan or purpose.

Both the legislative and executive branches of the government have from time to time recognized the need for reform. In 1946, for example, Congress included provisions for better budget control in the Legislative Reorganization Act, but the experiment was abandoned after a brief trial. Expenditure ceilings enacted for fiscal years 1969 and 1970 again proved ineffective since they could be readily adjusted to accommodate increases in spending. These rubbery ceilings did, however, help to prepare the ground for more meaningful reform. When the President called for a rigid limit of $250 billion on outlays for fiscal 1973, both the House and the Senate accepted the expenditure ceiling. But they were unable to agree on a method for reducing the previously enacted spending authority so that the $250 billion limit could in fact be realized.

Actions subsequently taken by the President to hold outlays for fiscal 1973 to $250 billion have been criticized on the ground that impounding of funds enables the administration to substitute its priorities for those established by the Congress. Concern over possible usurpation of congressional prerogatives is entirely understandable. However, this controversy should not divert our attention from the broad political consensus that has already emerged on the need to limit outlays. If the Congress does the job itself, there will be no occasion in the future for the administration to cut billions out of authorized outlays in order to achieve the overall level of spending that Congress agrees is appropriate.

Although last year's efforts to impose a legislative budget ceiling proved disappointing, they did prompt the Congress to ponder closely the need for budgetary reform and to create a Joint Study Committee on Budget Control.

This committee has made excellent use of the brief time it has been in existence. In a recently released report, it recommends specific and practical procedures by which Congress could control the level of federal outlays, the priorities among programs, and the size of any deficit or surplus. Bills to carry out these recommendations have now been introduced in both the House and Senate, with support from all members of the joint committee, as well as others in the Congress.

It would seem, therefore, that prospects for meaningful budget reform are now very good, perhaps better than at any time since the Budget and Accounting Act of 1921. I find the joint study committee's recommendations most encouraging, but I also think that they need to be supplemented with systematic and frequent review of the effectiveness of federal programs.

Traditionally, officials in charge of an established program have not been required to make a case for their entire appropriation request each year. Instead, they have had to justify only the increase they seek above last year's level. Substantial savings could undoubtedly be realized by zero-base budgeting, that is, by treating each appropriation request as if it were for a new program. Such budgeting will be difficult to achieve, not only because of opposition from those who fear that it would mean loss of benefits they now enjoy, but also because it would add heavily to the burdens of budget making. It may be, therefore, that Congress will rely initially on procedures that ensure reappraisal of each program only every two or three years. But whatever form it takes, a method must be found for screening out programs whose costs clearly exceed their benefits, while assuring a satisfactory level of performance for programs that contribute significantly to the general welfare.

The day is past—if indeed, it ever really existed—when only the well-to-do need concern themselves with economy in government. Perhaps there was a time when those who benefited from the status quo could block social reform by inveighing against governmental spending. But today Big Government is no longer a slogan for appealing to some and frightening others. For better or worse, it has become part of our lives. And those who would use government as an instrument of reform have perhaps a larger stake in eliminating wasteful programs than those who resist change.

We have passed the point where new programs can be added to old ones and paid for by heavier borrowing. With the economy expanding vigorously, with inflation persisting stubbornly, with our balance of payments in serious trouble, with two devaluations of the dollar just behind us, we clearly cannot afford to continue large budget deficits. It is sobering to reflect that in spite of the President's determined efforts to hold down federal spending, the budget he originally presented for this fiscal year called for outlays that exceeded estimated receipts by about $25 billion.

In principle, taxes can always be raised to pay for more public services, but the resistance to heavier taxation has become enormous. If we count outlays by all governments, state and local as well as federal, we find an increasingly large fraction of the wealth our citizens produce being devoted to the support of government. In 1929, total government spending came to about 10 percent of the dollar value of our national output. Since then the figure has risen to 20 percent in 1940, 30 percent in 1965, and 35 percent in 1972. I believe that most citizens feel that one-third of our national output is quite enough for the tax collector, particularly since the expansion in government outlays has not produced the kind of benefits they have a right to expect.

The key to rebuilding confidence in government is improved performance by government, and budgetary reform can move us powerfully toward this goal. Rational control of the budget by the Congress should improve our economic stabilization policies. It should facilitate judicious choice among governmental activities. It should improve evaluation of governmental performance. It should help us avoid abuses of power—whether they arise in the world of business, or labor, or government itself. And it should restore to the Congress some of the prestige that it has lost as a result of many years of neglect.

I trust that the members of this graduating class will join other citizens throughout the country to see to it that budgetary reform is carried out with the promptness and on the scale that this nation's interests require. Let us always remember that budgets are a means for promoting national objectives. For those of you who enter public service, better budgeting can offer more meaningful and rewarding careers. For all Americans, it can mean a rejuvenation of spirit as government becomes more responsive to our aspirations and more effective in fulfilling them.

The Congressional Budget Act
of 1974

It is a pleasure to meet with this committee as it undertakes its momentous responsibilities under the Congressional Budget Act of 1974. In recent years, federal spending has risen swiftly, deficits have become chronic, and the public debt has mounted. Our present grave problem of inflation stems from many causes, and inadequate fiscal discipline is prominent among them. You and your congeners in the House of Representatives therefore face a great challenge, but you also have a unique opportunity to reestablish order in our nation's finances.

The budget that the president recommends to Congress at the beginning of each session is the product of a systematic process aiming to establish an overall limit on outlays in relation to expected revenues, and to determine priorities within the totality of outlays. This process, as you know, has hitherto had no counterpart in the Congress. Instead, congressional decisions that determine the ultimate shape of the budget have been taken by acting separately—or at times by taking no action—on a hundred or more entirely independent measures. It is only after separate votes are cast on housing, education, defense, welfare, and whatnot that we put the pieces together and discover what kind of budget has emerged.

Thus, year after year, members of Congress have been voting for or against larger benefits to veterans, for or against better schools, for or against cleaner air, and for or against a host of other good things that government can help to provide.

Statement before the Senate Budget Committee, August 21, 1974.

But the Congress has not had the opportunity to vote on what total outlays should be, or whether an appropriation for a particular purpose is needed badly enough to raise taxes or to make offsetting reductions in other appropriations.

This fragmented congressional consideration of the elements that make up the budget has contributed materially to the almost uninterrupted succession of budget deficits. Since 1960, we have had a deficit in every fiscal year except 1969. True, some of these deficits occurred because of efforts to use the federal budget as a means of stimulating a lagging economy, but for the most part we have allowed deficits to happen without plan or purpose. Machinery for putting effective ceilings on expenditures, and for establishing priorities among alternative uses of federal revenues, has simply not been available.

By passing the Budget Act of 1974, the Congress has established a framework for exercising this much needed control, and has also indicated its firm resolve to do so. The Budget Act is a milestone in the reassertion of congressional authority and self-discipline. There is now real hope that we can avoid the massive increases of federal expenditure and the persistent deficits that have plagued us in the past.

The immense importance of your committee's new responsibilities may perhaps be more fully appreciated by reflecting on what has happened to the federal budget over the long sweep of our nation's history. Total expenditures did not reach the $100 billion level until fiscal 1962, or nearly 200 years after the founding of the republic. By fiscal 1971, nine years later, federal spending had risen another $100 billion and thus passed the $200 billion mark. In the budget as now projected, the $300 billion mark will be passed this fiscal year. Clearly, the pace of federal spending has been accelerating rapidly, and a pause for taking stock of where we are is overdue.

One result of the sharply rising curve of expenditures is that government has been assuming an ever larger role in the economic life of our people. In 1929, federal expenditures accounted for less than 3 percent of the dollar value of our total national output, and expenditures at all levels of government—federal, state, and local—amounted to about 10 percent of the national product. By 1950, the share of national output absorbed by government had risen to 23 percent. Since that time, governmental involvement in the economy has increased further; last year, federal expenditures alone accounted for 22 percent of our national output, and the combined expenditures of all governmental units for 35 percent.

A significant increase over the past four decades in the role of government in economic life was inevitable. A growing population, and the increasing complexity of modern urban life, gave rise to new and expanded governmental activities. This was also a period in which the United States came to occupy a position of leadership in international political affairs and in world economic development.

Some part of the rapid upward trend of federal spending, however, is attributable to widespread acceptance of the theory that social and economic problems can generally be solved by quick and large expenditure of governmental money. We have tried to meet the need for better schooling of the young, for upgrading the skills of the labor force, for expanding the production of low-income housing, for improving the nation's health, for ending urban blight, for purifying our water and air, and for other national objectives, by constantly excogitating new programs and getting the Treasury to finance them on a liberal scale before they have been tested.

The result has been a piling up of one social program on another, so that they now literally number in the hundreds and practically defy understanding. Not a little of our taxpayers' money is being spent on activities of slight value, or on laudable activities that are conducted ineffectively.

Another result of the rapid growth of federal spending has been a larger tax burden borne by our citizens and a blunting of economic incentives. Business capital investment in recent years has certainly been inadequate for a nation that is eager for rapid improvement in the general welfare. There is thus reason to believe that governmental spending and taxing may have gone beyond prudent limits.

Where the line should be drawn between governmental and private use of resources is, in the final analysis, a matter of judgment and of social values. However this question is resolved, it should be clear to everyone that federal spending, whatever its level, needs to be financed on a sound basis. Deficit financing by the federal government can be justified at a time of substantial unemployment, but it becomes a source of instability when it occurs during a period of high economic activity, such

293

as we have experienced in recent years. The huge federal deficits of the past decade added enormously to aggregate demand for goods and services, but they added little to our capacity to produce. They have thus been directly responsible for a substantial part of our present inflationary problem.

The current inflation began in the middle 1960s when our government embarked on a highly expansive fiscal policy. Large tax reductions occurred in 1964 and the first half of 1965, and they were immediately followed by an explosion of federal spending. New and substantial tax reductions followed in 1969 and 1971, and so too have massive increases of expenditures. In the last five fiscal years, that is, from 1970 through 1974, the public debt—including obligations of the federal credit agencies—has risen by more than $100 billion, a larger increase than in the previous twenty-four years.

In the fiscal year just concluded, the condition of the federal budget failed to improve sufficiently. True, the reported budget deficit declined to about $3½ billion—a much smaller deficit than in the three preceding years. But in a year of such powerful inflationary forces, the federal budget should have been in surplus. Moreover, when off-budget outlays and the expenditures of governmentally sponsored agencies are taken into account, as I believe they should be, the total federal deficit reached $21 billion last year, which is not much lower than the extraordinary deficits of the three previous fiscal years.

The financing of these huge federal deficits has contributed powerfully to the upward pressure on interest rates and the tension in financial markets, which have been so troublesome of late. The disturbing effect of federal borrowing on the flow of funds was illustrated dramatically earlier this month, when the Treasury went to the market to refinance some maturing debt obligations. Long lines of people formed at the doors of the Treasury and the Federal Reserve Banks to bid for the new securities offered by the Treasury. Half of the total of $4.4 billion sought by the government was obtained through noncompetitive bids—that is, from relatively small investors. A large share of these funds undoubtedly came out of deposit accounts, and thus further reduced the ability of our financial institutions—particularly savings banks and savings and loan associations—to support homebuilding activities.

Despite such concrete evidence, it is sometimes contended that the federal deficits of recent years have been only a minor source of economic or financial instability, since the amounts are small relative to total borrowing by the private sector. This is a faulty argument. To be sure, the rate of private credit expansion has substantially exceeded the rate of federal borrowing. But we must never confuse the power or responsibility of private citizens with the power or responsibility of government. Business firms and consumers have no way of acting in concert to prevent an inflationary expansion of credit, and their private responsibilities may conflict with national objectives. The basic responsibility for economic stabilization lies with the federal government. Unless our government exercises that function better than it has in the past, there will be little hope for restoration of stability in the general price level.

The central purpose of the Congress, besides providing for the nation's security, is to help find the way to a better life for the American people—among other things, reasonably full employment, a widely shared prosperity, and a stable purchasing power of their currency. None of these objectives will be achieved over any length of time without far stricter fiscal discipline than we have exercised in recent years. That is why your committee, together with the Budget Committee of the House, has such a great and unique opportunity to serve the nation's welfare.

I recognize that you have a good deal of preparatory work to do before you can begin exercising fully your responsibilities under the Congressional Budget Act of 1974. The importance of this preparatory effort should not be underestimated. A highly competent and thoroughly objective staff will need to be assembled to carry out the functions of the Congressional Budget Office. Good working relations will need to be established between your committee and the House Budget Committee and between both committees and the Office of Management and Budget. Procedures will have to be worked out for implementing the intricate steps in the budgetary process set forth in the Budget Act. Some flexibility is needed in congressional management of our enormously complex federal budget, and the Budget Act properly provides opportunity for waiver of procedures and deadline requirements. But unless the Congress undertakes its new responsibility with a firm determination to reserve the waiver privilege for unusual circumstances, the Budget Act may turn out to be a well-meaning but illusory gesture.

Full implementation of the new budgetary procedures, I understand, will begin in fiscal 1977—or two years from now. We dare not wait two years, however, for the additional fiscal restraint that is so urgently needed in the present inflationary environment. Strenuous efforts should be made immediately to pare budget expenditures in fiscal 1975 and to balance the budget in fiscal 1976.

I recognize that this committee is not yet in a good position to recommend to the Congress where expenditure cuts would be most appropriate. Nevertheless, in view of the special responsibility that has been assigned to you by the leadership of the Senate, you can justly use your good offices to press for restraint on federal spending. This is the most important single step that can now be taken by the Executive and the Congress to curb inflationary pressures and to restore the confidence of our people in their own and the nation's economic future.

The Financial Crisis
of New York City

I am here to discuss with this committee the financial crisis of New York City.

The difficulties now facing New York stem from the erosion of its financial position over the past decade. During this period the expenditures by the city's government grew rapidly while revenues failed to keep pace. To close the gap between its revenues and expenditures, the city relied increasingly on borrowed funds. Not only capital expenditures, but also the mounting deficits on current operations, were financed in this fashion. By the end of 1974, New York City's outstanding debt amounted to over $13 billion, much of which was in the form of short-term notes—that is, obligations maturing in a year or less.

As poor management of New York finances persisted, at first a few but in time more and more investors became concerned about the city's financial condition. During the past winter and spring the city began to experience very serious difficulties in rolling over its debt—to say nothing of adding to its outstanding indebtedness. In the absence of clear-cut remedial measures by the city, the possibility of default on the city's obligations became very real, and it was so portrayed almost daily in our newspapers.

The financial crisis confronting the nation's largest city prompted the government of New York State to offer financial and managerial assistance. Starting in April, the state put at

Statement before the Subcommittee on Economic Stabilization, Committee on Banking, Currency, and Housing, House of Representatives, October 23, 1975.

the city's disposal substantial sums that were not scheduled for payment until some months later. Then, around mid-June, the state legislature created a new instrumentality—the Municipal Assistance Corporation (MAC). This agency was empowered to sell up to $3 billion of its debt obligations, to make the proceeds of its borrowing available to the city, to wring some clarity out of the city's tangled finances, and to help develop a budgetary plan that could lead the city back to a balanced budget.

These measures, however, proved insufficient to restore investor confidence in the city's financial management, and even the new securities issued by MAC soon came under a cloud. To ward off imminent default by the City of New York, the state adopted firmer measures on September 9. These included creation of a state-dominated Emergency Financial Control Board to manage the city's finances, expansion of MAC's authority to issue securities, and a plan to arrange additional financing of $2.3 billion for the city. This financial package was designed to tide the city over until early December. It was hoped that by that time a strong program of budgetary restraints would be in place and that it would enable the city to resume the sale of its securities to the investing public.

But the new financial plan failed to elicit any enthusiasm on the part of investors. The financial community has remained skeptical about the city's ability to avert default and rebuild its financial strength. Moreover, the intertwining of the state's finances with the city's finances has troubled investors and has damaged the state's credit standing. The concern of market participants was heightened this past week by the extraordinary difficulties encountered in arranging for the city's refunding needs on October 17, and default was averted by only an hour or two. Thus, the stresses and strains that began to develop in the municipal securities market in the summer have become more acute with the passage of time.

Since the summer, and to an increasing degree in recent weeks, the participants in the municipal market—that is, investment bankers, securities dealers, and ultimate investors—have been attempting to reduce their exposure to the risk of loss. This has affected not only securities bearing a New York name, but also issues of some other state and local governments. Thus, many securities dealers have sought to cut back on their inventory of municipal securities. Underwriters of municipal issues have generally reduced their participation in new offerings, and some have withdrawn entirely from bidding syndicates. And investors—the ultimate buyers of municipals—have been tending to shift to higher-quality municipal securities or to categories of investment judged to be less hazardous.

Trading in the market for outstanding tax-exempt bonds has therefore slowed appreciably and the spread between bid and asked quotations has widened. These developments are characteristic of a period when investor confidence has been shaken, and they are indicative of a weakened market.

The behavior of investors and dealers in recent months has resulted in a rise of yields on municipal securities to the highest level ever experienced in the tax-exempt market. Yields for even the highest-rated borrowers have risen conspicuously, but a part of this increase is doubtless due to the enormous volume of municipal securities issued during the third quarter.

In the past two to three weeks, open-market interest rates have declined somewhat. The municipal market has benefited from this development, as well as from various indications that the federal government is becoming more concerned about New York's financial problems. Nevertheless, investors in municipal securities remain highly selective. The obligations of New York City, New York State, and certain of the state's agencies continue to be shunned by investors. And the effects of investor uncertainty have spilled over to other governmental units as well, some of which have not received any bids for their bonds or have rejected bids because the interest cost was deemed excessive.

If the weakness of the market for municipal securities were to persist and to spread further, many soundly run, creditworthy communities and public agencies could have difficulty—or suffer very heavy costs—in raising needed funds. This would tend to induce cutbacks or stretchouts in local spending programs. In addition, holders of municipal securities, which include many banks and other financial institutions, would to some degree be affected, as might the attitudes of others less directly involved. Hence, if the New York City crisis remains unresolved, and if the fate of New York State remains tied to the city's, the process of economic recovery now under way in our nation could be impaired.

In seeking ways to resolve New York City's crisis, the suggestion has occasionally been advanced that the Federal Reserve might serve as a source of emergency credit. No formal application for such credit has been received by the Board or the Federal Reserve Bank of New York. But I want to explain why we probably would have disapproved such an application had it been made.

As the ultimate source of financial liquidity in the economy, the Federal Reserve has certain powers to extend emergency credit even to institutions that are not members of the System. But the use of that authority is tightly circumscribed. The basic provision—contained in Section 13, paragraph 13, of the Federal Reserve Act—states that emergency loans with maturities no longer than ninety days may be made by the Federal Reserve Banks on the basis of promissory notes backed by Treasury or federal agency securities. To qualify for credit assistance under this provision of law, a local government would have to possess sizable amounts of unencumbered federal obligations. This would be an unusual situation for any distressed borrower and it obviously does not apply to New York City.

The lending authority under paragraph 3 of Section 13 of the Federal Reserve Act is broader, permitting the Board, in unusual and exigent circumstances, to authorize Reserve Banks to make loans on the kinds of collateral eligible for discount by member banks. Such paper may not have a maturity of more than ninety days and must afford adequate security to the Reserve Bank against the risk of loss. Furthermore, in view of restrictions of law and congressional intent, certain conditions must be met in order to permit the extension of emergency credit under this authority. Among these conditions is a requirement that an applicant has exhausted other sources of funds before coming to the Federal Reserve, that the borrower is basically creditworthy and possesses adequate collateral, and that the borrower's need is solely for short-term accommodation. It does not appear that New York City is now in a position to meet all these requirements. Certainly, its finances would hardly permit early repayment of emergency borrowings.

In addition to the emergency lending provisions in Section 13 of the Federal Reserve Act, the Reserve Banks have authority under Section 14(b) to purchase short-term obligations of state and local governments issued in anticipation of assured revenues, subject to regulations by the Board. Legislative history indicates that this authority was designed to assist the Federal Reserve Banks in meeting their operating expenditures, and also to enable them to make the discount rate effective when little borrowing took place at the discount window. There is nothing in the Federal Reserve Act or its legislative history to suggest that Section 14(b) contemplated the purchase of municipal securities as a means of aiding financially distressed communities.

The Congress, of course, could amend the Federal Reserve Act so as to relax the requirements for extending Federal Reserve credit to financially troubled governmental units. But the Board of Governors would have the gravest doubts about any such action. If loans were to be made to state or local governments, the Federal Reserve would have to involve itself in the activities of these governmental units, including particularly their expenditure budgets and the adequacy of their revenues. Moreover, since numerous demands for credit might ensue, the Federal Reserve would have to set standards of eligibility. Being thus placed in the position of having to allocate credit among governmental units, the nation's central bank would inevitably become subject to intense political pressures, and its ability to function constructively in the monetary area would be undermined.

The Board fully recognizes that the Federal Reserve System has the responsibility, subject only to restrictions under existing law, to serve as the nation's lender of last resort. Over the years, we have therefore developed contingency plans to deal with possible emergency situations. As I have already indicated in testimony before the Joint Economic Committee, our plans have been adapted recently to cope with the financial strains that might be associated with the default of a major municipality.

In that event, I assure you, the Board is prepared to act promptly. The contingency plan calls for lending to commercial banks through the Federal Reserve discount window beyond the amounts required by normal discounting operations. Credit provided in this manner would assist banks in meeting their temporary liquidity needs. Not only that, the proceeds of the special loans made at the discount window could also be used by the banks to assist municipalities, municipal securities dealers, and other customers who are temporarily short of cash because of unsettled conditions in the securities markets. In addition, the System would, of course, be ready to use its broad power to stabilize markets through open market purchases of Treasury or federal agency securities.

In the event this contingency plan has to be activated, the Board will make funds available on whatever scale is deemed necessary to assure an orderly financial environment. The Board recognizes that sizable extensions of Federal Reserve credit would run the risk of leading to a substantially larger expansion of bank reserves and the money supply than is consistent with longer-run monetary objectives. Clearly, therefore, any such expansion must be only temporary. In time, any excessive growth in bank reserves would need to be corrected through offsetting open market operations and through repayment of bank borrowing from the System.

There are also certain supervisory and examination questions that may arise with respect to banks in the event of a major municipal default. In this connection, the Board and other agencies have plans to revise procedures that apply to the valuation of defaulted securities, so that any writedowns may be postponed until the market has had a few months to stabilize and thus provide more reliable indications of their value.

Even so, a default might ultimately require writedowns that could seriously reduce the capital of some banks. In that event, the Federal Deposit Insurance Corporation has statutory powers to assist federally insured banks that might find their capital impaired by a decline in the value of securities in their portfolios. I understand that the corporation is prepared to implement, with appropriate safeguards, its contingency plans for dealing with insured banks that require a temporary infusion of supplemental capital for the above reason.

I think it evident from the scope of our contingency plans that we believe a default on debt obligations by New York City could produce serious strains in securities markets. For a time, it could also adversely affect municipalities that need to issue new debt. The like is true of financial institutions that hold such securities in significant volume, and also of individual investors who have part of their life savings at risk in these bonds. I still believe that the damage stemming from a default by New York City would probably be short-lived. Indeed, the possibility of such a default has already been discounted to a considerable degree by the market. But I am also aware of the uncertainty that inherently attaches to a judgment on this score;

and I recognize that a default, besides being a very serious matter for the city and state of New York, could have troublesome consequences for the nation at large.

The very fact that this committee and other committees of the Congress are holding hearings on New York City's finances indicates that concern is spreading that a New York default may injure the economic recovery now in process. I have said enough to indicate that I feel this possibility can no longer be dismissed lightly. That, however, does not ease the task that the Congress faces in dealing with the New York problem; for the precise issue is whether federal financial assistance to New York may not cause national problems over the long run that outweigh any temporary national advantage.

As this matter is debated by the Congress, the adverse effects of a New York City default will undoubtedly receive full attention—as they indeed should. I would only urge that the longer-run risks also be considered thoroughly. A program of federal assistance to the city may well lead to demands for similar assistance to other hard-pressed communities, even though their distress may have been brought on by gross negligence or mismanagement. Substantial federal aid—whether through insurance, guarantees, or direct loans—would compete directly with the already huge amounts of federal financing needs. Most important of all, the provision of federal credit for local governments would necessarily inject a major federal presence in local spending and taxing decisions.

These longer-run dangers have a vital bearing on our nation's future; but they can be exaggerated, just as the immediate consequences of a New York default can be—and perhaps are now being—exaggerated. It is entirely clear to me that if the federal government had previously yielded to the entreaties for aid that New York officials kept pressing, neither the city nor the state would have gone as far as they now have in restoring some hope for eventual order in the city's finances. Earlier intervention would have been a disservice to the people of New York as well as to the nation at large. But it also seems to me that the effort thus far made by both the state and the city is still inadequate. And while I take a more serious view of the potential economic consequences of a New York default than I did three months ago or even three weeks ago, I am not ready to recommend to the Congress that financial assistance to New York is now required in the nation's interest.

I was asked at a recent hearing what advice I would give if Congress were inclined to legislate assistance for New York. My reply was that stringent conditions should in that event be laid down, so that no municipality would seek federal financial aid unless such a request became unavoidable. I proceeded to list a half-dozen conditions; and, if I may, I shall now restate them somewhat more fully.

One essential condition prior to receipt of any federal assistance would be that the municipality has exhausted all other sources of funds. This would require, of course, that the municipality demonstrate that it is unable to obtain credit through the public issuance of securities, or through private placement of securities, or direct loans from banks or other private lenders.

A second condition that seems to me essential is that the state assume control over the finances of the municipality in difficulty. When a local government reaches the point where no source of funds is any longer available, its management of finances can no longer be relied upon. State control would mean that a local government has lost its fiscal authority, and this should serve as a powerful deterrent to other mayors or city councils across the nation from ever placing their municipality in such a position.

A third essential condition for federal assistance, I believe, should be that the state levy a special state-wide tax, the proceeds of which are pledged to cover one-half of the deficit faced by the municipality. The requirement of such a tax would materially strengthen the state's resolve to put whatever pressure is needed on the troubled municipality to work its way toward a balanced budget. It would thus ensure that the state will discharge adequately its own responsibility to enforce fiscal discipline on a troubled municipality. No governor or state legislature will welcome the prospect of levying a special state-wide tax for the benefit of a municipality that has mismanaged its affairs. But this very reluctance would provide some assurance that federal assistance would not be expected until an effective city-state program of remedial action, no matter how politically troublesome this may prove, has been developed.

Fourth, prior to receipt of federal assistance, a detailed financial plan would need to be presented for approval by the federal authority charged with administering the assistance program. Criteria for accepting a plan would have to be spelled out—such as the use of standard accounting procedures, unrestricted access by the federal authority to all local financial records, provision for retiring short-term debt other than that required to handle seasonal discrepancies between expenditures and receipts, and so on. Clearly, the plan should provide for restoration of sound municipal finances within a relatively short period and certainly within two fiscal years.

Fifth, a municipality that obtains a federal guarantee for the payment of principal and interest on its issuance of new securities should be required to pay an appropriate guarantee fee. The municipal security should be taxable, but tax-exempt bonds might be permitted in special cases—for example, if return to nonguaranteed status were thus eased. In such cases, the guarantee fee would naturally have to be much higher than if the security were taxable.

Sixth, and finally, the federal guarantee program should be of limited scope and duration. The total amount of guaranteed debt should be set at the lowest practical figure. The debt instruments should be of short maturity so that the guarantee may be reconsidered periodically. In order to minimize federal exposure to risk and to assure compliance with the approved financial plan, the federal government should have authority to withhold revenue-sharing funds from a delinquent municipality. At the end of a relatively short period, say three years, all federally guaranteed debt under the program should have expired.

If conditions along the several lines I have here suggested were included in a legislative plan for assisting troubled municipalities, the number of applicants that might seek federal aid would be severely limited. It is highly important to recognize that the issue of assistance to New York City goes to the very heart of our system of separation of powers between the federal and state governments—a system that, despite enormous economic and social changes, is still honored by our country. If there is to be any legislation on assisting local governments, it should at least be designed so that the longer-run risks to our federal system of government are kept to a minimum.

Before bringing this testimony to a close, I want to make two additional comments briefly.

First, recent attention to New York City's difficulties has brought to the fore certain shortcomings of our bankruptcy laws. It is highly important that the Congress enact legislation that would enable the judiciary to deal with a municipal default so that reorganization of outstanding debts, service or employee contracts, and other financial obligations may proceed in an orderly and expeditious manner.

Second, the behavior of financial markets has recently been disturbed by the grave uncertainties surrounding New York City finances. A quick but well considered decision by the Congress to assist or not to assist New York is now urgently needed. Almost any resolution of these uncertainties may be better than prolonged debate and controversy. Financial markets do not thrive in such an environment.

Moderation in Fiscal Policy

I am pleased to appear before the Committee to Investigate a Balanced Federal Budget of the Democratic Research Organization.

Our country is now confronted with a serious dilemma. Over 7 million people are still unemployed, and many of them have been seeking work for an extended period. More jobs are clearly needed—not only for workers who are now unemployed, but also for those who will soon be entering the labor force.

In the current inflationary environment, however, expansionist policies of the traditional type cannot be counted on to restore full employment. Recent experience in both our own and other industrial countries suggests that once inflation has become ingrained in the thinking of a nation's businessmen and consumers, highly expansionist monetary and fiscal policies do not have their intended effect. In particular, instead of fostering larger consumer spending, they may intensify inflationary expectations and lead to larger precautionary savings and sluggish consumer buying. The only sound course for fiscal and monetary policy today is one of prudence and moderation.

One of the urgent tasks facing our nation is to end the federal deficits that have been a major and persistent source of our inflation. Since 1960, the federal budget has been in deficit every year but one. The cumulative deficit in the unified budget over the past ten years, including the official estimate for the

Statement before the Committee to Investigate a Balanced Federal Budget of the Democratic Research Organization, House of Representatives, March 23, 1976.

current fiscal year, comes to $217 billion. If the spending of off-budget agencies and government-sponsored enterprises is taken into account, the aggregate deficit for the ten years amounts to almost $300 billion.

This sorry record of deficit financing means, of course, that we as a people have been unwilling to tax ourselves sufficiently to finance the recent sharp increases of governmental spending. In this bicentennial anniversary of our nation's independence, we would do well to reflect on the fact that it took all of 186 years for the annual total of federal expenditures to reach the $100 billion mark. This occurred in fiscal year 1962. Only nine years later, in fiscal 1971, expenditures already exceeded $200 billion. Four years from that date, in fiscal 1975, the $300 billion mark was passed. And unless expenditures are held under a very tight rein, federal spending will easily exceed the $400 billion level in fiscal 1977.

One aspect of the sharply rising curve of expenditures is that government has been assuming an ever larger role in the economic life of our people. In 1929, federal expenditures amounted to less than 3 percent of the dollar value of our total national output, and expenditures at all levels of government—federal, state, and local—amounted to about 10 percent of the national product. Last year, federal expenditures alone were about 25 percent of the dollar value of our national output, and the combined expenditures of all governmental units reached almost 40 percent.

Much of this increase in the role of government in our economy was made necessary by the rapid growth of population in recent decades, the increasing complexity of modern urban life, the explosion of military technology, and the enlarged responsibilities of the United States in world affairs. However, the trend of federal spending has also been significantly influenced by strong intellectual currents, both in our country and elsewhere, that keep nourishing the belief that practically all economic and social problems can be solved through the expenditure of public funds.

Where the line can best be drawn between governmental and private use of resources is, in the final analysis, a matter of social or philosophic values and of political judgment. But regardless of how this question is resolved, it should be clear to everyone that federal spending, whatever its level, must be soundly financed. The large budgetary deficits that have persisted since the mid-sixties—and in good years as well as bad years—added little to our capacity to produce, but they added substantially to aggregate monetary demand for goods and services. They were thus largely responsible for the ten-year stretch of accelerating inflation that culminated in the deep recession from which we are now emerging.

The President's budgetary program for the coming fiscal year, taken on an overall basis, would go far toward breaking the spiral of federal spending and bringing order to our fiscal affairs. The proposed budget would limit the rise of spending in fiscal 1977 to 5½ percent, compared with an average yearly increase of 12 percent over the previous five years. The federal deficit is projected to decline from $76 billion in the current fiscal year to $43 billion in the next, with a balanced budget finally in view by fiscal 1979.

Some well-meaning citizens are now urging the Congress to provide added fiscal stimulus in the interest of speeding the return to full employment. I would warn this group that still larger federal expenditures and a bigger deficit may fail of their purpose. A deeper deficit would require the Treasury to rely more heavily on credit markets, thus drawing on funds badly needed for homebuilding and for business capital formation. Worse still, a significantly larger deficit would revive fears of accelerating inflation and weaken the confidence of businessmen and consumers that is essential to the return of general prosperity.

Moderation in monetary policy is also needed to bolster confidence in the economic future. That is why the Federal Reserve has been so diligently seeking to foster a financial climate conducive to a satisfactory recovery, but at the same time to minimize the chances of rekindling inflationary fires. Since last spring, growth rates of the major monetary aggregates— while varying widely from month to month—have generally been within the ranges specified by the Federal Reserve in its periodic reports to the Banking Committees of the Congress.

The recent moderate increases in the monetary aggregates have been accompanied, as we expected, by a sharp rise in the turnover of money balances. The rising velocity of money has not, however, been associated with higher rates of interest or developing shortages of credit—as some critics of Federal Reserve policy had predicted. On the contrary, conditions in financial markets have eased materially. They are more comfortable now than at any time in the past two years, and thus remain favorable to continued economic expansion.

Before closing, I feel bound to say that fiscal and monetary policies alone cannot be expected to achieve our economic goals in the current economic and financial environment. It is not enough to ask what further fiscal stimulation, if any, or what further monetary stimulation, our economy requires. Nor is this even the basic question. We should rather be asking what governmental policies, covering as they might an enormous range of actions and even inactions, are most likely to strengthen the hope and confidence of our people. Let me briefly comment on some policies outside the monetary and fiscal area that, in my judgment, can make a significant contribution to the restoration of full employment and also to correcting the long-run inflationary bias in our economy.

First, governmental efforts are long overdue to encourage improvements in productivity through larger investment in modern plant and equipment.

Second, we should face up to the fact that environmental and safety regulations have in recent years run up costs and prices and have held up industrial construction across our land.

Third, a vigorous search should be made for ways to enhance price competition among our business enterprises.

Fourth, governmental policies that affect labor markets cry out for review.

Finally, we need to think through the appropriate role of a limited incomes policy in the present environment.

Under current conditions, the return to full employment will have to depend rather heavily on structural policies that serve to reinvigorate competition and release the great energies of our people. Such policies are not, however, a substitute for responsible fiscal and monetary actions. In order to strengthen the confidence of people in their own future and the future of our country, we in government will need to work constructively on all three policy fronts—fiscal, monetary, and structural.

Current Fiscal Requirements

It is a particular pleasure, Mr. Chairman—and I do not say that lightly—for me to meet with this committee. For many years, I joined other citizens in urging a reform of the budget process, so that tax and expenditure decisions of the Congress would become effectively linked. Passage of the Congressional Budget Act of 1974 was a major landmark in financial reform—comparable in importance, I think, to the Budget and Accounting Act of 1921 which rationalized budgetary procedures for the executive branch. In my judgment, the experience of the last two years confirms the wisdom of the 1974 innovation. The new element of order and discipline that this committee, your counterpart in the Senate, and the Congressional Budget Office have brought to fiscal deliberations has served the American people well. We finally have a mechanism for determining congressional priorities and relating expenditures to prospective revenues.

Today, I would like to share with you my views about evolving trends in economic and financial conditions and to spell out the implications, as I see them, of those trends for some of the critical economic policy questions that confront our nation.

This winter's unusual weather has, of course, greatly complicated the interpretation of statistical data. For a while, jobs, output, and sales were significantly affected by cold weather and interruptions of fuel supplies, especially in the eastern half of the country. And in parts of the West, drought conditions have

Statement before the Committee on the Budget, House of Representatives, March 2, 1977.

necessitated the rationing of water and may later affect some branches of agriculture and also the cost and availability of hydroelectric power.

These vagaries of the weather have left their mark on household budgets through their impact on incomes, fuel bills, and food prices. The overall economic effect, however, in all probability will prove considerably smaller than many news accounts initially suggested. The period of acute disruption of industrial and commercial operations was, after all, brief, and as we meet here today, production and employment appear to have recovered in most places. While I am sure that the hardships imposed on many American families by this winter's extraordinary weather will long be remembered, it seems most unlikely that the disturbance we have suffered will have large or lasting effects on the performance of our economy.

There is good reason, I think, to feel a sense of encouragement about the way in which underlying economic conditions are unfolding. Before the advent of inclement weather, the economy was already emerging from the phase of hesitancy that prevailed for a while last year. During the closing months of 1976, the demand for goods and services—except for inventory additions—accelerated, reflecting primarily a resurgence of consumer buying and a further strong advance in homebuilding. The improvement in sales volume enabled business firms to work off a good part of the excess inventories that had accumulated over preceding months when buying was fairly sluggish. With sales and stocks coming into better balance, the pace of orders and production began to quicken and the demand for labor strengthened. This reacceleration of the recovery was the consequence, in my judgment, of gradually cumulating strength in key sectors of our economy and an improved financial environment. I believe that we shall see evidence before long that the reacceleration has survived the weather disturbance, and I expect good gains to be recorded in general economic activity this year.

Emerging trends in the consumer sector were strongly favorable as this year began. The considerable expansion in jobs last year, also the decline in the rate of inflation and the enlarged liquid assets of households, served to improve consumer sentiment. It seems reasonable to think that it is those trends—rather than the transitory effects of bad weather—that will basically condition household behavior in the months ahead.

A quickening tempo, as I have noted, developed in late 1976 for both incomes and employment. This created the basis for more aggressive retail buying. Indeed, reliance on instalment credit to finance purchases of consumer durable goods increased in late 1976; and, strikingly, the personal saving rate for the fourth quarter fell to its lowest reading in several years.

One consequence of the buying surge was that inventories toward the close of last year fell below levels preferred by many business firms. In some instances further depletion of stocks has since then occurred because of the production curtailments occasioned by bad weather and fuel problems. Very possibly, therefore, considerable inventory investment by businesses lies ahead.

The major influences that affect residential construction are also favorable. Indeed, except for January's weather-related setback, housing activity has been in a strong upward movement since last autumn. The swelling of new housing starts in the fourth quarter of 1976—to a rate, incidentally, 30 percent greater than a year earlier—assures that work on homes under construction will be very active for a good many months to come. And some further rise in starts is a reasonable expectation, in view of the liquid condition of mortgage-lending institutions and the progressive correction of the imbalances in the housing market that arose during the early 1970s.

The outlook for business capital spending in 1977 is also promising, even though serious questions can be raised as to the likely adequacy of capital formation in our country over the longer term. So far in the current recovery, capital spending has been lagging; measured in constant dollars, it rose by only 3 percent through the final quarter of 1976. This contrasts with an average rise of 15 percent during the corresponding periods of earlier business-cycle expansions since World War II. However, the average rate of gain should be decidedly better during the next year or so.

This judgment is based on a number of considerations—the continuing improvement of product markets, the intentions of business firms to invest as disclosed by survey data, the increasing number of new firms that are starting up operations, the comparatively favorable cash position of corporations, and an impressive uptrend in capital-goods ordering. Contracts and orders for plant and equipment, a leading indicator of invest-

313

ment activity, spurted at an annual rate of more than 20 percent in the fourth quarter of last year, and monthly data covering new orders for nondefense capital goods show the rise continuing in January. To be sure, the level of capital-goods production is still far short of what we normally might expect at this stage of cyclical expansion, but we can at least anticipate that it will make a larger contribution to the advance of the general economy this year than it did in 1976.

It is much more difficult to reach a confident judgment about how exports and imports will impinge on our nation's economy this year. In 1976, both exports and imports rose considerably, but our export trade was held back by the weak expansion of many foreign economies. The rise in imports was far more pronounced, reflecting in significant part our increasing dependence on foreign sources of fuel. Some further decline in our trade balance and also in the broader current account balance is likely this year, but not nearly to the degree that occurred in 1976.

The challenge facing our exporters is formidable because of the continuation of less decisive recovery tendencies abroad than here at home. In some instances, less vigorous economic growth reflects actions taken by foreign officials to cope with severe inflationary problems and the accompanying imbalances in international payments. An important drag on recovery in numerous countries is the ongoing adjustment, as yet far from complete, to the quantum jump of oil prices since 1973. Thus, our export trade may be adversely affected for some time, particularly since the external indebtedness of many nations cannot continue rising as rapidly as it has in recent years.

But with the exception of these uncertainties relating to foreign trade, factors on the demand side generally seem to point to good growth in our nation's output this year. Buttressing that expectation is the fact that overall financial conditions in this country—an area in which the Federal Reserve System has a major responsibility—provide a satisfactory foundation for economic growth.

The basic objective of monetary policy in the recent past has been to promote conditions conducive to substantial expansion in economic activity, while guarding against the release of new inflationary forces. To that end, the Federal Reserve has fostered moderate rates of monetary growth. During the period extending from the cyclical trough of March 1975 to February of this year, M_1, the narrowly defined money stock—which includes only currency and demand deposits—grew at an annual rate of 5.6 percent. A broader monetary aggregate, M_2—which includes as well savings and consumer-type time deposits at commercial banks—increased at a 10.7 percent rate.

These increases in the stock of money have proved adequate to finance a large gain in the physical volume of output and employment. Indeed, the evolving stock of money could readily have accommodated larger growth in economic activity than actually occurred. In that connection, it is important to bear in mind that consideration of the stock of money alone is not sufficient for assessment of the adequacy of the economy's liquidity. Money has a second dimension, namely, velocity, or—in common parlance—the efficiency with which it is being used. For the narrowly defined money supply, efficiency of use has been improving with special rapidity in recent years, reflecting numerous innovations in financial technology that serve to reduce reliance on demand deposits for handling monetary transactions. In fact, during the span of the current recovery, the gains recorded in the efficiency of M_1 appear to have exceeded typical gains during corresponding periods of past cyclical upswings.

Major benefits have flowed from the Federal Reserve's carefully fashioned monetary policy. By holding resolutely to a course of moderation—a policy that at times has run counter to strongly voiced urgings that we be much more expansionist— we have helped in very significant degree, I think, to dampen inflationary expectations. This has strengthened public confidence—both here and abroad—in the value of our currency and in the future of our economy.

Mainly as a result of the lessening of inflationary expectations, interest rates have not increased as they usually do in a period of cyclical expansion. On occasion during the past two years, both short- and long-term interest rates have registered noticeable upward movements, but the general trend has been downward in the yields on securities traded in public markets and also in the interest charges on loans extended by financial institutions. In general, interest rates are appreciably lower now than they were at the beginning of the economic expansion—a fact that augurs well for the continuation of recovery. One of

315

the considerations brightening the housing outlook, for example, is that the average rate on residential mortgage loans across the country has come down almost 1½ percentage points from its earlier high. Also important to the housing outlook is the fact that the rates paid by mortgage-lending institutions to their depositors remain attractive relative to money market obligations, so that no threat exists—at least for the immediate future —of heavy shifts of funds out of such institutions.

Significantly, our nation's business enterprises have made good use of the prevailing financial climate to improve their liquidity. Corporations have issued a huge volume of long-term bonds, and they have used the proceeds largely to repay short-term debt and to acquire liquid assets. They have also greatly increased the volume of stock flotations above the depressed level during the recession. Supplementing these actions, business enterprises have followed generally conservative dividend policies, thereby retaining substantial amounts of current earnings for internal use. The consequence of this combination of moves is that corporate balance sheets have a much healthier look now than they did several years ago. The average maturity of outstanding corporate debt has been lengthened appreciably, and businesses now also have more equity relative to debt. This clearly puts business firms in a good position to expand the scale of their operations as opportunities arise. For a while the improvement in liquidity occurred mainly in the case of firms enjoying the highest credit ratings and therefore having the easiest access to longer-term funds; but the improvement has progressively become a generalized phenomenon.

The favorable condition of financial markets has been of important help as well to the nation's state and local governments. Record volumes of new tax-exempt bonds were sold in 1975 and 1976, in part to pay off short-term debt. Those repayments, together with progress made by many states and municipalities in strengthening their budgetary positions, have improved the standing of such governments with the investment community. Testifying to that is the fact that interest rates on municipal securities have not only declined; they have declined more sharply than interest rates on other fixed-income obligations. In addition, the spread between yields on higher- and lower-quality issues of municipal securities has narrowed. These developments suggest that the demand for goods and services by states and municipalities—which was relatively subdued during the past several years of difficult adjustment—will now expand somewhat more rapidly.

During the past two years, the nation's financial institutions have also strengthened their capability to be supportive of economic expansion. Commercial banks have materially improved their liquidity by doubling their holdings of Treasury securities and reducing reliance on volatile sources of funds. They have, moreover, retained a large share of profits to enhance capital positions, so that the ratio of capital to risk assets, which had declined steadily during the early 1970s, has risen appreciably. Other depository institutions have made similar progress in strengthening their capacity to respond to financing requests. Savings and loan associations, for instance, have repaid large amounts of debt besides adding heavily to their holdings of liquid assets. With savings inflows ample, thrift institutions have already stepped up their mortgage lending to a record level, and they clearly are going to have considerable scope to accommodate further the demands for mortgage credit in 1977.

In sum, both the background of favorable financial conditions prevailing at this time and the growth patterns that have been unfolding in key sectors of our economy justify considerable optimism about the immediate future. Indeed, it seems doubtful to me, as I have previously indicated, that any special efforts to stimulate growth—at least any of a conventional character—are now needed to assure broad economic expansion this year and on into 1978.

I realize that a majority of this committee, as well as the able members of President Carter's economic team, feel differently. I thoroughly respect their judgment as well as yours. In matters pertaining to the future, no sensible person can be at all certain that he has captured the truth. As things stand, I diagnose the condition of our economy somewhat differently, and it is my duty to advise you as I best can.

I believe that we can all agree that, in wrestling with the policy challenges that face our nation, no objective deserves higher priority than that of creating job opportunities for the millions of Americans who want to work but who nevertheless now find themselves idle. But while the goal we seek is clear, appropriate actions for dealing with unemployment are not easy to devise or to carry out.

By my diagnosis, as I have already noted, our economy faces a serious deficiency of business investment in fixed capital, rather than any generalized problem of demand deficiency. The underlying difficulty is that we have done many things over a span of years which have been damaging to the state of confidence—especially the confidence of the business community. Efforts at fiscal stimulation do not seem promising to me in these circumstances. Indeed, they could prove inimical to real progress, if only because they are likely to be perceived by many people as an extension of the loose budgetary practices from which so many of our troubles derive.

By and large, the American public is familiar with the sorry record of federal government finances in our generation. More and more of our citizens have come to appreciate the linkage between the record of persistent deficit financing and the debilitating inflation of recent years. The degree to which we have been unwilling to tax ourselves—even in good years—to finance the programs enacted by the Congress never ceases to astonish me, no matter how often I scan the figures. Only once since 1960 has the federal budget shown a surplus. The cumulative deficit in the unified budget over the past fifteen years, including the newly revised official estimate for the current fiscal year, comes to $308 billion. If the spending of off-budget agencies is also taken into account, as it should be, the aggregate deficit for the period amounts of $337 billion.

We have built momentum into the rise of federal expenditures by the enactment of "entitlement" programs relating to income security and health and by extending inflation escalator clauses to a significant range of federal programs. The merit of many of these responses to the needs of our citizens is indisputable, but the impetus thus imparted to budgetary expansion is nevertheless very serious. It underscores the imperative need for us to be extremely cautious in adding new programs to the budget. In stressing this principle, President Carter deserves your and the nation's full support. But it is equally important that the Congress ponder carefully any abrupt surrender of sizable amounts of tax revenue.

The inflation that has plagued the American economy since the mid-1960s is a complex phenomenon, and it is by no means solely the product of budgetary practices. But there can be little doubt that the chronic reaching of the federal government for both financial and real resources has been a major contributory element in inflation—indeed, the dominant one in my judgment. The federal government was a party—rather than the counterweight it should have been—to the demand pressures that began building up in the mid-sixties and that culminated in the speculative distortions of the 1973-1974 period. Inflation, by my assessment, not only sowed the seeds of the recession that ensued; it also is the basic explanation—precisely because it became so virulent—of why the recession that followed was so severe. Blinded by the explosive advance of prices—which for a while swelled nominal profits—businessmen were unusually slow in adapting their activities to the weakening pattern in consumer markets that had actually become quite well-defined during 1973. When businessmen finally recognized in the autumn of 1974 that their perception of market conditions had been mistaken, the response in scaling back operations was often drastic—in large part because distortions had been allowed to cumulate for such a long period.

A strong residue of caution has been evident in business circles since then. That caution—which explains, I believe, the relatively weak recovery in capital spending so far in this expansion—is an amalgam of several things. These include the rude discovery that the business cycle is by no means dead, a heightened worry about the troubles inflation can breed, apprehension about the cost and availability of energy supplies, a lingering fear that expansionist governmental policies could again lead to price controls, and growing concern about the costs of complying with existing environmental and safety regulations. In short, a confident business mood has been slow to emerge in the aftermath of recession, in considerable part for reasons that relate to our recent history of inflation and government's role in that history. The consumer mood is stronger; but consumers, too, have anxieties about inflation and inflation-inducing actions by government.

What this analysis suggests to me is that governmental consideration of economic policy should focus sharply on ways and means of strengthening the confidence of our people in their own and the nation's economic future. By focusing as we have on the size of a "stimulative" fiscal package, we inadvertently have been diverting attention from what I believe to be the main problem. At this juncture of history, government actions should

aim above all else at reassuring our citizens that the policy mistakes of the past will not be repeated. Indeed, from the viewpoint of the responsibilities of this committee, a consideration
of what not to do again ought, I believe, to serve as the critical
point of departure for policy formulation.

Starting there, I obviously cannot feel comfortable about
the official budget for fiscal 1977, or for that matter about any
budget which moves toward enlarging the federal deficit. This
prospective enlargement comes at a time—unlike that of 1975—
when private credit demands are rising. Thus, a troubling
departure is occurring from the normal pattern of gradually
diminishing demands for credit by the federal government as
recovery proceeds.

On the basis of the revised budget proposals submitted by
the administration, it would appear that federal borrowing in
public markets in the current calendar year could be $10 billion
or so higher than in 1976. The prospect that federal demand for
credit will run considerably higher than earlier seemed likely
has stirred uneasiness among credit market participants, as is
evidenced by the decline in prices of fixed-income obligations
that followed disclosure of the administration's intentions. While
a "crowding out" of private borrowers from credit markets does
not seem a serious threat, at least not for 1977, the enlarged
prospective competition of the federal government with private
borrowers—with the housing sector, for instance—is most un-
welcome. It may impart some upward tendency to interest rates,
and it will also make it more difficult for the Treasury to achieve
further progress in lengthening the maturity of outstanding debt.

I have felt obligated in the course of this statement to
explain to you why, on the basis of my interpretation of the
events that have occurred during recent years, I have reservations about budget moves that do not yet have the appearance
of breaking with the past. Whatever early action is taken in
the Congress with regard to the budget, I hope that the point
I have made about the vital need for confidence-building actions
will carry some weight in your continuing deliberations as the
year goes on. To give Americans confidence that the future
will be something other than a repetition of the past, government
must demonstrate in a persuasive way that it is regaining control
of our fiscal affairs.

The President's commendable goal of a balanced federal budget within four years might still be within reach even if the budget is now enlarged by the full amounts that have been recommended. The task of holding to that timetable will, however, be made more difficult by each and every enlargement of spending. This emphasizes the need for an especially cautious approach to requests for program increases—both now and in the future. In that regard, I particularly want to applaud the President's decision to go forward with a zero-base budget system for fiscal 1979, and also to review very critically the current practice of allowing off-budget outlays. These steps should serve to reduce, if not eliminate, programs that have outlived their usefulness.

Such a budgetary approach, it seems to me, has great potential for helping arrest the powerful upward push of federal spending. For the record, I would note that the Federal Reserve has for some time been conducting two pilot studies of the feasibility of adopting zero-base budgeting ourselves. One of those studies is going forward at the Chicago Federal Reserve Bank and the other in a division of the Board. While evaluation will take some time, I am inclined to think that we may be able to move to the recommended approach fairly rapidly, even though as an independent agency we have no formal obligation to do so.

In closing, I would like to come back for a moment to the workings of the new congressional budget system. I am aware, of course, that the proposal for a Third Concurrent Resolution for fiscal 1977 has been subjected to some fairly sharp criticism. To the extent that such criticism has been directed at the specific content of the resolution, it seems entirely proper. Indeed, as I have made clear here today, I take some exception myself to its basic thrust. The legitimacy of having a third resolution, however, does not seem to me to be open to question. If a judgment emerges after acceptance of a particular concurrent resolution that some significant change has occurred in national conditions, a reopening of that resolution for revision is a clearly proper and responsible action.

I would voice, however, one cautionary word. As a practical matter, if the Congress were to move in the direction of very frequent revision of concurrent resolutions, the essential discipline of the new budgetary process would be lost. It may

321

be useful to recall that the only previous effort by the Congress to operate with a formal legislative budget—under the Legislative Reorganization Act of 1946—foundered in part because liberal supplemental appropriations made the whole exercise of spending ceilings by concurrent resolution somewhat pointless. While I do not think there is great risk that we shall travel such a route again, I mention that bit of history because it is so vital that the new legislative budget process continue to evolve along the lines of its promising beginnings. The last two years have clearly demonstrated the value of the legislative budget as an instrument for bettering fiscal discipline. This committee has earned the nation's gratitude by its commitment to that objective.

PART FOUR

Sound Money and Banking

The Federal Reserve and the Banking System

It is a pleasure to be with you here in Boca Raton this morning. I am particularly pleased because this meeting gives me a timely opportunity to discuss with leading representatives of the banking community some of the concerns which have been uppermost in my mind since February when I assumed my present position.

The principal concern of a central banker is, of course, monetary policy. I have already expressed my views on this subject at some length in two recent appearances before committees of the Congress, and I shall not return to it this morning. What I should like to do instead is to discuss with you the Federal Reserve Board's administrative and regulatory policies.

Let me tell you, first, how we have altered our administrative procedures. Almost all of the independent agencies of the federal government, acting on the recommendations of the Hoover Commission, now centralize administrative authority in the head of the agency. In keeping with this strong trend, the Board recently delegated the bulk of its administrative responsibilities to me as chairman. I, in turn, have redelegated some of this authority to Governor Sherrill, who in the past has devoted considerable time and effort to this area. I expect that centralization of administrative control will significantly improve the efficiency of our procedures.

Other delegations of authority have been made to other members of the Board, to directors of its divisions and to the

Remarks before the 59th annual meeting of the Association of Reserve City Bankers, Boca Raton, Florida, April 6, 1970.

Reserve Banks, and still further delegations are contemplated. The result has been that relatively minor issues involving banking structure, foreign banking, and internal personnel procedures no longer consume much of the Board's time. We have been able to reduce our meetings from five days a week to three. And we can now devote these meetings largely to monetary and regulatory policy issues, besides attending to difficult or precedent-setting banking applications.

With regard to Federal Reserve actions affecting banking structure, we are taking steps to arrive at prompter action where this can be done without harm to the integrity of the regulatory process. To further this objective, the Board recently created the new post of program director for banking structure, and named Mr. Brenton Leavitt, deputy director of our division of supervision and regulation, to that post. He will be responsible for marshalling staff resources so as to expedite decisions on bank merger and holding company applications.

I should point out that progress in this area is all the more necessary because of the increasing number of banking applications coming to us. For example, during 1969, the Board issued decisions on 91 holding company applications, compared with 44 in 1968 and only 17 in 1965. During the first three months of 1970, we issued decisions in bank-holding company cases at a rate in excess of 150 per year. Streamlined procedures have been introduced to process this increasing flow of applications on a timely basis. Our current goal is to handle all but the most difficult cases within ninety days of acceptance. Considerable progress has already been made in this direction, and we aim to reduce processing time below ninety days as our procedures improve. Let me add that you can be of considerable help to us in reaching these goals by submitting applications which give at the outset all the factual information needed to reach a decision.

The Federal Reserve's current emphasis on centralization and delegation of authority has already enabled us to discharge our responsibilities with increased efficiency and speed. Even more important, however, than these present results, is the improved capability these arrangements have given us to deal with new problems flexibly and effectively.

I would like to convey to you now the trend of current thinking at the Federal Reserve on regulatory policies. There are three basic strands in the Board's approach to regulatory issues. *First,* we always aim to formulate policies that are consistent with the safety and soundness of the banking system. Innovations that significantly threaten either of these elements are clearly undesirable in the long run, whatever their short-term attraction may be. *Second,* as far as practicable, we are attempting to develop policies that will be consistent with market principles. Wherever we can, we wish to avoid introducing artificial constraints upon the free play of market forces. In this way the overall efficiency of our economy will be furthered. *Third,* our efforts are being directed at building a structure of regulatory policies that are consistent with effective monetary policy. Regulatory policies should provide a means for furthering, not hindering, the execution of monetary policy decisions. This is a basic and inescapable constraint within which the Federal Reserve must work.

These efforts to improve our administrative efficiency and to rethink our approach to regulatory decisions have been the result of a continuing process. This process did not suddenly commence on February 1. And, I can assure you it is one which will continue.

The changes within the Federal Reserve that I have been describing are fundamentally a response to changes in the financial environment during the past decade, especially the latter half of the decade. I would like to review with you what seem to me to be the major factors which have led to the new emphasis in Federal Reserve policies.

Bankers have had to function under an extremely tight monetary policy twice in the past five years. Though the banking industry has generally supported anti-inflationary policies in those years, the particular means and degree of the credit restraint to which the industry was subjected brought forth a stream of objections. Circumventing maneuvers by banks occurred not infrequently, and some of these elicited an eventual Federal Reserve response in the form of regulatory counteraction. These episodes were not calculated to endear either of our groups to the other. I shall explore with you a bit later what might be done during periods of tight money to prevent a recurrence of such episodes.

Significant changes have also taken place in the competitive environment of banking in the past ten years. Competition among commercial banks has increased sharply. Savings and loan associations, finance companies, and commercial paper issuers have grown in both size and number. Moreover, new debt instruments have proven highly successful in drawing savers directly into the financial markets and away from such traditional intermediary instruments as bank deposits. This trend toward increasing competition for funds seems likely to continue. I suspect that in the future you will have to work even harder to acquire the funds you need. But, I am hopeful that your efforts to find new sources of funds will not create the strains our relationship has recently experienced.

The decade of the 1960s has also been one of remarkable change in the structure of banking. We have seen a sharp rise in bank mergers, an expansion of branch systems and of overseas banking activities, and a notable increase in the number of bank-holding companies, especially of the one-bank variety.

These rapid structural changes have been in part a cause and in part a result of the increasing competition of which I have spoken. They have also been both a cause and result of changes in the statutory and regulatory environment. Liberalizations as well as restrictions have occurred. But, where limitations on structural change have been imposed—as by the 1966 amendments to the Bank Merger and Holding Company Acts, the imposition of interest-rate ceilings, and the expansion of the Reserve Board's regulations, especially D and Q— increased burdens have inevitably been placed on the relationship between banks and the Federal Reserve. I would hope that these strains will in the future be eased, where this can be done without injury to the public interest.

Another factor which has been instrumental in transforming the banking environment has been technology. The new science of computers and of data processing has had, and will continue to have, striking effects upon our entire society. We have yet to experience the full impact of this technological revolution. The past decade contains some hints, however, of the order of change we will be experiencing. The present check collection system, I am told, owes its survival to the advent of automated processing. The new technology has facilitated the growth of banks, but it has also created problems. Corporate treasurers have learned to manage their cash flows better through the use of automated bookkeeping. Demand balances have suffered as a result, placing additional pressure on banks to seek new sources of funds. In a comparatively short time an electronic payments mechanism will be a reality. As we move towards such a payments system, even greater alterations can be expected in the competitive environment and structure of the banking industry.

At the Federal Reserve we are preparing our communications system for the payments mechanism of the future. At this moment, we are in the final stages of installing a highly advanced computer switching apparatus which will link all Federal Reserve Banks and the Reserve Board. This apparatus should be operating by mid-year. It will provide banks and their customers with a means of moving money and securities at a higher speed than ever before. The computerized operation will permit the gradual removal of limitations on the volume of transfers now imposed on the Federal Reserve leased wire network by manual operations and outdated equipment. This nationwide electronic grid will also be of considerable benefit to the Federal Reserve itself. High-speed communications with the Reserve Banks will improve the timeliness and availability of our data. We expect this improvement in the flow of information to aid our assessment of economic and financial developments.

The changes I have been describing in the financial environment and in the Federal Reserve's efforts to meet these changes through improvements in its equipment and its administrative and regulatory policies must be seen against the broader economic and social setting which encompasses them. Significant changes in the financial environment are usually a reflection of far-reaching economic, technological, and social developments. Thus, the types of economic and social demands society will be making on the financial system will condition the types of activities in which both banks and banking regulators will be engaging. They will, therefore, partially determine the relationship between the regulators and the regulated. Within this setting, I believe ways can be evolved to enable banks and the

Federal Reserve to interact more harmoniously in furtherance of the public interest.

Let me tell you then what I think bankers might do to help our relationship in the future. After that, I shall say a few words about what the Federal Reserve Board can do on its part. Please remember that these are not the official views of the Board, but simply my personal observations. I trust that you will treat them as such.

One way to improve our relationship would be for you to pursue policies which are more compatible with overall economic stabilization efforts. As you know, these efforts require that restraints sometimes be brought to bear on credit-financed spending. In this connection, the task of economic stabilization might be easier if bankers considered reforming some of their lending techniques. I am referring in particular to the practice, which appears to have grown of late, of making binding commitments for large amounts of credit tied to a conventional "prime" rate. Such commitments tend to insulate a sizable sector of credit from the effects of monetary policy. If bankers were to limit their commitments to totals they felt sure they could finance in periods of tight money, and if they charged at least as much for commitment takedowns as they themselves were paying for additional funds, I suspect that some of our nation's battles against inflation would be easier to win.

Another matter which I think deserves more attention is the underlying trend in the quality of credit. The period since 1965 has been of the kind which historically has given rise to deterioration in credit quality, sometimes with unhappy consequences. It is hard to tell to what extent the quality of credit has suffered in recent years, for statistics in this area are fragmentary, and oftentimes of dubious significance. We at the Federal Reserve are trying to press ahead with studies in this field. At this stage, however, those of you in the very midst of the lending process are in the best position to perceive the drift of credit quality. I urge you to be watchful, and to share your assessment of the situation with us.

Lastly, I would urge you to be extremely sensitive to the importance of preserving a vigorous competitive environment both within and outside the banking industry. If you keep this caution in mind, you may save yourselves a good deal of grief at the hands of the bank supervisory agencies, the Justice Department, and the courts. There is much yet to be learned about the essential ingredients and prudent limits of vigorous banking competition, and you can help to further understanding by your comment and example. But, progress in this area needs to be conditioned by a deep awareness of the value that is placed upon truly competitive banking alternatives being available to our citizenry.

The increasing demands on banks for new and improved services create considerable pressure for increases in the size and diversity of banking organizations. It is vital, however, for bankers to remember that public fears of undue concentration of economic power in banks are easy to rouse and difficult to lay to rest. Our nation's economic, social, and political philosophies are not congenial to the creation of monolithic centers of power along the lines of Japan's *zaibatsu*. Bankers. have done very little to allay the fears of the American public, and of the Congress, that efforts to expand the scope of banking are leading us in this direction. Part of the problem here has been a seeming unwillingness on your part to have a sharp line drawn between banking and industry. I personally believe that a reasonable distinction can and must be made, difficult though that task may be. The one-bank holding company bill now before the Congress seems to me, however, to confine banks too narrowly. That it does so is at least partly a result of a gap in communication between the banking industry and the American people.

This communication failure is the greatest we have seen since the 1930s. The banking industry has simply failed to win public understanding and acceptance of its lending practices, its charges, and its aspirations. The result has been a rising level of suspicion and even antagonism. I think the time has come, indeed is past due, for making every possible effort to correct this unfortunate state of affairs. I urge you to take positive steps in this direction.

Now I should like to turn briefly to what I believe the Federal Reserve can do to serve the banks and the public interest more effectively. First, we need certainly to press forward with current efforts to improve our administrative efficiency. Next, I can assure you that we shall try to be sensitive to the effects of changes in the financial environment on the competitive position of the commercial banking industry. In that connection, let me remind you that in February of last year, in a statement dealing with the proper scope of banking activities, the Board expressed the view that "banks should be granted greater freedom to innovate new services and procedures . . ." when these activities are not inconsistent with the purposes of the governing statutes. I look forward to Board action in the spirit of this statement of principle as we consider the bank regulatory issues ahead of us.

I have mentioned before the importance of permitting market forces in banking as much free play as is consistent with the protection of the public interest. This is the kind of generality that is easier to express than to apply, for the pragmatic considerations of the moment often press in an opposite direction. In my view, however, banking is burdened with too many regulatory legacies of past circumstances in which pragmatic concerns overrode market processes. To cite a specific example, I regard interest-rate ceilings on deposits as one device that is overdue for serious reexamination. As a matter of personal economic philosophy, I would like to see an evolution away from reliance upon interest rate ceilings as an ancillary device of monetary policy, at least as far as instruments of the money market type are concerned. When and as circumstances permit, I believe an element of greater economic rationality would be introduced into the financial system if interest rates on such instruments were permitted to find their own level as a result of market forces.

Finally, the Federal Reserve needs to explore means of achieving a more equitable impact of monetary policy on all segments of the economy. The strongly adverse effects of a tight money policy on the housing industry, state and local government financing, and small businesses need hardly be amplified. The public, quite rightly, is especially concerned about housing, which has borne a large portion of the burden of tight monetary policy. Efforts to alleviate this situation must be made.

Among the various proposals now before the Congress, one would require the Federal Reserve to provide up to $3 billion a year to the Federal Home Loan Bank system to support the middle-income housing market. While the underlying intent is commendable, this proposal would undermine the Federal Reserve's ability to stabilize the economy and would eventually lead to our supporting other special segments of the economy. The consequence would be a drastic diversion of the Federal Reserve System from its historic and essential role of protecting the integrity of the dollar and promoting stable prosperity for our nation. I need hardly tell you that I am doing everything I can to promote wiser legislation.

The Federal Reserve has been accused of insensitivity to the nation's housing needs. This is by no means true. We are well aware of the plight of the housing industry and we have under way at this moment a major study of housing finance needs. Its results, I hope, will indicate what steps may dependably be taken to improve the housing situation. A great deal of study will have to be devoted also to other sectors of the economy, particularly municipal finance. Necessary changes are likely to be of a kind that take considerable time to put into effect. Some of them may make the banker's job easier, and some may make it more difficult; but, like all the ideas I have been expressing, they will stand the test of time only if they promote the long-run welfare of the nation as a whole.

Now seems to me a particularly apt time for us at the Federal Reserve to be reexamining our relationship with the commercial banking industry. At this moment financial markets and institutions are under somewhat less pressure than earlier. Money, bank credit, and savings flows are again beginning to expand moderately. There is reason to believe that changes in the financial environment will result in a relaxation of some of the constraints under which banks and their regulators have been operating. The decade before us promises to bring with it even greater changes in banking than the past ten years have brought. I firmly believe that we *can* learn from the hard-earned lessons of the past—that we can find ways to discharge our responsibilities in a spirit of greater harmony and thus bring out the best in both of our institutions. The ultimate benefactor will be not the banks, nor the Federal Reserve, but the public we both serve.

The Structure of Reserve Requirements

It is a pleasure for me, both as a citizen and as a government official, to join in the deliberations of this council. We share many common objectives and we face common problems. Of course, our views have not always agreed in the past, and I doubt if the future can or will be entirely different. It is important, nevertheless, that we make a conscientious effort to understand one another's perceptions of the problems we face. If we do so, we will generally find a path to fair and constructive solutions.

One gratifying demonstration of that fact has taken place in recent weeks. The Committee on Interest and Dividends recently issued guidelines on the so-called "dual prime rate." In response to my invitation, bankers from all over the country met with the committee and its staff to ponder the difficulties surrounding the prime rate in the current environment and to seek a solution that could best serve the public interest. I am especially grateful to two of your leaders, Eugene Adams and Rex Morthland, for giving so generously of their time and wisdom to make the lending rate guidelines fair and workable. And I also want to note that the banking industry has acted prudently in complying with the committee's request to move gradually and cautiously in adjusting the prime loan rate for large businesses. Such a moderate response adds to national confidence in the public responsibility of banking leaders.

Address before the Governing Council of the American Bankers Association, White Sulphur Springs, West Virginia, April 26, 1973.

335

Today, however, I shall say no more of the Committee on Interest and Dividends, but turn instead to my responsibilities as chairman of the Federal Reserve Board. You and I have a number of pressing problems demanding our immediate attention. But it is also essential that we focus on longer-range issues from time to time. I want to discuss with you one of those issues this morning—namely, the structure of reserve requirements.

This is a subject of substantial interest to the managers of commercial banks. It is also a matter of considerable importance to those of us concerned with the nation's economic and financial policy. For reserve requirements can influence in fundamental ways the effectiveness of monetary policy, the cost of financial intermediation, and the allocation of savings among competing financial institutions.

Let me begin by considering the role and purpose of reserve requirements in the functioning of monetary and credit policies.

Before the Federal Reserve System was founded, reserve requirements were imposed by legislation at the national and state levels as a means of protecting bank liquidity. That philosophy was retained in the original structure of reserve requirements established for Federal Reserve member banks. Higher requirements were set for reserve city banks than for country members, and still higher requirements were imposed on central reserve city banks. Vestiges of that initial structure remain, even today.

Required reserves, however, are not really an important source of bank liquidity. The reserves required to back deposits cannot be withdrawn to finance a rise in loan demand, and they can supply only a small portion of the funds needed to accommodate deposit losses. The true and basic function of reserve requirements is not to provide liquidity, but to permit the Federal Reserve to control the supply of money and credit so that monetary policy can effectively promote our national economic objectives.

To achieve good management over the supply of money and credit, reserve requirements must be met by holding assets whose aggregate volume is under the control of the Federal Reserve. Whatever their role may be in protecting bank liquidity, the reserve requirements set by the various states do not meet this test. This is a serious defect, since the principal reason for reserve requirements is their contribution to effective monetary policy.

Judged by this criterion, the present structure of reserve requirements leaves much to be desired. Reforms are needed to increase the precision and the certainty with which the supply of money and credit can be controlled. Reforms are needed to permit more variation in reserve requirements as an instrument of monetary policy. Reforms are also needed to distribute the burden of monetary controls more equitably among the financial institutions that participate in the payments mechanism.

The Federal Reserve Board has been concerned for some time with inequities in the structure of reserve requirements. Last November, we finally used our authority under Regulation D to carry out substantial improvements in the structure of reserves that are required to be held against the demand deposits of member banks.

As you know, the Federal Reserve Act specifies that the Board must distinguish between reserve city banks and other members in the establishment of reserve requirements. Until November 1972, the principal determinant of a bank's reserve status was its geographic location. Banks in principal financial centers were generally classified as reserve city banks; those in other locations fell into the country member category. A bank could, however, have its classification changed by appealing for special treatment based on the nature of its banking business.

With the passage of time, this system of reserve classification became increasingly outmoded and inequitable. Some large banks in cities of substantial size enjoyed the lower reserve requirement on demand deposits applicable to country members. At the same time, there were some small banks in major financial centers that had to carry the higher reserve requirement imposed on reserve city members. Over the years, exceptions had been granted in so many cases—each of them probably justified but different from most others—that the principles underlying the reserve classification of member banks could no longer be readily discerned.

The Board moved last year to eliminate these capricious elements in reserve classification by introducing a graduated reserve requirement—that is, by relating the reserve against demand deposits of each bank to the size of the bank. Under the new system, all member banks of a given size, whatever their location, are subject to identical reserve requirements.

This reform was a major step forward in the creation of a more rational and equitable structure of reserve requirements. Yet, much more remains to be done.

One of the principal steps needed is to apply equivalent reserve requirements to member and nonmember banks. At present, nonmember banks are not required to hold reserves in the form of deposits at the Federal Reserve Banks, as member banks do.

In many states, percentage reserve requirements for non-member banks are comparable to those for Federal Reserve members. However, the reserves required of nonmember banks usually may be carried as correspondent balances, or even in the form of government securities. When reserves are held as correspondent balances at a member bank, that bank is of course required to support these balances with reserves that consist either of vault cash or cash at the Federal Reserve. But in such a case the size of the cash reserve held by the member bank is quite small relative to the initial deposit at the nonmember bank.

The consequence of these differential reserve requirements is that shifts of deposits between member and nonmember banks alter the quantity of deposits at all commercial banks that can be supported by a given volume of bank reserves. Thus, the links between bank reserves, on the one hand, and bank credit and the money supply, on the other, are loosened, and the Federal Reserve's control over the monetary aggregates becomes less precise than it can or should be.

The magnitude of this problem is difficult to assess, since nonmember banks submit statistical reports to supervisory authorities infrequently. Annual data, however, suggest a substantial variability in the relative growth rates of member and nonmember banks. Over the past decade, increases in the volume of checking deposits at nonmember banks accounted for around 40 percent of the total rise in checking deposits. But the proportion was as low as one-tenth in 1962 and as high as three-fourths in 1969. Variations of this magnitude add to uncertainty about the effects of open market operations on bank credit and deposits, on the cost and availability of loanable funds, and hence also on the level of aggregate demand for goods and services.

This source of imprecision in monetary control has become more worrisome as the proportion of bank deposits held at member banks has declined. In 1945, 86 percent of total commercial bank deposits was held by member banks. The ratio had fallen to 80 percent by 1970 and to 78 percent by the end of last year.

In part, this trend reflects the relatively rapid growth of population in areas served by nonmember banks, particularly suburban areas. The major causal factor, however, is the competitive disadvantage that is imposed on member banks by requiring them to hold reserves against deposits in the form of vault cash or as deposits at the Federal Reserve. For nonmember banks, required reserves are, in effect, earning assets even when they are held as demand balances with other commercial banks, since these balances normally also serve as a form of payment for services rendered by city correspondents.

One consequence of this inequity is an incentive for member banks to withdraw from the Federal Reserve System, or for newly chartered state banks to avoid Federal Reserve membership. Since 1960, about 700 banks have left the System through withdrawal or mergers. Just over 100 state-chartered banks have elected to join the System since 1960; nearly 1,500 others receiving new charters chose to remain outside the System.

And the trend continues. During 1972, five banks with deposits of $100 million or more withdrew from Federal Reserve membership. Of the 212 new commercial banks receiving state charters last year, only 13 elected Federal Reserve membership.

Over the years, efforts have been made to reduce the competitive disadvantage faced by member banks and thereby make System membership more attractive. Permission to count vault cash in meeting reserve requirements clearly improved matters. The changes made in Regulation D last November were also helpful, because they reduced reserve requirements against demand deposits—particularly for small member banks that compete actively with nonmembers. Recently, a seasonal borrowing privilege at the discount window was established for member banks that have insufficient access to the national money markets. This, too, should make membership more attractive.

339

Nevertheless, there are limits to measures of this kind that can be taken under existing legislation.

The erosion of membership in the Federal Reserve System is therefore a serious problem. It reduces the precision of monetary control, as I have already noted. It may, in time, also weaken public confidence in the nation's central bank and in its ability to maintain a stable currency and a sound banking system. And it has already reduced the potential for using changes in reserve requirements as an effective instrument of monetary policy. When a large and increasing proportion of total bank deposits is left untouched by changes in the reserve requirements prescribed by the Board, that alone is a fact of some significance. The greater loss, however, arises because the Board must use changes in reserve requirements sparingly as an instrument of monetary policy, since an increase in required reserves would worsen the competitive disadvantage of member banks and thereby threaten a further erosion of membership.

This inhibition has been unfortunate, for there have been times when the prompt and pervasive impact of a higher reserve requirement would have been the best way to signal that monetary policy is moving toward added restraint on the availability of money and credit. In view of the divergence in reserve requirements between member and nonmember banks, the Federal Reserve has sometimes had to turn to other, perhaps less effective, measures to achieve its objectives.

These considerations argue persuasively, I believe, that reserve requirements on demand deposits at nonmember banks should be the same as those faced by Federal Reserve members. Continuation of the present state of affairs is inequitable, and it also weakens monetary control. These difficulties will become more acute in the years to come if corrective legislative action is not forthcoming.

The proposal to treat member and nonmember banks alike for reserve purposes is not new. Its substance was embodied in the recommendations of a congressional committee chaired by Senator Douglas in 1950, repeated in 1952 in the recommendations of a congressional committee chaired by Congressman Patman, endorsed by the Commission on Money and Credit in 1961, reaffirmed by the President's Committee on Financial Institutions in 1963, and restated again in the 1971 report of the

President's Commission on Financial Structure and Regulation. Since 1964, the Federal Reserve Board has repeatedly urged the Congress to bring all insured commercial banks under the same reserve requirements, and to provide all these banks with equal access to the discount window.

I am aware that this proposal is not viewed with favor by many segments of the banking community, and that is the major reason why this needed reform has been delayed. The proposal would be more palatable to bankers if some part of the Board's reserve requirement against demand deposits could be held in the form of an earning asset, such as U.S. Government securities. I do not want to rule out that possibility categorically. Simple honesty, however, compels me to state that, however attractive reserve requirements in that form may be from the standpoint of bank earnings, they cannot serve a useful function in monetary management. As I noted earlier, satisfactory control over the supply of money and credit requires that bank reserves be held in the form of assets whose aggregate volume is directly controlled by the Federal Reserve.

The principle that underlies the Board's recommendation is simple and straightforward—namely, that equivalent reserve requirements should apply to all deposits that effectively serve as a part of the public's money balances. Recent efforts of non-bank depositary institutions to evolve new modes of money transfer make adoption of this principle a matter of some urgency. If legislative action is delayed, we may soon find a much larger share of money transfers taking place at institutions outside the reach of the Board's reserve requirements.

As you know, participation in third-party transfers by non-bank financial institutions has already commenced. In Massachusetts and New Hampshire, mutual savings banks have begun to offer depositors an interest-bearing account subject to a negotiable order of withdrawal—a "NOW account"—that resembles closely an interest-bearing checking account. In California, savings and loan associations are seeking direct access to an electronic money transfer system operated by California banks. Access to the system would enable these associations to charge and credit the savings accounts of their customers in much the same way that checking deposits are handled at commercial banks. Other forms of third-party transfers are likely to spring up here and there.

The Board believes, and has so indicated in testimony to the Congress, that federal regulation should permit developments such as these to flourish, so that the range of services of depositary institutions to American families may be extended. The Board believes, however, that present trends could have significant adverse effects on monetary control unless reserve requirements established by the Federal Reserve are applied to all deposit accounts involving money transfer services. Failure to do so would also have damaging effects on competitive relations between commercial banks and nonbank thrift institutions.

Universal application of reserve requirements to all deposits providing money transfer services need not mean a uniform percentage requirement on all these deposits. There may be a reasonable basis for lower reserve requirements on savings accounts with third-party transfer privileges than for deposits that carry full checking account powers. There may also be a reasonable basis for retaining the principle of reserve requirements graduated by size of the depositary institution. Lack of uniformity of reserve requirements on similar deposits does, however, pose potential problems for monetary control.

There are other aspects of present reserve requirements that also deserve careful and continuing review in the light of our evolving financial structure.

The appropriateness of reserve requirements on commercial bank time and savings deposits has been a subject of debate over the years. It has been argued that cash reserves against time deposits are not essential for purposes of monetary control, and therefore should be abolished as an unnecessary impediment to intermediation. Yet, some observers take the position that reserve requirements for commercial bank time deposits should be increased to the same level as the requirements for demand deposits, so that shifts of funds between the two deposit classes would not alter the relation of bank reserves to bank credit and the money supply.

The merits of these conflicting arguments are difficult to evaluate. At present, there is no convincing evidence of frequent, or large-scale, shifts of funds between demand and time deposits of the sort that could be disruptive to financial markets and to the management of aggregate demand. Still, the potential for such shifts may be increasing with the proliferation of new financial services that facilitate transfers from one type of deposit to another.

Removal of reserve requirements against time deposits would, therefore, seem unwise at this time. And in any event, elimination of statutory authority to impose reserve requirements against time and savings deposits would take away a weapon of monetary policy that is potentially useful for containing increases in bank credit at a time when inflationary pressures are already strong and threaten to become still stronger.

As long as commercial banks are required to hold cash reserves against time and savings deposits, questions will persist about the desirability of similar requirements against savings accounts at nonbank thrift institutions. At present, extension of reserve requirements to savings accounts at nonbank intermediaries does not appear to be needed for reasons of monetary control. There have been times when shifts of funds between banks and nonbank intermediaries have had a disturbing influence on the mortgage market. But those shifts have not produced serious problems for monetary control, and they would not have been prevented by comparable reserve requirements at the two classes of institutions.

From the viewpoint of equity, the case for equal reserve requirements on time and savings deposits at all financial institutions is stronger. Even on this ground, however, it should be kept in mind that the diversified services that commercial banks offer their customers give them an advantage in bidding for time and savings deposits—an advantage that probably still remains after the costs of holding cash reserves are taken into account.

However, if recent trends continue, the increasing provision of money transfer services by nonbank thrift institutions will blur the distinction between commercial banks and nonbank intermediaries, just as it blurs the distinction between checking and savings accounts. As nonbank depositary institutions become more like commercial banks, the basis for differences in reserve requirements will be weakened and so too will the justification for differences in tax and regulatory treatment.

Public policy must take account of the competitive forces

that are altering the structure of our nation's depositary institutions and the character of the services they supply. The need for legislation authorizing identical reserve requirements on demand deposits at member and nonmember banks is of long standing. The time for bringing NOW accounts and any other deposits offering money transfer services under the Board's reserve requirements is clearly at hand. And if the distinctions between commercial banks and nonbank financial institutions gradually fade away, regulatory authority to equalize the treatment of time and savings deposits for reserve purposes will also be needed.

Enabling legislation to accomplish these ends should allow flexibility in implementation. The transition to a new and more appropriate system of reserve requirements should be designed so as to minimize the adjustment problems of individual institutions, and also permit the regulatory authorities to monitor the effects of changing reserve requirements on financial markets and on economic activity. Abrupt changes in the structure of reserve requirements are unnecessary and would probably be unwise. The need, as I see it, is for a gradual transition to a reserve structure that will accomplish two objectives: first, ensure adequate control over the supply of money and credit in the years to come, and second, establish an equitable sharing among financial institutions of the costs of monetary control.

Objectives and Responsibilities of the Federal Reserve System

It is a great pleasure to join you here today at the opening ceremonies of the Federal Reserve building that now graces the Twin Cities. The beautiful new home of your Federal Reserve Bank, with its truly unique architectural design, is the physical expression of the hopes and dreams of many people.

The directors of the Federal Reserve Bank of Minneapolis were looking to the future when they chose the site for this building. They had the courage and vision to make this new facility an integral part of the Gateway Redevelopment Area. In earlier times, the Gateway was known as the entrance to the vast Western prairies. Today, this Federal Reserve Bank can be the gateway to a brighter and better economic future for all Americans.

The business leaders of this great metropolitan area played a prominent role in the planning and construction of the new building. Joyce Swan, the former publisher of the Minneapolis Star and Tribune, was chairman of the board of directors of this Reserve Bank through 1968. In that capacity, he directed the early planning for the building. The late Robert Leach, a highly respected St. Paul attorney, succeeded Mr. Swan as chairman of the board, serving the Federal Reserve from early 1969 until his untimely death in December 1970. The present chairman, David Lilly, played a substantial role in bringing the project to completion.

Address at the Federal Reserve Bank of Minneapolis, Minneapolis, Minnesota, September 8, 1973.

The man chiefly responsible for the new building, however, is the late Hugh Galusha, the former president of this bank, whose career was cut short by a tragic accident in 1971. Hugh Galusha was a most remarkable man. He had the inquiring mind of a scientist, and at the same time the spirit of the frontiersman. He was venturesome, bold, joyous, and imaginative. He was not afraid of newness and challenge, as the unique structure to which he devoted so much of his energy indicates. His fine judgment led to the selection of the architect for the building—Gunnar Birkerts—and to the approval of its unusual design. He convinced skeptics at the Federal Reserve Board of the wisdom of his plan, and he did so in a gentle but persuasive manner.

Over the years, the Federal Reserve System has been fortunate in attracting outstanding men like Hugh Galusha—and his successor Bruce MacLaury—to devote their lives to public service at the central bank. The reason for this lies in the character of the Federal Reserve System and the vital role it plays in national economic policy.

The Federal Reserve was endowed by legislative mandate with a substantial degree of independence within government. Freedom from the daily pressures of the political process has given the Federal Reserve the opportunity to make the hard choices that continually confront those who are responsible for economic and financial policies. Over the years, the Congress has significantly enlarged the duties and responsibilities of the Federal Reserve System. The stature of our central bank has therefore grown within the counsels of government and in the minds of our people. Nowadays, the people of America expect the Federal Reserve to use its great powers to thwart—or at least to moderate—business recessions, and they also look to the Federal Reserve as the ultimate defender of the purchasing power of their currency.

To earn the confidence of the American people, the members of the Federal Reserve family have observed rules of conduct such as animate our great universities and our courts of justice. We have sought to foster a spirit of freedom and objective inquiry in the field of economic analysis. Our staff in Washington and the staffs of the individual Reserve Banks are encouraged to analyze economic and financial problems in the spirit of science and to express their findings freely. The directors of our Reserve Banks, who are drawn from every region and practically every branch of business in our country, provide a constant stream of up-to-date information on business and financial developments. When the presidents of the individual Reserve Banks meet with the Federal Reserve Board, as they do at very frequent intervals in our nation's capital, they have at their disposal a system of economic intelligence that cannot be matched by any organization or agency in our country or, for that matter, anywhere else in the world.

Concern for the general welfare, moral integrity, respect for tested knowledge, independence of thought—these are the basic assets of the Federal Reserve. They are the foundation on which our nation's monetary policy is constructed.

The Federal Reserve must, of course, account for its stewardship to the Congress and to the general public. We do so through news releases, publications, public addresses, and testimony before congressional committees. The information that our central bank discloses about its myriad activities vastly exceeds, both in promptness and detail, that of any other central bank. We do, of course, withhold for a time information that could cause embarrassment to a foreign government or that might enable the more alert members of the financial community to gain an early and unfair advantage over other citizens by becoming privy to the precise plans that the Federal Reserve has set in motion. Even here, once the need for delay in reporting has passed, full disclosure is made by the Federal Reserve, so that the Congress and the interested public may be in a position to appraise the System's policies and actions, and so that we ourselves may benefit from outside review and criticism.

It is precisely because of its openness and impartiality that the Congress has resisted occasional demands to bring the Federal Reserve under this or that administrative branch of the federal government. Both the Congress and the informed public have perceived the great damage that could be done to our nation's prosperity by weakening the independent voice of the Federal Reserve within our government. This sentiment, I believe, has been shared by every president since Woodrow Wilson's time, although the fervor of our presidents for the independence of the Federal Reserve may at times have been greater upon leaving office than when they themselves were still wrestling with the nation's economic problems.

Monetary policy in this country carries a heavy burden of responsibility for the maintenance of economic stability. Actually, our nation sometimes expects more from the Federal Reserve than we can reasonably expect to accomplish, in view of the imperfect tools with which we work and the complex problems that our nation faces.

During the past decade, our nation has generally experienced prosperity, but the prosperity has been marred for many of our people by persistent and rapid inflation. Many factors are responsible for this unhappy development—among them, a protracted and unpopular war, and abuses of market power by some of our business firms and trade unions. But I believe that the most important underlying cause has been the looseness of our federal fiscal policies. Federal spending has been rising with disconcerting speed during the past decade. Despite the costly war in Vietnam, new governmental programs have been enacted at a dizzy pace, almost without regard to their cost or to the state of public revenues.

Deficits have therefore mounted in both good years and bad. In fiscal 1965, a year of rapidly advancing prosperity, the federal deficit came to $1.6 billion. In fiscal 1973, a similarly prosperous year, the deficit amounted to $14.4 billion. In three of the past six years, the deficit came close to—or actually reached—$25 billion. Nor do even these figures tell the full story of how much federal money has been paid out to the public beyond what the government collected in taxes. Governmentally sponsored corporations, such as the Federal National Mortgage Association and the Federal Home Loan Banks, have also gone heavily into debt and poured out additional billions that are excluded from the budgetary totals. In the fiscal year just ended, the net borrowing by federally sponsored agencies exceeded $11 billion.

The continuance of large federal deficits at a time of rapid resurgence of the economy has inevitably stimulated private spending and aggravated upward pressures on the level of prices. In fact, our economy is suffering at present from stronger inflationary pressures than at any time since the outbreak of the Korean War. Prices have risen sharply since the beginning of this year, and they are continuing to rise.

In view of the huge expansion in production and employment that we have experienced during the past year, it would have been difficult to avoid an appreciable upward movement of the price level even with a balanced federal budget. But as the Fates would have it, several unusual factors combined to impart a new dimension to our inflationary problem this year. First, the devaluation of the dollar not only resulted in higher prices of imported goods; it also affected our price level by leading to some substitution of domestic for foreign products and by imparting a sharp impetus to foreign demand for our products. Second, our economic expansion has been accompanied by rapid expansion in virtually every other industrial country. The worldwide demand for capital equipment and industrial materials—goods for which the United States is a major supplier—has therefore burgeoned. Third, our current ability to expand output of basic industrial materials is narrowly limited—in large part because investment by producers of key materials has been held back in recent years by unsatisfactory profits and new environmental controls. Fourth, bad weather in a number of countries severely restricted agricultural production last year—at the very time when the demand for foodstuffs was rising rapidly in response to the worldwide expansion of incomes and employment. The concatenation of these special factors has played a decisive role in driving up prices this year.

The inflationary problem we are dealing with today is therefore quite complex, and we must be prepared for a further rise in prices in the months ahead. The resulting damage can be minimized, however, if aggregate monetary demand is restrained. The inflationary forces that now plague us will then have a better chance to burn themselves out.

The Federal Reserve is pursuing a course of monetary policy that is designed to minimize the threat of excess demand by restricting the growth of the monetary and credit aggregates. Monetary policy began to move in this direction in the spring of 1972, but at a pace that may appear in retrospect to have been too gradual. In any event, restrictive actions have multiplied both in frequency and impact in recent months. By now,

349

even skeptics in the financial community should be convinced that the Federal Reserve will not flinch in its determination to moderate substantially the pace at which money and credit supplies have been expanding.

A restrictive monetary policy cannot be carried out without causing difficulty for some business firms or households that seek additional credit. The homebuilding industry, in particular, is very sensitive to the level of interest rates and the availability of mortgage money. In view of the outflow of funds from thrift institutions into higher yielding market instruments, mortgage commitments have been diminishing and this is bound to affect homebuilding adversely in the months immediately ahead.

Early in 1970, anticipating precisely the kind of development that is now under way in the housing field, the Federal Reserve Board undertook a comprehensive study of the ways in which the chronic fluctuations of housing construction may best be moderated. Two years later, in March 1972, the Board presented its report to the Congress. The Board's recommendations for legislative action deserve more careful consideration than they have yet received. If the needed reforms come too late to help in the present difficulty, they can still serve the larger purpose of stabilizing housing finance over the long future. Meanwhile, the several housing agencies, which have been softening the impact of credit shortages on homebuilding activity, are in a position to continue to do so. And the Federal Reserve System, as the lender of last resort, will, of course, honor its obligation to provide emergency credit in the event of need. I might add that it appears unlikely that such a need will arise.

The time will surely come when monetary policy can again be less restrictive, but that time has not yet arrived. At present, there is no real alternative to a restrictive monetary policy. To be sure, if we permitted money and credit to expand at a more rapid pace, short-term interest rates would decline for a brief period. But in so doing we would be adding fuel to the inflationary fires now raging. Before very long, interest rates would rise again, and probably well beyond their present level, as both lenders and borrowers adjusted to the quickened pace of inflation. The simple and inescapable truth is that inflation and high nominal interest rates go together.

The Federal Reserve must therefore persevere in its present policy. Fortunately, there are some signs that our efforts are bearing fruit. For example, the narrowly defined money supply —that is, currency plus demand deposits—grew at an annual rate of 6 percent during the first half of 1973, compared with a growth rate of 7½ percent during 1972. In recent weeks, the growth rate has slowed further. During July and August, the money stock rose at an annual rate of only about 2 percent. These signs of better control over the growth of the money supply are encouraging, but the Federal Reserve will need more convincing evidence on moderation of the monetary and credit aggregates before it can responsibly relax its pressure on the monetary brake.

Of late, there have also been encouraging developments with respect to our international balance of payments. Our competitive position in world markets has dramatically improved over the past year, and the deficit in our trade accounts that was for some time a source of great concern has now all but vanished. In fact, we enjoyed a modest trade surplus in the month of July, and the outlook for our exports continues to be very promising. These developments have not gone unnoticed in the financial world, and the dollar has strengthened markedly in recent weeks in foreign exchange markets. Intervention in these markets by the Federal Reserve has helped to bring about this turn in the dollar's value. However, a more basic factor in the recent improvement in the value of the dollar relative to other currencies is the increasing recognition abroad that the American people are determined to bring inflation under control and that they will support any reasonable policy that promotes this objective.

Governmental efforts to stabilize the general price level must therefore persist until the forces of inflation are fully dissipated. Since direct controls over wages and prices in the present environment can provide only limited benefits, primary reliance in this struggle must be placed on monetary and fiscal policies.

Clearly, monetary policy must play a major role in the fight against inflation, but we should not expose the economy

351

to unnecessary risks by overburdening this tool of policy. Additional restraint through fiscal policy, in the form of reduced government spending or increased taxes, would be helpful even now. Particularly appropriate would be fiscal measures that could be quickly reversed if economic activity began to weaken, as sometimes happens after a prolonged period of economic expansion.

We also need to improve our instruments of monetary policy to gain better control over the monetary aggregates. More precise management of money and credit supplies could be achieved if the reserve requirements that apply to demand deposits of Federal Reserve member banks were extended to all commercial banks.

The present limitation of the reserve requirements imposed by the Federal Reserve to the System's member banks, apart from being inequitable, weakens monetary control. All demand deposits are a part of the nation's money supply, and they should be treated equally from the standpoint of reserve requirements. The difficulties already imposed on monetary policy as a result of the unequal treatment of demand deposits at member and nonmember banks will become more acute in the years ahead in the absence of corrective legislation. The Federal Reserve Board must therefore urge the Congress to give this problem its earnest consideration. The solution that we shall propose will not infringe in any significant way on our dual banking system, and yet it will enable the monetary authority to achieve more precise control over the monetary aggregates.

I need hardly say, in closing my remarks, that there is much unfinished business to attend to in our struggle to control inflation, to manage the nation's money supply, to stabilize housing construction, and to deal with a host of other economic and financial problems. I am optimistic, however, about the future of our nation's economy. Progress in moving toward equilibrium in our international payments accounts has been encouraging. So also has the recent evidence of moderation in the growth of monetary aggregates. And agricultural production in this region of our nation and elsewhere is now on the increase, offering hope that food supplies will soon be more plentiful.

The principal source of my optimism, however, lies not in

these general indicators of progress in dealing with economic and financial problems, but in my faith in our nation and its good people. Our country has been blessed with rich natural resources and our people have been endowed with the vision and energy to strive for a better life. Let us dedicate the new Federal Reserve building today to the brighter future that is the hope and dream of every American.

Maintaining the Soundness of
Our Banking System

This year, for the first time in decades, questions have been raised about the strength of our nation's, and indeed the world's, banking system. It is profoundly disturbing to me, as indeed it must be to all of you, that such questions should be raised.

Over the past century or longer, the American people have repeatedly demonstrated their determination to have a sound system of banking, and they have been willing to take whatever steps are necessary to assure it. The central role now played by American banks in international trade and finance imparts a new and global dimension to the need for confidence in our banking system. This international responsibility is made all the more compelling by the sudden and massive flows of funds to and from the oil-exporting countries. It is clearly of vital importance for the United States and the rest of the world that our commercial banks continue to measure up to the heavy obligation of financial stewardship now placed upon them.

In the past year, we have had the two largest bank failures in the nation's history. This fact has been widely noticed, as it deserves to be. But it is equally important to recognize that these failures did not cause any loss to depositors. Nor did they have serious repercussions on other banks or businesses. The ability of our financial system to absorb such shocks reflects

Address at the 1974 American Bankers Association Convention, Honolulu, Hawaii, October 21, 1974.

credit on the safeguards that Congress has developed in response to past experience.

One crucial element of our banking strength is federal insurance of deposits. Another major source of banking strength is the Federal Reserve System's ability and willingness to come promptly to the assistance of banks facing a temporary liquidity squeeze. The financial world understands that our banking system can be and will be supplied with funds in whatever amount is necessary to forestall a credit crunch.

Nonetheless, it is important to ask why, for the first time since the Great Depression, the availability of liquidity from the central bank has become such an essential ingredient in maintaining confidence in the commercial banking system. The economy is operating at a reduced, but still very high, level. Bank profits are generally satisfactory. There is no danger of withdrawal of deposits for purposes of hoarding. Very few of our banks should need to count on federal support in circumstances such as these. It is in order, therefore, to take a close look at recent trends in banking.

Commercial banking has been undergoing a profound evolution for well over a decade. The focus of bank management still embraces the traditional fiduciary responsibilities, but goals of profitability and growth have been receiving more and more attention. The recruitment and promotion policies of many banks nowadays emphasize entrepreneurial talent. Their internal controls are elaborately designed to weed out inefficient operations, and to stress the profits being generated by individual departments. Innovation has become one of the prime attributes of the pace-setting banks, and competition has sharpened appreciably in the process.

In seeking growth and profitability in an increasingly competitive environment, banks have generally succeeded in meeting the needs of their business customers more effectively. Deposit instruments have been tailored to meet the special needs of customers. New types of lending arrangements to serve business and institutional borrowers have proliferated. The capability of banks to assist their customers in financial management has also come to include "off balance-sheet" activities, such as bookkeeping, data processing, and financial advisory services. And as regional banks have entered national markets for loans and deposits, while local banks kept entering regional markets, the banking alternatives available to business firms have multiplied and the nation's money and credit markets have become more closely integrated.

For many years now, banks have been cultivating aggressively the area of consumer finance. Besides competing intensively for consumer deposits, they have been promoting installment credit and increasing home mortgage lending. Where possible, banks have expanded their branch networks to facilitate the quest for consumer business, and the result has been a dramatic increase in the number of banking offices relative to the nation's population.

The larger banking organizations have also been driving hard to acquire foreign business—by soliciting deposits, making loans, and conducting other financial activities through their foreign branches or subsidiaries. Foreign exchange operations have assumed a larger dimension in the workaday world of banking, and this activity accelerated once exchange rates were allowed to float and forward markets became essential for the conduct of international business.

The quest for profits and growth has led, moreover, to substantial changes in the structure of the banking system. Bank mergers and acquisitions of individual banks by multi-bank holding companies have resulted in consolidation of small units into larger organizations, which have often added financial strength to individual banks and enabled them to provide a broader range of services.

Nor is that all. One of the most notable manifestations of the drive for profits and growth has been the development of diversified bank-holding companies. These organizations now extend substantial amounts of credit through subsidiaries engaged in mortgage banking, factoring, consumer finance, leasing, and other specialized activities. Many smaller firms in these lines of activity have been rejuvenated through acquisition by bank-holding companies. De novo entry into these lines of activity has also been widespread, thereby leading to more vigorous competition. And since the nonbank subsidiaries of bank-holding companies enjoy the privilege of multistate operation, the growth of their activities has played an important role in the process of knitting together the nation's credit markets.

Clearly, the far-flung changes I have been describing have served the public in many ways. There is, however, another side of the ledger. The very forces that have produced innovative, highly competitive banking have also led to some trends that go far to explain the uneasiness that so concerns us in 1974. The most significant of these trends are, first, the attenuation of the banking system's base of equity capital; second, greater reliance on funds of a potentially volatile character; third, heavy loan commitments in relation to resources; fourth, some deterioration in the quality of assets; and fifth, increased exposure of the larger banks to risks entailed in foreign exchange transactions and other foreign operations. These developments have increased the vulnerability of individual banks.

The first of these trends—the attenuation of the equity capital base—is directly traceable to the recent rapid expansion of the banking system. In the years immediately following World War II, commercial banks were able to accommodate increases in loan demand mainly by reducing the portfolios of government securities accumulated during the war. Commercial bank deposits therefore failed to keep pace with the growth of the national economy. But by the early 1960s, as loan-deposit ratios kept rising and competition became keener, a faster rate of growth became necessary to enable banks to expand further their lending activities. Thus, during the decade ending in 1970, total assets of commercial banks increased at an average annual rate of 9 percent, in contrast to a 7 percent rate of growth in the dollar value of our gross national product.

Then, during 1971–1973, banking assets grew more than 15 percent per year. To some extent this faster growth was linked to the pace of inflation. But banking assets increased more than three times as fast as the price level, and about half again as fast as nominal GNP, which itself reflects the impact of inflation. To a large extent, therefore, the phenomenal pace of recent bank expansion reflects neither price level changes nor real economic growth, but an expansion of banking's share of total financing business, both at home and abroad.

Banks provided over half of total new financing during 1971–1973 in several key domestic areas, including the markets for consumer installment debt, corporate debt other than mortgages, and debt of state and local governments. Expansion in foreign markets has been even more dramatic. During these three years the assets of foreign branches and subsidiaries of American banks nearly tripled, reaching $117 billion. In fact, expansion abroad accounted for more than one-fifth of the growth in total assets of the U.S. commercial banking system during this period.

The diversified bank-holding company has also become an important instrument of growth for a relatively small number of banking organizations. Major banks or bank-holding companies now account for over half of the factoring business, a major portion of mortgage banking, and a significant part of consumer finance and leasing.

And so I now come to my point, namely, that this enormous upsurge in banking assets has far outstripped the growth of bank capital. At the end of 1960, equity capital plus loan loss and valuation reserves amounted to almost 9 percent of total bank assets. By the end of 1973, this equity capital ratio had fallen to about 6½ percent. Furthermore, the equity capital of banks has been leveraged in some cases at the holding company level, as parent holding companies have increased their equity investments in subsidiary banks by using funds raised in the debt markets. Thus, the capital cushion that plays such a large role in maintaining confidence in banks has become thinner, particularly in some of our largest banking organizations.

It has been no simple feat for banks to grow so rapidly. A key tool of management in the drive for expansion has been a shift in emphasis from managing assets to managing liabilities. This is the second of the recent trends that I mentioned earlier.

Liability management requires tapping of external sources for liquidity—that is, borrowing funds as needed to meet the demand for loans from present customers, to accommodate new borrowers, or to adjust to reserve drains. Asset management, by way of contrast, involves adjusting liquid assets in response to changes in the volume of deposits or loan demand.

The development of liability management has led the larger banks to operate on the premise that, within wide limits, additional funds can be acquired at any time as long as the market rate of interest is met. The presumed ability to acquire whatever funds might be needed has encouraged banks to seek new channels for profitable investment; it has also reduced incentives to maintain the liquidity of their assets. Recent experience has demonstrated, however, what banking prudence itself should have dictated; namely, that the funds on which liability management depends can be quite volatile, especially if the maturities are short, and that banks may therefore have to wrestle with uncomfortable—even though they be temporary —liquidity problems.

The shift to liability management has occurred on a vast scale. During the 1950s, commercial banks obtained the major portion of their new funds from increases in demand deposits or equity capital. In more recent years, on the other hand, about two-thirds of the new money raised by domestic offices of our banks has come from interest-bearing time accounts or nondeposit liabilities. Once the concept of liability management took hold, banks developed great ingenuity in tapping the markets for interest-sensitive funds.

Although the beginnings of modern liability management can be traced to the rejuvenation of the federal funds market in the 1950s, the major breakthrough came with the introduction of large negotiable certificates of deposit in early 1961. Private holdings of negotiable CDs now exceed those of any other money market instrument, including Treasury bills. Large, but non-negotiable, time deposits have also figured significantly in liability management. Commercial paper has become another vehicle of liability management; some bank-holding companies rely on it heavily to finance their nonbank subsidiaries. Still another method by which banks have attracted interest-sensitive funds is by borrowing Eurodollars from their foreign branches for use in domestic banking.

Taken together, these several types of interest-sensitive funds have assumed huge proportions. Not only have they become the principal means of financing expansion at many of our larger banking organizations, but the apparent efficiency of liability management has tempted banks to make advance commitments of funds on a generous scale. This is the third of the recent trends in banking that I previously mentioned.

Beyond question, loan commitments have a legitimate place in the array of services offered by banks. But they should be made with caution, since they constitute a call on bank resources that can be exercised at an awkward time. This fact has been driven home in recent months as banks were being called upon with increasing frequency to meet their commitments. Excessive commitments have raised problems for some thoroughly sound banks, and they also have complicated the Federal Reserve's efforts to bring aggregate demand for goods and services under control.

A fourth disturbing trend has been a deterioration, albeit moderate as a rule, in the quality of bank assets. During recent years, as the role of credit in financing private spending increased and as interest rates rose, the debt service requirements of business borrowers have generally grown more rapidly than their incomes, and the additional debt has resulted in a rise of debt-equity ratios. These changes accompanied the efforts of commercial banks to assume a higher proportion of the lending done in the country. It should not be surprising, therefore, to find some tendency toward deterioration in the quality of bank assets.

Finally, both in this country and abroad, the freeing-up of exchange rates has made dealing in foreign currencies both tempting and risky. Not a few conservative bankers who previously had a strong preference for stable exchange rates suddenly discovered that floating exchange rates offered a new opportunity for profit, and some went at it with more enthusiasm than awareness of the risks involved. The large losses that a number of banks in Europe and the United States have experienced as a result of excessive trading or unauthorized speculation in foreign currencies have not only caused embarrassment to these banks; they also have tarnished the reputation of the banking profession.

The confluence of the closely related trends I have just discussed—declining capital ratios, aggressive liability management, generous commitment policies, deterioration of asset quality, and excessive foreign exchange operations by some banks—explains much of the recent uneasiness about banking. Clear understanding of the current situation requires recognition of the interrelated effects of these banking practices on the state of confidence. An increase in doubtful loans is of consequence because it raises questions about bank solvency. Maintenance of solvency is closely linked, of course, to the adequacy of capital and reserves for losses. Similarly, heavy reliance on potentially volatile funds is not dangerous per se; it is dangerous only in proportion to doubts about ability to repay the borrowed money. Such doubts can undercut the basic premise of liability management—that needed funds can be raised as required from short-term sources. Extensive loan commitments are dangerous only when too many takedowns occur at the wrong time. And losses on foreign currency transactions have serious implications for the public only to the extent that they bulk large relative to the basic strength of the banks that experience them.

The developments I have sketched are in large part an outgrowth of the overheating experienced by our economy since the mid-sixties. This was also a period in which corporate profits failed to keep pace with expanding business activities. During the past year, in particular, the demand for business loans grew with extraordinary rapidity, as more and more corporations found it necessary to borrow heavily and to do so increasingly through the banking system. To a significant degree, many banks—especially the larger banks—have met the recent credit needs of hard-pressed sectors of the business community with a fine sense of public responsibility. But that is by no means the full story. Some carelessness also crept into our banking system, as usually happens in a time of rapid inflation, and that is why I have commented at such length on several disturbing trends in modern banking.

Even so, only a very small number of banks can be justly described as being in trouble. Despite all the strains recently experienced in credit markets, the banking system remains strong and sound. There is no reason to doubt the ability of our banks to meet their commitments, even in these trying times. But while faith in our banks is fully justified, it now rests unduly on the fact that troubled banks can turn to a governmental lender of last resort.

It goes without saying that the discount facility is available for use and that it should be used when necessary; but the banking system's strength should not depend heavily on it. In our free enterprise system, the basic strength of the banking system should rest on the resources of individual banks. I believe that bankers generally support this principle, and that their policies are already reflecting renewed respect for it.

It is not sufficient, however, to rely on a rethinking by bankers of their goals and responsibilities. This country, like others, depends on public regulation as well as private vigilance to assure the soundness of its banking system. While the profound changes that I have described were taking place, our bank regulatory system failed to keep pace with the need. To be sure, there has been a great deal of activity among the regulators. Examinations of America's 14,000 banks have continued to be made methodically by the federal supervisory agencies and the state banking authorities. And hundreds of regulatory decisions concerning bank mergers, holding company acquisitions, and the like have been handed down each year by hard-working regulators under federal and state statutes.

But the public attention devoted to adequacy of the safeguards provided by the regulatory system has waned appreciably since World War II. The traditionally interested parties—legislators, bankers, financial analysts, economists, and the bank regulators themselves—tacitly assumed that the sweeping financial reforms of the 1930s had laid the problem of soundness and stability to rest, once and for all. They have therefore concentrated on other matters, such as improving bank competition and adapting the banking system to changing needs for credit.

The stresses and doubts that have characterized recent financial experience are, however, bringing sharply back into focus the essential role of regulation and supervision in maintaining a sound system of banking. The regulatory agencies are responding to this need. At the Federal Reserve Board, concern about the adequacy of bank capital has been increasing. Recent decisions have also reflected a determination to slow down the expansion of bank-holding companies. As one recent ruling stated, "The Board believes that these are times when it would be desirable for bank-holding companies generally to slow their present rate of expansion and to direct their energies principally toward strong and efficient operations within their existing modes, rather than toward expansion into new activities." The purpose of this pause is not only to encourage—and where necessary enforce—a husbanding of resources, but also to provide a breathing spell during which both the Board and the banking industry can give the most serious thought to ways in which commercial banks and bank-holding companies should develop in the future.

In this connection, it is well to note the favorable action by Congress on the legislation requested by the Federal Reserve for authority to prevent, through cease and desist orders, unsound practices by bank-holding companies and their nonbank subsidiaries. I am glad to say that the banking industry supported this needed legislation.

A number of specific projects designed to strengthen the regulatory system are under way at the Board, including establishment of a new program of reporting and financial analysis for bank-holding companies, a critical appraisal of the current approach to bank examination, and concerted efforts to deal with problems relating to bank capital, bank liquidity, and foreign exchange operations. Similar projects, I understand, are under way at the other federal bank supervisory agencies.

I must say to you, however, that I am inclined to think that the most serious obstacle to improving the regulation and supervision of banking is the structure of the regulatory apparatus. That structure is exceedingly complex. The widely used term "dual banking system" is misleading.

As you know, each of the fifty states has at least one agency with responsibilities for supervising and regulating banks. Some states also have statutes relating to bank-holding companies. At the federal level, every bank whose deposits are insured is subject to supervision and regulation, but authority is fragmented. The comptroller of the currency charters and supervises national banks. The Federal Reserve System supervises state-chartered member banks, regulates activities of Edge Act corporations, regulates all bank-holding companies, and controls the reserves and other operating features of all its member banks. The Federal Deposit Insurance Corporation insures nearly all banks, but supervises only state-chartered banks that are not members of the Federal Reserve. The FDIC also has certain regulatory powers that apply to insured nonmember banks.

Those of you who have been intimately concerned with regulatory matters will realize that I have oversimplified, that our system of parallel and sometimes overlapping regulatory powers is indeed a jurisdictional tangle that boggles the mind.

There is, however, a still more serious problem. The present regulatory system fosters what has sometimes been called "competition in laxity." Even viewed in the most favorable light, the present system is conducive to subtle competition among regulatory authorities, sometimes to relax constraints, sometimes to delay corrective measures. I need not explain to bankers the well-understood fact that regulatory agencies are sometimes played off against one another. Practically speaking, this sort of competition may have served a useful purpose for a time in loosening overly cautious banking restrictions imposed in the wake of the Great Depression. But at this point, the danger of continuing as we have in the past should be apparent to all objective observers.

I recognize that there is apprehension among bankers and students of regulation concerning overcentralized authority. Providing for some system of checks and balances is the traditional way of guarding against arbitrary or capricious exercise of authority. But this principle need not mean that banks should continue to be free to choose their regulators. And it certainly does not mean that we should fail to face up to the difficulties created by the diffusion of authority and accountability that characterizes the present regulatory system. On the contrary, it is incumbent on each of us to address these problems with the utmost care. For its part, the Federal Reserve is now pushing forward with its inquiries.

The range of possible solutions is broad. Some will doubtless conclude that the proper approach lies in improved coordination among the multiple bank regulatory agencies, together with harmonization of divergent banking laws. My own present thinking, however, is that building upon the existing machinery may not be sufficient, and that a substantial reorganization will be required to overcome the problems inherent in the existing structural arrangement. I have no illusion that reaching agreement on these matters will be easy. But I have found much wisdom and a strong sense of responsibility among this nation's bankers. I therefore earnestly solicit your views. They will receive full attention as the Board searches for the best path to progressive but still prudent bank regulation.

Monetary Targets and
Credit Allocation

The Board of Governors of the Federal Reserve System appreciates the opportunity to comment on H.R. 212. This bill has far-reaching implications for the workings of our economy. It raises momentous issues with respect to monetary and credit policies, the role of the Federal Reserve System, and whether its traditional insulation from political pressures should continue. I therefore hope that this committee will take whatever time is needed to arrive at a full and just understanding of the proposed legislation.

Section 2 of the proposed bill requests the Federal Reserve Board and the Federal Open Market Committee to "direct their efforts in the first half of 1975 toward maintaining an increase in the money supply (demand deposits and currency outside banks) of no less than 6 percent at an annual rate, over each three month period. . . ." This section further requires the Board and Open Market Committee to report to the House and Senate Banking committees whenever the money supply deviates from the specified target for either technical or substantive reasons.

I want to make it clear at the outset that the Board fully supports the general objective of maintaining adequate growth of the monetary aggregates. Indeed, the Board and the Open Market Committee have adopted policies in recent months to encourage greater expansion in the whole family of monetary and credit aggregates. The Board is also well aware of its re-

Statement before the Subcommittee on Domestic Monetary Policy of the Committee on Banking, Currency, and Housing, House of Representatives, February 6, 1975.

sponsibility to the Congress, and we would welcome the opportunity of clarifying our actions and policies.

In our judgment, however, this purpose can be best served through congressional hearings or other communications with the Congress. As the members of the committee know, the Congress has not found it easy to legislate fiscal policy. If the Congress now sought to legislate monetary policy as well, it would enter a vastly more intricate, highly sensitive, and rapidly changing field—with consequences that could prove very damaging to our nation's economy.

In the past few years, the Federal Reserve System has paid more attention to the growth of monetary aggregates than it did in earlier times. We appreciate the fact that an expanding economy requires an expanding supply of money, that any protracted shrinkage of the money supply may well lead to shrinkage of economic activity, and that attempts to encourage growth in money and credit will lead to a decline of short-term interest rates when economic activity is weak. But, while the Federal Reserve recognizes all this, we are also mindful of the lesson of history that rapid growth of the money supply will lay the base for a new wave of inflation, and that interest rates on long-term loans will tend to rise when a higher rate of inflation is expected by the business and financial community.

As these comments indicate, the Board and the Open Market Committee pay close attention to monetary aggregates. We do not, however, confine ourselves to the particular monetary aggregate on which H.R. 212 focuses—namely, demand deposits plus currency outside of banks. The reason is that this concept of the money supply, however significant it may have been ten or twenty years ago, no longer captures adequately the forms in which liquid balances—or even just transactions balances—are currently held. Financial technology in our country has been changing rapidly. Corporate treasurers have learned how to get along with a minimum of demand deposits and to achieve the liquidity they need by acquiring interest-earning assets. For the public at large, savings deposits at commercial banks, shares in savings and loan associations, certificates of deposit, Treasury bills, and other liquid instruments have become very close substitutes for demand deposits. Nowadays, a corporate treasurer is likely to see to it that the size of his demand deposit is no larger than the working balance required by his bank. He knows that a telephone call to his bank will suffice to convert promptly any negotiable certificate of deposit in his possession into a demand deposit, and he is therefore apt to keep the bulk of his transactions and precautionary balances in the form of interest-earning assets—that is, certificates of deposit or other highly liquid paper.

Let me try to make what I've just said a little more concrete. During the final quarter of 1974, the narrowly defined money supply on which H.R. 212 focuses grew at an annual rate of 4.3 percent. Meanwhile, time and savings deposits of commercial banks, exclusive of large certificates of deposit, grew at a rate of 9 percent; the deposits of non-bank thrift institutions grew at a rate of 7 percent; credit union shares grew at a rate of 9 percent; large negotiable certificates of deposit issued by commercial banks grew at a rate of 26 percent, and so on. We at the Federal Reserve are concerned with all these aggregates because the narrowly defined money supply, taken by itself, is an inadequate—and at times a misleading—indicator of what is happening to the stock of highly liquid assets available to American families and business firms. Since the demands by the public for currency, demand deposits, savings deposits, and various liquid market instruments keep changing, monetary policy has to concern itself with a large family of monetary aggregates. The aggregate specified in H.R. 212 is only one of these.

Moreover, the condition of credit markets also weighs heavily in decisions on monetary policy. There is a school of thought that holds that the Federal Reserve need pay no attention to interest rates, that the only thing that matters is how this or that monetary aggregate is behaving. We at the Federal Reserve cannot afford the luxury of any such mechanical rule. As the nation's central bank, we have a vital role to play as the lender of last resort. It is our duty to avert liquidity or banking crises. It is our duty to protect the integrity of both the domestic value of the dollar and its foreign-exchange value. In discharging these functions, we at times need to set aside temporarily our objectives with regard to the monetary aggregates.

In particular, we pay close attention to interest rates because of their profound effects on the working of the economy. The Federal Reserve's ability to influence interest rates is far

369

more limited than is commonly believed; but in exercising whatever influence we do have, we must think of tomorrow as well as of today. If, for example, we presently encouraged a sharp decline of interest rates on top of the decline that has already occurred in recent months, we would run the risk of seeing short-term interest rates move back up while the economy is still receding. There is, moreover, a very real possibility that, as a result of such a policy, a monetary base would be established for a new wave of inflation in the future, and that market expectations of such a development would lead rather promptly to a rise of long-term interest rates.

It should be clear from these comments that the Board is deeply concerned about proposals to legislate monetary targets. Economic and financial conditions change, public preferences for liquidity change, and what constitutes an appropriate monetary response changes. Moreover, the rate of turnover of money—that is, the rate at which the public is willing to use the existing stock of money—is typically much more important than the size of the stock over periods of six months, a year, or even somewhat longer.

Changes in the public's willingness to use the existing stock of money are a highly dynamic force in economic life. The turnover or velocity of money depends heavily on the state of confidence, and varies widely in the course of a business cycle. If the public lacks confidence, increasing injections of money will tend to be offset by a decline in the turnover of money. The economy will not be immediately stimulated; but a large buildup of the money stock will lay the base for an inflationary upsurge in the demand for goods and services at a later time.

As these comments indicate, it would be unwise for the nation's monetary authority to concentrate on just one aspect of financial life—namely, the achievement of this or that rate of growth of the narrowly defined money supply, as specified by H.R. 212. There are also technical problems of importance on which I shall not dwell, but which I must at least call to the committee's attention. First, H.R. 212 assumes that the Federal Reserve can control the rate of growth of demand deposits plus currency in public circulation over periods as short as three months. This we are unable to do. All that we can control over such brief periods is the growth of member bank reserves;

but a given rate of growth of reserves may be accompanied by any of a wide range of growth rates of the narrowly defined money supply. A second technical problem is that measures of the growth of the money supply over periods as short as three months are surrounded by very considerable uncertainty—a fact that H.R. 212 overlooks.

In view of the formidable difficulties, both conceptual and technical, that surround the section of H.R. 212 that I have been discussing, it is the Board's judgment that congressional concerns with regard to money supply behavior will be better served by careful periodic review of the Federal Reserve's stewardship. I can assure you that we at the Federal Reserve are willing to report fully on the factors that have been influencing growth in money—both narrowly and more broadly defined—and also on how we evaluate monetary expansion in relation to economic and financial circumstances. This reporting could be done on a periodic basis, or whenever special circumstances warrant it.

Let us turn next to Section 3(a) of the bill, which makes it mandatory for the Board to allocate credit toward "national priority uses" and away from "inflationary uses." Certain broad categories of priority uses and inflationary uses are specified. The Board is given the power to add to or subtract from the listed categories by notifying both houses of Congress. If not disapproved within a sixty-day period, the Board's proposals would become effective.

It is important to note that this section of the proposed legislation amends the Credit Control Act. As the Credit Control Act now stands, the president must make a specific determination before the Board can regulate extensions of credit—namely, that this is necessary "for the purpose of preventing or controlling inflation generated by the extension of credit in excessive volume." This provision of law is eliminated by the proposed legislation. As we understand it, therefore, the proposed bill would require the Board to undertake immediately and maintain in force a program of credit allocation that may apply to any or all markets and any or all financial institutions. In carrying out this mandate, the Board would have available to it an extremely wide range of regulatory options, as currently enumerated in Section 206 of the Credit

Control Act. Supplementary reserve requirements on member banks of the Federal Reserve System would be specifically added to that list by Section 3(b) of H.R. 212.

Our financial markets are highly competitive and they have served our nation well over the years. Nevertheless, the Board recognizes that the workings of financial markets are imperfect. We have therefore been generally sympathetic to efforts aiming to improve the flow of credit into socially desirable uses through special federal credit agencies—as in the fields of housing, agriculture, and small business. In early 1972, the Board submitted to the Congress, after a thorough inquiry, recommendations for moderating fluctuations in the availability of housing finance. More recently, in September 1974, the Board circulated to all member banks a statement on appropriate bank lending policies prepared by the Federal Advisory Council—a statutory body established under the Federal Reserve Act. The Board felt that the council's statement could be helpful to commercial banks in shaping their lending policies under the conditions of credit restraint then prevailing.

But as we read H.R. 212, it envisages a comprehensive intrusion of the federal government into private credit markets, and thus goes much further than anything that has been seriously considered in the past. The bill delegates enormous and virtually dictatorial power to the Federal Reserve. Implementation of the bill could undermine the market system and wreck all chances for economic recovery. And it is even highly doubtful whether H.R. 212 could achieve the objectives being sought—that is, larger credit flows to certain uses, such as essential capital investment, small businesses, and agriculture, at low interest rates.

Decisions as to social priorities in the use of credit are inherently political in character. If such decisions are to be made at all, they should be made by the Congress—not by an administrative and nonpolitical body such as the Federal Reserve. After all, tilting credit in favor of some borrowers implies denying credit to someone else. Our economy has developed by relying mainly on the market to make such decisions. The market reflects the interaction of many thousands of borrowers and lenders. If the day ever arrives when governmental decisions are to be substituted for individual preferences expressed in the marketplace, then the priorities should be set explicitly by the Congress.

The specifications of H.R. 212 are so vague and general that they would inevitably involve the Board in political judgments—an area in which it obviously has no special competence. For example, the bill requires the Board to allocate credit toward "essential and productive investment." But how are we to evaluate the credit needs of public utilities relative to the needs of defense contractors? Are we to favor the credit needs of "small business and agriculture," as the bill requires, even if that means that large corporations will be denied the credit needed to keep their employees working? Are we to favor the automobile manufacturer who turns out cars that suit our concept of what is socially desirable and punish the manufacturer whose cars fail to pass our test of social utility? And since the bill requires the Board to move credit away from financial activities such as corporate acquisitions, would we have to deny credit to finance a merger of two firms, even though such a merger is expected to result in a strong enterprise that can better expand job opportunities in its area? Questions such as these may be multiplied by the hundreds and thousands.

Moreover, would it really be wise in an interdependent world to discourage loans to foreigners? Such a policy would handicap our exporters and importers; it would lead to retaliation by other countries; it could cause goodwill towards our nation to vanish; and it would surely diminish, as the entire bill before us would tend to do, confidence in the dollar.

I must add that administration of the credit control program envisaged in H.R. 212 would be enormously complex and costly. I doubt whether it is even feasible. In view of the variety of financial channels available to borrowers and lenders, controls would have to be comprehensive if they were to be at all effective. They would need to include not only the banks but also other institutional lenders, such as the thrift institutions, finance companies, insurance companies, and pension funds. They would need to cover financing through the public markets for debt and equity securities. They would need to embrace the entire network of trade credit. They would have to regulate access to lending and investing alternatives abroad.

Such a task has not been attempted in the history of this country—not even in wartime.

The ultimate difficulty is that a comprehensive allocation program would disrupt the orderly processes of financial markets. It could well create serious industrial imbalances and depress sharply the economic activity of many industries and communities. In the Board's judgment, there is no good substitute for the decision-making process provided by our highly developed, sensitive, and intensely competitive financial system.

Nevertheless, as noted earlier, the Board recognizes the worthwhile nature of special governmental efforts to strengthen market processes or supplement private credit flows—as in the case of housing. The need for such special efforts varies with economic and overall financial conditions. The need is most evident in periods of general credit restraint, when the supply of credit falls short of demand. On the other hand, when credit conditions are easing, as at present, market processes typically assure that credit for commercially feasible projects of a productive and socially useful character will be in reasonably ample supply.

There is no evidence that a significant amount of credit is being squandered on wanton or speculative enterprises. In the latter part of January, the Board addressed an inquiry to a sample of banks to gauge their response to the principles suggested earlier by the Federal Advisory Council—recognizing, of course, that credit and economic conditions change. The inquiry covered questions on the demands by bank customers for the kinds of loans specified by the Federal Advisory Council as well as questions on bank policies with respect to approval or disapproval of such loan requests.

Not all of the banks have as yet replied, but we do have responses from about 80 percent of the sample on the questions pertaining to credit demands and credit policies. On the basis of a preliminary tabulation of these results, about three-fourths of the banks report that loan requests for purely financial or speculative purposes, a category that figures prominently in H.R. 212, were significantly fewer in December 1974 than in previous years or that none were in fact received. Moreover, about 90 percent of the banks report that they have become more restrictive in their attitude toward such loans.

Our preliminary assessment of the survey thus suggests that bank loan policies are generally consistent with the Federal Advisory Council's statement. I believe that even in absence of this statement, most banks would have put in place similar policies, in view of the limited funds available to them, their risk exposure, and their sense of obligation to the local community and the nation. As soon as tabulation and analysis of this special inquiry are completed, the results will be forwarded to this committee and made available to other interested parties.

I believe that allocation of credit among competing uses is becoming a less serious problem for our banks. For credit demands have diminished, interest rates have declined substantially from their peaks of last summer, and many banks and other financial institutions have recently improved their liquidity positions.

I realize that some might argue that H.R. 212 would increase the flow of funds to high priority areas, and perhaps even reduce interest rates for those areas. Such an argument would have to assume that a comprehensive, leak-proof credit control program can be devised and enforced. That is impossible in a complex economy possessing highly developed credit and money markets. Inflation, if nothing else, will lead lenders to seek every possible avenue to increase their yields. Gray markets will flourish, as borrowers also attempt to protect themselves against credit shortages. In addition, both lenders and borrowers will inevitably turn to foreign credit markets. The ones who would probably suffer most are small businesses and home buyers. In short, the Board firmly believes that credit allocation, as envisaged in the proposed legislation, will injure our economy, besides failing to achieve the purposes it seeks to promote.

In addition to the already substantial list of regulatory measures available under the Credit Control Act, H.R. 212 enables the Board to impose reserve requirements on assets with a view to rechanneling credit flows. The bill would permit the Board to require a member bank to maintain, besides the reserves required to support its deposits, a supplemental cash reserve whose size would depend on the distribution of the bank's loans and investments. A supplemental cash reserve would be held against loans and investments other than the so-called "national priority uses," while a reserve credit would be given for "national priority" loans and investments. The total of any such credit, however, could not exceed a bank's supplemental reserve.

Suggestions for redistributing credit flows through differential reserve requirements on bank assets have been advanced from time to time during recent years. The logic of these proposals may seem simple and even appealing. Banks would be encouraged to channel more funds into high priority uses, and away from others, because the structure of reserve requirements would make it profitable to do so. A market device—rather than compulsion—would thus be employed to accomplish a desired social objective.

Careful reflection on the implications of these proposals, however, reveals that they would seriously weaken the capacity of the Federal Reserve to control the growth of the monetary aggregates. Furthermore, while they would impose enormous administrative costs on the banking system, they would be rather ineffective in redistributing credit flows among the various sectors of the economy.

As this committee knows, a major function of the Federal Reserve is to control the growth of bank reserves so as to maintain a rate of expansion of monetary aggregates that is consistent with the economy's needs. That is what reserve requirements are for. To exercise this function effectively, there must be a reasonably precise relation between the volume of bank reserves, on the one hand, and the volume of money and bank credit on the other.

I have noted on a number of occasions that the Federal Reserve's control over the monetary aggregates is already less precise than it can or should be because of differences in reserve requirements on the deposits of member and non-member banks. The consequences of these differences is that shifts of deposits between member and nonmember banks alter the total quantity of commercial bank deposits that can be supported by a given volume of bank reserves.

Differential reserve requirements on assets would introduce yet another element of uncertainty in the link between bank reserves and the monetary aggregates. Every shift in the composition of bank loans and investments between "national priority" and other uses would alter the total quantity of bank deposits that could be supported by the existing volume of bank reserves, and therefore lead either to a contraction or an expansion in bank assets and liabilities. Since changes in the structure of bank assets from one reserve period to the next could hardly be predicted, the Federal Reserve would have much greater difficulty in judging what additions to total reserves were needed to achieve any desired growth rate of the monetary aggregates. H.R. 212 would thus weaken further the Federal Reserve's control over money and credit.

This would be a large price to pay, even if reserve requirements on the assets of member banks could be used effectively to rechannel credit flows. There is every reason to believe, however, that reliance on reserve supplements and credits for this purpose would set off myriad adjustments in other lending markets—adjustments that would tend to frustrate the intended effects of the program.

Let us see how markets would react. To the extent that member banks were induced by differential reserve requirements to shift funds toward certain priority uses, yields on those assets would decline, while yields on other classes of loans and investments would rise. The many lenders to whom the asset reserve requirements did not apply—such as nonmember commercial banks, mutual savings banks, life insurance companies, pension plans, and so on—would therefore be encouraged to direct their loanable funds away from projects of the priority type. Borrowers displaced at member banks, meanwhile, would turn to other lenders or to the open market for credit, thereby forcing up yields and thus encouraging individuals and other lenders to supply them with funds. These offsets would be so substantial, in my judgment, that they would largely negate the results of the supplemental reserve requirements. Moreover, I need hardly say that exemption of nonmember banks from the provisions of Section 3(b) would induce some, perhaps many, member banks to change their status.

Finally, this committee should consider carefully the administrative costs and problems that would be encountered in any serious effort to implement a supplemental reserve program effectively and equitably. Very likely, it would be necessary to require that member banks report detailed data on the structure of their assets on a daily basis, just as they now do for deposits. Otherwise, a bank could acquire an asset eligible for a reserve credit one day and sell it to another lender the next—thereby benefiting from the reserve credit, but contributing nothing meaningful to expansion of credit supplies of the desired kind. Also, it might well become necessary to attach supplemental reserve requirements and credits to particular loans, rather than to the dollar amount of loans in any given category, and this would require the development of elaborate bookkeeping systems for keeping track of many millions of individual loans.

In conclusion, let me state once again that the Board recognizes that adequate expansion of money and credit is needed to cushion recessionary forces and to encourage early recovery in economic activity. I must warn you, however, that the course of monetary policy cannot be guided effectively by a single measure of the money supply, as this bill would require. A careful weighing of the behavior of various monetary and credit aggregates is essential.

The Board also recognizes that the nation's best interests are served when credit flows are channeled into productive uses and away from speculative channels. The market itself is a good disciplinarian in this respect, though it often works with a lag. Developments in credit markets of late have been moving in a constructive direction. Banks and other business enterprises have come to recognize that decisions made in a euphoric inflationary environment are not always those that contribute most to their own benefit or that of the national economy. If inflationary pressures continue to unwind this year, as I believe they will, managerial talent will be concentrated more intensively on efficiency in business enterprise, and participants in financial markets will seek to avoid the speculative excesses of the recent past.

The Independence of the Federal Reserve System

It is a pleasure to be here on this beautiful campus and to join the audience in honoring the graduating class of Bryant College.

In earlier and calmer times, it was customary for a commencement orator to address the principles of life that he thought would be most helpful to members of the graduating class. Such pronouncements are less fitting in our turbulent age, which has sharply narrowed the gap in knowledge—if not also in wisdom—that once separated the generations.

Yet each of us, and here your elders may have some advantage, has had opportunity to reflect with more than ordinary care on his own range of responsibilities. I therefore want to share with you today a few thoughts about the Federal Reserve System, which serves as our nation's authority for controlling the supply of money and credit.

Industrial nations, including our own, nowadays rely heavily on monetary policy to promote expansion of production and employment, to limit any decline that may occur in overall economic activity, or to blunt the forces of inflation.

There are two major reasons for the emphasis on monetary policy. In the first place, manipulation of governmental expenditures has proved to be a rather clumsy device for dealing with rapidly changing economic developments. Secondly, the process of reaching a consensus on needed tax changes usually turns out to be complex and time-consuming. Experience has

Commencement address at Bryant College, Smithfield, Rhode Island, May 22, 1976.

thus taught us that alterations of fiscal policy, once undertaken, frequently have a large part of their economic effect too late to be of much value in moderating fluctuations in business activity.

Even when the economy is booming, legislatures are rarely willing to increase tax rates or to restrain the rising curve of governmental expenditures. Such reluctance also limits the discretionary use of fiscal measures to counter the forces of recession that develop from time to time in a free enterprise economy. Once reduced, tax rates cannot easily be increased again, and new expenditure programs to stimulate a lagging economy all too often are the source of a new inflationary problem later on.

Fortunately, monetary policy is relatively free of these shortcomings. Flexibility is the great virtue of instruments of monetary and credit policy. Changes in the course of monetary policy can be made promptly and—if need be—frequently. Under our scheme of governmental organization, the Federal Reserve can make the hard decisions that might be avoided by decision makers subject to the day-to-day pressures of political life. And experience indicates that the effects of substantial changes in the supply of money and credit are rather speedily transmitted through financial markets to the workshops of the economy—that is, our factories, mines, construction yards, and the range of service establishments.

The founders of the Federal Reserve System were well aware of the dangers that would inhere in the creation of a monetary authority subservient to the executive branch of government—and thus subject to political manipulation. Senator Nelson Aldrich, chairman of the National Monetary Commission, whose investigations of central banking laid the basis for establishing the Federal Reserve System, was deeply impressed with the need for a strong monetary authority capable of exercising discipline over the financial affairs of a nation. Carter Glass, chairman of the House Banking and Currency Committee when the Federal Reserve Act was passed in 1913, reported that the committee regarded the Federal Reserve Board "as a distinctly nonpartisan organization whose functions are to be wholly divorced from politics." That view was fully shared by President Woodrow Wilson, who was extremely careful to avoid any suggestion of interference with the newly created monetary authority, thereby setting a precedent that has been usually followed by succeeding presidents.

The concept of independence of the monetary authority within the structure of government is congenial to the basic principles of our Constitution. As Alexander Hamilton put it in one of the Federalist Papers, our system of government is based on the precept that partitions between the various branches of government "ought to be so contrived as to render the one independent of the other." Such a division of power, according to another of the Federalist Papers, is "essential to the preservation of liberty."

The principle of independence of the monetary authority within the structure of our federal government was embodied in the original Federal Reserve Act in several ways. First, individuals appointed to the Federal Reserve Board by the president were to have ten-year terms, and they could be removed from office only for cause. A president could not, therefore, remove a Board member from office simply because he disagreed with his views, and the term of office was long enough to minimize the threat of covert political pressure on Board members. Moreover, the law provided for staggered terms in order to avoid presidential "packing" of the monetary authority.

Second, the newly created Federal Reserve Board was required to report on, and to account for, its actions to the legislative branch of government, not to the administration.

Third, the operations of the Federal Reserve System were to be financed from its own internal sources, and thus protected from the political pressures that may be exercised through the congressional appropriations process.

Fourth, power was to be diffused within the Federal Reserve System, so that the interests of borrowers, lenders, and the general public were to be recognized and blended in the new regional Federal Reserve Banks.

In the years that followed creation of the Federal Reserve System, experience—particularly during the Great Depression— suggested that the degree of independence assigned to the monetary authority was insufficient. The Banking Acts of 1933 and 1935 sought to rectify this and other defects in the financial structure.

Under the new legislation, the secretary of the Treasury and the comptroller of the currency, who originally were *ex officio* members of the Board, were relieved of this responsibility. The terms of the members of the Board were lengthened from ten years to twelve years, and then to fourteen years, to insulate the Board still more from political pressures. A new agency—the Federal Open Market Committee, including representatives of the regional Federal Reserve Banks as well as members of the Board located in Washington—was established to conduct open-market operations, which by the early 1930s had come to play a major role in implementing monetary policy. Moreover, the principle was reaffirmed that funds used by the Federal Reserve to finance its operations were not to be construed as government funds or as appropriated money. All of these legislative changes strengthened the ability of the Federal Reserve System to resist efforts by the Treasury, or the White House, or any other agency in the executive branch to influence unduly the course of monetary and credit policy.

Senator Carter Glass once stated that intelligent and fearless performance of the functions of the monetary authority "involves as much of sanctity and of consequence to the American people as a like discharge of duty by the Supreme Court of the United States." We at the Federal Reserve have in fact sought to model our conduct on that of the Supreme Court.

In the exercise of our adjudicatory responsibilities, the members of the Board scrupulously avoid any contact with interested parties. In our deliberations on monetary and credit policies, not the slightest consideration is given to questions of political partisanship. Every member of the Board, and every member of the Federal Open Market Committee, weighs the issues of monetary and credit policy solely from the viewpoint of the public interest and the general welfare. My colleagues at the Federal Reserve are highly qualified individuals possessing a diversity of skills essential to the management of the nation's financial affairs. They live and work under a Spartan code that avoids political entanglement, conflicts of interest, or even the appearance of such conflicts. At the same time, the members of the Board, particularly its chairman, maintain close contact with members of the Executive and the Congress in order to assure that the activities of the Federal Reserve are appropriately coordinated with what other branches of government are doing.

Our system of monetary management, I believe, is thus working in the way the founders of the Federal Reserve intended. Nonetheless, there are now, as there have been over the years, some well-meaning individuals in our country who believe that the authority of the Federal Reserve to make decisions about the course of monetary policy should be circumscribed. The specific proposals that have been put forth over the years differ greatly, but they usually have had one feature in common—namely, control by the executive branch of government over the monetary authority.

A move in this direction would be unwise and even dangerous. It is encouraging to find that, despite occasional outbursts of temper, a majority of the Congress share this belief. I doubt that the American people would want to see the power to create money lodged in the presidency—which may mean that it would in fact be exercised by political aides in the White House. Such a step could create a potential for political mischief or abuse on a larger scale than we have yet seen. Certainly, if the spending propensities of federal officials were given freer rein, the inflationary tendency that weakened our economy over much of the past decade would in all likelihood be aggravated.

The need for a strong monetary authority to discipline the inflationary tendency inherent in modern economies is evident from the historical experience of the nations around the world. Among the major industrial countries, West Germany and the United States appear to have achieved the greatest success— albeit woefully insufficient success—in resisting inflationary pressures in the period since World War II. It is no accident that both countries have strong central banks. In some other countries, where the monetary authority is dominated by the Executive or the legislature, inflationary financial policies have brought economic chaos and even extinguished political freedom.

It is, of course, essential that the monetary authority observe the spirit as well as the letter of our laws. In our democratic society the independence of a governmental agency can never be absolute. The Federal Reserve System is thus subject not only to the provisions of the Federal Reserve Act, but also to the Employment Act and numerous other statutes. The original design of the Federal Reserve System recognized this duty by requiring the Federal Reserve to account for its stewardship to the Congress. The oversight responsibilities of the Congress for the conduct of the monetary authority do not, however, require congressional involvement in the details of implementing monetary policy. The technical complexities of adjusting monetary or credit instruments to the needs of a modern industrial economy are far too great to be dealt with by a large deliberative body. At the same time, there is a significant role for the Congress in setting forth the economic and financial objectives that the monetary authority is expected to observe and honor.

Over the past year, the Congress has been exercising its vital oversight function through a new and more systematic procedure, spelled out in House Concurrent Resolution No. 133. That resolution requires the Federal Reserve to report to the Congress at quarterly intervals on the course of monetary policy, and to project ranges of growth in the major monetary and credit aggregates for the year ahead.

We at the Federal Reserve regard the dialogue between the monetary authority and the Congress stimulated by the Concurrent Resolution as constructive. It has given the Congress a better opportunity to express its views on the appropriateness of our actions. It has also provided us at the Federal Reserve with an opportunity to explain fully the reasons for our actions, and to communicate to the Congress and to the public at large our firm intention to adhere to a course of monetary policy that is consistent not only with continued economic expansion at a satisfactory rate, but also with further gradual unwinding of inflationary tendencies.

Such a course of policy, I believe, is the only option open to us if we as a nation are to have any hope of regaining price stability and maintaining a robust economy. Our country is passing through a fateful stage in its history. Economic, social, and political trends of the past several decades have released powerful forces of inflation that threaten the vitality of our economy and the freedom of our people.

Defeating the forces of inflation requires determined action. Greater discipline is needed in our fiscal affairs, and structural reforms are required to improve the functioning of our labor and product markets. But all such reforms would come to naught in the absence of a prudent course of monetary policy. At this critical time in our history, any interference with the ability of the Federal Reserve to stick to a moderate rate of monetary expansion could have grave consequences for the economic and political future of our country.

The Proper Limits of Openness in Government

During the past decade we have witnessed profound changes in the attitudes of Congress, the courts, and the public generally toward "secrecy" in government. Since the passage of the Freedom of Information Act in 1966, the public has had broad access to government documents, and almost daily one reads of new legislative proposals or judicial decisions that would require agencies of government to make public some aspects of their business that previously had been kept confidential. The balance between the needs of government to carry on certain aspects of its business in confidentiality and the right of the public to know what is going on in government is nowadays more frequently being struck on the side of disclosure. At a time when antiestablishment feeling is running high, there seems to be little inclination to consider what limits the national interest should impose upon openness in government.

The acceleration of the trend toward greater disclosure is unquestionably part of our nation's reaction to Vietnam and Watergate. By 1972, a large section of the American public, including many members of the Congress, already felt that information vital to understanding the Vietnam war and its proper financing had been withheld or distorted by the executive branch. The shocking revelations that soon followed of the Watergate crimes and other excesses at the highest level of government diminished still more the credibility of government.

Address at the 1976 International Monetary Conference, San Francisco, California, June 19, 1976.

The very fact that serious misconduct by high government officials had been so recently concealed under spurious claims of national interest has naturally resulted in widespread public skepticism about the need for confidentiality in any phase of government business.

It has now become a popular saying among articulate advocates of disclosure that the government's business is the people's business, and that the people's business should be carried on in public. But this is a slogan, not a reasoned argument. Moreover, it is a dangerous slogan, because it obscures the practical need to conduct some of the work of government in private. The efforts to dispel mistrust in government by exposing more of the process to contemporaneous public view are undoubtedly well-meaning, but they run a serious risk of impairing the ability of government to carry out certain of its necessary activities effectively.

The trend toward increased openness in government should be of special significance to the banking industry. Historically, banking and bank supervision have been subject to a high degree of confidentiality. The process of bank examination, in particular, has been surrounded with elaborate safeguards intended both to protect the privacy of bank customers and to preserve public confidence in individual banks and the banking system as a whole. Yet during the past ten years a number of laws have been enacted—and a mass of regulations promulgated under congressional mandates—requiring banks to make greater disclosure to their customers and security holders, and in recent months there have been several significant attempts in Congress to breach the confidentiality of the supervisory process. These events mark a serious departure from tradition with respect to banking matters, and both bank regulators and bankers must come to terms with these changing attitudes.

At the Federal Reserve we have been deeply concerned about two disclosure issues that have confronted us recently. One of these involves the disclosure of examination reports in connection with a congressionally ordered study of the bank supervisory process. The other involves disclosure of certain aspects of our decision-making process—in particular, the application to the Federal Reserve of one or another of the "Government in the Sunshine" bills that may soon become law.

I would like to discuss each of these issues in some detail, because I believe that the positions we have taken indicate areas in which the public interest requires some limits on openness in government.

To be fully effective, the process of bank supervision—and by this I mean the process by which the banking agencies detect problems or potential problems in banks and attempt to remedy or prevent them—depends heavily upon an atmosphere of free communication between bank officials and examiners. While our laws have not yet recognized an enforceable privilege for such communications—similar to that which attaches to the relation between a lawyer and client or a doctor and patient—there are significant protections in this area. For example, an examiner or some other agency employee who makes an unauthorized disclosure of information obtained in the examination process may be subject to criminal penalties. Even the Freedom of Information Act expressly recognizes an exemption for documents relating to the bank examination process.

The banking agencies traditionally have gone to great lengths to protect the confidentiality of examination reports. They have done so for three principal reasons: First, public disclosure of problems surrounding a bank could threaten such swift erosion of public confidence in the bank that the ability of supervisors to remedy those problems might be destroyed. Since the main purpose of bank supervision is to prevent bank failures, public disclosure of the results of the examination process could run directly counter to the very objective that the supervisors are attempting to achieve. Second, bank examination reports typically will contain confidential information about bank customers that could damage the legitimate interests of those customers if it were disclosed publicly. We feel a very deep obligation to maintain confidentiality in this area. Finally, we believe that if examination reports were made public, bankers would be less candid in discussing their problems with the examiners, who in turn would be less candid in their appraisal of bank portfolios and bank managements. The effectiveness of the examination process itself would thus become impaired.

The Federal Reserve has recently had its commitment to

the principle of nondisclosure of examination reports tested. You may recall that in January of this year two of the country's largest newspapers published highly confidential information from examination reports and internal supervisory memoranda relating to so-called "problem" banks—that is, institutions which had received or were receiving special supervisory attention. These disclosures set off a number of inquiries in Congress. In January, the late Congressman Wright Patman proposed that the General Accounting Office conduct a far-reaching study of the bank supervisory process—a request that was subsequently supported by Mr. Reuss, the chairman of the House Banking Committee, and by Mr. St Germain, an influential subcommittee chairman. At about the same time, Mr. Proxmire, the chairman of the Senate Banking Committee, proposed a similar study by GAO, to be conducted under the general direction of the committee staff. In each case the focal point of the study was to be on the bank examination process, so that disclosure of examination reports would be required. A subcommittee of the House Government Operations Committee similarly indicated its intention to conduct such a study through its own staff, again focusing on the examination process. It sought authority in this connection to subpoena the comptroller of the currency to produce examination reports of more than sixty national banks.

In response to these congressional intiatives, we at the Federal Reserve informed the two banking committees that we would welcome a meaningful inquiry into the performance of our bank supervisory responsibilities, but that we strongly opposed disclosure of bank examination reports. In order to permit such a study to go forward, we proposed a means by which GAO could look into the performance of our bank supervisory functions without the need for disclosure of the identities of individual banks or bank customers. We further offered to work with the committee in developing a procedure by which information on the bank supervisory process and the health of the banking system could be supplied on a regular basis to assist the committees in performing their oversight responsibilities.

Our staff negotiated at length with GAO, both on the issue of disclosure of examination reports and on the scope of the study itself. We explored a number of possible ways of providing information from examination reports without disclosing the identities of banks or their customers, but GAO would not accept any such limitations. The negotiations finally resulted in an agreement under which GAO will have access to examination reports of a sampling of state member banks on a carefully controlled basis. The security of these materials will be closely guarded. GAO will not be permitted to remove from our premises either the examination reports, copies or extracts of reports, or notes or other work papers generated by GAO itself during the study, and all such materials will be kept under lock at the Board. When GAO completes its study it will prepare a report to the Congress, but that report may not identify any bank, bank official, or customer, and it may not be framed in such a way as to permit such identification. Furthermore, GAO must give us an opportunity to review its report in draft form, so that we will be able to insure that no improper disclosure of examination report information is made.

I am pleased to say that both Mr. Reuss and Mr. St Germain of the House Banking Committee have accepted our agreement with GAO. More important, they have assured the Comptroller General that no attempt will be made to compromise the agreement by requiring disclosure of confidential information. An important precedent has been established, therefore, in support of our position that bank examination reports should not be a subject of congressional staff study. Indeed, the fact that the comptroller of the currency and the FDIC had previously agreed to a GAO study, and that we too were involved in negotiations with GAO, finally persuaded the House Government Operations Committee not to issue a subpoena to the comptroller for the production of bank examination reports in connection with the study being conducted by its staff.

We have by no means satisfied all demands for access to examination reports. With increasing frequency other agencies of government with investigative or law enforcement responsibilities are looking to the bank examination process as a means of obtaining information to carry out their responsibilities. It has been our practice in the past, when access to examination reports has been sought by other agencies in connection with specific allegations of wrongdoing, to allow carefully limited access under conditions intended to protect both banks and their customers from unwarranted invasions of privacy. Furthermore, when our examiners uncover evidence of crime in the course of their examinations, they regularly refer such matters to the proper authorities. However, we do not believe it appropriate for other agencies to use the examination process as a means of prospecting for evidence of possible wrongdoing in areas beyond our jurisdiction. I say this not because we want to protect bankers or bank customers from lawful investigation into possible misconduct, but because we firmly believe that the principal objective of the examination process, namely, maintenance of a safe and sound banking system, would be injured by burdening that process heavily with other tasks.

I would now like to turn to the question of disclosure of the Federal Reserve's internal decision-making process. This question has received considerable public attention recently because of a decision by a federal district judge in Washington ordering the Federal Open Market Committee to make available to the public, immediately after each meeting of the FOMC, the guidelines agreed upon at that meeting for market operations by our New York bank during the succeeding month. In addition, the court ordered that segregable factual portions of the minutes of two FOMC meetings be made promptly available to the plaintiff in that judicial proceeding.

We have appealed certain aspects of the court's order, and I am therefore limited in the extent to which I may comment upon the case. But I can say that even if the district court's interpretation of the Freedom of Information Act is upheld, I believe the public interest would not be served by immediate disclosure of FOMC strategy. Our open-market activities are watched closely by some of the sophisticated money market specialists. Based upon their observations they make judgments about the current direction of monetary policy, and they shape their strategies in the securities market on the basis of these judgments. While their guesses are often astute, there is sufficient uncertainty to cause them to temper their aggressiveness.

If FOMC plans were disclosed immediately, however, market professionals would know at once the key determinants of our open-market operations over the next four or five weeks. Sophisticated and experienced market participants, equipped with financial resources to act quickly, would be far better situated to interpret and trade on this information than members of the general public. Needless to say, the Federal Reserve has not the slightest interest in assuring profits for speculators in stocks or bonds—the ones who would inevitably be the chief beneficiaries of immediate disclosure. And there is still another difficulty with premature publicity. Not only would the large speculators gain trading advantages, but—being armed with these new insights—they would be apt to engage in more aggressive market behavior. As the response of market rates to Federal Reserve actions was accentuated by such behavior, the result could well be greater short-run volatility in interest rates. Exaggerated shifts in market expectations and interest rates caused by premature disclosure of FOMC strategy may in turn require adjustments of policy simply to maintain orderly conditions in financial markets. Our ability to control bank reserves and to make effective use of open-market operations might therefore be weakened.

While the case just discussed raises questions about the timing of the release of FOMC market strategy, I am even more deeply concerned about the prospect that Board deliberations prior to decision may be opened to public scrutiny. One of the principal legacies of Watergate is a deep public cynicism about the process of government decision making. Many people seem willing to assume that confidentiality in the decision-making process promotes improperly motivated or even corrupt decisions. The response to that attitude has been a drive to force government agencies to conduct their deliberations in public sessions. This movement has rallied under the banner of "Government in the Sunshine."

There are several versions of "Sunshine" bills presently pending in Congress, and I am continually amazed at how little public attention these bills have received. The basic structure of these bills is similar: they would require multimember federal agencies to conduct their deliberations concerning agency business in an open forum, accessible to the public. While the bills all recognize certain exemptions from open meetings, they require that if a meeting is to be closed pursuant to an exemption, notice must be given of the subject matter of the meeting and a verbatim transcript must be made and retained. Following each closed meeting, the agency would be required to release to the public those portions of the transcript not covered by an exemption. Any member of the public could bring a court challenge to the validity of the agency's action in closing a meeting, and the court could order the entire transcript to be disclosed. This provision alone offers frightening potential for innumerable lawsuits, each of which would require individual defense.

The obstructionist dangers in this legislation do not stop there: they extend to the greater part of the substantive business of the Federal Reserve. Our deliberations on monetary policy issues involve highly sensitive questions of great national concern. The close scrutiny that is given our statements and actions in this area is itself an indication of the sensitivity of the matters with which we deal. We are keenly aware that financial markets may react dramatically, based solely upon nuances or shades of meaning in our decisions; and our public statements are drafted with great care because of this.

Similar observations apply to our bank supervisory and regulatory functions. We very often have before us detailed information about the financial and managerial condition of bank-holding companies or about individual banks and their customers. Sometimes we must deal with crisis situations that may call for emergency action. It is unthinkable to me that the national interest would be served by discussion of these issues in public. Indeed, the Congress has thus far concurred in this judgment by delineating various exemptions from the requirement for open meetings. But it is no answer that certain meetings may be closed, for as long as we must keep a verbatim transcript of such meetings the threat exists that the substance of these meetings may be made public.

The underlying premise of the "Sunshine" legislation is that if the public is permitted to observe the decision-making process in action, the integrity of decision making will be assured and public confidence in government will be enhanced. This, however, is a vastly oversimplified view of the manner in which the government works, and I believe it is a simplistic view of the way in which government should work. The advocates of this view ignore the fact that debate conducted on a stage is different in tone and quality from debate conducted in private. The simple fact is—and I think that even the supporters of

"Sunshine" legislation ought to concede this—that debate carried on before a public audience tends to take on some characteristics of the theater, rather than serve as a search for truth and wisdom, and that the debaters themselves tend to become performers pronouncing predetermined positions, rather than participants in a deliberative process seeking to develop their own ideas and persuade their colleagues.

The advocates of "Sunshine" also overlook the fact that many actions of the Federal Reserve are quasi-judicial in nature. At almost every meeting we are called upon to adjudicate the rights of private parties seeking to engage in certain new activities or to extend the scope of their existing authority. In such matters we conduct ourselves much as judges would. It is a firm rule, for example, that Board members will not discuss the merits of an application with interested parties prior to Board action on the application. Historically, the deliberations of appellate courts on cases coming before them have not been conducted in open session. I see no convincing rationale for treating our adjudicatory deliberations differently. Of course, once decisions on applications before us have been reached, they are promptly announced and reasons for approval or denial are set forth.

There is a serious danger, I believe, that a "Sunshine" law may have the unintended effect of diminishing the quality of decision making in an agency such as the Federal Reserve Board. The Board has a long tradition of free discussion. We have important decisions to make, and we have been extremely fortunate to have Board members and staff of high intellectual competence. Our deliberations are characterized by deep respect for one another's opinions, and by an atmosphere that welcomes completely free expression by both Board members and staff. A fundamental precondition to the free exchange of ideas is an atmosphere in which new or unpopular ideas—or even wrong ideas—can be put forth for discussion without fear of embarrassment or recrimination.

As we attempt to decide difficult issues, many things are said in our Board meetings that might well not be said if we were in public session or if each word spoken were subject to later public disclosure. This is not to say that "evil" views are being expressed; it simply means that the goal of fully informed decision making can only be achieved if the participants are free to bring to light all considerations that may bear upon their actions. Were we forced to conduct our deliberations under circumstances where highly sensitive matters could not be discussed in private, the quality of our decision making would unquestionably deteriorate and the public interest would ultimately be disserved.

Although the Board has at times been accused of being overly secretive in performing its responsibilities, I believe that charge is not based upon fact. We make far more information available to the public about our activities than any other central bank. Very few of the world's central banks regularly inform their national legislature of their plans for the future course of monetary policy, and none does this as often as the Federal Reserve. Not only do we appear frequently before committees of Congress—Board members have testified twenty-five times already during 1976—but we deal constantly with inquiries from Congress and the public about the substance of our work. In our responses we strive to be as forthcoming and helpful as we can. In the bank regulatory area, unlike many other agencies, we have for many years published written decisions explaining our actions in application proceedings, such as those involving bank-holding company and merger actions.

I believe we must face the problem presented by the "Sunshine" legislation realistically. Certain of the "Sunshine" bills and associated congressional reports define the term "meeting" so broadly that a bare quorum of the Board—four members—literally could not converse informally about any aspect of the Board's business without being required first to issue notice to the public and thereafter to conduct a public discussion or hold a closed discussion with the tape recorder running. In certain instances, these requirements would apply even to discussions between only two Board members.

In conclusion, I fail to see how the national interest would be served by circumscribing actions of the Board in an endless array of recording requirements. In such circumstances we could not be expected to maintain the quality of thorough analysis and thoughtful care that has marked our work over the years. If the Board were exempted from the verbatim transcript requirement, our difficulties with the "Sunshine" legislation would be substantially reduced. However, if any of the "Sunshine" bills as now written becomes law, an agency such as ours would be in an almost impossible position. On the one hand, we could operate under the law as enacted with the virtual certainty that some of the destructive consequences I have indicated—and I have not even mentioned international complications—will occur. On the other hand, we could go through the motions of adhering to the law's requirements but, as a practical matter, resort to "underground" procedures that would effectively circumvent the law. That would be a cruel dilemma, but I would have no hesitation about the choice. I must and do reject circumvention as a suitable course for the Federal Reserve. We will have no part in any such dubious exercises.

In sharing with you my views on some of the disclosure issues that have come before the Board recently, it has been my purpose to question the premise that disclosure is a desirable end in and of itself. I particularly question the premise that disclosure is the cure for bad government. To be sure, it is more difficult for corruption and malfeasance to occur when the public has easier access to the inner workings of government. But there are legitimate and important reasons for permitting certain processes of government to operate in reasonable confidentiality. In striving to renew the public's trust in government, we should recognize that such trust ultimately will depend not upon the public's observation of the process of government decision making, but upon their perception that their government is comprised of men and women of intelligence and integrity making reasonable decisions in the public interest.

The Condition of the Banking System

As you know, Mr. Chairman, I attach special importance to this meeting today at which I shall report to you, on behalf of the Board of Governors, on the condition of the banking system.

This hearing, the first of its kind for this committee, is an outgrowth of our shared judgment—the committee's and the Board's—that there ought to exist an official forum for objective and systematic review of our banking system. Certainly from the Board's standpoint, there has been a regrettable lack of balance at times in the past several years in public discussion of banking matters. It is our hope, which I am sure you share, that hearings of this kind will contribute to better understanding of the performance of the nation's banking system and in so doing will bring individual banking problems into better perspective.

A few years ago it would have been difficult to generate broad interest in the kind of review this committee is now initiating. The reason, obviously, is that from the standpoint of the public the nation's banking system was adjusting well to the general growth of the economy. During the decade of the 1960s, bankers progressively shed much of the caution that had carried over from the great Depression and—freed, as they came to be, of some of the restraints imposed on them—they began to do things that were impressively creative.

That history of change during the 1960s is reasonably well known, and I need not dwell on it. In brief, what bankers did was to reach out for new business far more aggressively

Statement before the Committee on Banking, Housing, and Urban Affairs, United States Senate, March 10, 1977.

than they had formerly. To that end, they devised new techniques—many highly ingenious—for gathering deposits and making loans. They opened offices at a rate much more rapid than the growth of the nation's population, and increasingly extended their operations to new geographic areas and functions. Banks that previously served only local markets sought to become regional in scope; regional banks moved to establish a national presence; and our nation's largest banks looked more and more to opportunities abroad. As long as such growth was outwardly free of signs of strain—as it generally was for more than a decade—the development met with broad approval. Complaints were few—except, of course, from banking's competitors, who were understandably unenthusiastic about banking's new display of entrepreneurial energy and talent. Consumers and businessmen could only be pleased by the enlarged range of banking services and the more intense competition among financial institutions.

There is, however, another side to the ledger. As often happens with evolutionary change that is essentially constructive, the pendulum swung too far too quickly. Excited by the profit gains which the drive for growth yielded in the 1960s, a good many bankers paid less heed than they should have to traditional canons of banking prudence.

Most importantly, the growth of loans and investments in the banking system proceeded much more rapidly than did additions to the base of equity capital. Commercial bank assets increased at an average annual rate of 9 percent in the decade of the 1960s and at the even more rapid rate of 15 percent in the first three years of the 1970s. In both periods, the rate of growth of bank assets appreciably exceeded the growth in the dollar value of the nation's production—a fact indicative of the determined efforts banks were making to enlarge their share of total financing activity.

The consequences of the hard push for growth was that, by the end of 1973, equity capital was equivalent to only about 6½ percent of total bank assets—down sharply from 9 percent at the end of 1960. Moreover, the equity capital of banks had been leveraged by some parent holding companies which used funds raised in debt markets to increase equity investment in their subsidiary banks.

That thinning of the capital cushion would have been reason enough for some uneasiness about banking trends as we moved into the 1970s. But there were other reasons as well. Of key importance was the particular way in which asset growth was achieved. The 1960s witnessed the birth and rapid spread of so-called liability management by banks—a technique that in practice involved heavy reliance on borrowed funds, often very short-dated funds, to accommodate loan requests. Thus, uneasiness was engendered not only by the rapid expansion of assets relative to equity but also because that expansion rested so heavily on volatile resources.

The unease was accentuated by the fact that, in addition to the rapid growth of loans, commercial banks proceeded with a rapid buildup of commitments to their customers to make additional loans in the future. A suspicion, moreover, that banks had to some extent compromised previous standards of asset quality in their drive for growth added to concern in the early 1970s. So, too, did realization that the holding company device had carried bankers into terrain that was relatively unfamiliar. Finally, the advent of widespread floating of currencies produced keen awareness that many of the nation's larger banks, by virtue of their international involvement, had become exposed to additional risks. In sum, as the decade of the 1970s began, apprehension was emerging—and this was not confined to banking regulators—that the innovations and developments of the 1960s, welcome as they were in many respects, posed some formidable challenges.

Such uneasiness as existed in the public mind with respect to trends in banking remained relatively mild, however, until 1974. The failure of U.S. National of San Diego in October 1973, followed some months later by the well-advertised difficulties of Franklin National and Bankhaus Herstatt, both ending in failures, transformed the incipient unease into serious apprehension. Indeed, for the first time since the 1930s major doubts began to be voiced here and there about the soundness of our nation's, and indeed the world's, banking system.

The unhappy closing in our country of two large banks—U.S. National and Franklin National—was handled by the regulatory authorities in a manner that caused a minimum of disturbance to their customers and no loss at all to their depositors.

401

Even so, public concern about banking continued. In fact, it still lingers on in some degree, having been nurtured since 1974 by a succession of troubling events and revelations.

Financial strains associated with the quantum jump in oil prices—involving as they did huge borrowing by oil-deficit nations—have contributed to unease about the health of banking. So too has the severity of the recent recession—itself the product of an inflationary environment that fostered widespread speculation. The slump in business activity triggered a number of major business bankruptcies entailing some well-publicized loan losses for banks. The recession, moreover, laid bare the financial weakness of many real estate investment trusts, which, as is well known, are heavily in debt to our nation's banks. And the recession also played a part in exposing New York City's financial difficulties, thus bringing to acute national consciousness the risk exposure of commercial banks—particularly, but by no means exclusively, the large New York banks—to the vicissitudes of municipal finances.

All of these events have at times made for nervousness about the condition of banking, and that situation may not change quickly. A number of the problems impinging on banks —for example, those related to international oil financing and those having to do with New York City—are almost certain to keep coming back into the headlines. Then, too, loan losses and loan problems often continue months or even years after a recession in economic activity has ended. The recent recession illuminated the bad credits, indeed to a large extent caused them, but considerable time will be required for troubled debtors to work out their financial difficulties. Hence, the total amounts of questionable loans, and the number of banks classified as problem banks because of a sizable volume of such loans, may not diminish rapidly even in an upbeat economy. We ought to expect that and not be surprised by such disclosures.

On behalf of the Federal Reserve, I am pleased to report that our analysis leads to the conclusion that the nation's banking system has passed well beyond the worst of its recent difficulties and is in fact regaining strength steadily. This is the product of several influences—among them, corrective actions taken by the banks on their own initiative, supervisory pressure for better performance, and the recovery that is under way in the general economy.

All of the widely used measures of bank-capital position have shown definite improvement since 1974, reflecting a combination of much slower growth in banking activity and sizable additions to capital resources. Total loans and investments of commercial banks have increased at an annual rate of approximately 5½ percent during the past two years, only about a third of the pace that prevailed in the opening years of this decade. A major part of the slowdown reflects, of course, the subsidence of credit needs occasioned by the state of the economy and the increased reliance of business firms on public debt markets. But there also has become discernible a greater sense of caution and selectivity on the part of bankers in extending credit. Meanwhile, in order to bolster their capital, banks have raised substantial sums in the longer-term debt market, and they have also added to their equity base both by stepping up sales of new stock and by continuing to pursue conservative dividend policies.

Fortunately, our nation's banks have enjoyed relatively good profits, in part because of a new cost-consciousness that has manifested itself not just in go-slow policies affecting the scope of operations but in some instances also in personnel reductions—something that until recently was wholly uncharacteristic of the banking industry. Earnings of banks have been big enough, taken in the aggregate, to absorb the large loan losses that have occurred in lagged response to the recession and yet permit moderate gains in net income. This performance of profits has been a key factor, of course, in enabling banks to strengthen their capital position by retaining a large part of earnings. It is also worth noting that in many of the larger banks, profits have been bolstered by exceptional income gains growing out of international activities.

The ratio of bank equity to total assets that I mentioned earlier as having fallen to 6½ percent at the end of 1973 recorded no significant deterioration thereafter. It tended to stabilize in 1974, then improved modestly in 1975, and modestly again through the middle of 1976, when it approached 7 percent. Other available measures of the status of bank capital—those that take debt capital into account as well as equity and which

403

focus on risk assets rather than total assets—show either equal or greater strengthening. In particular, the ratio of total capital —that is, equity plus subordinated debt—to risk assets rose by more than a full percentage point between the end of 1974 and mid-1976, when it reached 10.2 percent. Significantly, this improvement in bank capital positions has occurred for all size classes of banks, from the smallest to the biggest.

The growth of bank assets has not merely slowed, but— as is typical in strength-rebuilding phases of the kind now proceeding—there has been a decided improvement in the composition of newly acquired bank assets. Between the end of 1974 and the end of 1976, commercial banks added enormously to their holdings of U.S. government securities—in all, about $47 billion. This emphasis on liquid assets has strengthened the general quality of bank asset positions. Moreover, in view of the chastening experience so many banks have had, loan officers have typically been exercising greater care in extending new credit.

Besides the improvement in asset composition, there has been a diminished emphasis by banks on accommodating expansion of their portfolios by relying on short-term borrowed funds. The total of so-called managed liabilities of large banks declined between December 1974 and December 1976, despite a substantial rise in the overall liabilities of these banks. The relative dependence on borrowed funds that are potentially very volatile has thus decreased. At present, the average ratio of managed liabilities to the total assets of large banks is some six percentage points below the high recorded in the summer of 1974.

As I stated earlier, it would be unrealistic, even with the improvement now occurring in asset quality, to expect a rapid change in the loan-loss experience of banks. Banks for some time will continue to wrestle with the legacy of loans that turned sour during the recession. Complete information on loan-loss experience is not yet available for 1976. But such data as we do have indicate a flattening tendency in the net loan losses of commercial banks, measured as a percentage of loans. That is an encouraging change from 1975, when loan losses climbed sharply. Strengthening the impression that a turn for the better has occurred is the fact that during 1976 a decline was recorded in the proportion of past due loans of national banks. Moreover, preliminary data for 1976 on bank assets classified by bank examiners as substandard or worse also suggest that the dollar amount of classified loans is no longer rising. Thus, some signs of improvement in bank loan experience have appeared, and these should multiply as expansion of the economy continues and gives support to the financial position of bank customers.

Essentially the same stabilizing tendencies are evident with regard to banks classified by banking agencies as being in the "problem" category. When a bank is placed in such a category, this simply means that it requires special supervisory attention. The number of such banks increased sharply in 1974 and 1975, but it has since then remained substantially unchanged. For purposes of evalution, it is important to bear in mind that the composition of these lists changes frequently as difficulties are identified by the regulators and resolved by the institutions. Thus, no inference of a lack of progress in overcoming specific problems should be drawn from the recent relative stability in the overall number of banks on such lists. In particular, the recent stability of numbers does not mean that there is a set of chronic "hardcore" cases that defy remedy. We should, moreover, keep in mind the fact that the overwhelming majority of our commercial banks do not require special supervisory attention.

The so-called problem banks represent only a small percentage of the total number of commercial banks in the United States—less than 5 percent even at the worst readings of recent years. And, of course, the number of banks that actually fail is a small percentage of so-called problem banks. The incidence of failure in the banking industry is, indeed, very much smaller than in other lines of business. In the difficult period from 1973 through 1976, there were only thirty-nine bank failures in the United States and most failing institutions were relatively small. As a rule, the supervisory agencies were able to arrange takeovers of the failed institutions by healthy banks. Few were liquidated; thus services to customers were generally uninterrupted, and losses to depositors on uninsured balances were minimal.

The Federal Reserve Board expects the gradual improve-

ment that is under way in the condition of the banking system
to continue. Our anticipation that the general economy will expand at a good rate during 1977 and on into next year is, of
course, critical to that judgment. But other important reasons
also suggest further strengthening in the banking situation.

By no means the least of these is the sobered mood of
bankers. The difficulty experienced by some banks in issuing
certificates of deposit at times during 1974 or 1975 has clearly
left its mark. So has the embarrassment that certain institutions
suffered in having to pay a premium rate on their certificates of
deposit. Fresh is the memory, also, of the cost and strain many
banks experienced in making good on liberally granted commitments to extend credit. Such things as these, combined with
the shock of heavy loan losses, appear to have significantly
altered the psychological framework within which banking
decisions are made. Liability management no longer seems
quite so wondrous to many bankers, and there is clearly a new
degree of appreciation that commitments to lend ought not to
be undertaken lightly. Having learned the hard way that the
business cycle is, after all, very much alive, most bankers are
likely for a time to apply stricter standards than they did a
few years ago in making credit judgments. All in all, the banking industry is exhibiting considerable caution, which extends
both to the traditional range of banking operations and to the
nonbanking activities of holding companies. This should help
to clear up old problems and avoid new ones.

Not only bankers, but also their customers, are in a more
sober mood and this, likewise, bodes well for progress towards
a healthier banking industry. Business managers in particular—
stung by their own discovery that the business cycle is not yet
dead and that huge risks are entailed in enlarging balance-sheet
totals through short-term borrowings—have been hard at work
putting their houses in order. They have sold sizable amounts
of both long-term bonds and equity securities and have used
the proceeds of these sales largely to reduce short-term bank
debt and increase their liquid assets. Those developments, together with the continuing improvement of corporate earnings,
certainly ought to result in fewer new bad-loan problems for
banks and also should help progressively in cleaning up existing
problems.

I can, moreover, assure this committee that the Federal Reserve Board will make every effort to see to it that the current trend toward a strengthened banking situation continues. The Board in its regulatory and supervisory actions is adhering basically to the cautionary thrust that was formally initiated in the spring of 1973.

There has been no significant departure, for instance, in our "go-slow" policy toward expansion of bank-holding company activities. The list of activities generally permissible for these companies has not been expanded since early 1974, and the Board has recently determined that two requested activities are not to be permitted. Individual companies have been allowed to expand into new areas only when the Board has been satisfied with their financial condition and managerial capabilities. On the other hand, companies whose asset composition, capital, or liquidity raises doubts ought by now to know that the Board will be extremely skeptical of proposals that divert financial or managerial resources to new undertakings. Partly as a result of pointed denial of various applications to undertake new investments—through which the Board has signalled to the market its "go-slow" policy—the number of requests filed with the Federal Reserve has sharply diminished in the past two years. Moreover, in some instances in which applications for expansion have been approved, the authority to proceed has been made conditional on improvement of the applicant's capital base.

The Board intends to continue using such leverage in the interest of assuring further improvement in the condition of the banking system. The capabilities of the Federal Reserve to exercise a constructive influence on banker attitudes and actions are numerous, even though our power to deal with certain problem areas is inadequate. Perhaps of greatest significance is the fact that the examination and supervisory process is being strengthened by expanded and more timely surveillance, thereby enhancing our ability to identify problems and to respond to them at an early stage. Parallel developments to strengthen monitoring and follow-through capabilities are under way in the office of the Comptroller of the Currency and at the Federal Deposit Insurance Corporation. Coordination of efforts among the three agencies is, of course, frequent.

The conclusion of the Federal Reserve Board that the condition of the banking system is improving does not mean that we are taking anything for granted or that we see no problems. The wiser attitude that now appears to prevail among bankers needs to be tested as the expansion in economic activity proceeds. Memories—however painful—can sometimes be short. Should we find that the lessons of the recent past—concerning capital adequacy, excessive reliance on volatile funds, or expansion into unfamiliar areas—are no longer generally respected by bankers, the Board will be ready to take whatever action seems appropriate.

Nor, even now, despite steady improvement in real estate markets, do we have any complacency about the involvement of banks and bank-holding companies in real estate investment trusts (REITs). Many of these trusts have avoided bankruptcy only because of the forbearance of creditors, and from the strained and often touchy relationships that inevitably exist in such a situation sudden flare-ups of trouble are always possible. A number of REITs face a significant increase of maturing medium-term debt later this year and in 1978. This situation demands close attention, with the prospect that more REIT-related losses lie ahead for banks and that it will be a long while before the messy problems in that area have been resolved.

Much the same is true of the financial difficulties of New York City in which the New York banks have such a substantial stake. The working assumption must be that a solution calming to financial markets will be devised, but simple prudence demands that the Federal Reserve System, because of its responsibility for containing shocks to financial markets, be alert to any sudden untoward turn in that troublesome situation.

Another area of concern with respect to the soundness of our banking system is the continued attrition in Federal Reserve membership. In 1976, 46 banks chose to give up membership and 8 banks left the System as a result of mergers with non-members. Over the past eight years a total of 427 member banks have withdrawn from the System, and an additional 91 have left as a result of merger. These banks have left mainly because of the high cost of the non-interest-earning reserves that they are required to hold as members of the Federal Reserve. Not a few of the banks that dropped out of the System, being financially weak, faced a desperate need to cut costs and improve profits. At present 60 percent of insured commercial banks, accounting for about 25 percent of deposits, are outside the Federal Reserve System.

Unless the trend toward nonmembership is reversed, the soundness of the banking system will be jeopardized by the fact that so many banks will not have direct access to the Federal Reserve discount window. The availability of the discount window—as was demonstrated dramatically in 1974— is an important element contributing to the stability of our banking system. There should be no assumption that correspondent banks will always be able to afford assistance to nonmembers. This is a problem that warrants priority attention by this committee and the full Congress.

The Board also would like to see this committee focus as soon as it reasonably can on gaps that continue to exist in the supervisory powers of the agencies that regulate banks. On January 31 of this year, the Board, as you know, forwarded to this committee a regulatory reform bill that we believe would contribute materially to better bank supervision.

Our draft bill proposes, among other things, the creation of a statutory interagency bank examination council that would establish uniform standards and procedures for federal examination of banks. The bill would also place statutory limits on loans to insiders. As the committee is aware, problems with insider loans have been a major contributing factor in a number of bank failures. In addition, we see a need for change in existing "cease and desist" authority. At present the Board cannot remove bank or bank-holding company officers for anything less than a showing of personal dishonesty. We believe that authority for removal, with appropriate safeguards, ought to extend as well to gross managerial negligence.

The bill we have proposed would also permit out-of-state acquisition of large banks in danger of failure. When adverse developments trigger deposit losses that seriously weaken a bank, it may be necessary in the public interest to combine the weakened institution with a larger and stronger bank. As you know, this recently occurred in New York and California, where large in-state banks were available to acquire the problem banks involved. Had institutions of the size of Franklin National or

U.S. National failed in certain other states, no in-state bank would have been large enough to acquire them. In such circumstances, the ability to arrange acquisitions across state boundaries would become urgent.

These specific legislative changes would be helpful. From a broader perspective, it is vital to make membership in the Federal Reserve more attractive—perhaps by providing for lower reserve requirements or allowing the System to pay interest on the reserve balances that member banks maintain. Moreover, in view of the expanding presence of foreign banks in the United States—with assets here that now exceed $75 billion—the Board believes it important to subject foreign banks to the same federal rules and regulations that apply to domestic banks. To strengthen our banking system, we therefore urge adoption by Congress of legislation on foreign banking such as the House of Representatives passed last year.

I have dwelt thus far on the condition of the banking system in relation to the activities that banks carry on in our domestic markets. A proper assessment must take into account as well the role of our banks abroad. That role has expanded enormously, and the pace of growth has been especially fast in the last several years. The indebtedness of foreigners to U.S. banks and their foreign branches rose annually during the past three years by about 20 percent. It is important to recognize in this connection that most of the expansion in foreign lending by our banks has been made possible by funds raised abroad.

As the world economy keeps getting bigger, some year-to-year increase in the international loan portfolios of U.S. banks is a normal occurrence. But the recent pace of bank lending to foreigners goes beyond anything that can be explained in terms of the growth of either world economic activity or international trade. In addition, it reflects three developments: first, the enormous rise of financing needs around the world that was occasioned by the quintupling of oil prices; second, the willingness of American banks to respond to those financing needs; third, the growth of multinational corporations and the internationalization of banking through the Eurocurrency markets.

The sharp increase of oil prices did not in and of itself give rise to a need for financing activity of the kind American banks have been engaged in. Theoretically at least, the OPEC group, recognizing the severe payments imbalances they had caused, could themselves have become bankers on a major scale. We know, of course, that they largely avoided the route of extending credit directly to the countries that were buyers of their oil, but instead funneled their huge surpluses into a variety of financial assets—chiefly bank deposits. They thereby shifted the banking opportunity—and with it, of course, the burden of credit evaluation—to others, which meant mainly the large American and European banks that the OPEC group used as depositories. The fact that things might have happened otherwise is something we should not forget, since in the years immediately ahead—if serious oil-related payments imbalances persist—it may yet be necessary to urge upon the OPEC group a much more active role as bankers than they have so far played.

American banks, as is well known, responded along with other banks to the "recycling" challenge, serving since 1974 a very substantial intermediary role between the OPEC group and the countries whose external payments had deteriorated because of OPEC pricing. The fact that loan demand within the United States was relatively weak in 1975 and 1976 undoubtedly has been a factor helping to sustain an unusuallly high rate of foreign lending activity by our banks.

The sharp increase of oil prices, to say nothing of the worldwide recession, caused extensive dislocations in the world economy; but much more serious difficulties would have occurred if commercial banks here and elsewhere had not acted as they did. There simply was no official mechanism in place in 1974 that could have coped with recycling of funds on the vast scale that then became necessary. The supportive role that American and other commercial banks played in this situation thus prevented financial strains from cumulating dangerously, and this role continues even now. Certainly, our export trade and the general economy have been helped—and are being helped—by banking's role in international lending.

This is not to say there have been no excesses or that expansion of international lending by American banks can continue at an undiminished pace. Even though losses on foreign loans have been small—indeed, relatively smaller than on domestic loans—the Federal Reserve Board is concerned about the enlarged risk exposure of our banks. I personally have voiced apprehension about various aspects of these international lending activities in both private and public discussion.

The rapid expansion of credit to the non-oil "less developed" countries (LDCs) warrants particularly close attention. The total indebtedness of such countries to American banks alone approximated $45 billion at the end of 1976. These countries also owe substantial sums to foreign banks, official institutions, and others. The fact that the aggregate external indebtedness of these countries may run to something like $180 billion has been well publicized.

Of course, total debt figures—and more importantly the interest charges flowing from them—need to be viewed in the context of the levels of production and exports of the non-oil LDCs. Looked at in those terms, they are decidedly less worrisome. Nevertheless, the ratio of the external debt to exports and also the ratio of the external interest burden to exports have deteriorated for most non-oil LDCs in recent years, although some stabilizing tendencies did emerge in 1976. In some countries, such ratios have reached levels which justify serious concern and which point to the need for determined stabilization policies. In the absence of such policies, difficulties may be encountered in rolling over existing debt or borrowing to meet new requirements.

This situation demands a heightened sense of caution on the part of our banks in managing their international loan portfolios, and such caution does in fact appear to be emerging. Here, too, though, the Board will be watchful of developments. As part of a broader effort to improve knowledge of international lending activities, we are currently engaged in a joint project with other central banks to obtain a more accurate size and maturity profile of the indebtedness to banks of individual countries. Such data should prove useful to bankers as they proceed to evaluate credit requests by foreigners. The Board has communicated its intent to be both helpful to banks and watchful of their activities. The latter point is currently being signalled, for example, by an informal survey of bank practices in defining, monitoring, and controlling risk in international lending.

The Board's judgment about the condition of the international loan portfolios of American banks is not easily summarized. We have been concerned with the rapidity of the rise in foreign lending, and we believe that here and there a slowing must occur—to rates of growth, generally, that are consonant with expansion of the debt-servicing capabilities of individual borrowing countries. Such slowing, it should be appreciated, may well involve some problems for the international economy, since the structural payments imbalances that have occasioned such heavy bank lending to foreign countries are not going to disappear rapidly. The inference is clear that a strong cooperative effort is more than ever necessary—involving, among others, official international agencies, the Group of Ten countries, OPEC, the non-oil LDCs, and the private banks. Unless we succeed in devising sound financial alternatives, serious strains in the world economy may develop.

In closing, let me say that I am sensitive to the fact that the statement I have made this morning—despite its length—by no means reviews the condition of our banking system as fully as would be desirable. Some of the matters I have touched on are extremely complex and that inherently creates risks that relatively brief treatment may give rise to misunderstandings.

I particularly hope that the emphasis I have placed on the need for caution in credit extension will not be misunderstood. In banking, as in other pursuits, a fine line exists between being too cautious and not being cautious enough. At the Federal Reserve Board, we certainly do not want caution to be overdone in the sense of having our bankers be unresponsive to the needs of creditworthy borrowers, either at home or abroad. Nor do we as supervisors, despite our obligation to be watchful, seek to substitute our judgments for those of on-line bankers in deciding who should get credit. We have neither the capacity nor the desire to play such a role.

The legitimate credit needs of our citizens and our businesses must be met if our economy—and indeed the world economy—is to prosper. It is precisely for that reason that the Federal Reserve is pursuing a policy of adding steadily to our banking system's resources, and yet doing so on a scale that will not reignite the fires of inflation. Our banks are in a good position to serve the needs of their communities. They have been extending impressive amounts of credit to consumers, to farmers, and to those in need of mortgage credit. As the demand for business credit strengthens, that too will be reasonably accommodated. I hope that in dwelling on other considerations this morning, I have created no misimpressions about this critical matter.

The Importance of an
Independent Central Bank

It is a pleasure for me to be here on the campus of Jacksonville University to join in honoring this graduating class. I say that most sincerely. Having spent the greater part of my life as a university teacher, I always take satisfaction in the scholastic achievement of young men and women. This is rightfully a proud moment for you, and I very much appreciate being able to share it.

Today, I would like to talk to you about an issue that has been important throughout much of recorded history and which is certain to influence your lives—for better or worse. I refer to government's management of money—a function than in our country is lodged by statute with the Federal Reserve System.

No nation whose history I am familiar with has succeeded in managing the stock of money perfectly. Few, indeed, have even managed it well. And those societies that have been least successful have paid dearly for their ineptitude. Debasement of the currency had a great deal to do with the destruction of the Roman Empire. In our own times, excessive creation of money has released powerful inflationary forces in many countries around the globe. And once a nation's money is debauched, economic stagnation and social and political troubles usually follow.

Each of you in this assemblage, whatever your age, has experienced at first hand some of the consequences of monetary

Commencement address at Jacksonville University, Jacksonville, Florida, August 13, 1977.

stress. For a dozen years now, our nation has been subjected to a relentless siege of inflation that has conferred undeserved windfall gains on some and undeserved hardships on others. In terms of social well-being, these capricious pluses and minuses by no means cancel out. Young people wanting to buy a home these days know that the price of decent shelter has soared almost out of reach. Parents across the country know the shocking extent to which tuition costs have ballooned. And woe to anyone who has major medical expenses and is not adequately insured.

Those, moreover, are merely among the most readily visible consequences of inflation. There are other less apparent effects that are even more pernicious. Once a nation's economy has been gripped by inflation, it becomes virtually impossible to maintain an environment in which jobs are plentiful and secure. The economic recession of 1974–1975, in the course of which unemployment climbed to a level above 8 million persons, would not have been nearly so severe—and indeed might not have occurred at all—had it not been for the inflationary distortions of the preceding several years.

That is clear, I think, from the sequence of events. Double-digit inflation severely drained many family pocketbooks, reduced consumer confidence, and led to more cautious consumer spending. Businessmen, however, were slow in responding to the weakening of consumer markets. They seem to have been blinded by the dizzying advance of prices and by the effect of that advance on their nominal profits. They thus continued aggressive programs of inventory expansion and capital-goods expansion longer than was prudent, thereby causing economic imbalances to cumulate to major proportions. By the time the weakening of consumer markets was fully recognized by businessmen, the need to scale back had become enormous. The worst recession in a generation ensued.

The only positive aspect of that traumatic episode is that it finally opened the eyes of many economists and public officials to the fact that inflation and unemployment are not alternatives for our economy. The message is now clear that inflation in time causes serious unemployment. Understanding of that relationship is gradually tending, I believe, to make public policies more sensible.

Some of you in this audience may be wondering, I suspect, whether the Federal Reserve may not have something to do with the inflation we have been experiencing. It may fairly be asked: Has not the Federal Reserve been creating too much money? And may not this be one of the causes of our inflation?

That question is, indeed, often put to me, and I welcome it because of the opportunity it affords to clarify the nature of the dilemma our country faces. Neither I nor, I believe, any of my associates would quarrel with the proposition that money creation and inflation are closely linked and that serious inflation could not long proceed without monetary nourishment. We well know—as do many others—that if the Federal Reserve stopped creating new money, or if this activity were slowed drastically, inflation would soon either come to an end or be substantially checked.

Unfortunately, knowing that truth is not as helpful as one might suppose. The catch is that nowadays there are tremendous nonmonetary pressures in our economy that are tending to drive costs and prices higher. This, I should note, applies not only to our country, nor is it anymore just a phenomenon of wars and their aftermath as tended once to be the case. Rather, powerful upward pressures on costs and prices have become worldwide, and they persist tenaciously through peace-time periods as well as wars.

This inflationary bias reflects a wide range of developments that have been evolving over a span of decades in both governmental and private affairs. Foremost among these developments is the commitment of modern governments to full employment, to rapid economic growth, to better housing, improved health, and other dimensions of welfare. These are certainly laudable objectives, but they have too often caused governmental spending to outrun revenues. Other developments—such as the escalator arrangements that various economic groups have achieved through their efforts to escape the rigors of inflation—have speeded the transmission of inflationary impulses across the economy. What we as a people, along with other nations, have been tending to do is to subject available resources to increasingly intensive demands; but we at the same time have sought to insure that incomes do not get eroded when excessive pressures on resources generate inflation. This amounts, unfortunately, to creating upward pressures on costs and prices, and then arranging to perpetuate them. That is the awesome combination that fighters against inflation have to try to counter.

Theoretically, the Federal Reserve could thwart the non-monetary pressures that are tending to drive costs and prices higher by providing substantially less monetary growth than would be needed to accommodate these pressures fully. In practice, such a course would be fraught with major difficulty and considerable risk. Every time our government acts to enlarge the flow of benefits to one group or another the assumption is implicit that the means of financing will be available. A similar tacit assumption is embodied in every pricing decision, wage bargain, or escalator arrangement that is made by private parties or government. The fact that such actions may in combination be wholly incompatible with moderate rates of monetary expansion is seldom considered by those who initiate them. If the Federal Reserve then sought to create a monetary environment that seriously fell short of accommodating the nonmonetary pressures that have become characteristic of our times, severe stresses could be quickly produced in our economy. The inflation rate would probably fall in the process but so, too, would production, jobs, and profits.

The tactics and strategy of the Federal Reserve System—as of any central bank—must be attuned to these realities. With sufficient courage and determination, it is nevertheless within our capacity to affect the inflation rate significantly. We may not, as a practical matter, be able to slow monetary growth drastically within any given short time span, but we do have considerable discretion in accommodating the pressures of the marketplace less than fully. We are, indeed, often engaged in probing and testing our capacity to do just that. And, while we must be cautious about moving abruptly, my colleagues and I in the Federal Reserve System are firmly committed to a longer-term effort of gradual reduction in the rate of growth of money—something that is reflected in the progression of steps we have been taking to lower permissible growth-ranges for the money supply. Slowly undernourishing inflation and thus weakening it seems the most realistic strategy open to us. We believe that such an effort—especially if Congress becomes less tolerant of budget deficits—will ultimately create a much healthier environment for the determination of wages and prices.

The capacity of the Federal Reserve to maintain a meaningful anti-inflationary posture is made possible by the considerable degree of independence it enjoys within our government. In most countries around the world, central banks are in effect instrumentalities of the executive branch of government—carrying out monetary policy according to the wishes of the head of government or the finance ministry. That is not the case in this country because the Congress across the decades has deliberately sought to insulate the Federal Reserve from the kind of political control that is typical abroad. The reason for this insulation is a very practical one, namely, recognition by the Congress that governments throughout history have had a tendency to engage in activities that outstrip the taxes they are willing or able to collect. That tendency has generally led to currency depreciation, achieved by stratagems ranging from clipping of gold or silver coins in earlier times to excessive printing of paper money or to coercing central banks to expand credit unduly in more modern times.

With a view to insuring that the power of money creation would not be similarly abused in our country, the Congress has given our central bank major scope for the independent exercise of its best judgment as to what monetary policy should be. In fact, Congress has not only protected the Federal Reserve System from the influence of the executive branch; it also has seen fit to give the System a good deal of protection from transitory political pressures emanating from Congress itself.

Probably the two most important elements making for Federal Reserve independence are the following: First, the seven members of the Federal Reserve Board serve long and staggered terms and can only be removed for "cause." This arrangement severely limits possibilities for any "packing" of the Board and enables members of the Board to act without special concern about falling out of grace politically. Second, the Federal Reserve System finances its activities with internally generated funds and therefore is not subject to the customary appropriations process. This arrangement is intended to assure that the congressional "power of the purse" will not be used in an effort to induce System officials to pursue policies that they otherwise might consider poorly suited to the nation's needs.

The Federal Reserve has thus been able to fashion monetary policy in an impartial and objective manner—free from any sort of partisan or parochial influence. While the long history of the Federal Reserve is not faultless, its policies have consistently been managed by conscientious individuals seeking the nation's permanent welfare—rather than today's fleeting benefit. Significantly, this country's record in dealing with inflation—albeit woefully insufficient—has been much better generally than the record of countries with weak central banks. Indeed, I would judge it no accident that West Germany and Switzerland, which in recent years also have managed their economy better than most others, happen to have strong and independent monetary authorities like ours.

The degree of independence which Congress has conferred upon the Federal Reserve has been a source of frustration to some government officials since the Federal Reserve Act first became law. Certainly, from the standpoint of the executive branch, it would at times—perhaps often—be more convenient to instruct the central bank what to do than to reckon with the System's independence. In the end, however, the country would not be as well served. The Federal Reserve, it needs to be emphasized, seeks earnestly to support or to reinforce governmental policies to the maximum extent permitted by its responsibilities. When the System's actions depart, as they occasionally have, from the way in which the executive branch would wish it to act, that is generally because the System tends to take a longer-range view of the nation's welfare. Actually, most of the time, monetary and fiscal policies are well coordinated and mutually reinforcing; in other words, they are the product of continuing and fruitful discussions between members of the administration and Federal Reserve officials.

Not only is dialogue continuous with the executive branch of government, but Federal Reserve officials appear frequently before congressional committees—something that works, on the one hand, to keep Congress informed as to System activities and which, on the other, affords senators and congressmen an effective means of registering approval or disapproval of Federal Reserve policy. In practical terms, the economic policy dialogue that is always in process within our government produces a thorough exploration of options. It may fairly be said, I believe, that the System's independence results in a more thorough discussion and thrashing out of public issues than would otherwise occur.

Despite the salutary influence that the Federal Reserve's independence has had on our nation's economy, legislative proposals that would place the System under tighter rein keep being introduced in Congress. The proposals that have been put forth over the years cover a wide range—for example, to enlarge the size of the Board, to shorten the terms of its members, to enable the president to remove board members at will, to diminish or eliminate the role of Federal Reserve bank directors, and to subject the System to the congressional appropriations process or to audit by the Government Accounting Office. In recent years, there have also been proposals calling for numerical forecasts of interest rates or other sensitive magnitudes, which if ever undertaken by the Federal Reserve, could unsettle financial markets, besides misleading individuals who lack sophistication in financial matters.

The shortcomings of these individual proposals matter less, however, than what appears to be their common objective, namely, to reduce the Federal Reserve's independence and to restrict its scope for discretionary action. That, I believe, is the real thrust of the diverse efforts to "reform" the Federal Reserve System. It is perhaps of some significance that such proposals not infrequently come from individuals who are basically dissatisfied with what they regard as excessive Federal Reserve concern with battling inflation.

The element of populism in all this is strong—particularly the preoccupation with maintaining low interest rates. It makes no difference how often Federal Reserve officials repeat that the System's continuing objective is the lowest level of interest rates compatible with sound economic conditions. That is not enough. What is desired is assurance that interest rates will be kept permanently down, or at least not be allowed to rise significantly.

The Federal Reserve cannot, of course, give that kind of assurance. In a period of rising demands for funds, a determined effort by the System to keep interest rates down could quickly turn the Federal Reserve into something akin to the engine of inflation that it was during the early Korean War period when the System unwisely tried to keep interest rates down so that the cost of financing the federal debt would not escalate. Actually, the consequences now would almost certainly be far worse than they were a quarter century ago because the public has become far more sensitive to inflation.

Long-term interest rates, in particular, tend to respond quickly nowadays to changing inflationary expectations. Once the financial community perceived that the Federal Reserve was pumping massive reserves into commercial banks with a view to creating monetary ease, fears of a new wave of inflation would spread quickly. Potential suppliers of long-term funds would then be inclined to demand higher interest rates as protection against the expected higher rate of inflation. Borrowers, on the other hand, would be more eager to acquire additional funds, since they would expect to repay their loans in still cheaper dollars. In short, heightened inflationary expectations would soon overwhelm markets in today's inflation-conscious environment by actually causing long-term interest rates— which are generally more important to the economy than short-term rates—to rise. The policy of seeking lower interest rates by flooding banks with reserves would thus be frustrated. And I need hardly add that adverse effects on production, employment, and the dollar's purchasing power would follow.

The Federal Reserve System, I assure you, will not be deterred by the drumbeat of dubious propositions concerning money and interest rates. We are determined to continue on a path of further gradual unwinding of the inflationary tendencies that have become so deeply embedded in our economic life. We are determined to continue promoting the expansion of our economy and yet control the supply of money so as to prevent a new wave of inflation. Such a policy, I firmly believe, is the only responsible option open to us.

I hope that I have succeeded today in conveying some sense of the importance to you as individuals and to the nation generally of the Federal Reserve's role in our government. Fortunately, despite the criticism that is not infrequently voiced by some members of Congress, the Congress as a whole has kept the Federal Reserve's role in a clear perspective and has fully protected the essentials of Federal Reserve independence.

That will continue to be the case only if you who are graduating today and other citizens develop a full understanding of what is at stake.

Vital Issues of Banking
Legislation

It is a great pleasure for me to be here today and to have the privilege of addressing this gathering.

I thought I might usefully speak to you about some of the legislation pending in the Ninety-fifth Congress. This is a busy season for banking legislation. Bills under consideration deal with such diverse subjects as nationwide NOW accounts, the financial burden of Federal Reserve membership, the operation of foreign banks in this country, the restructuring of bank supervisory and regulatory authority, and revision of the Truth in Lending statute. There are, moreover, various proposals in the congressional hopper that aim in one way or another at circumscribing the Federal Reserve's scope for independent judgment and decision.

I cannot, of course, cover this morning all the banking legislation that is now pending. But I welcome this opportunity to comment on some of the major bills that have been introduced, and also to indicate why we at the Board are so deeply concerned about the character of numerous proposals that keep being advanced under the banner of "reform."

Let me say something first about S. 2055—the legislative package that combines authority for nationwide NOW accounts with measures to lighten the burden of Federal Reserve membership. As you know, this bill was voted out of the Senate Banking Committee in early August and may soon be debated on the Senate floor.

Address at the eighty-third annual convention of the Kentucky Bankers Association, Louisville, Kentucky, September 12, 1977.

I am well aware that some of you have serious reservations about this bill. Indeed, I have heard from many bankers around the country who object to some of its key provisions—particularly the contemplated extension of NOW-account authority—and who urge the Federal Reserve to withdraw its support of the measure. The impact on earnings of paying interest on transactions balances is obviously of concern—and properly so—to commercial banks, especially those for which the checking accounts of individuals make up a large portion of total deposits.

Let me assure you that we at the Federal Reserve Board recognize the importance of good bank earnings. We well know that unless earnings are reasonably satisfactory, commercial banks will not be able to serve their communities or the national economy in an effective manner. We also believe that bank earnings will be adversely affected for a time during the transition to a NOW-account environment. That has certainly been the experience with NOW accounts in New England.

Why, then, it may fairly be asked, does the Federal Reserve support nationwide NOW-account authority?

The reason essentially is that we think it is important to bring a sense of order to a development that has the look of inevitability about it but which to date has proceeded in haphazard fashion. The simple fact is that by one means or another depositors have been increasingly successful in earning interest or its equivalent on their transactions balances. Such interest is implicit in the banking services that are provided bank customers without charge or below cost. Beyond this, and on a growing scale, many customers of financial institutions are already receiving interest in cash on transactions balances—not only in the New England states where NOW's are authorized, but throughout the country. This is the consequence, as you well know, of recent financial innovations that enable individuals as well as corporations to move funds readily between interest-bearing accounts and checking deposits or between money market instruments and checking deposits. Congressional inaction will not stop the spread of interest payments on what are in effect transactions balances; it would simply mean that the movement will go forward without guidance at the national level, attended by inefficiency and competitive distortion. My colleagues and I thus see S. 2055 as a vehicle for guiding this development in a gradual and orderly fashion while limiting the adverse effects on bank earnings.

I well understand the displeasure that commercial bankers feel over the fact that S. 2055 would in effect confer checking-account authority on thrift institutions while leaving intact their ability to pay savings depositors a higher rate of interest than can commercial banks. To be sure, all depository institutions that decide to offer NOW accounts under the new authority would do so on the same terms, so that the troublesome interest-rate differential would be eliminated for that category of deposits. However, since NOW accounts would expand the powers of thrift institutions to a point where they could offer depositors the attractions of "one stop banking," the extension of parity should not be limited to newly created NOW accounts. Both logic and equity suggest that thrift institutions should enjoy either NOW-account authority or the interest-rate differential— but hardly both.

The difficulty of overcoming opposition to any modification of the differential must not, however, be underestimated. This was evidenced by the failure of the Senate Banking Committee to accept an amendment by Senator Lugar, which would have restored the power that bank regulatory agencies had until late 1975 to adjust the differential without ratifying action by the Congress. I have indicated to Senator McIntyre, the distinguished sponsor of the NOW-account legislative package, the desirability of removing the ratification requirement because it constitutes an impediment to timely adjustment of deposit interest-rate ceilings as circumstances change. Even though Senator Lugar's amendment failed in committee, this moderate step toward less rigidity with regard to the differential deserves sympathetic consideration by the Congress at large. Senator McIntyre's support of the amendment was particularly encouraging. I hope that interested parties will continue to press the issue.

In your continuing assessment of S. 2055, I would urge that you weigh carefully the point I have made about the disadvantages inherent in letting interest payments on what are essentially transactions balances continue to spread in haphazard, piecemeal fashion. Neither individual bankers, nor

427

their nonbank competitors, nor state legislatures, nor bank regulators, nor the Congress itself are likely to stand still. On the contrary, actions that serve to expand the payment of interest on transactions balances by all types of depository institutions will continue to multiply. It is my strong conviction that ultimately both the general interests of the nation and the particular interests of commercial banks will be poorly served if the changes we have been witnessing are not subjected to orderly direction.

The transitional problems faced by financial institutions in adapting to NOW accounts will not be easy, but they ought to be less troublesome in most parts of the country than they have been in New England. I say this in part because the New England experience is available as a guide. It surely should be possible to avoid repeating some of the mistakes—particularly the mistakes in pricing—that were made by various institutions in that region. Indeed, it seems clear from the statistical evidence that depository institutions in Connecticut, Maine, Rhode Island, and Vermont have generally been able to profit from the earlier NOW-account experience in Massachusetts and New Hampshire. Banks and thrift institutions in the New England states that were relative latecomers to the NOW experiment have tended to pursue more cautious marketing and pricing strategies, and their earnings have consequently stood up better.

There are also other reasons for thinking that New England's experience is not likely to be repeated in other regions. For one thing, competition between commercial banks and thrift institutions appears to be somewhat more vigorous in New England than in most parts of the country. Then, too, S. 2055 is deliberately structured to minimize transition costs and protect bank earnings. It limits eligibility for NOW accounts to individuals. It gives regulatory agencies discretion to set a lower interest-rate ceiling for NOW's than currently prevails in New England. It authorizes the payment of interest on reserve balances held at the Federal Reserve, including reserves against the NOW accounts. It anticipates lower reserve requirements on NOW accounts than on demand deposits. It allows more room for reductions in the reserves required of member banks, especially the smaller banks. And it delays the effective date of nationwide NOW-account authority for one year after the enactment of legislation.

These things in combination make it seem likely that depository institutions across the country will be able to maintain their earnings reasonably well as they move to NOW accounts. I would note especially that the one-year waiting period will afford banks time for rational planning of their operational systems and marketing strategies for NOW accounts. Without this array of provisions designed to maintain earnings strength, the Federal Reserve Board, I assure you, would not be willing to support the NOW-account proposal.

That there will nevertheless be some net cost to many commercial banks in making the transition to NOW's also seems clear. That is why we at the Board have been at such pains to keep this cost down and that is also why we have been so insistent on combining the NOW-account proposal with action to lighten the financial burden of Federal Reserve membership.

Member banks are already very sensitive to the cost disadvantage they suffer vis-à-vis nonmembers because of the more onerous reserve requirements they have to meet. This has resulted in recent years in a significant erosion of membership—particularly on the part of smaller banks. There is no question at all in my mind that this membership erosion would accelerate if we were to go forward with nationwide NOW's without taking simultaneous action to lighten the burden of membership. That is the reason, of course, the Board has worked so intensely to obtain authority to pay interest on reserve balances and to be in a position to lower reserve requirements—particularly for the smaller banks.

A healthy, effective central bank is not a matter of parochial concern—of importance only to Federal Reserve officials and member banks. The Federal Reserve serves the entire financial community and indeed the nation at large. It would be in no one's interest to see its vitality sapped. Unless the erosion of membership is arrested, a steadily diminishing portion of commercial bank deposits will be lodged with members and the execution of monetary policy will therefore become less and less precise. Other things trouble me still more. Provision of lender-of-last-resort facilities was a critical reason for establishing the Federal Reserve System. I do not like to contemplate the ultimate consequences for the soundness of our banking structure if fewer and fewer banks enjoy ready access to the System's discount window.

Declining membership could also threaten the insulation of the Federal Reserve System from day-to-day political pressures. The System's independence from such pressures will remain sustainable, I believe, only as long as the System continues to have balanced representation of membership among all sizes of banks across the country. But membership attrition has been most acute among smaller banks—those with deposits of less than $100 million. If the exodus continues and the remaining members are only the larger banks, the Federal Reserve will then be perceived by the public as a big banker's bank. This would almost certainly generate disenchantment with the System. In time, the Federal Reserve's independence—which enables it to base monetary policy on long-range considerations as well as those related to the short term—would diminish if not entirely end.

I hope that these comments on key provisions of S. 2055 may suffice to show why we at the Board view the bill on balance as a constructive and desirable piece of legislation. I said before that I know many of you have reservations about it, and I understand the reasons for those reservations. I nevertheless believe that it would be the better part of wisdom to retain an open mind toward this legislative effort and seek to improve it rather than scuttle it.

Let me now turn to other items in the legislative mill. I noted earlier that the banking bills under consideration this year include the usual array of measures to "reform" the Federal Reserve System. The Federal Reserve Reform Act of 1977 recently cleared the House Banking Committee in a form greatly different from the measure originally proposed. Fortunately, the most troublesome features of the bill were eliminated during the committee markup and this is an encouraging fact. One of the defeated provisions—that dealing with so-called lobbying communications—would have placed very broad restrictions on the right of Federal Reserve officials to communicate with bankers about legislative matters. Indeed, were it ever to become law, there would be a serious question whether I or any of my colleagues would be able to address an assemblage such as this in the manner I am doing. Other rejected provisions would have required the Federal Reserve to publicize at quarterly intervals numerical forecasts of interest rates and other sensitive financial variables. Forecasts of interest rates by the nation's central bank may seem harmless at first blush, but any such pronouncement by the Federal Reserve would in practice carry implications for debt markets that could generate wide and unsettling swings in security prices.

The wish to have us make such pronouncements is somewhat puzzling. My best guess is that preoccupation with interest rates—particularly with trying to influence the Federal Reserve to keep interest rates down—often tends to blur judgment. Populist emphasis on low interest rates appears to be a key reason for the steady stream of proposals that in one way or another would enlarge opportunities for exerting political influence upon monetary policy. A less independent Federal Reserve—particularly one that would be less concerned about inflation and thus more generously accommodative of credit demands—clearly remains an objective of many people.

A perennial favorite for the past quarter century of those who would like to see the Federal Reserve enjoy less independence is the proposal to subject the System to audit by the General Accounting Office. Indeed, a bill giving the GAO sweeping authority to audit the Federal Reserve—as well as the Federal Deposit Insurance Corporation and the Comptroller of the Currency—was introduced in the House last January. In the course of the recent markup by the House Government Operations Committee, a number of provisions were wisely incorporated in the bill with a view to affording some protection against disclosure of confidential information. Even so, the measure retains major deficiencies and ambiguities, and we thus feel compelled to oppose it. Incidentally, the bill is expected to be on the calendar for floor action very soon, possibly this week or next.

The bill raises serious questions of public policy. The Federal Reserve Banks have never been subject to GAO audit. The exempted status of the Board dates back to the Banking Act of 1933. The complete exemption of the Federal Reserve System from GAO audit since 1933 thus complements the original exemption of the Federal Reserve from the appropriations process. These exemptions have conferred on the Federal Reserve a heavy responsibility to conduct its affairs with the highest standards of probity; they have also enabled the System to determine its internal management free from political pressures. Exemption from GAO audit is one of the main pillars of Federal Reserve independence.

In exempting the Federal Reserve from customary appropriations and auditing procedures, the Congress has recognized the special political vulnerability that a central bank tends to develop if it in fact comports itself as it should in carrying out its monetary function. It is simply a fact of life that whenever a central bank imposes monetary discipline, it almost always generates a good deal of opposition. Those displeased with Federal Reserve performance would surely have greater leverage in their efforts to get monetary policy changed if the System were subject to customary appropriations and auditing procedures. I do not mean to suggest that our stewardship should be beyond examination. Accountability by the Federal Reserve is obviously essential, and we believe that the arrangements Congress has fashioned across the decades achieve thorough accountability within a framework of safeguards that take account of the special vulnerability to which central banks are everywhere subject.

What concerns the Board most about proposals for a GAO audit is that such auditing may become a device through which pressure is brought to bear directly on the formulation of monetary policy. To be sure, the pending GAO audit bill excludes a broad range of monetary policy deliberations and transactions from the proposed audit, but it does not flatly and unambiguously exclude all monetary policy matters. For example, the Committee Report indicates that the GAO would have authority to audit and evaluate discount-window transactions to the extent that such transactions are related to the supervisory function of the System—as distinct from its monetary policy function. This is an extremely fuzzy distinction, and it could easily become a vehicle for GAO intrusion into monitoring monetary policy—an area in which that venerable institution has neither experience nor expertise, to say nothing of responsibility.

It is to the credit of the pending bill that it recognizes the need to protect sensitive and confidential information concerning private parties. But I am by no means satisfied that the bill's provisions in this regard are adequate. Except for records pertaining to monetary policy, the GAO would be given access to "all books, accounts, records, reports, files, memorandums, papers, things, and property belonging to or in use by the entities being audited, including reports of examination of banks or bank-holding companies . . . together with workpapers and correspondence relating to such reports . . . ." These materials obviously include a great deal of sensitive information. And while the bill prohibits the GAO from identifying individuals and institutions in its public reports to Congress, all such information could still be made available to congressional committees sitting in executive session. Experience suggests that this limitation is scant guarantee that sensitive and confidential information about banks and their customers would not find its way into the public domain. Great damage could thus be caused to banks, individuals, and business enterprises. In self-protection bankers might soon become less forthcoming to examiners, while their work in turn might become infected either by timidity or by zealotry because of the potential for disclosure. The integrity of the entire bank examination process could therefore be undermined.

Ultimately, as I have tried to suggest, the exemption of the Federal Reserve from GAO audit can be properly understood only in the context of the importance that congressional shapers of the Federal Reserve System have attached to insulating this nation's central bank from day-to-day political pressures. That present audit arrangements for both the Board and the Federal Reserve Banks are thorough and effective has, I believe, been demonstrated by Federal Reserve officials in public testimony time and time again. It is a fact, moreover, that besides the auditing reports that go to the Congress each year, a great deal of detailed information about Federal Reserve activities and operations is supplied to congressional committees in response to a steady stream of inquiries. When one also takes into account the scope of the public oversight hearings conducted by the House and Senate Banking Committees, the need for a GAO oversight role is doubtful at best. If the Congress should nevertheless want to go to the considerable expense of an

additional audit by the GAO, I certainly hope that such legislation would not allow the GAO to involve itself in any way
with monetary policy procedures or deliberations, and that it
would also fully protect sensitive and confidential information
concerning banks and their customers.

I am mindful that my remarks have been lengthy, particularly for the opening session of a working convention. Even so,
there is much in the field of banking legislation on which I have
not commented. For example, the Senate Banking Committee
will soon consider a proposal to establish a Federal Bank Commission that would assume responsibility for the supervisory
and regulatory work now carried on by the three banking
agencies. In the Board's considered judgment, removal of the
Federal Reserve's supervisory and regulatory responsibilities
would at times seriously lessen the effectiveness with which
monetary policy is carried out, and that is one basic reason—
among others—why we are opposed to it. I regret that I cannot
discuss this bill fully today, but I hope that you and other
bankers in our country will make the effort to familiarize yourselves with the issues surrounding it.

In closing, I would like to touch on one more matter. In
recent weeks, banking practices have become prominent in the
general news, and as a result are coming under special congressional scrutiny. Chairman St Germain's subcommittee, for
example, has already embarked on hearings dealing with a range
of banking practices—among them, correspondent bank relations, bank policies relating to loan collateral, and bank policies
relating to overdraft facilities. Chairman Proxmire has scheduled hearings on similar topics toward the end of this month.
Specific legislation directed at some of the banking practices
that have recently received public attention will soon be
considered.

I deem it premature to make any kind of judgment as to
how sustained the legislative interest in such matters will be
or to what specific ends it will be directed. My hope is that a
sense of calm deliberation and balance will be maintained—
difficult though this may be at present. We cannot remind ourselves too often that haste can easily make for bad legislation.

For several years, the Federal Reserve has been in the fore-
front of efforts to obtain added enforcement authority for fed-

eral banking agencies. Our efforts in that direction in no sense imply an unfavorable view of banking. Like other industries, banking is not free of problems, but it is my judgment that generally high standards of behavior prevail in banking. The Federal Reserve's long-standing interest in greater enforcement authority simply reflects our belief that some gaps in supervisory authority exist and that improved enforcement powers are appropriate.

The Ninety-fourth Congress did not give much attention to our initiative. This year, however, after full and calm deliberation, the Senate passed S. 71—a regulatory and supervisory bill that embodies more stringent rules on insider loans, strengthens cease-and-desist as well as officer-removal powers, and provides a range of cash penalties for violations of banking law or regulation. At present, the absence of an effective range of penalties at times causes undue restraint on the enforcement procedures of bank regulators.

Perhaps legislative remedies beyond those contained in S. 71 are needed. I certainly have an open mind on this question. But I would urge full deliberation before wider legislative remedies are enacted. The banking legislation that I have reviewed with you or alluded to this morning is quite enough for the Congress to handle in the remainder of this year.

I have talked a long time and I certainly dare not burden you with anything else. May I just express my appreciation once more for the privilege of visiting with you.

PART
FIVE

International Finance

The Par Value Modification Act

The Board of Governors of the Federal Reserve System strongly supports enactment of the Par Value Modification Act. Prompt passage of this bill will fulfill an important commitment undertaken by the United States as part of the Smithsonian Agreement reached by the Group of Ten countries on December 18, 1971.

The Par Value Modification Act proposes a new par value for the dollar in the International Monetary Fund. We will thus have a new official dollar price of gold: an ounce of gold will in the future be carried on the books at thirty-eight dollars instead of thirty-five dollars as at present. The act does not deal with the issue of convertibility, and therefore does not affect the present suspension of convertibility of dollars into gold or other international reserve assets.

The proposed change in the par value of the dollar will have several financial and accounting consequences. First, the value of the Treasury's gold and other reserve assets will be written up by 8.57 percent, or about a billion dollars. Second, the Treasury will be able to issue new gold certificates to the Federal Reserve Banks for this amount, and its cash balance will rise to the extent that it does so. Third, the dollar value of subscriptions and contributions to several international financial organizations will need to be increased.

The net result of the various financial and accounting adjustments, as the secretary of the Treasury has informed this

Statement before the Committee on Banking, Housing, and Urban Affairs, United States Senate, February 24, 1972.

committee in detail, will somewhat improve the Treasury's cash position and leave both budgetary expenditures and the overall dollar assets and liabilities of the U.S. Government roughly unchanged.

If these consequences were the sole results to be expected from the Par Value Modification Act, there would be no need to rush its passage. But much more than this is involved. As this committee knows, the proposed change in the par value of the dollar was an integral part of the Smithsonian Agreement. Failure to pass promptly the Par Value Act could provoke a renewal of disorderly conditions in financial markets and place in jeopardy the Smithsonian Agreement itself. It is no exaggeration to state that the realignment of currencies which the Smithsonian Agreement achieved is absolutely essential to the reinvigoration of our foreign trade and the eventual restoration of equilibrium in our balance of payments.

The international monetary crisis we experienced in 1971 was by far the most severe since World War II. It had its roots in events that stretch back over many years, during which a persistent deficit developed in the U.S. balance of payments. The crisis came to a head last summer when increasingly unfavorable reports on our foreign trade released a wave of speculation against the dollar that eventually engulfed foreign exchange markets. The speculation expressed a growing belief that there would soon have to be a substantial upward revaluation of at least some major currencies against the dollar— or, what comes to the same thing, that the dollar would need to depreciate in terms of other major currencies.

On August 15, the President announced a new policy for dealing decisively with the domestic problems of inflation, inadequate productivity, and unemployment, which were weakening confidence in the American economy. Recognizing that curbs on domestic inflation would not suffice to restore equilibrium in the balance of payments, the President sought also to achieve a realignment of currencies and better access to foreign markets for American producers. To set the stage for useful international negotiations, a temporary surcharge was therefore imposed on imports and the convertibility of dollars into gold or other reserve assets was suspended.

As expected, dollar prices of most of the major foreign

currencies rose on the exchange markets. Foreign governments, although caught by surprise, soon sought in various ways to adjust to the new monetary and trade conditions. Some imposed restrictions on inflows of funds while permitting their exchange rates to appreciate in a controlled manner. Others resorted to rather comprehensive financial controls in an effort to maintain pre–August 15 exchange rates, at least for trade transactions. Only a few countries permitted their exchange rates to move more or less freely.

The pattern of exchange rates that evolved after August 15 thus failed to meet American objectives. Worse still, restrictions on international transactions were proliferating, with a few countries even imposing restrictions or subsidies on trade itself. Businessmen both here and abroad faced acute uncertainty regarding the exchange rates and governmental restrictions under which trade would be carried on in the future. This uncertainty aggravated recessionary forces already evident in Europe and Japan. It also affected adversely the profit expectations of American companies engaged in foreign operations or foreign trade, thereby inhibiting investment expenditures and economic expansion in the United States.

In these circumstances, the dangers were growing of a recession in world economic activity, of increasing recourse to restrictions on international transactions, of a division of the world economy into restrictive blocs, and of serious political frictions among friendly nations. Prompt resolution of the crisis was clearly necessary, and intensive international discussions therefore got under way in the autumn of 1971.

The settlement negotiated at the Smithsonian meeting of last December provided for an average appreciation of the currencies of the other Group of Ten countries against the dollar of about 12 percent. Agreement was also reached on a widening of margins for exchange rate variation. Later, a number of other countries decided to revalue their currencies upward against the dollar, but most of the developing countries have elected to maintain their exchange rates against the dollar at the pre–August 15 levels.

Trade agreements were recognized by the participants in the Smithsonian Agreement as relevant to the achievement of lasting equilibrium in the international economy. Negotiations on trade matters of immediate concern to the United States, and which were under way at the time of the agreement, have since been completed with Japan and the European Community—but not with Canada. The new trade measures should improve the climate for certain U.S. exports. For the longer run, the prospects are now promising for widespread support of comprehensive multilateral negotiations on reducing barriers to trade in both industrial and agricultural products.

For its part in the settlement, the United States agreed to drop the import surcharge and related provisions of the investment tax credit, and to facilitate the realignment of exchange rates by proposing to Congress a change in the par value of the dollar in terms of gold.

Thus, the Par Value Modification Act is before you to honor a critical commitment made in behalf of the U.S. Government at the Smithsonian meeting. The American negotiators would have preferred to achieve the desired appreciation of foreign currencies without doing anything about the official dollar price of gold. Other countries, however, refused to countenance such a passive role by the United States in a multilateral adjustment of exchange rates.

Active participation by the United States in the exchange rate realignment was expected by other countries for various reasons. Some countries regarded it as politically or financially unacceptable to reduce the price of gold in terms of their own currencies—as would have been required if the exchange rate realignment had left the par value of the dollar in terms of gold unchanged. And virtually all countries took the position that no nation should be immune from changing its par value when its balance of payments is in disequilibrium. In our judgment, a negotiated realignment of exchange rates would have been unattainable if the United States had refused to consider a change in the par value of the dollar.

As already noted, the Par Value Modification Act proposes an increase in the official dollar price of gold from thirty-five dollars to thirty-eight dollars an ounce, that is, by 8.57 percent. This exact increase reflects a compromise outcome of the negotiations on the realignment of exchange rates. A price significantly higher than thirty-eight dollars per ounce was never seriously considered. An increase of less than 8½ percent would have failed to bring forth a realignment of exchange rates as large as the readjustment that was finally accepted. The primary objective of the U.S. negotiators at the Smithsonian meeting was to achieve a substantial upward revaluation of the currencies of other industrial countries against the dollar, and this result was achieved.

It should be noted in passing that under the two-tier system for gold, agreed to in March 1968, the official price of monetary gold and the free market price of gold are effectively separated. For all practical purposes, gold in official reserves is now a different entity from gold that is bought and sold in free markets for industrial, artistic, or hoarding purposes. In particular, the market price of gold has no bearing on the change in the official price of gold proposed in the Par Value Modification Act.

Looking to the future, let me turn briefly to the probable effects of the Smithsonian Agreement. Since dollar prices of foreign currencies are now substantially higher than before, the growth of our imports will tend to slacken and domestic production will be stimulated. On the other hand, the lower price of dollars abroad will make it possible for our exporters to quote lower prices in terms of foreign currencies. Similarly, the lower price of dollars will tend to stimulate foreign investments and travel in the United States.

There is thus every reason to expect the realignment of exchange rates to bring about, in time, a substantial improvement in our foreign trade balance and in our overall balance of payments. Just how large the improvement will be, and how long it will take for the full improvement to be realized, cannot be predicted with certainty. The experience of other countries indicates that large exchange rate changes will produce large shifts in the balance of payments; but it also indicates that two years or so may need to elapse before the full extent of the favorable shift is realized.

While the Smithsonian realignment will have its largest effects on our exports and imports, there should also be favorable effects on other components of the balance of payments, including capital flows to and from the United States. Such capital flows have already been affected. The enormous outflow of speculative funds from the United States came to an end when the Smithsonian Agreement was announced. Since December 18, there has been a small net return flow of funds.

Besides serving to reinvigorate our foreign trade and otherwise improve the balance of payments, the Smithsonian Agreement has increased confidence both at home and abroad in the stability of the world economy. This confidence will be buttressed by passage of the Par Value Modification Act.

The Smithsonian Agreement provided not only for a realignment of exchange rates and other measures of immediate concern, but also "that discussions should be promptly undertaken, particularly in the framework of the IMF, to consider reform of the international monetary system over the longer term." This unfinished business is most important. If we are to avoid a repetition of crises while preserving a monetary framework conducive to the healthy expansion of trade and investment, we must work with other countries to build a new and stronger international economic order.

In the area of exchange rates, the wider margins agreed to in December should prove helpful, especially in moderating short-term capital flows and thereby permitting somewhat greater scope for differences in interest rates among countries. For the longer run, procedures for changing par values will need to be flexible enough to prevent the buildup of large and persistent imbalances in trade and payments among countries.

A searching reevaluation is also needed of the roles to be played by gold, reserve currencies, and special drawing rights in settling international accounts. Various proposals for modifying the operations of the International Monetary Fund require study and discussion. The circumstances under which the dollar may again be convertible into international reserve assets will have to be reviewed carefully. And determined new efforts will be required to reduce impediments to the international flow of goods, services, and capital.

The issues are many and complex. It will take time to resolve them. But the unfinished business of international monetary reform requires that we get on with the job without delay. Early action by the Congress on the bill before you will set the stage for much needed progress in both the international monetary and international trade areas.

I have discussed at some length the Smithsonian Agreement because it has given rise to the present hearing. But I cannot conclude this statement without warning that neither the Smithsonian Agreement, nor passage of the bill before you, nor any international monetary or trade reforms that may follow, can of themselves do more than move us toward the objectives of renewed vigor in foreign trade and equilibrium in the balance of payments.

To assure success in these objectives of foreign economic policy, we must have skillful and fully responsible management of monetary and fiscal affairs. The objectives of our foreign economic policy and of our domestic economic policy are interdependent. For the sake of both the one and the other we will need to concentrate on stepping up sharply the productivity of our resources and on regaining prosperity without inflation.

Some Essentials of
International Monetary Reform

On August 15 of last year, in the face of an unsatisfactory economic situation, the President of the United States acted decisively to alter the nation's economic course. The new policies, especially the decision to suspend convertibility of the dollar into gold or other reserve assets, were bound to have far-reaching consequences for international monetary arrangements. New choices were forced on all countries.

The next four months gave all of us a glimpse of one possible evolution of the international economy. Since exchange rates were no longer tied to the old par values, they were able to float—a prescription that many economists had favored. However, last fall's floating rates did not conform to the model usually sketched in academic writings. Most countries were reluctant to allow their exchange rates to move in response to market forces. Instead, restrictions on financial transactions proliferated, special measures with regard to trade emerged here and there, new twists crept into the pattern of exchange rates, serious business uncertainty about governmental policies developed, fears of a recession in world economic activity grew, and signs of political friction among friendly nations multiplied.

Fortunately, this dangerous trend toward competitive and even antagonistic national economic policies was halted by the Smithsonian Agreement. Despite recent developments in Vietnam, which may cause some uneasiness in financial markets

Address before the 1972 International Banking Conference, Montreal, Canada, May 12, 1972.

447

for a time, the Smithsonian realignment of currencies is, in my judgment, solidly based. It was worked out with care by practical and well-informed men, and I am confident that the central banks and governments of all the major countries will continue to give it strong support.

Developments in the American economy since last December have been encouraging. Aggregate activity in the United States has begun to show signs of vigorous resurgence. Price increases have moderated, and our rate of inflation has recently been below that of most other industrial countries. Moreover, the budget deficit of the federal government will be much smaller this fiscal year than seemed likely three or four months ago. These developments have strengthened the confidence with which businessmen and consumers assess the economic outlook. International confidence in turn is being bolstered by the passage of the Par Value Modification Act, by the convergence of short-term interest rates in the United States and abroad, and by some promising signs of improvement in the international financial accounts of the United States.

With the Smithsonian Agreement and other indications of progress behind us, it is necessary now to move ahead and plan for the longer future. The Smithsonian meeting was preeminently concerned with realigning exchange rates. It did not attempt to deal with structural weaknesses in the old international monetary system. Yet they must eventually be remedied if we are to build a new and stronger international economic order.

We all have to ponder this basic question: Given the constraints of past history, what evolution of the monetary system is desirable and at the same time practically attainable? For my part, I should like to take advantage of this gathering to consider some of the elements that one might reasonably expect to find in a reformed monetary system.

First of all, a reformed system will need to be characterized by a further strengthening of international consultation and cooperation among governments. Our national economies are linked by a complex web of international transactions. Problems and policies in one country inevitably affect other countries. This simple fact of interdependence gives rise to constraints on national policies. In a smoothly functioning system, no country can ignore the implications of its own actions for other countries or fail to cooperate in discussing and resolving problems of mutual concern. The task of statesmanship is to tap the great reservoir of international goodwill that now exists and to make sure that it remains undiminished in the future.

Sound domestic policies are a second requirement of a better world economic order. A well-constructed international monetary system should, it is true, be capable of absorbing the strains caused by occasional financial mismanagement in this or that country—such as are likely to follow from chronic budget deficits or from abnormally large and persistent additions to the money supply. But I doubt if any international monetary system can long survive if the major industrial countries fail to follow sound financial practices. In view of the huge size of the American economy, I recognize that the economic policies of the United States will remain an especially important influence on the operation of any international monetary system.

Third, in the calculable future any international monetary system will have to respect the need for substantial autonomy of domestic economic policies. A reformed monetary system cannot be one that encourages national authorities to sacrifice either the objective of high employment or the objective of price stability in order to achieve balance-of-payments equilibrium. More specifically, no country experiencing an external deficit should have to accept sizable increases in unemployment in order to reduce its deficit. Nor should a surplus country have to moderate its surplus by accepting high rates of inflation. Domestic policies of this type are poorly suited to the political mood of our times, and it would serve no good purpose to assume otherwise.

I come now to a fourth element that should characterize a reformed monetary system. If I am right in thinking that the world needs realistic and reasonably stable exchange rates, rather than rigid exchange rates, ways must be found to ensure that payments imbalances will be adjusted more smoothly and promptly than under the old Bretton Woods arrangements.

The issues here are many and complex. There was a consensus at the Smithsonian meeting that wider margins around parities can help to correct payments imbalances, and should prove especially helpful in moderating short-term capital movements—thereby giving monetary authorities somewhat more scope to pursue different interest-rate policies. Our experience has not yet been extensive enough to permit a confident appraisal of this innovation. It is clear, however, that no matter how much the present wider margins may contribute to facilitating the adjustment of exchange rates to changing conditions, the wider margins by themselves will prove inadequate for that purpose.

We may all hope that at least the major countries will pursue sound, noninflationary policies in the future. We should nevertheless recognize that national lapses from economic virtue will continue to occur. In such circumstances, changes in parities—however regrettable—may well become a practical necessity. Moreover, even if every nation succeeded in achieving noninflationary growth, structural changes in consumption or production will often lead to shifts in national competitive positions over time. Such shifts will also modify the pattern of exchange rates that is appropriate for maintaining balance-of-payments equilibrium.

In my judgment, therefore, more prompt adjustments of parities will be needed in a reformed monetary system. Rules of international conduct will have to be devised which, while recognizing rights of sovereignty, establish definite guidelines and consultative machinery for determining when parities need to be changed. This subject is likely to become one of the central issues, and also one of the most difficult, in the forthcoming negotiations.

Let me turn to a fifth element that should characterize a reformed monetary system. A major weakness of the old system was its failure to treat in a symmetrical manner the responsibilities of surplus and deficit countries for balance-of-payments adjustment. With deficits equated to sin and surpluses to virtue, moral as well as financial pressures were very much greater on deficit countries to reduce their deficits than on surplus countries to reduce surpluses. In actual practice, however, responsibility for payments imbalances can seldom be assigned unambiguously to individual countries. And in any event, the adjustment process will work more efficiently if surplus countries participate actively in it. In my view, all countries have an obligation to eliminate payments imbalances, and the rules of international conduct to which I referred earlier will therefore need to define acceptable behavior and provide for international monitoring of both surplus and deficit countries.

Sixth, granted improvements in the promptness with which payments imbalances are adjusted, reserve assets and official borrowing will still be needed to finance in an orderly manner the imbalances that continue to arise. Looking to the long future, it will therefore be important to develop plans so that world reserves and official credit arrangements exist in an appropriate form and can be adjusted to appropriate levels.

This brings me to the seventh feature of a reformed international monetary system. It is sometimes argued that, as a part of reform, gold should be demonetized. As a practical matter, it seems doubtful to me that there is any broad support for eliminating the monetary role of gold in the near future. To many people, gold remains a great symbol of safety and security, and these attitudes about gold are not likely to change quickly. Nevertheless, I would expect the monetary role of gold to continue to diminish in the years ahead, while the role of special drawing rights increases.

The considerations which motivated the International Monetary Fund to establish the SDR facility in 1969 should remain valid in a reformed system. However, revisions in the detailed arrangements governing the creation, allocation, and use of SDRs will probably be needed. In the future, as the SDRs assume increasing importance, they may ultimately become the major international reserve asset.

Next, as my eighth point, let me comment briefly on the future role of the dollar as a reserve currency. It has often been said that the United States had a privileged position in the old monetary system because it could settle payments deficits by adding to its liabilities instead of drawing down its reserve assets. Many also argue that this asymmetry should be excluded in a reformed system. There thus seems to be significant sentiment in favor of diminishing, or even phasing out, the role of the dollar as a reserve currency. One conceivable way of accomplishing this objective would be to place restraints on the further accumulation of dollars in official reserves. If no further accumulation at all were allowed, the United States would be

required to finance any deficit in its balance of payments entirely
with reserve assets.

I am not persuaded by this line of reasoning, for I see
advantages both to the United States and to other countries
from the use of the dollar as a reserve currency. But I recognize
that there are some burdens or disadvantages as well. And in
any event, this is an important issue on which national views
may well diverge in the early stages of the forthcoming negotiations.

I come now to a ninth point concerning a new monetary
system, namely, the issue of "convertibility" of the dollar. It
seems unlikely to me that the nations of the world, taken as a
whole and over the long run, will accept a system in which
convertibility of the dollar into international reserve assets—
SDRs and gold—is entirely absent. If we want to build a
strengthened monetary system along one-world lines, as I certainly do, this issue will have to be resolved. I therefore anticipate, as part of a total package of long-term reforms, that some
form of dollar convertibility can be reestablished in the future.

I must note, however, that this issue of convertibility has
received excessive emphasis in recent discussions. Convertibility
is important, but no more so than the other issues on which I
have touched. It is misleading, and may even prove mis-
chievous, to stress one particular aspect of reform to the ex-
clusion of others. Constructive negotiations will be possible
only if there is a general disposition to treat the whole range
of issues in balanced fashion.

We need to guard against compartmentalizing concern
with any one of the issues, if only because the various elements
of a new monetary system are bound to be interrelated. There
is a particularly important interdependence, for example, between improvements in the exchange rate regime and restoration
of some form of convertibility of the dollar into gold or other
reserve assets. Without some assurance that exchange rates of
both deficit and surplus countries will be altered over time so
as to prevent international transactions from moving into serious
imbalance, I would deem it impractical to attempt to restore
convertibility of the dollar.

My tenth and last point involves the linkage between
monetary and trading arrangements. We cannot afford to over-

look the fact that trade practices are a major factor in determining the balance-of-payments position of individual nations. There is now a strong feeling in the United States that restrictive commercial policies of some countries have affected adversely the markets of American business firms. In my judgment, therefore, the chances of success of the forthcoming monetary conversations will be greatly enhanced if parallel conversations get under way on trade problems, and if those conversations take realistic account of the current and prospective foreign trade position of the United States.

In the course of my remarks this morning I have touched on some of the more essential conditions and problems of international monetary reform. Let me conclude by restating the elements I would expect to find in a new monetary system that met the test of both practicality and viability:

- First, a significant further strengthening of the processes of international consultation and cooperation;
- Second, responsible domestic policies in all the major industrial countries;
- Third, a substantial degree of autonomy for domestic policies, so that no country would feel compelled to sacrifice high employment or price stability in order to achieve balance-of-payments equilibrium;
- Fourth, more prompt adjustments of payments imbalances, to be facilitated by definite guidelines and consultative machinery for determining when parities need to be changed;
- Fifth, a symmetrical division of responsibilities among surplus and deficit countries for initiating and implementing adjustments of payments imbalances;
- Sixth, systematic long-range plans for the evolution of world reserves and official credit arrangements;
- Seventh, a continued but diminishing role for gold as a reserve asset, with a corresponding increase in the importance of SDRs;
- Eighth, a better international consensus than exists at present about the proper role of reserve currencies in the new system;
- Ninth, reestablishment of some form of dollar convertibility in the future;

- And finally, tenth, a significant lessening of restrictive trading practices as the result of negotiations complementing the negotiations on monetary reform.

I firmly believe that a new and stronger international monetary system can and must be built. Indeed, I feel it is an urgent necessity to start the rebuilding process quite promptly. It is not pleasant to contemplate the kind of world that may evolve if cooperative efforts to rebuild the monetary system are long postponed. We might then find the world economy divided into restrictive and inward-looking blocs, with rules of international conduct concerning exchange rates and monetary reserves altogether absent.

As we learned last fall, a world of financial manipulations, economic restrictions, and political frictions bears no promise for the future. It is the responsibility of financial leaders to make sure that such a world will never come to pass.

The Need for Order in
International Finance

I plan to comment tonight on the need for order in international finance. My choice of topic does not require lengthy justification. For more than a decade now, we have been besieged by problem after problem in the working of international financial mechanisms. Strain and turbulence have, in fact, been so constant a feature of the international financial scene in recent years that I suspect they are coming to be widely regarded as the normal state of affairs.

I do not share any such mood of resignation. In the first place, governments around the world now have a better understanding of the troubles caused by inflation—both in their own economies and in international dealings—than they had only a few years ago. As a result, not a few countries have been adjusting their economic policies with a view to curbing inflation. In the second place, financial institutions—particularly commercial banks—are now giving closer attention to the volume and character of their foreign lending. And in the third place, the International Monetary Fund has been gaining in prestige and is already exercising a more constructive influence than seemed likely a year or two ago. These are promising trends, and if we build on them we can in time reattain the financial stability that is so vital to orderly expansion of the international economy.

Certainly, we all know of the great difficulties that plagued financial relationships among countries during the 1930s. Those

Address at the annual dinner of the Columbia University Graduate School of Business, New York City, April 12, 1977.

difficulties generated pessimism about the capacity of nations ever again to achieve orderly arrangements for the conduct of international finances. And that pessimism was deepened by the frightful disruption of the world economy during the war. Yet, it was the genius of that age to devise the structure of Bretton Woods and to strengthen that extraordinary structure with our own Marshall Plan. Within a framework of established financial rules, a great liberalization of the world economy occurred and world trade and output flourished. Although we tend to forget it now, the postwar period was a time of quite impressive stability in world finance until the early sixties.

That experience should serve to remind us that difficulties do yield to determined effort. Our present problems in the sphere of international finance, while different from those of a generation ago, surely are no greater. They too can be dealt with effectively if once again we perceive the wisdom of some subordination of parochial interests and if nations marshal the will to live by new rules of responsible behavior.

Quite obviously, the overriding problem confronting us in world financial matters today is the massive and stubborn imbalance that prevails in payments relations among nations— a condition arising importantly, although by no means exclusively, from OPEC's action in raising the price of oil so abruptly and so steeply.

This year alone OPEC's revenues from international oil sales are likely to total something on the order of $130 billion. What is most significant about that figure is that it represents an enormous explosion of revenues in such a short time. In 1972, before OPEC's aggressive pricing policy began, receipts of the OPEC group from international oil sales totaled less than $14 billion, with most of the rise since then representing higher prices rather than enlarged volume. For the great majority of OPEC's customers—both affluent and needy alike—it has been the rapidity of the massive change that has been so troublesome. To be sure, OPEC members have dispensed some aid to less developed countries, but so far the grants have been very selective and quite small relative to the size of the international problem that OPEC has created.

The imposition of the enormous tax that the OPEC group has in effect levied on the world economy has been met, as you know, partly by transferring goods and services to OPEC members and partly by deferring such transfers through borrowing arrangements. OPEC's absorption of goods and services for both consumption and development purposes has been expanding, with the consequence that OPEC's collective current-account surplus has shrunk considerably from its peak level of more than $65 billion in 1974. Only five of the thirteen OPEC nations in fact are currently running sizable payments surpluses. Contrary, however, to earlier widespread hopes that the aggregate OPEC surplus would continue to decline—perhaps nearing elimination by the end of this decade—it seems at present to be eroding slowly, if at all. This year it could easily run above $40 billion, marking the fourth consecutive year that OPEC's trading partners as a group will have to seek substantial loans or grants to help meet their oil bills.

Continuation of a surplus for the OPEC group at such a high level reflects several influences: first, the further increase that occurred this January in OPEC oil prices; second, growing demand for oil as recovery of the world economy has proceeded; third, insufficient energy conservation by many non-OPEC countries, including most notably the United States; and fourth, a slowing of import absorption by the OPEC group—in some instances because bottleneck problems of one kind or another are being encountered, in other instances because development plans have come to be viewed as excessively ambitious. The apparent stickiness of the OPEC payments surplus at a high level, buttressed by what is now a significant stream of income from investments, implies large-scale financing requirements for OPEC customers for a considerable period ahead. The prospect of such persistent financing needs, year after year, is especially worrisome.

Great as must be our attention to these OPEC-related problems, we dare not lose sight of the fact that our international payments mechanism is now under stress for reasons that go beyond the extraordinarily high price of oil. The payments deficits of various nations, both industrial and less developed, can be traced to extensive social welfare and development programs undertaken in the early 1970s and financed by heavy governmental borrowing, often directly from central banks. Even when the internal stresses resulting from inflation were aggravated by the oil burden and by weaker exports, there was little or no adjustment of economic policies in numerous instances, thus causing external positions to deteriorate sharply. There were conspicuous exceptions, of course, particularly on the part of countries that historically have the greatest sensitivity either to inflation, or payments imbalance, or both. A wide diversity of payments imbalances thus developed around the globe, accentuated for a time by differences in the severity with which recession affected national economies and, more recently, by differing inflation and recovery trends.

The current pattern of international payments imbalances, in short, is something far more complex than an OPEC phenomenon alone. Essentially, what prevails is a problem within a problem. The non-OPEC group of countries collectively not only has a massive structural deficit vis-à-vis OPEC. In addition, serious payments imbalances exist within the non-OPEC sector itself, with a few nations experiencing sizable surpluses on their current account while many others suffer deficits that reflect many factors besides the way in which the burden of costly oil imports happens to be distributed around the globe.

A great deal of effort has been devoted by scholars to the task of trying to estimate how long the present severe imbalance of international payments accounts could persist in the absence of deliberate new policy actions. The results of these exercises generally are not reassuring. They point to the distinct possibility that huge borrowing needs—that is, needs that are uncomfortably large in relation to the debt-servicing capabilities of many countries—could persist at least through the remainder of this decade.

The potential trouble in this set of circumstances should be obvious. If OPEC surpluses on current account should continue on anything like the present scale, they would inevitably be matched by deficits of identical magnitude on the part of other nations. And if some countries outside OPEC should also have sizable and persistent surpluses, as now appears to be the case, the aggregate deficit of the remaining countries will be still larger. Under such circumstances, many countries will be forced to borrow heavily, and lending institutions may well be tempted to extend credit more generously than is prudent. A major risk in all this is that it would render the international credit structure especially vulnerable in the event that the world economy were again to experience recession on the scale of the one from which we are now emerging.

To minimize the risks that face us, there is a clear need for a strong effort involving all major parties at interest. In order to achieve relatively smooth expansion of the world economy, five conditions are essential: first, the aggregate of payments imbalances around the world needs to be reduced far more rapidly than currently observable trends imply; second, the divergences that now exist among countries with regard to their balance-of-payments status need to be narrowed; third, protectionism must be scrupulously avoided by governments; fourth, private financial institutions need to adhere to high standards of creditworthiness in providing whatever volume of international financing occurs during the next few years; and fifth, official credit facilities need to be significantly enlarged.

The realization of these conditions requires diligent pursuit of stabilization policies by countries that have been borrowing heavily in international markets. The obstacles to speedy adjustment on the part of these countries are well known. Resistance stems chiefly from the political difficulty of gaining broad acceptance of the painful things that must be done to restrain inflation and to achieve energy conservation. Countries thus find it more attractive to borrow than to adjust their monetary and fiscal policies; and if they can do this without having lenders write restrictive covenants into loan agreements, so much the better. That is why countries typically prefer to tap foreign credit markets to the maximum extent possible rather than borrow from the International Monetary Fund which, in aiding countries that experience significant payments disequilibrium, makes credit available only after the borrower has agreed to follow internal policies judged appropriate by the Fund. Commercial banks, as a practical matter, have neither the inclination nor the leverage to impose restrictive covenants on sovereign governments.

In these circumstances, admonition alone is likely to accomplish little in prodding countries with large payments deficits to take affirmative action. There are, however, limits dictated by financial prudence beyond which private lenders will be unwilling to go. More than one country has recently found that its ability to borrow in the private market has diminished. The fact is that commercial banks generally, and particularly those which have already made extensive loans abroad, are now evaluating country risks more closely and more methodically. Credit standards thus appear to be firming; and as information about borrowing countries improves, we can reasonably expect the market to perform its function of credit allocation more effectively.

As some of you may know, the Federal Reserve is currently engaged in a joint project with other central banks to obtain a much more complete size and maturity profile of bank credit extended to foreign borrowers, country by country. That information, which is being gathered under the auspices of the Bank for International Settlements, will be shared with private lenders, but even so it will fill only a fraction of the existing informational gap.

What we need is a more forthcoming attitude on the part of borrowing countries in regularly supplying information to lenders on the full range of economic and financial matters relevant to creditworthiness. I realize that much of the needed information is not even collected in some countries, but such a condition should not be tolerated indefinitely. Logically, the BIS—having links with the central banks of the principal lending countries—could take the lead in setting forth a list of informational items that all countries borrowing in the international market would be expected to make available to present or prospective lenders. Compliance could then become a significant factor in the ability of countries to secure private credit, particularly if—as I would judge essential—bank regulators in the various lending countries explicitly took account of compliance in their review of bank loan portfolios.

Imperfect or incomplete information, as I think we all recognize, makes for inefficient markets and heightens the risk of disruptive discontinuities if some previously unknown but pertinent fact suddenly comes to light. In the market for bank credit, a continuous flow of factual information will produce gradual as distinct from abrupt changes in assessments of creditworthiness. This should induce earlier recourse to the IMF by countries experiencing payments difficulties than was usually the case in the past. Even now, as lenders are becoming better informed and somewhat more cautious in extending foreign credit, a tendency toward earlier recourse to the IMF appears to be emerging. It seems likely, therefore, that more countries that need to adjust their economic policies will henceforth do so sooner and probably also more effectively. By so doing, the unhappy alternative of resorting to protectionism will be more readily avoided.

Private banks—both in this country and elsewhere—played a very substantial role in "recycling" petrodollars between the OPEC group and other countries, especially those whose external payments position was weakened by the higher oil prices. Had the banks not done so, the recent recession would have been more severe than it was, since there was no official mechanism in place that could have coped with recycling of funds on the vast scale that became necessary in 1974. But with many countries now heavily burdened with debt, bankers generally recognize that prudence demands moderation on their part in providing additional financing for countries in deficit. For that reason, they understandably wish to see an increase in the relative volume of official financial support to countries that continue to have large borrowing needs.

Bankers are not alone in wanting to see countries in deficit pursue adjustment policies more diligently. This interest, in fact, is widely shared by economists and other thoughtful citizens who see an urgent need for healthier and more prosperous economic conditions around the world. The interests of the international economy and of private lenders thus converge and point to the need for a much more active role by the Fund.

The leverage of the Fund in speeding the process of adjustment would clearly be enhanced if its capacity to lend were greater than it is now. One reason why countries often are unwilling to submit to conditions imposed by the IMF is that the amount of credit available to them through the Fund's regular channels—as determined by established quotas—is in many instances small relative to their structural payments imbalance. That will be so even after the scheduled increase in IMF quotas becomes effective. To remedy this deficiency, the Fund is currently seeking resources of appreciable amount that could be superimposed on the framework of the quota system. Negotiations are in progress with several countries of the OPEC group as well as with the United States and other industrial nations whose payments position is comparatively strong. Such a supplementary Fund facility should induce more deficit countries to submit to Fund discipline. But in no case must it become a substitute for an adequate adjustment policy by borrowers or serve as a bailout for private banks. If negotiations for such a facility are completed soon, which appears possible, high priority should be given to prompt ratification by our Congress and the legislatures of other countries.

The ability of the Fund to act forcefully in speeding the adjustment process will be strengthened in still another way once the five-year effort of amending the IMF's Articles of Agreement is completed. At present the Fund normally immerses itself in urging appropriate policies on a country only when that country applies for financial assistance. Under the revised Articles, the Fund could take the initiative in determining whether individual countries are complying with formally prescribed obligations to foster orderly economic growth and price stability. This authority, once available, will enable the IMF to broaden progressively its oversight role even when a country is not an applicant for a loan.

As the number of countries brought within the reach of the Fund's influence increases—either because of the enticement of enlarged lending facilities or because an IMF "certificate of good standing" becomes essential to further borrowing from private lenders—the outlook for correction of balance-of-payments deficits would be considerably improved. But that outcome will also depend on full appreciation by private lenders of the need to avoid actions that tend to undercut Fund efforts.

This does not mean that Fund judgments are to replace those of private lenders in the determination of which countries should be accommodated with private credit. Nor do I even mean to suggest that the texts of the Fund's country evaluations are to be handed around in the private banking community. Were that to become a practice, I am sure the quality of such reports would suffer by becoming less explicit and less frank. But some sharing of Fund information—within the limits imposed by requirements of confidentiality—may still become feasible, the most logical conduits perhaps being the central banks of the countries in which the major private lending institutions are located.

Fund country reports are transmitted to central banks as a matter of routine, and—as I previously indicated—new factual information about individual countries is now being developed, and more may well be developed later, by the BIS. Private lenders might want to discuss with the staffs of central banks the flow of such information, and this could be done—as would surely be the Federal Reserve's practice—without advising whether or on what scale a loan should be made to this or that country. Such a consultative process, especially if it also involved frequent interchange of information among the leading central banks, would go quite far in preventing any inadvertent circumvention by private banks of the efforts of the IMF to promote financial stability.

The suggestions I am exploring with you for improving the adjustment process obviously will not work unless broadly shared agreement develops that international financial affairs require a "rule of law" to guide us through the troubled circumstances that now exist. Such a rule cannot be codified in detail, but it is essential that there be broad agreement that parochial concerns will be subordinated to the vital objective of working our way back to more stable conditions in international finance. And if the IMF is to play a leadership role in pursuing this objective, it is not only private parties that must avoid weakening the IMF's efforts. Governments also—indeed governments especially—must be prepared to forgo their own quite frequent inclination to do things inconsistent with the effective pursuit of Fund objectives. There have been too many instances in which the government of a country negotiating a stabilization program with the Fund's officials has attempted to circumvent the Fund by seeking instead a loan from another government or by exerting outside political pressure on Fund officials in an effort to make loan conditions as lenient as possible. If the rule of law in international monetary affairs is ultimately to prevail, all countries—there can be no exceptions—must fully respect the IMF's integrity.

Our first requisite, therefore, is for a new sense of commitment by governments as well as private parties to a responsible code of behavior. I believe that understanding of this need has been growing—certainly within our own government. And, of course, the working of the marketplace—tending now to make credit less readily available to some foreign borrowers—is helping to foster a new set of attitudes.

As I noted earlier, the payments difficulties of countries outside the OPEC group reflect many factors besides the way in which the burden of oil costs happens to have been distributed. It is important that adjustment proceed along several paths in this vast part of the world.

First, countries whose external position has been weakened by loose financial policies are going to have to practice some fiscal and monetary restraint, either of their own volition or because they find it obligatory to do so in order to maintain access to international credit facilities, including those of the IMF. In individual instances, the adjustment process in such countries may at times also entail allowing some depreciation of the foreign exchange value of their currencies.

Second, since the burden of adjustment cannot and should not rest with deficit countries alone, those non-OPEC countries that are experiencing significant and persistent current-account surpluses must understand that they too have adjustment obligations. In saying this, I do not mean to imply that we should urge such countries to pursue expansionist policies that could undo or jeopardize the hard-won progress that some of them have made in curbing inflation. That would be both wrong and unwise. What I mean is simply that such countries should not actively resist tendencies toward appreciation in the value of their currencies in foreign-exchange markets. Such appreciation will aid other countries by facilitating access to the markets of the countries in surplus; and at the same time it will make imported goods and services available at a lower cost to the citizens of the surplus countries, thus reinforcing their constructive efforts to control inflation.

Third, practically all non-OPEC countries—the deficit and surplus countries alike—must treat energy conservation as a key element of their economic policy. This is something to which the United States in particular must give the closest attention. We are by far the largest single consumer of energy in the world, and we have so far been notably laggard in addressing the energy problem. This year imported oil will probably account for over 40 percent of domestic consumption of petroleum, up from 22 percent in 1970. Our passive approach to energy policy, besides endangering the nation's future, has aggravated strains in the international financial system, because we are directly responsible for a large part of the OPEC surplus. And, of course, our huge appetite for oil has added to the leverage of those OPEC members that have been most reckless in urging a still higher price of oil. The energy program being prepared by President Carter unquestionably will entail sacrifices by many of our citizens. It is essential, however, that we at long last recognize that a decisive conservation effort must be a major part of our nation's economic policy.

If, in fact, we can build momentum into payments adjustment by the non-OPEC group of countries along these three paths—that is, internal discipline by countries in deficit, non-resistance to exchange rate appreciation by countries in surplus, and determined energy conservation by all—the favorable consequences will be enormous. To the extent that energy conservation is effective, the present serious imbalance of the non-OPEC group of nations vis-à-vis OPEC will be reduced. Beyond that, there will no longer be such extremely large differences in the balance-of-payments status of the non-OPEC nations. Consequently, the risk of disruption of the international financial system would be greatly reduced, and we could have greater confidence that progress will be realized around the world in reducing unemployment and otherwise improving economic conditions.

There is a critical proviso, however, to this optimistic assessment—namely, that the OPEC group, seeing their surplus decline as a result of foreign conservation efforts or their own increasing imports, will not seek to compensate for the decline by a new round of oil-price increases. Obviously, if they were to do so—and if they could make the action stick—the whole exercise of trying to reduce the massive payments imbalances traceable to the oil shock would be rendered futile.

Effective oil conservation and the development of other sources of energy would, of course, militate against such an outcome to the extent that those efforts lessened OPEC's market leverage. That is important for the longer run, but particularly in the years immediately ahead it is vital that the

465

members of OPEC recognize that their economic and political future cannot be divorced from that of the rest of the world. Besides practicing forbearance with regard to the price of oil, it would be very helpful if they made larger grants of assistance to the less developed countries and also expanded the volume of loans and investments made directly abroad—so that the intermediation of American or European commercial banks may be substantially reduced. Fortunately, there are various signs that the more influential members of OPEC are becoming increasingly aware that their self-interest requires a major contribution along these lines. The OPEC group has become a large factor in international finance, and there is some basis for confidence that they will play a constructive role in the reestablishment of order in the international financial structure.

In the course of my remarks tonight, I have touched on a number of actions that either need to be taken or avoided to achieve a new sense of order in international finance. Let me conclude by sketching or restating the responsibilities, as I see them, of the major participants in the international financial system:

First, in order to contribute to a more stable international system, the IMF must act with new assertiveness in monitoring the economic policies of its members. To give the Fund added leverage for such a role, its resources must be enlarged. But those resources must be used sparingly and dispensed only when applicant countries agree to pursue effective stabilization policies. In view of the clear need for better financial discipline around the world, this would be a poor time for a new allocation of SDRs—or, in plain language, printing up new international money.

Second, national governments must encourage and support the IMF, so that it can become an effective guardian of evolving law in the international monetary sphere. Governments need to resist the temptation to circumvent the Fund by seeking bilateral official loans or to embarrass the Fund by exerting political pressure on Fund officials. Commercial and investment bankers also need to recognize that their actions must not undercut IMF efforts to speed adjustment. The IMF, in its turn, will have to equip itself to handle appropriately its new and larger responsibilities.

Third, a better framework of knowledge for evaluating the creditworthiness of individual countries is badly needed. Among other things, central banks could work together through the BIS and establish a common list of informational items that borrowing countries will be expected to supply to lenders.

Fourth, commercial and investment bankers need to monitor their foreign lending with great care, and bank examiners need to be alert to excessive concentration of loans in individual countries.

Fifth, protectionist policies need to be shunned by all countries.

Sixth, countries with persistent payments deficits need to adopt effective domestic stabilization policies.

Seventh, non-OPEC countries experiencing large and persistent payments surpluses also need to adjust their economic policies and they can probably best do so by allowing some appreciation of their exchange rates.

Eighth, all countries, and especially the United States, need to adopt stringent oil conservation policies and, wherever possible, speed the development of new energy sources.

Ninth, the members of OPEC must avoid a new round of oil-price increases. They also need to play an increasingly constructive role in assisting the less developed countries and in the evolution of the international financial system.

Observance of these do's and don'ts would go a significant distance, in my judgment, in meeting the formidable challenges that now confront us. But we shall undoubtedly need to be ready to improvise in the fluid and complex area of international finance. I have no illusions that the ideas that I have presented here tonight can serve as a rigid blueprint. I hope, however, that they will have some value in suggesting directions in which governments, private lenders, and official institutions need to move. By working together towards a rule of law in international finance, we shall be contributing to a stable prosperity both for our own citizens and those of our trading partners.

The Redirection of
Financial Policies

I am deeply honored, Mr. Chancellor, that you invited me to join this distinguished audience in paying tribute to Karl Klasen.

This occasion has very special meaning for me, inasmuch as Karl Klasen and I have headed our respective central banks over almost precisely the same span of time, each of us having begun service in early 1970.

The period since then has been one of the most eventful in the annals of international finance, and that inevitably has involved frequent and close contact between the two of us.

Our seven years of collaboration have left with me a deep appreciation of the talent and the intellectual integrity which Karl Klasen possesses. I shall miss his official counsel, and yet I count myself fortunate in having been able so often in the past to avail myself of the wisdom and the warm supportive friendship of such a colleague.

I have no difficulty in singling out Karl Klasen's premier achievement as President of the Bundesbank. That has been his determined, unwavering endeavor to foster understanding that there can be no durable prosperity, either in the Federal Republic or in the world community at large, if inflation is not controlled more effectively than it has been. Karl Klasen's skillful articulation of that truth—and the bold actions he has taken to give it meaning—place him squarely in the great tradition of responsible financial leadership so continuously evident in your country since Dr. Erhard's currency reform of 1948.

Remarks at Chancellor Helmut Schmidt's dinner honoring Dr. Karl Klasen, Bonn, Germany, May 11, 1977.

The Federal Republic's achievement—under the guidance of men such as Dr. Klasen—in dealing with inflation more successfully than any other major country has not been lost on an observant world. By your example, others know what can be done where intelligence, determination, and persistence prevail. At this critical juncture in the worldwide struggle against inflation, your achievement is a powerful counterweight to any mood of resignation or defeatism.

Indeed, I am inclined to think that the intellectual climate around much of the globe is slowly changing in a positive way. Only a few short years ago expansionist convictions and policies were in ascendancy almost everywhere, the simple creed being that governmental budget deficits and easy money were safe and effective stimuli whenever an economy failed to perform at its full potential. Country after country—mine included—has been learning the hard way that economic matters are far more complex, and—what is especially promising—policies are begining to be modified accordingly.

The British Prime Minister has summarized the bankruptcy of mechanical Keynesianism perhaps more effectively that anyone else. "We used to think," he said in addressing the British Labour Party Conference in Blackpool last September, "that you could just spend your way out of recession . . . I tell you in all candor," he continued, "that that option no longer exists, and that insofar as it ever did exist, it worked by injecting inflation into the economy. And each time that happened the average level of unemployment has risen. Higher inflation, followed by higher unemployment. That is the history of the last twenty years."

Those words of Mr. Callaghan's are remarkably perceptive. Though directed to Britain's special problems, they have broad applicability throughout the world. They capture the essential truth that policies for stimulating employment on which we have relied in the past—such as budget deficits and easy credit—do not work well in an environment that has become highly sensitive to inflationary fears and expectations. In such an environment the consuming public in its apprehension about the future will tend to raise its saving rate and thus may frustrate governmental policies aimed at stimulating the economy. Businessmen, too, having learned that profits can erode quickly when inflation is not effectively contained, will tend to become more cautious about undertaking new projects. Mr. Callaghan thus put his finger on the vital point: inflation is the key global problem with which we must cope if we are to regain a lasting prosperity.

Conventional thinking about stabilization policies is inadequate and out of date. Our quest must be for new policies tailored to the need for coping with inflation and unemployment simultaneously. Our approach almost certainly must be less aggregative in its orientation than it has been. More and more, we need to focus on particular structural impediments to increased economic activity and to work at building a social consensus that leads to responsible price and wage behavior by private parties. This does not necessarily mean that we must forswear all use of conventional devices in dealing with unemployment. But to the extent that such tools are employed, they must be used more judiciously than has been characteristic of the past. Policy makers everywhere must become alert to the need for prompt reaction if signs emerge that excessive stimulation is occurring. President Carter's recent decision to withdraw his proposal for a tax rebate in the face of evidence that the tempo of economic activity in the United States was accelerating more rapidly than had been expected is illustrative of precisely the kind of flexibility in economic policy making that has become essential.

A very general shortcoming of the 1972–1974 period—compounding the oil trauma of that time—was the slowness of policy makers in many countries in appreciating just how rapidly pressures were mounting on available resources. The consequence was that they permitted inflation to run totally out of control. When the distortions that arose in the process eventually culminated in the worst recession in a generation, the shock to the psychology of both consumers and businessmen was profound. The blow was particularly severe because so few of the current generation of business managers had experienced an economic decline of comparable severity. They had, indeed, been tutored to believe that the business cycle as it once existed was dead—that any recession that might occur would prove to be brief and mild, because of the countercyclical weapons possessed by modern governments.

Here in Germany you were wise enough in 1972 and 1973 to take relatively prompt moderating action on both the fiscal and monetary fronts, a fact that goes a long way in explaining, I believe, the comparatively favorable price experience you are now enjoying. But in many other countries the response was tardy, creating extremely vulnerable conditions that continue even now to plague recovery efforts.

Moderation in the pursuit of economic growth is particularly crucial if a much-needed revitalization of capital formation is to occur in the global economy. In the United States, business investment, although accelerating now, has lagged conspicuously so far in the current cyclical expansion relative to its behavior in earlier recoveries. And experience in the United States appears to be representative of what is happening in many other countries. This is a worrisome development because it is weakening the general recovery pattern and also because it suggests the distinct possibility that a condition of inadequate capacity could develop at a later stage of this expansion.

The present lag in capital formation can be traced to various causal factors, but two are of preponderant significance. One is the substantial residue of caution that lingers on among businessmen because of the rude discovery that the business cycle is still very much alive. Inflation worries—more specifically, apprehension about the degree to which inflation will be controlled—constitute the second major inhibiting influence on capital spending in industrial countries. Forward planning simply cannot proceed rationally in an environment in which business managers are unable to assess cost and profit prospects with any confidence over the long time horizons that are frequently involved in new investment projects. Inflation raises the risk premiums that businessmen attach to new undertakings; and the higher those risk premiums become, the more likely it is that the volume of investment will be depressed.

Fortunately, there are now numerous signs of an emerging consensus internationally that greater price stability is a key requisite to the achievement of sustainable economic growth and lower unemployment. Last autumn's Communiqué of the Interim Committee of the International Monetary Fund—urging as it did that industrial nations not only concern themselves with inflation but actually give it priority attention in their economic policies—provided striking testimony to the changing attitude of policy makers. Such emphasis would have been unthinkable in the days when the expansionist creed was in vogue. This new understanding of causal linkage between inflation and unemployment is reflected in the Communiqué just issued upon completion of the London summit meeting. Expressions of intent accomplish nothing of themselves, of course, but it is of great significance that major governments have at last come to perceive the appropriate direction in which they should be moving.

Because excessive creation of money, historically, has always been associated with inflation, it also is of great significance, I believe, that more countries are coming to experiment with new techniques for achieving better control over monetary expansion. Here, too, the Federal Republic can rightfully claim to have played a pioneering role. The Bundesbank, acting in December 1974, became the first central bank to announce publicly an explicit target for monetary expansion in the coming year. The Federal Reserve System shortly followed the Bundesbank in making public its monetary projections, and a number of other countries have since then done so as well.

One key value of monetary growth targets is that they force both central bankers and private parties to think more systematically than they otherwise might about the amount of inflation that is being financed at any given time. Our longer-term objective within the Federal Reserve, and I believe the like applies to the Bundesbank, is to achieve a rate of growth in monetary aggregates that is ultimately consistent with stability of the general price level. In the United States, we are, of course, a long way from that goal; and as a practical matter, we cannot move to it rapidly because of the risk of deflecting the economy from its present path of recovery. But it is helpful in our continuing monetary policy deliberations in the United States to have set our sights on what we need to achieve, and during the past two years we have in fact adjusted our growth ranges for monetary expansion gradually but persistently downward. In short, I believe that such growth targets provide a meaningful framework for fostering monetary discipline, and it is my hope that more and more countries will follow the German initiative.

The serious inflation of recent years has had pernicious effects not only within individual countries; beyond that, it has greatly complicated the task of maintaining orderly international relations.

I am aware, of course, that many people ascribe the present condition of serious payments imbalance among countries and the related bouts of unease in foreign-exchange markets almost exclusively to the burden of higher oil prices. But troublesome as the oil shock has been, it by no means fully explains the payments stresses that presently exist. The fact is that the troublesome payments deficits of many countries, both industrial and less developed, can be traced in large measure to extensive social-welfare and development programs undertaken in the early 1970s and financed by heavy governmental borrowing, often directly from central banks. Even when the internal troubles resulting from inflation were aggravated by the oil burden, there was little or no adjustment of economic policies in numerous instances. Faced with the political difficulties of gaining acceptance of the stringent measures required to restrain inflation and achieve energy conservation, many countries opted instead to borrow heavily from private external sources. Generally speaking, such borrowing entailed no obligation on the borrower to effect adjustments in the policies that had given rise to the need for special financing.

What is clearly required now is a financial environment in which countries needing to borrow will have less opportunity to do so if they are reluctant to reform their economic policies. Adjustment efforts of many countries must be intensified, so as to reduce their abnormally large deficits. To that end, private lenders need to understand the importance of taking greater initiative on their own in insisting that countries desiring to borrow commit themselves to meaningful stabilization goals; they must also avoid letting themselves be used as sources of funds by countries seeking to circumvent IMF discipline. This is a time that calls for especially close coordination of the efforts of private lenders and the IMF in the interest of seeing to it that international debt creation proceeds prudently and that adjustment policies are intensified.

In particular, so that countries needing to borrow have greater inducement to submit to Fund stabilization prescriptions, it has become clear that the Fund's lending capacity should be enlarged and that it should have added flexibility to make loans whose size is not limited by the quota structure. This has been agreed to in principle both by the IMF's Interim Committee and the London Summit conferees, and early implementation of a special lending facility can now be anticipated. This facility will be established on the sound principle that loans will become available only when an applicant country has agreed to pursue effective economic stabilization policies.

In focusing, as I have, on the need for adjustment by countries whose external position has been weakened by loose financial practices or by failure to adapt realistically to the burden of higher fuel costs, I do not mean to suggest that they alone have adjustment obligations. Countries enjoying payments surpluses have responsibilities as well, both the OPEC group and others.

Certainly, the non-OPEC countries as a group cannot go on indefinitely with payments deficits vis-à-vis the oil producers, totaling $40 billion or so a year. That would entail a serious risk of irreparable damage to the international economy. To the extent, therefore, that non-OPEC nations find ways to cut oil imports or to enlarge sales to oil producers, it is vitally important that the members of OPEC not try to compensate for any resulting slippage in their surpluses by a new round of oil-price increases.

And, just as clearly, the non-OPEC surplus countries too must contribute to the international adjustment process. Here, though, I think the progress that has already been made is sometimes not fully appreciated. The rapidity with which the large U.S. current-account surplus of two years ago has wilted away is worth noting. And here in the Federal Republic, your current-account surplus has fallen from about $10 billion in 1974 to a moderate level currently, thus reflecting a more rapid rise in imports of goods and services than in exports. You have reason to take pride in your record of responsibility toward your trading partners, especially in the degree of willingness you have shown in letting the value of the mark appreciate—an appreciation that in 1976 alone totaled some 15 percent.

I recognize that the appreciation of the mark in foreign exchange markets has entailed political risks in the Federal

Republic. But your policy has been enlightened in terms of international needs, and I believe it has also been wise domestically in helping to consolidate the hard-won progress you have achieved in curbing inflation.

The Federal Republic has been fortunate indeed in having leaders of the vision of Chancellor Schmidt and Dr. Klasen to serve it in the troubled and turbulent times in which we live. And it is a stroke of good fortune that a man of Otmar Emminger's experience and character stands ready to assume the presidency of the Bundesbank. I join you all in wishing Dr. Emminger, whom I have had the privilege of knowing for a quarter century, every success in continuing the Federal Republic's struggle for a durable prosperity. And I have no doubt that he will meet the challenge he now faces, provided he keeps firmly in mind Dr. Klasen's great lesson to his countrymen: that monetary order is the backbone of a nation and that an independent central bank is essential to such order.

INDEX

478

AEI Associates Program

The American Enterprise Institute invites your participation in the competition of ideas through its AEI Associates Program. This program has two objectives:

The first is to broaden the distribution of AEI studies, conferences, forums, and reviews, and thereby to extend public familiarity with the issues. AEI Associates receive regular information on AEI research and programs, and they can order publications and cassettes at a savings.

The second objective is to increase the research activity of the American Enterprise Institute and the dissemination of its published materials to policy makers, the academic community, journalists, and others who help shape public attitudes. Your contribution, which in most cases is partly tax deductible, will help ensure that decision makers have the benefit of scholarly research on the practical options to be considered before programs are formulated. The issues studied by AEI include:

- Defense Policy
- Economic Policy
- Energy Policy
- Foreign Policy
- Government Regulation
- Health Policy
- Legal Policy
- Political and Social Processes
- Social Security and Retirement Policy
- Tax Policy

For more information, write to: AMERICAN ENTERPRISE INSTITUTE
1150 Seventeenth Street, N.W., Washington, D.C. 20036

The Author

Arthur F. Burns is Distinguished Scholar in Residence at the American Enterprise Institute, in Washington, D.C. Also, he is Distinguished Professorial Lecturer at Georgetown University, in Washington, D.C., and since 1969 John Bates Clark Professor of Economics Emeritus at Columbia University, in New York. He has had a long and notable career both in academic and in public life. He has been affiliated with the National Bureau of Economic Research since 1930 and served as its president from 1957 to 1967. From February 1970 until March 1978, he served as Chairman of the Board of Governors of the Federal Reserve System. Prior to his Federal Reserve service, he was Counsellor to the President (1969–1970) and Chairman of the President's Council of Economic Advisers (1953–1956). His principal publications include: *Production Trends in the United States Since 1870* (1934); *Measuring Business Cycles,* with W. C. Mitchell (1946); *Economic Research and the Keynesian Thinking of Our Times* (1946); *Frontiers of Economic Knowledge* (1954); *Prosperity Without Inflation* (1957); *The Management of Prosperity* (1966); *Full Employment, Guideposts, and Economic Stability,* with Paul A. Samuelson (1967); *The Defense Sector and the American Economy,* with Jacob K. Javits and Charles J. Hitch (1968); and *The Business Cycle in a Changing World* (1969).